Common Places

Common Places

Mythologies of Everyday Life in Russia

Svetlana Boym

Harvard University Press
Cambridge, Massachusetts
London, England

Library of Congress Cataloging-in-Publication Data

Boym, Svetlana, 1959–
    Common places : mythologies of everyday life in Russia / Svetlana Boym.
        p.   cm.
    Includes index.
    ISBN 0-674-14625-5 (alk. paper)—ISBN 0-674-14626-3 (paper : alk. paper)
    1. Soviet Union—Social life and customs.   2. Russia (Federation)—Social life and
customs.   3. Popular culture—Soviet Union.   4. Popular culture—Russia (Federation)
I. Title.
DK266.4.B69   1944
947.08—dc20   94-19893
                                                                                                                  CIP

To my parents, Musa and Yury Goldberg

Acknowledgments

I began thinking about common places when I first went back to Russia, my native country which I had left nine years before. Writing helped me make sense of my round trips between Russia and United States; conversely, each new border crossing forced me to revise my project.

No book on common places can be written by any one person alone. Many memorable walks with Moscow writer and critic Maya Turovskaya—around the Golden Fountain of the Moscow Exhibition of Achievements and in New York's Central Park—inspired me to think about banality and bad taste seriously. I have benefited greatly from the generosity and support of many of my colleagues at Harvard. William Mills Todd III helped me from the beginning and shared with me his generous insight, erudition, and intellectual rigor. Susan Suleiman encouraged me to think about the pleasures and traps of autobiographical reading. Donald Fanger, Jurij Striedter, Judith Ryan, and Barbara Johnson supported and inspired me in many ways. Elaine Scarry made me think creatively about objects and artifacts as well as flowers and gardens. Stanley Cavell provoked me to consider the uncanniness of the ordinary in more than one context.

I am grateful to Michael Holquist for his sharp insights and unfailing intellectual challenge and to Jeffrey Brooks for his meticulous comments and tough criticism. Over the years I have enjoyed many friendly and stimulating dialogues with Katerina Clark, Marjorie Perloff, Thomas Lahusen, Greta Slobin, Catherine O'Connor, Irina

Paperno, Mikhail Yampolsky, Dmitri Shalin, Catherine Theimer
Nepomnyashchy, Musya Glanz. Thanks also to my fellow film buffs
Vida Johnson, Andrew Horton, and Nancy Salzer for the many cinematic experiences we shared. I have also benefited greatly from the
discussion of my work at various forums, particularly the seminar at
the Center for Literary and Cultural Studies, Russian Research Center
at Harvard, the symposium on postcommunism at the Center for
Cultural Studies at the University of California, Santa Cruz, and the
seminar on private life at the University of California at Berkeley. I
am thankful for comments from Stephen Greenblatt, Michael Flier,
Vladimir Brovkin, Yuri Slezkine, Eric Naiman, Anne Nesbit, and
Joseph Koerner.
    The work on the book was sustained by the generous support of
several institutions. A postdoctoral fellowship from the American
Council of Learned Societies and Social Science Research Council for
1990–91 allowed me to think seriously about the shape of the book
and begin my research. IREX short-term grants in 1989 and 1992 as
well as a grant from the Clark Fund of Harvard University in 1993
made it possible for me to travel to Russia and to complete the
primary research for my project.
    I was fortunate to enjoy the cordial hospitality of many writers,
artists, film makers, and intellectuals in Russia, among whom it was
possible to understand each other "with half-words." They are Zara
Abdullaeva, Daniil Dondurei, Lev Karakhan (and his colleagues from
the journal *Art of Cinema*), Ekaterina Degot', Joseph Bakshtein,
Dmitrii Prigov, Tatiana Arzamasova, Lev Evzovich, Evgenii Sviatsky,
Viktor Misiano, Natalia Ivanova, Nadezhda Azhgikhina, Asya
Kolodizhner, Leonid Gurevich, Semion Aranovich, Lana Go-
goberidze, Alexei Uchitel', Nadezhda Vasil'eva, Liubov' Arcus,
Arkadii Dragomoshchenko, Alexander Etkind, Igor Kon, Sergei
Sholokhov, Alla Gerber, Yelena Trofimova, Larisa Rezun-Zvezdochetova.
    My friends and fellow-exiles from various parts of the world
rewarded me with another kind of imagined community necessary
for writing this book. Greta Slobin, Alicia Borinsky, Ewa Lajer-
Burchardt, and Giuliana Bruno shared laughter, intellectual pleasures, and hot meals. My French cousin Kristian Feigelson was a
fellow-traveler to Russia. Paul Holdengräber's bibliomania helped to
sustain my graphomania, and Felix Roziner's generous story-telling

and encyclopedic passion for collecting the relics of the Soviet language were always inspiring.

I am grateful to my editor Lindsay Waters of Harvard University Press for his enthusiastic encouragements and intellectual stimulation. My warm thanks also to Alison Kent for her help and to my manuscript editor Anita Safran for her insight and patience with my endless rewritings. My graduate students and research assistants were my first readers: John Henriksen, Golfo Alexopoulous, Rosemary Peters, and Kim Thomas helped with the manuscript in most creative ways.

An exceptional debt of gratitude is owed to Mark Shteinbok, a brave and creative photographer whose artistic and journalistic eye helped me see what I wished to write about.

Dana Villa's special kindness, subtle support, and good sense of humor helped me to survive my American everyday life and made my private space as aesthetic as possible. Finally, the book is dedicated to my parents, whose voices, memories, jokes, and songs are recorded throughout.

Contents

Introduction
Theoretical Common Places

There used to be a saying among Soviet intelligentsia—"to under-stand each other with half-words." What is shared is silence, tone of voice, nuance of intonation. To say a full word is to say too much; communication on the level of words is already excessive, banal, almost kitschy. This peculiar form of communication "with half-words" is a mark of belonging to an imagined community that exists on the margin of the official public sphere. Hence the American metaphors for being sincere and authentic—"saying what you mean," "going public," and "being straightforward"—do not trans-late properly into the Soviet and Russian contexts. "Saying what you mean" could be interpreted as being stupid, naïve, or not streetwise. Such a profession of sincerity could be seen, at best, as a sign of foreign theatrical behavior; at worst, as a cunning provocation. There is no word for authenticity in Russian, but there are two words for truth: *pravda* and *istina*. It is possible to tell the truth *(pravda),* but *istina*—the word that, according to Vladimir Nabokov, does not rhyme with anything—must remain unarticulated. In this form of indirect communication, quasi-religious attitudes toward language, devices of romantic poetry, revolutionary underground conspiracies, and tactics of dissident intelligentsia strangely converge.

Communication with half-words secures the unspoken realm of cultural myths and protects the imagined community from outsiders and, in a way, from its own members. Among the dissidents of half words very little dissent is permitted. If all at once those other halves of words were to be spoken, intimate gatherings of friends might end—in fistfights.

At the risk of disturbing some of the imagined communities that I myself once cherished, I will try to describe them in a language foreign to them, in more than half-words. I write from the double perspective of a cultural critic and a former Leningrader, a resident of a communal apartment who often forgot to turn off the lights in the communal closet, earning severe scoldings from the watchful neighbors. This is a poignant historical moment, when all the imagined communities of Soviet culture are in a twilight phase. Some members of the post-Soviet intelligentsia perceive it as the end of a millennium of Russian culture, not merely of the Soviet Union but of the whole Russian literature-centered empire, with its centralized cultural text and shared double-speak.

In all the voluminous discussion one subject is generally left out: the everyday mythologies and rituals of ordinary life. They are hidden behind political, ideological, or artistic screens, deemed irrelevant for the heroic conception of the national identity in Russia or for Soviet ideology, inscrutable to many Western political scientists and journalists. The inner workings of the culture thus remain a mystery. In Russia, a country which during the past two centuries went through extreme calamities, wars, revolutions, and epochs of terror, everyday existence has often been precarious for the majority of the population. At the same time, in Russian intellectual tradition as well as in Soviet official ideology, a preoccupation with everyday life for its own sake was considered unpatriotic, subversive, un-Russian, or even anti-Soviet. Conversely, a central thread is an unusually strong, almost Romantic, fear of banality and "lack of culture," of anything that smacks of middlebrow or middle-class values. In this respect, both the Russian dream described by many Russian philosophers and writers, as well as the Soviet vision of the future, were radically different from the mythical American dream, which was based on the American lifestyle rather than on education, spiritual or ideological commonality, or the cultural canon.

I intend to put at the center what is marginal to certain heroic or apocalyptic self-definitions of Russian culture: the attitudes toward ordinary life, home, material objects and art, as well as expressions of emotion and ways of communication. In Russia the history of relations between culture and nation, art and life, society and individual, public and private, commodity and trash, often diverges from familiar Western European or American versions of modernity. To examine these differences is one subject of this book.

We might think, for instance, that banality is a global phenomenon and the banal is the banal is the banal. Vladimir Nabokov insists, however, on the originality of Russian banality and on its untranslatability. In his view, only Russians were able neatly to devise the concept of *poshlost'*—a word that encompasses banality, lack of spirituality and sexual obscenity.[1] In a similarly patriotic manner the distinguished linguist Roman Jakobson claims that the Russian word for the everyday—*byt*—is culturally untranslatable into Western languages; according to Jakobson, only Russians among the European nations are capable of fighting "the fortresses of byt" and of conceptualizing a radical alterity to the everyday (byt).[2] Russian, and later Soviet, cultural identity depended on heroic opposition to everyday life.

One could compile a *Dictionary of Untranslatables* that would include all the words that are (or were proudly claimed to be) culturally untranslatable into another language.[3] Perhaps every cross-cultural study should begin with a glossary of untranslatables and cultural differences, to prevent the transformation of a culture into a mere exotic movie backdrop or kitsch object. Until recently, many words used in Western public and private spheres lacked Russian equivalents: among them are the words for "privacy," "self," "mentality," and "identity."[4] The distinction between "policy" and "politics" is also incomprehensible in Russian, since they both translate as *politika*.

Conversely, various Russian thinkers from the nineteenth to the twentieth century insisted with a great zeal on the untranslatability of certain Russian words into Western languages. Among such specifically Russian words are *sobornost'* (a spiritual community, from *sobor*, which refers both to cathedral and to a gathering)—the Russian mythical alternative to private life, advocated by nineteenth-century Slavophile philosophers and contemporary nationalists—and the Russian form of compassion, *sostradanie*, literally co-suffering. And, of course, one could never forget Russian *toska*—a form of acute homesickness and yearning, celebrated in poems and heartbreaking gypsy romances. On a more heroic note, the Russian word for a feat, *podvig*, was also thought to be unique: it emphasizes dynamic heroic

impulse, courage and self-sacrifice, not merely a specific accomplishment suggested in the English word "feat." Perhaps the untranslatable Russian everyday depended too much on this Russian *podvig*
and its near-inability to acknowledge the ordinary.

My book is organized around several Russian cultural "untranslatables" that reflect common places of everyday life. I write "common
place" as two words when I wish to preserve all the multiple historical significations and poetic allusion of the word, from public architecture to topography of memory. I write it as one word ("commonplace") when I have in mind the modern derogative use of the term
in reference to a worn-out banality, or cliché. (The distinction between "common place" and "commonplace" is not wholly translat-
able into French, Spanish, or Russian, whereas in English the derogatory use of the term prevails, and the historical memory of different
"common places" is forgotten.)

Mythologies are cultural common places, recurrent narratives that
are perceived as natural in a given culture but in fact were naturalized
and their historical, political, or literary origins forgotten or disguised.[5] In Russia and the Soviet Union, where there is a long tradition of extreme political, administrative, and cultural centralization,
those mythologies played a particularly important role. Myths are
discernible in a variety of literary and historical texts as well as in
everyday practices. A myth fragment could slip into a love letter in
verse memorized in a Soviet high school, or into a reference to a
slogan that used to hang in front of the entrance, or a mildly political
joke told by a friend in the break between a lecture on "scientific
atheism" and a seminar on "the history of the Communist Party." To
understand Russian mythologies it is not enough to trace their origins
in intellectual history, state policy, or actual practice. It is necessary
to remember that they function in the culture as magical incantations,
memorized or paraphrased but rarely interpreted critically. Cultural
myths could also be defined as cultural obsessions. Looking for everyday mythologies one is tempted to see certain continuities in the
history of concepts between Russian and Soviet intellectual traditions—continuities which, however, reveal themselves to be paradoxical. My aim is neither to perpetuate cultural myths nor merely
to demystify them, but to identify them, to show how they were
appropriated by various ideologies, both Communist and nationalist,
and how they seduced native and foreign scholars and might have

obscured a cultural tradition that is in truth diverse and hybrid. Myths are sites of a shared cultural memory, of communal identifica-tion and affection; and while they shaped the national imagination, they did not always correspond to actual everyday practices and people's preoccupations.

One of the prominent Russian myths of the past two centuries is the myth of the national unity of Russian culture based exclusively on the heritage of the great literary classics of nineteenth and twenti-eth centuries. (The actual list of national literary geniuses has been altered several times throughout the twentieth century, but the myth of a unified canon survived.) "Culture" will be used both in its traditional sense as literature and the arts (which could be linked to the imagined community of a nation) and in a broader anthropologi-cal sense, as a way of making sense of the world and a system of patterns of behavior and signs. We will examine together the philo-sophical and literary texts, mass entertainments, and popular arti-facts. We will walk down the streets of Moscow and Leningrad, eavesdrop on domestic life, and examine jokes, films, TV programs, popular songs, and even the realm of post-Soviet advertising—new Russia's Wild West. At the center of our concern is the utopian topography of Soviet daily existence and its secret corners, from the Palaces of Culture to communal apartments, from public subways in the magnificent Stalinist style to not-so-private closets. These are spaces of illegitimate privacy, of forbidden kitschy souvenirs, of prac-ticed indirection. The study of the Russian everyday reveals some centuries-old mechanisms of cultural survival, arts of minor compro-mise and resistance. This book is not about Soviet politics or Russian art but about the unwritten laws of everyday existence, about every-day aesthetic experiences and alternative spaces carved between the lines and on the margins of the official discourses.

Rubber Plants and the Soviet Order of Things

Let us begin with the picture of Stalinist domestic bliss entitled *The New Apartment* (1952). In the center stands a middle-aged woman, a heroine of the Great Patriotic War and proud mistress of the new apartment, looking as if she is about to break into a Russian folk dance. Nearby is her son, a good boy and exemplary Young Pioneer. A portrait of Stalin takes the place of the father. The gazes of this

Laktionov, *The New Apartment* (1952)

Soviet family do not meet; the mother looks toward the invisible source of light, the bright future perhaps; the son looks up at his proud mother; and Stalin looks in the opposite direction, watching the half-open door, guarding the limits of the visible. The scene seems to be set in some familiar totalitarian sit-com: the characters wear the appropriate Soviet uniforms and freeze in theatrical poses known from films and paintings, as if awaiting prerecorded applause. This is not merely a private family festivity but a celebration of the Soviet collective in miniature; we see the friendly neighbors on the threshold exhibiting their healthy kittens, and bicycles ready to roll in the long corridors. There is little separation here between public and private; rather, the painting depicts a single fluid ideological space. The furniture in the room is very sparse, and private objects are limited to books by Soviet classic authors (including the revolutionary poet Vladimir Mayakovsky), a radio set, toys, a political poster emblazoned with "Glory to Our Beloved Motherland," a globe with the largest country of the world colored in bright pink, a mandoline, and a sickly-looking rubber plant in the foreground.

The painting is neither reflective nor self-reflective: people and objects hardly cast any shadows here, and there is no mirror hidden in the corner. The scene flaunts its perfect bright visibility and transparency of meaning. The painter of the new apartment is not presenting himself on the canvas, not meeting our glance, and not questioning the rules of representation. *Las Meninas* this is not! Yet *The New Apartment* is an icon of Soviet civilization in the way Velázquez's *Las Meninas,* in Michel Foucault's discussion of the painting, is an icon of the early modern "order of things."[6] It is the way the culture wishes to see itself and to be seen, without thinking about the act of seeing. This is a perfect Socialist Realist genre scene, not an accurate portrayal of a Soviet apartment. It reminds us of nineteenth-century paintings of the Academy and tells us more about Soviet iconography than about Soviet domestic life.

It is difficult to imagine what could have been considered ideologically incorrect in a painting that is so carefully, and so moderately, ideological. Yet its seamless surface was censored twice, from two different angles. When the painting was first exhibited in the early 1950s, it was the rubber plant in the foreground that rubbed critics the wrong way. After the Twentieth Party Congress of 1956, the

albums of Soviet art published in the early 1960s displayed the
painting without the portrait of Stalin, which was then deemed to be
in bad taste. In the early attack, the painting was accused of celebrating the petty bourgeois values of philistinism and banality embodied
in the rubber plant, and of "putting a varnish" on Soviet reality.[7]
Although both the painting and the Socialist Realist criticism of it
appear to be perfect examples of what Milan Kundera calls "totalitarian kitsch," the picture fell victim in the war against two specific
varieties of kitsch, thus demonstrating how the critique of kitsch and
banality can itself become kitschified. But what is ideologically incorrect about rubber plants? What made this minor *locus amenus* of the
urban domestic space so unnatural?

When I explained *The New Apartment* painting to my American
students, they attempted to figure out what specific thing about this
plant made it a symbol of bad taste. But no knowledge of horticulture
could help. There was no official hostility to exotic flora as such: the
sumptuous Moscow subway, one of Stalin's major urban projects, is
ornamented with exuberant palm trees and other plants that have
never grown in Russia. In this tropical utopia of a Communist underground city, even the climate was changed for the better. But the
rubber plant in the private corner of the communal apartment had
different ideological roots. It was regarded as the last sickly survivor
of the imagined bourgeois greenhouses, or a poor relative of the
ubiquitous geranium in the windowboxes of middle-class residents;
geraniums were purged and physically eradicated in Stalin's time.
Here the Socialist Realist art critics of Stalin's era borrowed a slogan
from the radical campaigns against "domestic trash" led by the leftist
artists of the 1920s. In 1929 the State Academy of Arts planned to
organize an exhibit of petit-bourgeois elements in art and antiaesthetic elements in the workers' everyday life. It was a kind of Soviet
forerunner of the Nazi exhibit of degenerate art, although the style
of this "degenerate art" was radically different. Moreover, the Soviet
exhibit was not so much about degenerate art as about degenerate
everyday life. The campaign "Down with Domestic Trash" was
launched by the newspaper *Komsomol Truth* in response to Vladimir
Mayakovsky's poems, and it proposed to "burn the little idols of
things" and create a new avant-garde environment. Mayakovsky decried the effeminate interiors of the new Soviet middle class, with
their gramophone records, lace curtains, rubber plants, porcelain

elephants, and portraits of Marx in crimson frames. His counterrevolutionary flora and fauna included all sorts of petit-bourgeois birdies of bad taste, from suspiciously chirping yellow canaries to sweet-singing nightingales. (After Mayakovsky's suicide in 1930 Stalin proclaimed him to be "the greatest poet of our epoch" and officially canonized him; no wonder his book appears in the programmatic new apartment of the picture-perfect Soviet family.) By the mid-1930s the attempt to bring revolutionary art into daily life while trashing domestic life and philistinism temporarily subsided, following the decisive trashing of the avant-garde itself. The new acquisitiveness of the Soviet citizens, the heroes of labor, was cautiously encouraged in official writings, partly to justify and disguise the legitimation of social inequality, special privileges, and spacious private housing allocated to the Stalinist elite.[8] Yet there is a tension in the official depiction of domestic space, and hence its ideal iconography is unstable and often inconsistent.

The New Apartment painting was exhibited in 1952–1953, when massive show trials of "cosmopolitans" in Soviet Russia resulted in the persecution and murder of thousands of Jews. Perhaps the brightly lit scene of moving into the new apartment is so paranoiacally codified because behind the threshold, in the unrepresentable space of cultural memory, lurks another scene—that of removing someone from their old apartment—the scene of arrest and home search that was an everyday occurrence of the Stalinist perestroika of life from the 1930s to the 1950s.

The rubber plant, it turns out, has roots in American mythology of the 1950s as well, but there it has quite a different meaning. A popular song of the times, entitled "High Hopes," tells about an optimistic ant's attempt to shift a rubber plant. In this song the plant is a symbol of natural obstacles overcome by confidence and hard work on the way to the American dream. So the "rub" is not inherent in the rubber plant. Its root is not in nature but in cultural mythology.

Back in the new apartment, the portrait of Stalin is located on a straight diagonal from the rubber plant; it almost seems that the "great leader of the people" is deliberately turning his eyes away from this bourgeois flower of evil. (In the 1960s Stalin's portrait was cropped out of the picture, having become a kind of historical embarrassment implicating the painter and his audience in the regime. Eliminating the controversial portrait of the leader, and with it the compromising mass collaboration with Stalinism, was an attempt to remove Stalin and still preserve his carefully watched, brightly lit and "varnished" world.) Since this is a didactic painting we are supposed to learn a lesson from it, and the real lesson is that the everyday is as natural as the rubber plant, history and ideology are as changeable as the portrait of Stalin, and the relationship between them is as seamless as the painting.

The rubber plant, an iconographic blemish on the image of Socialist Realist domestic bliss and one of the few true-to-life objects in the painting, can function as a trigger of cultural memory and a key to the archeology of Soviet private and communal life. The archeology of the everyday can offer neither a complete reconstruction of the past nor a single authorial explanation for it. It only helps to interpret material ruins—a house plant, a pink elephant with a broken tusk, a rusty bust of Lenin found at a flea market in a provincial town, a monument to a forgotten party leader littered with dead leaves, the basement of a church turned into the workers' club turned into a commercial firm, and so on. Such ruins suggest incomplete narratives, poetic allegories, twisted plots of history; they never point to one single, straightforward script of events. Walter Benjamin compares archeological digging to the operations of memory: in both cases the archeologist "must not be afraid to return again and again to the same matter: to scatter it as one scatters earth, to turn it over as one turns the soil. For the matter itself is only a deposit, a stratum which yields only to the most meticulous examination what constitutes the real treasure hidden within the earth; the images, severed from all earlier associations, that stand like precious fragments of torsos in a collector's gallery—in the prosaic rooms of our later understanding."[9]

From this perspective we learn to be suspicious of such seemingly transparent, brightly lit, and picture-perfect reconstructions of history as *The New Apartment*. A "thick description" of archeological ruins might occasionally offer deeper insights into another culture, its unwritten laws of operation and invisible spaces, than could comforting taxonomy, statistics, or scientific periodization.[10] The name of the first traveler to the island of Utopia in St. Thomas More's account was Raphael Hythlodaeus, which can be translated as "expert in trifles" or "well-learned in nonsense."[11] The expert in Soviet mythology has to be an expert in trifles, has to have a feel for the nonsensical, in order to understand how the utopian Soviet designs were put into practice and how they were translated into ordinary language.

Instead of demonizing the banal or discussing the "banality of evil," which often takes for granted the evil nature of banality, I will try to trace the history of wars against banality and explore the various maps of public culture and private life, along with the conflation of banality and everyday life. My aim is not to perpetuate Russia's exceptional fate or Russian exoticism but to examine everyday life cross-culturally and show that what seems most habitual, natural, and human cannot simply be taken for granted.

Many words that seem to belong to our common language and to describe the ordinary themselves require a careful cross-cultural reconsideration. "Banality," "cliché," "kitsch" (in their national varieties), and even the "common place" itself have gone through a startling historical transformation. Perhaps what both Russia and the West have in common is a modern perception of a crisis of communality, a search for the lost community that takes a variety of shapes and forms. In other words, we have to begin with an archeology of the common place itself.

Archeology of the Common Place: From Topos to Kitsch

Common place refers to both the organization of space and the organization of speech. This trope has degraded through history: from the noble Greek *topos,* a site of classical argument, it has turned into the modern commonplace, the synonym for a cliché. Common places *(koinos topos)* date back to the ancient art of memory; they were familiar sites in a building or on a habitual walk through the city, to which one attached memory images. They also preserved the traces of occult topography of the ancient Theater of Memory and provided a common spatial arrangement for the architecture of the world, the interior designs of memory, and, occasionally, of the cosmological theater of the universe. The art of memory was invented— or remembered—by Simonides of Ceos, the first professional poet in ancient Greece, the first one to take money for his poetry.[12] In Aristotle's writings common places (topics) are seen exclusively as devices of rhetoric and refer to arguments used by a skillful orator or politician.[13] In Renaissance rhetorical treatises classical common places are rediscovered as the memory of antiquity, their rhetorical role is reestablished, and they are regarded as necessary elements of a learned and elevated style. "Common place" could refer to a quotation of ancient wisdom; the quotation marks—two severed heads—were not always marks of originality and individual authorship, rather, they "decapitated" an individual author or, from another point of view, they authenticated his participation in the cultural commonality. In the sixteenth century studious young men were supposed to collect quotations of ancient wisdom in books; in the eighteenth century sensible young ladies cherished their "books of commonplaces" with dried flowers and perfumed letters from "dear friends." But in the nineteenth century the attitude toward the common place changed drastically: from something to be collected, it turned into something to be avoided. People still collected aphorisms—literally "off boundaries" *(apo-horos)*—and maxims, but not for long.

A certain anxiety surrounds the definition of common place in the eighteenth and nineteenth centuries. As the derogatory connotation of the word "common" gained ground, so did a philosophical nostalgia for a more idealized, purified, and euphorically positive redefinition of commonality—from the Kantian *sensus communis,* which fostered the judgment of the beautiful, to the early American conception of commonwealth, to the Saint-Simonian (and later Marxist) political ideal of a new world order founded on the communes and culminating with communism. Communality usually becomes precious at the moment it is perceived to be in crisis. (But we need not fall into an elegiac mode and lament the Golden Age of the Common Place, conceived as some kind of pastoral Arcadia. Under close historical scrutiny, neither the collectivity of primitive societies, called by Marx "primitive communism," nor the Greek polity, idealized by many twentieth-century philosophers as a pretechnocratic paradise of democracy, nor the peasant communes in Russia would qualify as this kind of ideal community.) The crisis of the common place is accompanied by a resurgence of utopian thought. "Utopia" is full of linguistic ambiguity; it can refer to "no place" or to a "good place"; the "u" can be a Latin negation *(u)* or a Greek euphoric affirmation of goodness *(eu)*.[14] Utopia is the ultimate insular conception of the ideal Common Place.

Kant attempts to draw a clear distinction between the usual formulation of common sense, which borders on vulgarity, and a philosopher's conception of a "common human understanding." *Sensus communis*—often used in Latin to distinguish it from its slippery colloquial counterparts in modern European languages—is what allows a human being to perceive, through reflexive aesthetic judgment, the universal purposefulness of nature. *Sensus communis* emerges through the blurred images of intuition, which are not private but shared: "Humanity means both universal feeling of sympathy and the ability to engage universally in very intimate communication."[15] At times it seems that Kant's concept of *sensus communis* in itself is not a concept but a *sense*, a poetic metaphor for the problematic hide-and-seek of human commonality. What is "common" to all humanity is not the primary sensory reflexes, "languid affects," but precisely the ability to detach oneself from the senses in order to apprehend the beautiful. Sympathy is a step toward the perception of the beautiful. Yet this perception, and the experience of human commonality, become more and more indistinct, and the shapes of the beautiful more blurred. The last paragraphs of *The Critique of Aesthetic Judgment* declare that in future centuries it will be ever more difficult to form a concept of the beautiful and of the common.

In earlier eighteenth-century discussions *sensus communis* is connected to Roman understanding of common morality and civic duty.[16] In Kant it is linked to the judgment of taste—specifically to aesthetic taste. "Taste" itself, used primarily as a metaphor, is taken directly from the numerous culinary treatises of the seventeenth century, suggesting an important connection between the arts of cooking and the arts of thinking. From the so-called skepticism of tastes, best expressed in the universally famous Roman proverb, "there is no arguing about tastes," we move toward a more refined concept of "good taste." The imposition of the ideals of good and bad on the range of sensual pleasures has connections to moral philosophy.[17] There is a classical and classicizing element in the notion of taste, one which dates back to the Greek conception of "ethics of measure," from Pythagoras to Plato: the ethics of proportion, restraint, and balance. "Common places," thus, are the sites of ancient good taste. The cultivation of good taste and the increasing emphasis on cultural distinction, rather than a distinction of birth, grew more important in the seventeenth and eighteenth centuries. The history of the idea of taste parallels the history of absolutism in Spain, France, and

England, and it is closely bound up with the development of the third estate.

With the Romantics, the idea of good taste is superseded by the idea of genius, which drastically affects the conception of the common place. At the turn of the eighteenth century a virtual "revolution in the common place" took place. One result of this change has been the modern crisis of cultural consensus, a crisis in the very understanding of the human community and commonality. Romantic aesthetics for the first time drew a sharp opposition between commonality and originality, triviality and authenticity. The common place, once merely a trope of normative classical rhetoric, a mark of learned elevated style shared by the privileged aristocrats of taste, took on a literal meaning associated with a public place, which in turn became a vulgar site. Formerly an aristocratic privilege, common place turned into "commonplace"; it became devalued and associated with unoriginality and ordinariness. Romantic originality was an enterprise dedicated to forgetting the complex rhetorical structure of the common place.

Romanticism thus brought about a degradation of the common place, which became synonymous with cliché, the word that embodies the devaluing effects of modern technology and mechanical reproduction. The French *cliché* referred originally to the typographic plate that allows multiple printings of pages, and also to the photographic negative. It is a modern word par excellence, which moves from technology to aesthetics. The reproducibility of the cliché and the availability of mass reproduction form a necessary background for the Romantic search for newness and for the cult of individual self-expression. Cliché ensures the proliferation of a work, but deprives it of an aura surrounding the uniqueness of the masterpiece. Cliché both perpetuates and prostitutes, both provides a grid for originality and devalues it.

We live nowadays in a "clichégenic society"; it is our inescapable cultural predicament. "One of the main reasons that clichés manage to evade reflection and its potential relativization, lies in the fact that they are as catching as laughter, or if you want, as stuttering."[18] Clichés preserve traces of cultural institutions, one of which is the very institution of the common sense that is a foundation of capitalist society. Moreover, in modern society clichés constitute the necessary incantatory noise of the everyday. They provide a guarantee of everyday survival that would not otherwise be possible in our age of oversaturation of information and stimuli. Clichés protect us from facing the catastrophe, the unbearable, the ineffable; thus for the major inexplicable areas of human existence—birth, death, and love—we have the maximum number of clichés. Responses to death and declarations of love are the most clichéd and ritualistic in every culture. Clichés often save us from despair and embarrassment by protecting the vulnerability and fragility of our way of life and social communication. In social situations we often blush and recite cliché excuses, cliché formalities, or no less cliché informalities, in order to cover up a frightening realization of the limits of language. One can estrange the common place, but then one has to estrange one's own estrangement.

Throughout European history the many levels of the "common place" were gradually forgotten, together with the art of memory itself. No longer a part of ancient art or of the rhetorical organization of the world, the common place was devalued and literalized. But on the ruins of the classical common place, the dreams of ideal communality—in art, politics, and society—emerged with a new force, taking their various shapes from the aesthetic *sensus communis,* whether communist utopia or democratic commonwealth. The new topographies of an ideal communality also produced its converse, the "bad communality": Palaces of Culture versus the Shopping Malls of Kitsch, architectural utopia versus communal apartments and housing projects, the sublime versus the banal. According to American modernist critic Clement Greenberg, not the "beautiful" of aesthetic judgment but the "agreeable" of kitsch has produced the "universal culture" of the twentieth century.[19]

"Kitsch," the Bavarian slang word that possibly translates as "sketch" or "cheap stuff," has received its share of cultural critique.[20] It was described as "the debased and academic simulacra of the genuine culture" (Greenberg), "a parody on catharsis" (Theodor Adorno), and a "sentimentalization of the finite ad infinitum" (Hermann Broch).[21] In this view kitsch is not merely bad art but also an unethical act, an act of mass manipulation. It blurs the boundaries between art and life and stands in the way of artistic autonomy. Kitsch appears as a sort of modern parasite, a virus of art and modernization to which there is no single antidote or counterconcept. Many critics attempted to discern the stylistic elements that charac-

terize kitsch and shape the structure of bad taste—the propensity
toward ornamentation, eclecticism, and sentimentality. But kitsch is
not merely a sum of stylistic features; in fact, the specific examples of
kitsch given in critical studies are often problematic. Through them
the critics betray their own cultural tastes and times. Greenberg's
example of kitsch is Ilia Repin's battle scenes, which, he claims,
merely imitate the effects of artistic battles and battles of consciousness and turn into didactic objects of official Stalinist art. Much as
one might agree with his assessment of Soviet reframing of Repin's
art, however, the fact is that Repin never painted any battle scenes.
Possibly Greenberg is confusing Repin with another painter or re-
hearsing someone else's clichés and effects of criticism. Clearly, particular examples of kitsch change from country to country, from one
historical context to another, and an uncritical choice of kitsch artifacts can turn the critique itself into kitsch.[22]

Much more important than specific stylistic devices are the mechanisms of kitschification. Greenberg writes: "If avant-garde imitates
the processes of art, kitsch . . . imitates its effect."[23] Kitsch manipu-
lates through objectification of the effects of art, and through ready-
made formulas that function like premodern magical incantations
known to trigger specific emotional responses. Such responses often
have the effect of mass hypnosis, even if a particular consumerist
kitsch item advertises individual improvement. This sort of individualism is mass-produced and ready-made, available to the many at a
discount price. The mechanisms of kitsch are directed toward pacify-
ing and sweetening the contradictions of human existence. Kitsch
neither resolves nor critically exposes the conflicts; instead, it offers
fragile bridges of commonplaces over the unbridgeable abyss. "Kitsch
expresses the sensibility of a public that no longer believes in hell, but
still worships paradise," writes Yaron Ezrahi.[24]

What is at stake in the modernist Western critiques of kitsch of the
1930s–1950s is, first of all, the responsibility of the intellectual, the
intellectual's response to the uses of kitsch by the culture industry and
by the totalitarian state, in both its fascist and Stalinist models.
Hannah Arendt, in her report on the Eichmann trial, presents Adolf
Eichmann as a kind of fascist kitschman who speaks exclusively in
officialese, "because he was genuinely incapable of uttering a single
sentence that was not a cliché."[25] Even at his execution Eichmann

came up with cliché phrases from funeral oratory—he surrounded himself with clichés to protect him against the words and worlds of others, against life and death. In Arendt's view, Eichmann's story, "the lesson of this long course in human wickedness," is the "lesson of the fearsome, word-and-thought-defying banality of evil." The psychological "normality" of Eichmann, diagnosed by Israeli psychiatrists, and even his conventional morality are particularly frightening: from the "banality of evil" to the "normality of evil" is only one step. (In prison Eichmann refused to read Nabokov's *Lolita,* considering it an "immoral book," a judgment which Nabokov would probably have taken as an ironic compliment.) In Arendt's discussion ethical and aesthetic judgments converge; Eichmann's inability to use words in an imaginative and individual manner reflects on his inability to think critically. The modernist critique of the banality of evil offers a powerful, if controversial, defense of the ethical foundation of aesthetics, as well as of the aesthetic judgment of morality.[26]

At the same time that intellectuals launched their critique of kitsch, artists and poets began to search for another sort of banality, which does not necessarily qualify as "evil." In the mid-nineteenth century artists developed a fascination for bad taste and the *démodé.*[27] Baudelaire declared his desire to "invent a cliché," thus offering us a paradox of the Romantic ideal of poetic invention that both defies and responds to the modern challenge of technological anonymity.[28] Baudelaire's fascination with bad taste is a reaction against bourgeois propriety and good taste that has less to do with aesthetic judgment than with moralistic common sense. The bourgeois good taste that Baudelaire attacked was a kind of "kitsch in good taste" to which he opposed the vulgarity of the grotesque and of low-class entertainment. For post-Romantic French poets and writers banality offered the infinite pleasures of writing, as well as an exploration of the limits of culture and the exotic journey from "high" to "low."[29] The English aesthetes, led by Oscar Wilde, cultivated artifice and artificiality, challenging Victorian good taste in art and life. They also claimed to be superior aristocrats of taste, going beyond the dull bourgeois norms of "good," "bad," and "evil." In the twentieth century the Surrealists cherished the ordinary marvelous, old-fashioned and useless "found objects" that prompted "profane illuminations." Surrealist art is excluded from Greenberg's definition of the "good avant-garde." Surrealists were the "bad boys" of the avant-garde because they were excessively seduced by bad taste.

Finally, in the 1960s, art criticism began to catch up with art and belatedly paid homage to "camp sensibility," which could be defined as kitsch in quotation marks, or aestheticized bad taste. Susan Sontag describes camp as a taste for everything "off," old-fashioned, out-of-date, *démodé*, all those things which, "from a 'serious' point of view, are either bad art or kitsch."[30] Camp sensibility is based on the eroticization of daily life; its key metaphor is that of life as theater, of "being-as-Playing-a-Role." Camp celebrates "a triumph of the epicene style" and playful reversals of gender and sexual impersonations, often associated with gay sensibility. Sontag remarks that "camp taste is by nature possible only in affluent societies, in societies or circles capable of experiencing the psychopathology of affluence."[31] "Camp sensibility" coincides with Pop art, which plays with the signs of commercial culture and with modernist theoretical clichés about the autonomy of art. Flirting with kitsch is a way of exploring the boundaries of art and of institutionalized good taste, which itself can turn into a cliché.

"None of us is superman enough to escape kitsch completely. No matter how we scorn it, kitsch is an integral part of the human condition," writes Milan Kundera, author of one of the most powerful invectives against both totalitarian and democratic kitsch.[32] The "we" of this sentence is seductively inclusive—it is at once the "we" of the universal brotherhood of kitsch-people and the "we" of the ironic critics of kitsch; it includes those who live it and those who scorn it. In Kundera's description of kitsch sentimental and political images blur, and so do the ironies and nostalgias of critics. Kitsch is defined by Kundera as a "dictatorship of the heart," as the "universal brotherhood of men" who celebrate a life in which the existence of shit is denied. The writer's own generalization suggests that not even he is "superman enough" to claim a space outside kitsch. Kundera's prophetic verdict on the human condition enacts the paradox of kitsch, its simultaneous repulsion and seduction, power and weakness, its ability to universalize and to discriminate

I will not attempt to get to the very heart of kitsch—a cheap holiday balloon heart made of red foil paper—and pierce it with a sharp critical arrow. Such heart-breaking criticism is both too violent and too sentimental. To confront the phenomenon of kitsch does not

necessarily mean to discern its essence and to universalize the structure of bad taste. On the contrary, seek to understand kitsch as an
experience and to recover precisely what kitsch tries to cover up: its
history, its cultural mythology, and its contexts.

The history of kitsch is as different in Eastern and Western Europe
as is the history of modern art. What is a countercultural discourse
in one part of the world can turn into officialese in the other. In our
cross-cultural exploration of banality and kitsch we will find some
untranslatable cultural aspects of the commonplace and of bad art,
as well as of their critique. In Russia the word "kitsch" was adopted
in the 1970s in a special sub-genre of books on Western mass culture.
It is characteristic of various foreign words in Russian that the word
in translation is less insulting than the native equivalent. This is true
of "banality" *(banal'nost')* as well as of "kitsch." Furthermore, kitsch
is mistranslated in Russian, and its critical history is virtually unknown. Whereas many modernist critics emphasized that kitsch is not
merely bad art but an unethical act, in the Russian usage kitsch has
no moral connotations. The Russian word *poshlost'* partly overlaps
both banality and kitsch, but it has its own dramatic cultural history
connected to the Russian encounter with Western "progress," the
pace of change and modernization.

Sontag's "camp," in contrast, would not include Russian artists
until the late 1980s. In Russia the metaphor of camp would be
definitely unpopular; nobody would like to be in any sort of camp
voluntarily. The mark of self-imposed aesthetic exclusionism turns
into its opposite—an image of enforced political isolation—when it
crosses the American-Russian border. Sontag's examples of supposedly shared and recognizable "camp sensibility" now appear dated;
one of the few that I was able to recognize, *Swan Lake,* I would
hardly call playful: for me it is associated with official Soviet culture.
The postmodern elements in late Soviet and post-Soviet art, which
will be explored in the last chapter, have little to do with the "psychopathology of affluence" and consumerism; they relate instead to
the psychopathology of totalitarian daily life. Hence the communality
of camp is culturally exclusive; not everyone can share the same
quotation marks.

The common place is not as transparent as it might seem; it is a
barricade, a battleground of warring definitions and disparate discourses—philosophical, political, aesthetic, and religious. By the

twentieth century the common place has turned into a complex pal-
impsest, a museum of the Romantic ruins of authenticity and of
modern homesickness. The common place is where the Romantic
poet stages his rebellion and where the modernist searches for anonymity; in the twentieth century it has sharply contrasted political
meanings, from the communist paradise of the common citizen to the
commercial bliss of the common consumer. The common place is a
mythical site from which intellectuals perpetually displace themselves,
only to write elegies to the lost communality.

A Labyrinth without a Monster

The everyday is a modern concept that grew out of the secularization
of the worldview, the disintegration of the many levels of the common
place, the division of the spheres of experience, and the emergence of
the middle class. The ordinary—the trivial and the quotidian—is very
difficult to map and to frame, whether by art, by theory, or by history.
Banality tends to incorporate framing and detachment into its own
machine of dailiness and to domesticate the irony. Stanley Cavell
speaks about the "uncanniness of the ordinary" that both resists and
invites philosophical discussion.[33] The commonplaces of our everyday life seem natural to us and it is this "naturalization" that leads
to many cultural mistranslations.

   Today the renewed interest in the study of the everyday in history
and social studies performs different functions in different cultural
contexts; it can go against the grain of heroic national self-definitions
or, conversely, play into the national dream; it can help to recover
forgotten histories of modernity (such as histories of women's work,
of private life)[34] or contribute to the forgetting of the major catastrophes of the twentieth century—such as the Holocaust—as the contemporary debates in Germany on the TV series "Heimat" and the
Alltagsgeschichte of Nazi time have demonstrated.[35]

   Michel de Certeau has written a history of the creation of the
everyday, a history of the separation of theory from practice and of
art in the singular from arts in the plural. He demonstrates how in
seventeenth-century France "savoir" (knowledge) is gradually disas-
sociated from "savoir-faire" (knowledge of skills); in a similar fashion, "art" becomes divorced from the "art of" (saying, doing, inhabiting space, walking, cooking, and other activities of the body and

techniques of the self). Certeau focuses on the rhetoric of everyday practice, on daily uses of discourse (and not only of discourse), on *ruses* and *braconnages*—acts of minor subversion of the official codes of behavior.[36] These daily tactics and strategies undermine purely theoretical concepts and allow a more multifaceted understanding of contemporary culture—not only Culture with a capital "C," but cultures in the plural. Certeau pays attention to the daily materiality of existence: ways of mapping space, walking around the city, marking time, preparing foods.

The everyday is at once too near us and too far from our understanding; we only become aware of it when we miss it in times of war or disaster, or when it manifests itself in excess during spells of boredom. Maurice Blanchot writes that the everyday is a "suspect that always escapes the clear decision of the law (the suspect: anyone and everyone, guilty of not being able to be guilty.)"[37] The everyday has its own temporality that Blanchot calls "eternullity," something like the eternal evanescence, or transient survival. The everyday is amorphous, unformed and informal, yet it is also the most conservative mode of preservation of forms and formalities. It is at once about spontaneity and stagnation.

The everyday tells us a story of modernity in which major historical cataclysms are superseded by ordinary chores, the arts of working and making things. In a way, the everyday is anticatastrophic, an antidote to the historical narrative of death, disaster, and apocalypse. The everyday does not seem to have a beginning or an end. In everyday life we do not write novels but notes or diary entries that are always frustratingly or euphorically anticlimactic. In diaries the dramas of our lives never end—as in the innumerable TV soap operas in which one dénouement only leads to another narrative possibility and puts off the ending. Our diaries are full of incidents and lack accidents; they have narrative potential and few completed stories. The everyday is a kind of labyrinth of common places without a monster, without a hero, and without an artist-maker trapped in his own creation. The labyrinth of the everyday is not the rhetorical labyrinth described by Jorge Luis Borges, which is like an imagined "book of sand" that leads everywhere and nowhere.[38] Rather it is like a shopping mall with no exit, or a bifurcating corridor in a communal apartment leading to the endlessly partitioned rooms. We often novelize the labyrinth of the everyday by creating a hero and a monster, a lover and her thread, in order to make sense of it.

In Russia the secular conceptions of the everyday were not completely developed, so the everyday kept its place in the hierarchical quasi-religious structure of sacred and profane, good and evil. The monster of Russian dailiness has never entirely disappeared. Many everyday experiences and minor arts of survival were taken up by the critical theorists of kitsch and unnecessarily demonized or reified. In the most radical of these theories, as expressed by the Soviet radical artists of the 1920s, the everyday—as it is and used to be—was synonymous with bad art and counterrevolutionary banality and had to be recreated in accordance with the revolutionary "dictatorship of taste." Although the prospect of practicing revolutionary avant-garde art instead of living everyday life might seem very appealing in theory, it soon became clear that theory and practice differ—a realization that is at the core of the problem of the everyday.

It has become a commonplace saying, but I will nevertheless repeat it, that literary metaphors in Russia are taken too much to heart, while the facts of daily life are treated highly metaphysically. In Chekhov's story "The Literature Teacher," the geography teacher Ippolitov obsessively repeats textbook banalities ("the Volga falls into the Caspian sea . . . Horses eat oats"). The revolutionary inventor in Mayakovsky's last play, *The Bathhouse,* holds the most radical attitudes toward such clichés. In response to the question, "Does this wretched Volga river still flow into the Caspian Sea?", he answers: "Yes, but it won't be doing so for long."[39] The revolutionary inventor is called upon to save the world from these stifling clichés once and for all. And this is not merely a rhetorical or poetic device or pure avant-garde fiction. Indeed, the Soviet government attempted to violate natural common places and to cause rivers to flow in the opposite direction. It was one of Stalin's most overwhelming construction plans, now considered a major environmental disaster. One reason for studying Russian cultural myths and Soviet psychopathology of everyday life is to find the invisible connections between the commonplaces of individual life and the national dreams.

The Soviet Union, a country of which no precise map ever existed and where physical geography was always a political science, is no longer on the map of the world. This book will not deal exclusively with the distinct features of Soviet civilization or of the international totalitarian culture, which certainly deserves a great deal of attention. Rather, it will examine some enduring Russian cultural myths that developed over a long duration of historical time and survived revolutions, civil wars, perestroikas, and coups. ("Russian" here is not the term of ethnic purity and refers to all ethnic groups which for better or for worse happened to share Russian and Soviet Russian history.) At the same time, this is not to say that things do not or will not change. Change, however, requires understanding the process of cultural myth-making: it should not be conceived as a mere change of portraits in one of the rooms in the old building of Moscow University, which is now for rent. (Before the Revolution there was a portrait of Tsar Nikolai II, later supplanted by Lenin, Stalin, and subsequently Brezhnev—only Gorbachev did not insist on the adoration of his image. In 1991, however, the space came to be occupied by a portrait of L. Ronald Hubbard, the author and founder of *Dianetics*, whose disciples were willing to pay hard currency for the honor.) It remains to be seen who will be the next cultural icon.

The Mythologist as Traveler

After his trip to the Soviet Union in 1927 Walter Benjamin suggested that citizens should look at their country in the context of a map of neighboring states; especially, "all Europeans ought to see, on a map of Russia, their little land as a frayed nervous territory far out to the West."[40] Yet Benjamin's advice to the Western intellectual was hardly ever taken to heart. Before the mid-1980s the Soviet Union belonged to the so-called Second World, a *demi-monde* of cultural criticism. Too implicated in the battles of the Cold War, the USSR became de-materialized; it appeared to some to be merely an evil object lesson of ideology, a media special effect. It fell between the First and Third worlds and was marginal to the recent debates around Eurocentrism. Conversely, the journey to Soviet Russia had been a mythical topos of several generations of left intellectuals in the West, a kind of "spiritual home," a home of the revolutionary communist ideal, as Jacques Derrida reminds us in his recent antitravelogue, "Back from Moscow, in the USSR."[41] From the other side, the dream of the West, of a mythical belonging to the "Western democratic public sphere," occasionally accompanied by a vicarious infatuation with Western consumer goods, were characteristic for many intellectuals in the

East. Perhaps it is this mythical idea of home that the Easterners locate in the West and Westerners locate in the East, the utopia that neither side wishes to radically undermine, that prevents a critical dialogue from happening. They tamper with each other's fantasy worlds shaped—but not necessarily predetermined—by differences in actual cultural experiences. Both sides were frequently disappointed by the mythical "homecoming," East and West alike, and frightened by their own uncanny mirror images. While some Western intellectuals nostalgically hum "back in the US/SR," many Russian intellectuals wish to go just up to the bar: "back to the US." A rock song popular in post-Soviet Russia echoes the Beatles' original in its refrain: "Bye-bye, Amerika—where I will never go."

Because of Russia's peculiar threshold position between Europe and Asia, the national identity crisis plays a very important role in Russian intellectual history, and one of the central conflicts in it is the relationship between Russia and the West. Hence, the anti-Western discourse of Russian exclusivity, of Russia's chosen role to save the West. It is time to question the mythical binary opposition of Russia and the West.[42] James Clifford writes that modern ethnographic histories of cross-cultural relationships "are condemned to oscillate between two metanarratives: one of homogenization, the other of emergence, one of loss, the other of invention."[43] Instead of lamenting the loss of Russian pure good taste or attempting to turn Russia into a truly Western country, it is important to question the conception of culture as a system of exclusive internal relationships with guarded national borders. Cultural specificity is not synonymous with cultural or national purity; most cultures, including the Russian, are inventively eclectic.

Perhaps the only way to explore cultural myths and commonplaces is to travel back and forth across the borders of one's own community. A cultural mythologist has to be a cross-cultural mythologist. We have to be prepared to be stopped at customs, to have our cultural baggage inspected, and still hope to make the flight. Jet lag is a necessary condition for the mythological exploration. Russia exerted a particular fascination for many foreign travelers: it was the limit of the Western world and its experimental lab, the exotic land of communist utopia and absolutist dystopia, of revolution and stagnation. Traveling to Russia was a way of testing one's beliefs and attitudes toward one's own country. Travelers' accounts, while quite unreliable as historical documents, are exemplary texts of cross-cultural mythology. In the 1830s a French nobleman, the Marquis de Custine, came to Russia fleeing a French revolution and ended up becoming an anti-monarchist who escaped an absolutist regime. Some hundred years later, André Gide and Walter Benjamin, among many others, came to discover the communist utopia, only to go back with changed views of France and Germany and of utopia as such. Benjamin's account of traveling along the icy and slippery streets of Moscow, where he collected facts and material artifacts that defy ideological maps, inspired my own journey. In a way this book is about my return to my native country, which I try to mediate through the writings of others, through art and kitsch. I left Leningrad, USSR, as a political refugee, never to come back, and ten years later returned as an American tourist. During those ten years the country and my native city changed their names, and I have changed mine. Now I cross the borders back and forth and feel like a perpetually traveling "resident alien."

During my last trip back to the former Soviet Union, I discovered that the generation to which I was supposed to belong has just acquired the name of "octoderasts" *(vos'miderasty)*. Those who entered public life during the post-Stalinist thaw of the late 1950s and early 1960s and experienced an internal crisis when the Soviet tanks entered Prague in 1968, were called the "sixtniks," with the diminutive-endearing suffix "nik," as in "no-goodniks" in the *Clockwork Orange* version of Sovietspeak. By contrast, those of us born in the late 1950s, after Stalin's death and around the cheerful time of the first International Youth Festival in Moscow, got their suffix from "pederasts"—the word in the Soviet criminal code for homosexuality. Whereas the sixtniks were romantic and optimistic, the octoderasts, the children of "stagnation," are skeptical, ironic, and disbelieving. They were the last Soviet generation, the last one to go through proper Soviet schooling with patriotic songs and military games, Pioneer camps and collective farms, all of which by now have become antique. They matured during the times of the Immortal Generalissimus Brezhnev, when the sixtniks fell silent or joined the establishment, and entered public life during glasnost' with their critique of the thaw. Perhaps generations acquire names once they begin to lose their historical momentum; the "children of perestroika," those who are twenty now, who know Marx-Engels-Lenin primarily from the "antique sales" on Arbat Street, appear indifferent to the never-ending intellectual debates about the end of history or the end of art, the death of the intelligentsia or the death of empire. Immune to the minor nostalgias their parents and elder brothers and sisters are occasionally prone to, they prefer *Terminator 2*. I spent the 1980s in the United States, so it is hard to say whether I would even belong to the octoderasts, but it is possible that they remain one of my imagined communities.

In Chapter 1 I collect the mythologies of Russian and Soviet everyday and reflect on a number of concepts that various Russian or Western intellectuals have claimed to be culturally untranslatable. This includes the Russian hatred of daily routine and stagnation, embodied in the words *byt* and *poshlost'; meshchanstvo*—the Russian middle class that, more (or less) than a social class, is rather a moral (or immoral) category of despicable philistines; Russian Culture in the singular and with a capital "C"; and the Stalinist campaign of mass culturalization *(kul'turnost'),* which represents an ideological "civilizing process" combining table manners with Marxism-Leninism. I will also consider why there is no Russian word for privacy or for authenticity but two words for truth, and how those linguistic features were explored and exploited by Russian and Soviet writers and critics. Why is it that the Russian idea of personality is opposed to the Western conception of individual identity, and why is it that the Russian soul is not supposed to have a private life? Finally, I will examine Soviet songs from the 1930s to the 1990s—from the "March of the Aviators" to "Good-bye, Amerika"—the songs that celebrate various ways of escaping Soviet everyday life and carving alternative spaces of cultural survival.

Chapter 2 will explore living in common places and its central archeological site, the communal apartment, stronghold of Soviet civilization and the ruin of communal utopias (not to be confused either with the communes or with voluntarily shared apartments). After examining the utopian topography of the socialist city and some comical artistic visions of communal life, we will visit a few of the old communal apartments in Leningrad-St. Petersburg and later go to my own (now destroyed) communal apartment. We will look behind the scenes at the class wars of the neighbors, at the rituals of secrecy and obsessive collecting of "domestic trash" that defy many sociological theories of object, fetish, commodity, and popular taste.

I dedicate Chapter 3 to writing common places, and particularly to the literary disease of "graphomania"—a writing obsession that was particularly dangerous in a country where the national identity depended on the correct interpretation of literature, and where violation of literary behavior was frequently deemed politically subversive. Why is graphomania a Russian and Eastern/Central-European national disease? Why is it much less prominent in other European countries and even less so in the United States? Will graphomania vanish together with the prestige of great literature?

The last chapter, "Postcommunism, Postmodernism," begins with the events of the 1991 military coup and the relationship between disaster and the everyday, between apocalyptic visions and banality. From walking the city streets at the time of glasnost' and the euphoria of the recovery of history, we will move to the post-Soviet versions of the "end of history" and to totalitarian nostalgia. We will examine postmodernism in post-Soviet art—from the carnival of kitsch in the Russian cinema and new documentaries to tactile conceptualism in the works of women artists. And finally, we will look at born-again cultures of post-Soviet entrepreneurs and examine TV soaps and recent commercials—perhaps the most unintentionally surreal and postmodern of all everyday arts. In this proliferation of "post" suffixes perpetuated by Western and Russian critics—posttotalitarian, postcommunist, post-Soviet, postmodern—what happens to the memory of the common place?

Television comes to the collective farm, 1990 (photo by Mark Shteinbok)

1

Mythologies of Everyday Life

Byt: "Daily Grind" and "Domestic Trash"

In his suicide note the Soviet revolutionary poet Vladimir Maya-kovsky lamented: "the love boat has crashed against *byt.*" The poet who dreamed of the radical reconstruction of life and art, at the end failed in the arts of daily survival in postrevolutionary Russia. He attributed his failure neither to the counterrevolutionaries nor to Stalinist bureaucracy, neither to the women who did not live up to his love nor to the public that betrayed him, but to the monstrous daily grind—byt. The words of the poet became a Soviet proverb; the phrase has the catchy quality of a punchline from a cheap melo-drama, and the ring of cultural tragedy. Everyday speech itself offers a number of dramatic metaphors for this attitude: "byt eats me up," for instance.

The opposition between *byt,* everyday existence (everyday routine and stagnation), and *bytie* (spiritual being) is one of the central common places of the Russian intellectual tradition. It is often under-stood as the opposition between everyday life and "real" life, which is always everywhere. Two distinguished theorists of Russian culture, Boris Uspensky and Iurii Lotman, insist that the binary opposition between *byt* and *bytie* dates back to Russian Orthodox Christianity and remains a fundamental feature of the culture at least until the nineteenth century. They point out the crucial difference between the Western medieval "world beyond the grave" and its threefold divi-sion of heaven, purgatory, and hell, and the Russian medieval order, based on a fundamental duality. Hence in Russia the everyday could not have been perceived as a neutral sphere of human behavior where the conceptions of "civil society" and private life might have originated.[1] Lotman explores the "semiotics" of everyday behavior of Russian nobility in the eighteenth and nineteenth century, but his emphasis is always on semiotics and structures rather than on the everyday resistance to them. Everyday behavior is described according to a literary model extracted from specific texts. While striving for scientific coherence, Lotman's approach fails to confront the contingencies and double-entendres of daily life, as well as the digressions and incoherences in the literary texts—digressions that might tell us more about the nature of the everyday life than systemic models.

The question is, do these theorists *describe* Russian culture or *perpetuate* its cultural mythology? Why is there such a national insistence upon the uniqueness of the Russian conception of the everyday, and a desire to live out what appears to be a common romantic metaphor of the battle against the ordinary?[2]

Originally byt referred only to the way of life or everyday existence; it is a word with a common Indo-European root connected to being and habitat.[3] It was the Symbolists of the late nineteenth century and the early revolutionaries that used byt to designate the reign of stagnation and routine, of daily transience without transcendence, whether spiritual, artistic, or revolutionary. Byt, the ordinary way of life, began to be seen as the order of chaos and contingency that precludes any illumination. It is this conception of the everyday that Roman Jakobson deemed untranslatable into the European languages. The brief sketch of poetic and political demonization of the everyday that follows includes discussions of Russia's messianic role in the world, revolutionary dreams of radical reconstruction of daily life culminating in the campaign against domestic trash in the 1920s, Stalinist "culturalization" and post-Stalinist wanderlust, as well as a 1990s retelling of the fairy tale about Ivan the Fool fighting the fortresses of byt.

It has been suggested that Muscovite culture developed out of the experience of East Slavic peasants in the nearly impossible conditions of life in the northern forest and in response to external aggression; hence it is characterized by "a strong tendency to maintain stability and a kind of closed equilibrium, risk-avoidance, suppression of individual initiative; informality of political power, and the striving of unanimous final resolution of potentially divisive issues."[4] This con-

servationist mentality did not seek to preserve a traditional or idealized Slavic "way of life" but to preserve life itself; it was an expression of sheer human survival.[5] If byt, the way of life, exemplifies the
collective Muscovite and later Russian mentalities—survivors of a
long duration of time, wars, uprisings and revolutions—so does the
opposition to byt, the anti-byt discourse as developed by Russian
poets and intellectuals since the nineteenth century; it is at the core
of many Russian and Soviet self-definitions. Nineteenth-century
Westernizers and Slavophiles, Romantics and modernists, æsthetic
and political utopians, and Bolsheviks and monarchists all engaged
in battles with byt. For many of them what mattered was not physical
survival but sacrifice, not preservation of life but its complete transcendence, not the fragile human existence in this world but collective
happiness in the other world. Many of them, speaking in the name
of the people *(narod)* and invoking traditional peasant communes
(obshchina), in fact promoted ideals that appear radically opposite to
the aspirations expressed by the "common people" themselves.

The leading philosopher of the "Russian idea," Nikolai Berdiaev,
insists that the Russian identity rests on an extra-ordinary, messianic
foundation. Russians, in Berdiaev's view, are the "chosen people" and
also "a People of the End." Such a people need not be concerned
about the process of everyday living and common survival, which is
often more difficult than imagining some kind of "future perfect." In
a culture in which the eschatological and the apocalyptic are closely
linked to the conception of national identity, there can be very little
patience for the ordinary, transient, and everyday. Russia itself is
frequently personified in poetry as a flying troika that leaves the limits
of this banal world and runs away without aim or restraint. In
Alexander Blok's *fin-de-siècle* vision, Russia is a pure spirit dancing
to a sad song about escaping the everyday.[6] And as she dances, a
wandering apocalyptic horseman lurks in the twilight. Russia is thus
defined by her perpetual nomadic spirit, wanderlust, and a liberation
from dailiness. In this iconography byt is perceived not simply as
unspiritual but also as non-Russian in the higher, poetic sense of what
it means to be Russian.[7]

Thus there is a radical difference between the American dream of
private pursuit of happiness in the family home, and the Russian
dream, which, at least in the conceptions of Dostoevsky and his great
admirer Berdiaev, consisted of spiritual homelessness and messianic

nomadism. No wonder that in Dostoevsky's *Crime and Punishment* the expression "going to America" is synonymous with committing suicide—quite another way of thinking about the New World. Of course, this apocalyptic struggle between byt and bytie did not remain uncontested. The popular commercial fiction that emerged in late imperial Russia and was forbidden after the Revolution often celebrated brave social climbers, people of everyday knowledge who dwell on daily trifles and minor erotic pursuits. Russian writers from Pushkin to Tolstoy and Chekhov have discovered the power of detail and the repetitive waves of everyday narrative.[8]

Some members of the intelligentsia launched a powerful critique from within of the intelligentsia's philosophy of life, on the grounds that it had little to do with the actual study of philosophy or with the ability to live a decent life. In the words of Mikhail Gershenzon, writing in the collection of essays *Landmarks:*

> The intelligentsia's *byt* is terrible, a true abomination of abandon and isolation, no discipline at all and no consistency, not even in external appearance . . . idleness, untidiness, Homeric uncleanliness and indecency in private life, dirt and chaos in the family and in sexual relations, naïve irresponsibility in work, in social matters unlimited propensity towards despotism and a complete lack of respect toward the other's personality. In the face of authority either proud challenge or obliging complaisance—not collective . . . but personal.[9]

Gershenzon questions the intelligentsia's romantic stance against the everyday, its refusal to develop a critical subjectivity and self-conscious personality. Yet even in this invective against the Russian intelligentsia's ideals, Gershenzon assumes a special intimacy of relations between the intelligentsia and the people; the members of the intelligentsia are not in danger of becoming European-style egoists or petty bourgeois who cultivate their everyday existence for its own sake.[10]

After the October Revolution of 1917, the war on "petit-bourgeois everyday life" enters a new phase with the dream of New Byt created by poets and politicians. Here the poet Nikolai Zabolotsky sings an anachronistic yet avant-garde hymn to the baby New Byt:

> The sun rises over Moscow
> Old women are running in awe
> where could they go now?

The New Byt is at the door.
The baby is big and well-groomed
he sits in the cradle like a sultan.

. . . . .

The baby becomes strong and virile
He walks across the table
and jumps right into Komsomol.[11]

New Byt is a kind of a miracle baby, whose iconography reminds us of an atheistic baby Christ. The poem was written only three years before the question of the "perestroika of byt" was to be taken away from the poets and given to the Central Committee of the Communist Party and its *ukazes*.[12] Paradoxically, the Soviet construction of the new byt—on the grounds that the everyday had to be created anew—is itself based on the old idea concerning the opposition between byt and bytie. The dream of New Byt reflects a series of rather uncanny continuities between the ideology of nineteenth-century Russian intelligentsia and early Soviet left theorists, and even more inappropriately, between left theorists and Stalinist bureaucrats (inappropriately, because the latter were often responsible for the physical extermination of the former).[13] The style of the new byt varied from violent to lyrical.

The Soviet iconography of New Byt was based on a complete restructuring of both time and space; from Gastev's utopian schedules of everyday life to the total design of the new communist space (the all-people's house-commune) to the construction of new men and women. But can everyday life be contained by the utopian topography? It is not surprising that hardly anywhere else in the modern Western world was such a precise construction of "ideologically correct" everyday life devised in the twentieth century, and nowhere else were there so many deviations from this utopian construct. Andrei Sinyavsky writes that the conception of "a Soviet way of life," or a new byt, is "an oxymoron, a marriage of mutually exclusive concepts"; since "a way of life" suggests something enduring and stable, tied to habit, to traditions and to basic forms of existence, and therefore it cannot be new or revolutionary.[14] Perhaps this very contradiction in terms became a Soviet way of life.

I will focus on the last bold attempt to implement a utopian avant-garde design in real life. In 1922–1928 Mayakovsky wrote a series of poems that shifted the focus from the heroism of the Civil War to the antiheroic everyday life—yet the militant rhetoric persists. These poems feature all the key words for our discussion of everyday mythologies: *meshchanstvo* (philistines, middle class), *poshlost'* (banality, obscenity, and bad taste), and *kul'turnost'* ("cultured behavior"). Trash does not stand for "rubbish" but for its opposite, cozy domestic objects that belong to the culture of the postrevolutionary pseudo-aristocrats, these same *meshchane, obyvateli,* and *nouveaux riches.* Here is how Mayakovsky presents the family scene of the new Soviet philistines with aristocratic pretensions:

> On the wall is Marx
> The little frame is crimson
> Lying on *The News,* a kitten is getting warm
> And near the ceiling
> Chirps
> A frantic little canary[15]

A rather innocent domestic setting turns into a battleground where the ferocious struggle for the New Byt must take place. The philistines' wish is to turn the revolutionary struggle into a cozy communist idyll, and revolutionary gains into a collection of private fetishes. Mayakovsky uses his magic poetic powers to wake up the Sleeping Beauty of the Revolution and stage a "rebellion of things":

> From the wall Marx watches and watches
> And suddenly
> Opening his mouth wide,
> He starts howling:
> The revolution is tangled up in philistine threads
> More terrible than Vrangel is philistine byt
> Better
> To twist off canaries' heads—
> So communism
> Won't be struck down by canaries[16]

Karl Marx is "framed" by Soviet philistines in the little red corner where icons used to be kept. The enraged "leader of the international proletariat" demands a heroic revolutionary feat, a symbolic sacrifice—the strangling of that dangerous petit-bourgeois yellow canary. (Mayakovsky uses the common Romantic device of personification to save Marx from philistine fetishism.)[17]

In response to his poems the newspaper *Komsomol Truth* launched the campaign "Down with Domestic Trash" in 1928–1929, to implement in real life Mayakovsky's poetic battle with the daily grind. The newspaper appealed to its new readers, the young Soviet men and women. It attempted to create a kind of interactive Soviet public sphere where readers would join in trashing old-style domesticity and report to the paper their own feats of burning "little idols of things." The campaign slogans proclaimed: "Let us stop the production of tasteless bric-à-bracs! With all these dogs, mermaids, little devils and elephants, invisibly approaches meshchanstvo. Clean your room! Summon bric-à-brac to a public trial!"[18] The campaign recreated the rhetoric of the Civil War and cultural revolution: "Our struggle against domestic trash has moved into a new phase . . . it is necessary to destroy the fortresses of the enemy so that evil will be eradicated completely."[19] The cry was, down with the "dictatorship of the workshop of faience figurines" and onward with the "dictatorship of [revolutionary] taste." The campaign was led by left art theorists close to the Constructivists. It was a campaign for a new topography of the home: an ideal revolutionary home, not a fetishistic refuge of bourgeois coziness.

One of the campaigners wrote that the "taste of the masses" had been formed under "Asiatic conditions of autocracy, when an abyss separated art for the ruling class and art for the people."[20] Hence contemporary conceptions of mass taste were irrelevant for the revolutionaries. The sweetly realistic faience figurines sold in GUM (the State Department Store) and *lubki* (popular eighteenth-century comic engravings recreated in a folkloric style by Soviet artists) were the main "devils of domestic trash," hated by the campaigners for the new byt but often beloved by the masses.

The attacks on domestic trash went hand in hand with the anti-religious campaign, on the one hand, and the campaign to promote physical culture and sport, on the other.[21] The objects of domestic trash were called "little idols" *(bozhki)* because they inspired counterrevolutionary idolatry. These little idols could take the shape of popular figurines of devils or porcelain elephants.[22] Pieces of furniture that were singled out for their "ugly aesthetics" were certain "fat-bellied" chests of drawers.[23] The adjective "fat-bellied" personifying the petit-bourgeois object is particularly revealing. What could be worse than to be "fat-bellied" at a time of national infatuation with sports and physical fitness, so often displayed in collective parades on the public squares—though not in front of the mirror in one's private room. The "fat-bellied" commode was unaesthetic and unhealthy; it was not "fit" to decorate the worker's room. The new concept of beauty was opposed to meshchansky pseudo-luxury and over-crowdedness of unhealthy objects. The new beauty was expressed in Mayakovsky's catchphrase: "Elegance is 100 percent utility, comfort of clothes, and spaciousness of dwellings."[24] The marriage of physical fitness and beauty and the obsession with hygiene was the shared "family value" of three diverse political cultures of the 1930s: United States, Nazi Germany, and Soviet Russia.

Women were often derided as the preservers of coziness and collec-tors of useless petit-bourgeois objects for the domestic hearth. In response to this accusation, two women readers offered the most radical programs of house-cleaning and self-purification. Here is what comrade Cherniakova proposed:

> Dear women home-makers! I accepted the challenge of *Komsomol-skaia Pravda:* I tore off the walls postcards and paintings. I put them in the stove. I broke the statuettes representing naked vulgar women in improbable poses . . . I broke the bric-à-brac—all these peasant-guys and dolls. I carried them to the trash. . . . This kind of beauty is not in my head. The room is so good and so full of light now! Having done this I appeal to all women homemakers to follow my example.[25]

What is characteristic of this euphoric and self-righteous scene of destruction is that comrade Cherniakova was not satisfied with just cleaning up her own house. Moreover, she was not able to do it quietly, "in the privacy of her own home," to use the American metaphor. She did it in order to write about it, to put the "privacy of her own home" on public trial, to expose her self-righteousness, and to get published. The letter ends with an appeal to the readers to follow her example. This new Soviet public sphere imagined by *Kom-somol Truth* resembles a premodern potlatch, when the members of a rival tribe burn their furniture as a public sacrifice so that the neighbor will be obliged to burn more.

Many other readers and editors shared with one another and with the larger public similar scenes of domestic destruction. One cautious person self-defensively presented a list of art reproductions in his room, wondering whether the editors of the newspaper would deem them in good taste. In a letter entitled "What Will You Give Us Instead of Trash?" reader Galkin from the village of Amvrosievka wrote:

> Everyone writes "down with"! I have already thrown out everything
> . . . I agree that there is little new in art and that mass production
> is trash, but nobody has shown specifically how to decorate the
> apartment. For instance, I have on my walls reproductions of the
> paintings *Factory* (from a Berlin gallery), *Peasants Visiting Lenin,*
> *The Last White Guards in Kuban,* portraits of Lenin and Marx.[26]

The reader's last name—Galkin, from *galka,* "jackdaw"—and the name of the village, Amvrosievka, most likely derived from "ambrosia" or gods' nectar—sound suspiciously fictional. What kind of pastoral Soviet Arcadia, what land of the new byt with pictures of Leninist peasants did this reader come from? Then again, in the Russian and Soviet context reality could be stranger than fiction. The reader confesses he is afraid to be placed on the "black list of culturelessness."

Komsomolskaia Pravda put its own editorial byt on trial and condemned the office ashtray. The editorial board decided to get rid of the old ashtray with a picture of two horses, a reduced version of the Russian troika (this was not because of the evils of smoking: the idea of smoking as a health hazard belongs to another era). Instead of the old one the editors purchased a new ashtray in GUM that depicted sportsmen, thereby discarding old-fashioned pseudo-Russian hobbies like sleighing and horseback-riding and substituting more modern athletic pursuits. The editors commented that they did not find the picture on the new ashtray more aesthetically pleasing, but this was all they could find in the Soviet store, and besides, the new ashtray was more functional.

The campaign for the new byt touched just about every trifle of daily decoration, every souvenir, every figurine, every postcard. In an article entitled "What Are We Demanding from a Plate?" the answer was "we demand that the plate fulfill its social function." During the cultural revolution, in "the parade of things every object has to be in line."[27] *Komsomolskaia Pravda* published "ideologically correct" postcards with abstract drawings and "ideologically incorrect" postcards with reclining half-dressed modern-day naiads. The naiads—

rare examples of early Soviet erotica—were to be put on trial.[28] The postcard, a minimal expression of the desire to decorate or to communicate, turned out to be rather ill-suited for the new byt. Mayakovsky's long poem "Vladimir Ilich Lenin" gives us a different view of the revolutionary interior decoration: "There are two of us in the room; me and Lenin—a photograph on the white wall."[29] This is not only a poem about the poet's communion with the Party Leader but also about the ideal revolutionary habitat, with bare walls adorned with the one true revolutionary icon—a black-and-white photo of Lenin, whom Sergei Tretiakov called "the greatest anti-fetishist of all."

The war against the reification and objectification of pleasures and experiences of life was also a war for the sake of war, a nostalgia for the warlike spirit and nomadic lifestyle of the true revolutionary. The new furniture, for instance, had to be folding and portable, as if ready for a journey or a military campaign in a literal sense. El Lissitsky compares the room of the future "to the best kind of traveling suitcase." He writes that for a modern person it is enough to have in an empty room a mattress, a folding chair, a table, and a gramophone (the gramophone here is an unusual concession to popular demand).[30]

Despite the powerful rhetoric and enthusiasm that characterized the campaign against domestic trash, its leaders turned out to be the losers in the battle for public taste. Moreover, some of the organizers of the campaign were eventually driven into exile or had to stop their activities forever. In the 1930s the intrusion into the everyday is more than rhetorical—the home search became a haunting image of the new Stalinist perestroika of everyday life. At that time, when the home search became a common practice, the burning of domestic trash no longer came up in the press. The style of Stalinist new byt turned out to be the style of GUM, of pseudo-Russian *lubok*, of the Soviet version of middle-brow culture, the main enemy of the Constructivists. Yet some of the slogans of the campaign, including occasional attacks on porcelain elephants and rubber plants, remained in the eclectic arsenal of the Stalinist critics.

Vera Dunham writes that a special pact, a "big deal," was made after World War II between the Soviet government and its ordinary citizens, the new Soviet middle class.[31] The postwar hero and heroine had grown tired of the frugality and heroic asceticism of the previous generation. There was a new passion for artifacts, for homeyness, and for femininity. This is a description of a girl's nook in the student dorm of the early 1950s: "Over the bed a lot of colored postcards were tacked up, with views of Naples, Venice, the sea, and naked mermaids. Several brightly embroidered pillows were neatly arranged on the bed. Her small nightstand was covered with pink paper, scalloped at the edge."[32] Here, reborn, are the artifacts of the much-cursed old byt of the times of the New Economic Policy (NEP): ornaments, pinned-up postcards representing the exotic lands to the west of the Russian border, and the pink-papered nightstand. Pink was the hot color of the season, as Vera Dunham points out, and so were purple and orange. But pink is particularly interesting: neither white nor red, it blurs the revolutionary opposition between the two—not the color of blood, nor of the revolutionary banner, but rather the color of the feminine blush. What could be more abject for the old guard of the revolutionary intelligentsia!

Vera Dunham ends her book with a strong indictment of the new Soviet man—neither a revolutionary idealist, a builder of the utopia, nor a purist intellectual, but a Soviet meshchanin, an incurable petit-bourgeois of a type that survived from the 1930s to the 1970s: "From the right and from the left, it would seem, from the top and from the bottom, private acquisitiveness is celebrated—cut crystal goblets for the rich, clattering pots for the poor, and pans for Ivan Ivanovich—so marking the triumph of the canary."[33] Mayakovsky's emblem of petit-bourgeois domesticity is still chirping, a sound that provokes recurrent urges to save revolutionary idealism. The moralizing invective against the Soviet middle class continues, "from the left and from the right, from the top and from the bottom," bringing us back to the opposition between the avant-garde revolutionary intelligentsia and the counterrevolutionary daily grind. And it is this permanent dualism of the material and the ideal, in their ethical as well as aesthetic dimensions, that needs to be rethought. Does that impulse to decorate a nook in a shared collective dorm—to protect the merest bit of privacy—deserve to be condemned out of hand? On what grounds and from whose perspective?

In the 1960s the Soviet intelligentsia rebelled against what they perceived as compromised Stalinist coziness and recreated the spirit of nomadic romanticism characteristic of the 1920s. There were songs about trips "in search for the fog and the smell of taiga," and stories of romances of alpinists, geologists, and flight attendants. A new campaign against domestic trash was proclaimed. It was another romantic crusade against domestic coziness, not only pink lamp-shades and porcelain elephants but also soft couches and armchairs, love-seat sofas *(lyra),* and plush curtains—against, in short, the feathering of domestic little nests. In the 1970s, after the Soviet tanks had driven into Prague, the intelligentsia retreated into the private domain and reexamined its own "kitchen communities" of the 1960s. Some *intelligents* became dissidents and experienced violent intrusions of privacy and KGB home searches; others conformed to the life of stagnation; and a few emigrated to capitalist lands where "privacy" is protected by law and elevated to the status of a state religion. It is from there that they observed the collapse of the Soviet civilization.

In the middle of the perestroika of the late 1980s one of the prominent Soviet satirists wrote that Russians recognize themselves in the folkloric character of Ivan the Fool, the youngest son of the family. He spends most of his time napping on the warm top of the large Russian stove, but occasionally wakes up to perform great heroic feats. Ivan the Fool is a great hero, but he does not know how to live between his heroic deeds. The byt, the everyday, is a more dangerous enemy for him than a multiheaded dragon with flaming tongues. Russia worships her heroes and praises their impracticality, their ability to overcome "water and fire" alongside their inability to cope with the daily routine. The heroic conception of Russian culture and its messianic mission is responsible for the ostracism of the everyday. Perhaps it is not the monster of byt that has to be beheaded but rather the cultural myth that pits everyday life against the national dream.

In the fairy tale Ivan the Fool always gets the same mysterious assignment: "to go nobody knows where, to find nobody knows what," and he finds a firebird and becomes the hero of all the people. But his heroic feat—*podvig*—has become as banal as his naps on the heated stove. Perhaps he actually never reaches the place "nobody knows where" and always goes for the predictable firebird, instead of taking another fork at the crossroad, confronting everyday contingencies and drifting beyond the limits of fairy-tale land.

Poshlost': Banality, Obscenity, Bad Taste

After making love with her new acquaintance in the resort town of Yalta, the heroine of Anton Chekhov's short story "A Lady with a Dog" begins to cry, and then declares that she has become "a *poshlaia* woman."[34] Her lover orders a piece of melon brought to him on a porcelain saucer with a golden rim. He is embarrassed by her tears, which are not in good taste for a conventional, cool, and blasé resort romance. Yet it is the shame and the lure of poshlost' that turn this Western-style casual adultery into a typical Russian love story, complete with tears, grey dresses, autumnal landscapes, and nostalgia.

Poshlost' is the Russian version of banality, with a characteristic national flavoring of metaphysics and high morality, and a peculiar conjunction of the sexual and the spiritual. This one word encompasses triviality, vulgarity, sexual promiscuity, and lack of spirituality.[35] The war against poshlost' is a cultural obsession of the Russian and Soviet intelligentsia from the 1860s to 1960s. Perhaps nowhere else in the world has there been such a consistency in the battle against banality. In Dostoevsky, poshlyi is an attribute of the devil (or at least of his dreamline novelistic apparition), while Alexander Solzhenitsyn uses it to characterize Western-oriented youth. In everyday speech a "poshliak" (boor or slob, with a diminutive pejorative suffix) is not a servant of the devil or a "Western spy" but only a man who frequently uses obscene language or behaves like a common womanizer.[36] Poshlost' has also a broader meaning, close to byt, when it refers to the incommensurable everyday routine, obscene by virtue of being ordinary and evil by virtue of being banal.

Vladimir Nabokov insists on the originality and untranslatability of Russian banality. In his view, only the Russians were able to devise the concept of poshlost', and they could do it because of the "good taste in Old Russia." (This is perhaps one of the least ironic sentences in Nabokov, bordering on the banal.) Poshlost', according to Nabokov, is an "unobvious sham"; it is "not only the obviously trashy but also the falsely important, the falsely beautiful, the falsely clever, the falsely attractive."[37] But the moment the famous literary ironist, who takes so much delight in describing poshlost' in his novels, attempts to come up with antidotes to it, he too is in danger of falling into the traps of Russian banality. In identifying poshlost'

as a key critical category, Nabokov inadvertently identifies *with* the
Russian intellectual obsession—the critique of banality. The epidemic
of poshlost' is often attributed by critically minded intellectuals to
Russia's encounter with the West and with "progress." What is at
stake in the Russian taste wars is not merely social prestige but
national pride.

In Nabokov's visualization the first "o" of poshlost' is "as big as
the plop of an elephant falling into the mud and as round as the
bosom of a bathing beauty on a German picture postcard."[38] His
defining examples are mainly German: Bavarian bathing beauties,
picturesque swans, and the lacy curtains of Hansel and Gretel as
described by Gogol. Yet while the Germans lived poshlost', the Russians learned to mock it (especially "educated, sensitive and free-
minded Russians," acutely aware of the "furtive and clammy touch
of poshlost'"). Nabokov's humorous, passionate, and occasionally
infuriating invective is directed at imitations of the European middle-
class middle-brow culture, as well as at the American ads.[39] Nabokov
has aestheticized the Russian word and turned it into a perfect artifact of national criticism, but without inquiring about its history.
What are the origins of this allegedly unique version of national
banality?

Until the nineteenth century the adjective "poshlyi" does not have
any derogatory connotation and is not connected with taste, morality,
sexuality, or the devil, but simply refers to something old and traditional. Poshlost' comes from *poshló*: something that has been, has
occurred, or has passed. Among the old meanings of the word are
"traditional," "ancient"; thus poshlyi people can refer to ancestors,
and a poshlyi route means an old thoroughfare.[40] There is an important connection between poshlost' and the merchant class—*kuptsy*, at
the higher level, and *meshchane* at the lower level of urban dwellers
(the mythical Russian equivalent of the petite bourgeoisie).[41] According to a tale that circulated in Russia in the seventeenth century, when
Elizabeth of England refused the marriage proposal of Ivan the Terrible, he was not particularly angry. "She is only a common woman
(poshlaia devitsa)," he remarked proudly.[42] "Common woman" here
does not mean a common whore, but rather a woman of inferior
(possibly not sufficiently aristocratic), merchant origins. Ivan, of
course, was tracing his genealogy from the great Prince Rurik, a
Viking who became the first East Slavic ruler. (One thing to be regret-

ted about this legendary and uncommon instance of matchmaking is that it could have resulted in a great Shakespearean comedy.)

One of the first literary uses of the word "poshlyi" occurs in Pushkin. In the course of a high-society ball, blasé aristocrat Eugene Onegin casually and carelessly flirts with the blond beloved of his best friend, the romantic poet Lensky: "Onegin goes with [poshel] Olga, leads her, sliding casually, leans and whispers to her some trivial [poshlyi] madrigal."[43] Although the word is used in the old sense of "old and common," its context anticipates the modern adventures of Russian banality.[44] In the episode of Onegin's flirtation, aesthetics and ethics appear intertwined: poshlyi refers to a minor form of writing that pays a ritualized "compliment to a lady"; at the same time, the word also applies to conventional codes of courtship in high society. Not only is the madrigal poshlyi, but the context of its usage is poshlyi as well.[45] In this case, Onegin's poshlyi behavior leads to what can be considered a moral transgression without any transgression of social etiquette: after his banal flirtation with Olga, he is challenged to a duel in which he kills his friend Lensky, who lived out romantic clichés without self-estranging irony.

Another usage of this adjective occurs in Pushkin's *The Queen of Spades*. One of the archetypal plots of Russian literature, it is the story of a young man murdering, or imagining the murder of, an old woman. The old woman (often referred to as "old hag") is perhaps one of the most sacrificial heroines in Russian literature. The young man, of German descent, is the modern hero par excellence; he needs to get rid of her in order to proceed with his metaphysical search culminating in either madness or redemption. The word poshlyi here, as in *Eugene Onegin*, stands for an intricate tangle of aesthetics, everyday life, and Pushkin's ironic flirtation with German Romanticism. Poshlyi appears again in the context of the highly theatrical high-society ritual—the ball. Young aristocrat Tomsky, like Onegin, flirts with a woman (Lisa) who is in love with another man. Tomsky draws for Lisa a verbal portrait of Hermann: "The portrait sketched by Tomsky was similar to the image that she composed for herself, and, having read the newest novels, this already trivial (poshloe) face scared her and stirred her imagination."[46]

Here again, poshlyi is used derogatorily or at least ironically. Hermann, though not a poet, is another Romantic epigone—a little Russian Napoleon of German descent, or a banal imitation of Mephistopheles. If Hermann is to be seen as a Romantic poet-in-life, he ranks only second class. At the same time, he is the first in a series of poshlyi German characters, embodiments not only of German banality but also of a xenophobic Russian mentality, who will populate the works of Gogol and Dostoevsky.

Yet Pushkin's attitude toward the commonplace is quite ambiguous; there is a certain nostalgia for the common ways. But these common ways in Pushkin, contrary to Nabokov's assertion of "good taste in old Russia," are hardly native: they carry a French accent and are translated from Chateaubriand: "Il n'est de bonheur que dans les voies communes"—one of Pushkin's favorite quotes ("there is no happiness but in the common ways"). Pushkin uses synonymous expressions in three languages—"vulgar," "poshlyi," and "voies communes," suggesting various nuances in his attitudes toward the commonplace.[47] What constitutes the native literary language at this point in Russian history is not determined; Pushkin in fact is the one who sets the limits. He is an enemy of linguistic and cultural purity.[48] His common ways are not the ways of national salvation; they are both Russian and European, culturally specific but not exclusionist. The European commonplace is in crisis, and Pushkin is the first to reenact this crisis on Russian soil.

In fact, the history of the Russian word "poshlost'" parallels the history of the French word for banality. Like *banal* initially, *poshlyi* is neither morally nor aesthetically valorized, and only in the nineteenth century, in the epoch of the Romantic cult of genius and authenticity, did it acquire its present-day connotations. At first, the word had to do with the feudal communality and order. Yet the mourning for that lost communality lasted longer in Russian culture than in France, and everyday life was never conceived by the Russian intellectual as something entirely secular. The sexual, spiritual, and artistic spheres are delineated differently than they are in the West, and everyday life, casual love, and spiritual waste remain linked. Poshlost' and its vehement critique are at the core of the definition of Russian identity, both national and cultural. The usage encompasses attitudes toward material culture and historical change, and it determines ethical values, particularly with respect to sexuality and occasionally with respect to femininity, since poshlost' is occasionally personified as a *salon madame* of loose morals. The "lady with a dog" wept because for a moment her sexuality seemed to have had a life of its own, with no pretense or disguise of anything other than itself—and that is what made it immoral. *Fin-de-siècle* poet Zinaida Gippius sums up Russian views on sex as such: "Something is not right! not this way! ugly! or banal [poshlo]! or a sin! or torturous! or ridiculous!"[49] Is the coupling of banality and sexuality a uniquely Russian phenomenon?

Although none of the European languages so clearly incorporates sexuality into the conception of banality as contemporary Russian does, sexual implications played an important role in the history of the denigration of the English word "common." In nineteenth-century English a "common woman" signifies virtually the same as a "common whore." In fact, one of the earlier synonyms of the word "banal"—trivial, which dates back to the seventeenth century—comes from the Latin "trivialis," a crossroads where prostitutes waited for clients.[50] The denigration of the common place comes down to the female figure of a prostitute, a peculiar Muse of modernity (of course it is not she, but her artist pimps, who get to collect all the honoraria). While the sexual connotation of commonality and triviality seems to disappear in the European languages by the mid-nineteenth century, it becomes accentuated in Russian. Yet poshlost' does not refer explicitly to prostitutes, who are often represented as saintly in both Dostoevsky and Tolstoy. Prostitutes are extreme enough to be redeemed; the real danger lies in everyday sexuality, which presents a larger cultural threat. The fear of poshlost', however, is not merely a fear of sex; rather, it is a fear of sexuality as a separate and autonomous sphere of existence—separate from love, religion, and social preoccupations. Poshlost' is not exactly prostitution, but rather a taste for the obscene, or for excessive sentimentality. In his fictional autobiography, for example, Tolstoy writes that at the time of his youth serious conversations with girls about love were considered to be poshlost'. They violated conventions of aristocratic good taste, male friendship, and rules of conversation.[51]

The connection between poshlost' and the devil might suggest that the term is an umbrella covering many areas of Russian life that refer to low culture, often interpreted in quasi-religious terms as the sinful realm of the devil. Yet the problem with poshlost' is that it trivializes both high culture and low folk culture and blurs the distinctions between cultural levels. Poshlost' risks "prostituting" national culture, turning tradition into fashion, love into sexuality, spirituality into triviality. But how did a word that simply referred to the past and to old and habitual things undergo such a negative metamorphosis?

At the core of the problem of poshlost' is the paradox of repetition and of tradition. Repetition and convention are fundamental for human survival, for the operation of memory and the preservation of culture, for the development of artistic and ordinary language. Poshlost', however, is perceived as a repetition gone sour, a convention turned into a worn-out cliché, a tradition reduced to an infinitely exploitable set of devices that puts a closure on aesthetic and critical experimentation and on experience. But how is it possible to distinguish between good and bad repetition? How do we draw the line between the conventions that constitute our cultural situation, and the trivialization that creates culture's malignant doubles?

Poshlost', like beauty, is in the eye of the beholder, and among its early beholders and discoverers were those writers and intellectuals of the nineteenth century who attributed it to Russia's encounter with modernization and progress, regardless of whether they thought this progress was too slow or too fast. The point is that it was an encounter with a different rhythm and pace of life, a confrontation with rapid change. And this speed of change is what is so difficult to comprehend. Iurii Lotman and Boris Uspensky write that the "binary model" characteristic of the Russian culture affected the conceptualization of the new as well as of the old.

> Duality in the absence of a neutral axiological sphere led to a conception of the new not as a continuation, but as a total eschatological change . . . Under such conditions, the dynamic process of historical change has a fundamentally different character; change occurs as a radical negation of the preceding state. The new does not arise out of a structurally "unused" reserve, but results from a transformation of the old, a process of turning it inside out. Thus repeated transformation can in fact lead to the regeneration of archaic forms.[52]

In this semiotic *vision* of Russian culture (which frequently appears more visionary than semiotic), there is no space for multiple layers of historical memory. The "past" is limited to "old," to the most immediate history being negated by the "new." The evil of poshlost', for some Russian cultural critics, consists precisely in its fuzziness:

poshlost' refers to a whole variety of "impure" phenomena such as the mixed and eclectic low-brow urban culture—neither the aristoc-racy-intelligentsia nor the people—and in fact it jeopardizes the clear contrast between the two and threatens the intellectual's idealization of the people's culture and its national purity.

Contrary to Nabokov's assertion, a comparative study of banality and its critical conceptualizations shows that the Russian concept, with all its cultural specificity, is not unique.[53] Moreover, Nabokov's own claim of exceptionally "good taste" in good old Russia is para-doxical, since the very notion of good taste is a foreign concept alien to old Russia, where taste is associated with the West and the Western concept of civilization.

Nabokov's definition of poshlost' as a peculiar moral-aesthetic hy-brid is quite similar to Hermann Broch's conception of kitsch. Defined as a "sentimentalization of the finite ad infinitum," kitsch is not merely anti-art or bad art, but acts to diffuse the integrity of art and of artistic autonomy.[54] Broch's essay on German kitsch was published a few years before Nabokov's book entitled *Nikolai Gogol,* and Nabokov's poshlost' is like a Russian half-sister of Broch's kitsch, much as the two strive to formulate their separate national identities and concepts of good taste. Nabokov's essay on poshlost' uses Ameri-can, French, and German examples; it praises Russian conceptual powers but is written in English from the perspective of an émigré. The remembrance of the good taste lost is a subtle expression of nostalgia of an aging, Western-educated, St. Petersburgian aristocrat and exiled critic of world poshlost'.[55]

Nabokov's path-breaking study of poshlost' reenacts some of its "unobvious shams." On the one hand, much was made of its Slavic root and native evolution, in the fight for cultural unity and a spiri-tual aristocracy of taste launched by the writers of Russian nobility and later by the Russian intelligentsia. On the other hand, throughout the nineteenth century poshlost' is frequently used in relation to the West and to Russian imitations of it. The fear is that foreign influence can turn native culture into mere fashion. In fact, poshlost' is fre-quently linked to a kind of theatricality in manners, behavior, and self-fashioning.[56] Discussions of poshlost' complicate the usual binary description of Russian culture and put a brake on the Russian na-tional tendency of perpetually swinging between extremes, less be-tween good and evil than (as the Russian saying goes) between two evils. ("Between two evils, choose the third.") My examination of poshlost' will therefore oscillate between the familiar notion of the banality of evil and the less familiar banality of good, and a third danger, the banality of the discourse about or against banality.

Literary Charms of Poshlost': Gogol and Chekhov

While the Russian intelligentsia launched a war on poshlost', the writers derived a great deal of pleasure and understanding of Russian life from describing and savoring it. Poshlost' had been defined in opposition to the creative force in art, but in fact the relationship between the two is symbiotic and paradoxical. Preoccupation with poshlost' and the poshly writer—a.k.a. graphomaniac—carries over from the nineteenth into the twentieth century and brings together Pushkin, Gogol, Chekhov, Zoshchenko, Bulgakov, and our contemporaries Tolstaya, Sorokin, Prigov, and others. The literary texts offer us a large variety of nuances of poshlost' and attitudes toward it—from denunciation to infatuation, from satire to tenderness. Gogol and Chekhov are two early bards of poshlost' who reveal its delights and confinements, its connection to home and homelessness, love and boredom.

Gogol proudly wrote that Pushkin had told him that no other writer "had such a gift of exhibiting so clearly the poshlost' of life, had known how to sketch with such skill the poshlost' of the poshlyi person."[57] The poshlost' of life is the major source of his artistic inspiration, and the embodiment of the evil spirit that he is trying to exorcise.[58] Gogol's fascination with this phenomenon will be later interpreted as his "realism." The debate concerning poshlost' is a key in the polemic between Belinsky and Gogol. Belinksy prefers to substitute more elevated and socially significant terms like "reality" and "truthfulness." He considers Gogol's gift not merely that of "clearly exhibiting the poshlost' of life but rather a gift of exhibiting the phenomena of life in their fullness, reality, and truthfulness *(istinnost)*."[59] Poshlost' is a key term in the transformation of the Romantic aesthetic into the aesthetic of realism. Gogolian poshlost' is slightly ideologically incorrect—precisely what irritated Belinsky. Gogol is fascinated with the materiality of life and the materiality of language in their most banal details and interjections.

As if looking for a home for poshlost', Gogol gives us a variety of scenes of domesticity, from his early works such as *Mirgorod* to his *Petersburg Tales* and *Dead Souls*. All those domestic scenes, whether elegiac or ironic, are seen through the eyes of an estranged narrator. Always on the road, always displaced and "abroad," Gogol gives us bittersweet descriptions of old-fashioned domesticity, as well as vignettes of new and foreign-fashioned Russian "private life." Traveling from the house of the old-fashioned landowners in Malorussia (presently the Ukraine) to the fashionable Manilovs we can trace the *perepeteias* of domestic poshlost'.

In *The Old-Fashioned Landowners* the narrator presents an elegiac image of the patriarchal life of Malorussian gentry, offering us a glimpse of the picturesque ruins of idyllic domesticity. Although the word poshlost' is not used in this story, the story is precisely about "poshlyi ways"—old common ways of living that offered a common happiness without romantic passions, intellectual self-reflections, or other evil excesses. The story is about the old ways of inhabiting the world before the Romantic revolution in the commonplace. It is also a tale of the writer's ironic nostalgia for the patriarchal way of life and for writing conventional bucolic idylls about it. The life of the Malorussian Philemon and Baucis is depicted as a "lowly bucolic idyll," a reign of habit protected from "the creatures of evil spirit," a little world in which desire "does not cross the fence." Their house has tiny warm rooms filled with boxes and chests, and walls covered with cheap eighteenth-century pictures covered with flies. The life of the old-fashioned landowners consisted of endearing rituals, gastronomic indulgencies—cakes with pork fat, poppyseed tarts, pickled red mushrooms, smoked fish—accompanied by extremely serious conversations about other delicious trifles. Although Afanasii Ivanovich occasionally jokes with Pulcheria Ivanovna, she hardly ever laughs, but occasionally smiles pleasantly. Laughter and irony do not coexist with idyll.

One detail endows this anachronistic domesticity with aesthetic potential. The house of the old-fashioned landowners has squeaking doors that sing for the homeless traveler—a song that ranges from comic to pathetically mournful.[60] Gogol's singing doors compose a kind of elegy to a world that is dying out, and embody an old-fashioned charm. These sounds constitute curious metapoetic moments within Gogol's text: they seem to echo the nuances of the narrator's own attitude in its amplitude of fluctuation—from light irony to melancholy, from nostalgia to pathos. *The Old-Fashioned Land-owners* is a narrative of mourning not only for Pulcheria Ivanovna and Afanasii Ivanovich, but also for simple-minded good old Slavic poshlost' before its linguistic and cultural corruption. In relation to the story, the term can be used in an almost pre-nineteenth-century sense. At first glance, it is a native Slavic poshlost' rather than the "common ways" translated from French, yet the roots of nostalgia for the old countryside are commonly European. The "good taste of old Russia"—to quote Nabokov again—can be understood here in a more literal sense of the word, as a discerning palate rather than a sense of aesthetic judgment.[61]

From the home of old-fashioned bucolic Russian poshlost' we move to the house of Manilov *(Dead Souls)*, the site of a more modern, Europeanized poshlost'. Manilov's estate, featuring a blue-and-green gazebo called The Temple of Solitary Meditation, with a pond "animated" by two quarreling peasant women, is an example of the English cult of home and domesticity transplanted onto Russian soil. This is embodied in Manilov's private family rituals: the conversations with his children named, in perfect classic fashion, Alkid and Femistoklus, and his delicious games with his wife, of feeding each other little pieces of candy or apple along with diminutives of endearment. Manilov and his wife are the "softest" among the poshlye heroes of *Dead Souls*. Their worthlessness appears harmless, their poshlost' insignificant, yet extremely revealing. Manilov's "pleasant smile," unlike the "pleasant smile" of Afanasii Ivanovich and Pulcheria Ivanovna, "has too much sugar in it." The excess here is part of the evil charm of poshlost'. Likewise, the surfeit of blond curls, blue eyes, and sweet manners are described as effeminate. Hence Manilov's poshlost' is characterized by an oversweetened dose of effeminacy and European pseudo-sophistication—a combination that will become crucial in later variations.

For Nabokov, the most appropriate mannerism of Manilov's is his habit of shaking out his pipe and arranging the ashes in symmetrical piles on the window sill—"the only artistic pleasure he knew."[62] Manilov's theatricalized amiability and imitative sophistication leave no room for irony or creativity. He can only sweetly and inefficiently inhabit the clichés of prefabricated European domesticity. His spouse, the product of a "lady's pension education, which puts its major emphasis on French, dancing, and knitting little surprises for the future husband" is an even more grotesque embodiment of modern poshlost'.[63] Madame Manilov's supreme artwork is one of her surprises, a minute, embroidered toothpick cover, an implement of advanced European oral hygiene. The little cover is a model of sublime cuteness. (It can perhaps be compared to a contemporary British artifact, a cover for a toilet-paper rack, an article sold in the English countryside.) A hundred years after Manilov's wife, these kinds of endearing, useless objects are no longer handmade surprises—they are mass-produced and sold in shopping malls. Madame Manilov's poshlost' prefigures the sweet kind of middle-class kitsch.

However, Manilov's character has a demonic side too. The man produces a dual impression: on the one hand, of an extremely sweet and pleasant nature, and, on the other hand, of "the devil knows what" *(chert znaet chto takoe)*. "The devil knows what" is a perfect linguistic monster, at once a cliché and a suggestive evocation of the devil. (The cliché can also be "God knows what," but Gogol, a subtle stylist, chooses the devil.) The character who truly embodies the "devil knows what" is "our Mr Chichikov," the prototypical Russian capitalist and dealer in "dead souls." Chichikov is everybody's friend of a friend, a mask of a "gentleman pleasant in all respects" and in some ways, "a man without qualities." Chichikov is a master of modern banality and of nearly postmodern simulation. According to Nabokov, he is "the ill-paid representative of the Devil, a travelling salesman from Hades, our Mr Chichikov of the firm Satan & Co."[64] His chameleon-like character, his own lack of reality as well as the surreality of his trade, are of a devilish elusiveness. Chichikov deals in dead words and dead souls—his own, and those of the others.

The relationship between the devil and poshlost' in Gogol is itself rather elusive.[65] Although evil held a special fascination for Gogol, his demon, a little folkloric devil, sometimes appears to be a linguistic monster, a writer's seducer and tormentor. All the vast terrain of poshlost' discovered and explored by Gogol cannot be presented entirely under the devil's banner. Gogol is largely responsible for the cultural adventures of poshlost' in Russia. Under Gogol poshlost' expands its territory: it begins to encompass domestic culture and Western fashions. It is also linked to the literary evolution and changing understanding of realism, as well as to the changing understanding of evil and its possible impersonations. Gogol's artistic texts reveal the great potential of poshlost' and its exhilarating literary powers.

In Chekhov, poshlost' is beyond good and evil. Poshlost' cannot be described from a single moral perspective, as in Tolstoy's novels. Boris Eikhenbaum wrote that Chekhov belongs to an alternative current of Russian literature—the secondary, provincial literature of the tradition of Pisemsky and Leskov that survived in the backward, godforsaken places in Russia. This tradition "did not teach or preach anything"; it did not focus on the "cursed questions" of Russian boys in a Dostoevskian fashion, but merely described the immutable Russian everyday.[66] Indeed, Chekhov is suspicious of the very divisions between things big and small, between major historical dramas and daily boredom.

In Chekhov's works poshlost' is part of the immutable daily grind. It is what makes life livable but not necessarily worth living. It is both worthlessness and a guarantee of survival. Poshlost' cannot be personified in any particular devilish or grotesque character; it is rather the force that blurs and undermines both characters and story line. If there is an overall structure common to Chekhov's stories, it consists in the tension between the desire to desire and the desire not to desire, or between the narrative of desire and the boredom of narrative. There is a point at which boredom is experienced as poshlost'—when it becomes painful, guilt-ridden, and inescapable. Chekhovian poshlost' can also be examined spatially as confinement, the imposition of a limit that can be hypothetically transgressed or reaffirmed. Many stories and plays unfold as if on the threshold of this walled edifice, usually a domestic space of common sense, contentment, and common ways, whose inhabitants dream of escape and very often end up escaping their dreams.

Poshlost' in Chekhov moves from a spiritual realm to the realm of human relationships, especially relationships between men and women. Many stories are about the crisis of a romance, and about classical Russian ways of speaking about love. In that respect it is possible to say that Chekhov follows up on Tolstoy's most repeated sentence from the opening line of *Anna Karenina,* about happy and unhappy families. Happy life is a realm of clichés; Chekhov writes stories about unhappy families and unhappy bachelors whose subtle unhappiness is too boring and insignificant, too undidactic for the melodramatic or metaphysical imagination. Chekhov's friends often teased him that his characteristically laconic stories were all about people who once upon a time were young, fell in love, got married, and were unhappy.[67] "The Literature Teacher" fits perfectly into this reductive and seemingly banal formula, although the poignant details and ironic precision of the story make it anything but banal. The story is a perfect romance between a young schoolteacher and a seventeen-year-old girl, Manusia Shelestova, the daughter of an impoverished landowner. The story has all the clichés of courtship and prerequisites for romance: a declaration of love in the garden, hasty kisses and blushes, and expectations of eternal happiness. The dénouement too is happy: the heroine agrees, the bridegroom is ready, and happiness, which "seems possible only in a novel," appears to materialize. The beginning of family life is happy as well; the schoolteacher can hardly wait for the working day to end so he can go home to his industrious and "positive" little wife and help her around the house. The only strange and estranging character in the story is Nikitin's friend, the geography and history teacher Ippolit, a confirmed bachelor who speaks in dry clichés about things that "everyone knew," maxims from secondary-school dictations: "The Volga falls into the Caspian Sea . . . Horses eat oats and hay." On his deathbed Ippolit forgets everything but those minimal expressions of worldly wisdom—his is a banality bordering on madness. At first glance it seems that Ippolit's dry minimalist clichés about life, death, and marriage are contrasted with the charming trivialities of the newlyweds' family rituals and romance. Yet Ippolit helps to lay bare the clichés and to estrange the pleasant naturalness of Nikitin's everyday.

The death of this odd bachelor subtly shifts the tone of the story and its perspective on quiet family happiness. The "little plump wife" and her "little fluffy cat," sleeping in a warm bed dreaming of marmalade, can no longer be regarded in the same light. Something unsettles the tranquility of the domestic life: "He began to think that the illusion had exhausted itself, and a new, anxious conscious life had already begun, the life that does not get along with peace and personal happiness."[68] The last sentence pits "conscious life" against family happiness, an opposition that will be at the center of modernist aesthetics and ethics. At the end of the story the word poshlost' recurs several times—the stifling, humiliating poshlost' that drives the happy schoolteacher mad: "My god, where am I? I am surrounded by poshlost' and more poshlost': dull, worthless people, pots with sour cream, jars with milk, cockroaches, stupid women . . . there is nothing more dreadful, insulting and sad than poshlost'. I have to escape, escape today, otherwise I will go mad."[69]

Thus in Chekhov's stories the pursuit of domestic happiness often turns into a pursuit by poshlost'. In contrast to Tolstoy's conception, family life in Chekhov is not a site of a spiritual rebirth but the cradle of banality. Chekhov's stories are mostly about two kinds of common unhappiness: those in which the romance was possible but was never consummated because of stifling daily routine, and those in which the romance was consummated and the protagonists have to escape the stifling inertia of the happy ending.[70]

The ending of "The Literature Teacher" suggests that the only way to escape poshlost' is literally to escape domestic life, to run away to Moscow. In Chekhov's last story, "The Bride," the structure is reversed, and the perspective shifts from the male to the female character: domestic "happiness" is only suggested, while the escape from it is actually realized. The heroine of the story, with the promising name Nadia (Nadezhda means hope), becomes aware of the imminent poshlost' of her future family life at the moment when she and her fiancé, the handsome and corpulent Andrei, take a tour of their new house with its freshly painted floors, Viennese chairs, and a large oil painting in a golden frame. The painting represents a nude beside a purple vase with a broken handle—reflecting the new taste of the time, with its slight but very proper erotic overtones. Nadia is nauseated by the legitimate sexual advances of her future husband in the midst of their bright blue living room, before the decadent nude lady and her purple vase. When he embraces her and holds her around the waist, Nadia sees only poshlost', "stupid, naive, unbearable poshlost'."[71] Poshlost' here encompasses the promises of marital bliss, domestic coziness, and artistic tackiness. Poshlost' is the limit of available narratives, at once comforting and stifling, like the dark blue walls of a nicely decorated house with no exit.

Nadia escapes to the city, literally over the dead body of the idealistic student Sasha, who stirred her imagination but whose own beliefs seemed to be rather vague and unoriginal at the time. Yet the ending of the story is, if not happy, at least hopeful; it offers the hope of a different narrative for a "new woman" and her uncommon life.[72]

Is escape, spatial dislocation, the paradigm of fleeing home the only way to fight poshlost'? Is the poshlost' of life at all escapable? What narrative ironies does one encounter in the Chekhovian universe on the road that leads away from poshlost'?

In "A Lady with a Dog" the discourse on poshlost' and vulgarity is poetically revaluated. Instead of escaping the triviality of romance, the story offers some tender redefinitions of it. Here the clichés of romance lead not to an ironic dénouement but to a tender and open-ended love story. Gurov is a typical Russian, middle-class, middle-aged man in a mid-life crisis (to put it in contemporary American clichés). He has been married forever, and has been forever unfaithful; his view of women is a grab-bag of vulgar clichés about "the lower race." Hence Gurov can be called a poshliak. The word poshlost' is used by Anna Sergeievna after their first sexual encounter. She calls herself a "poshlaia woman," which is here synonymous with a fallen woman. Her confession brings tears to her eyes, yet the melodramatic potential of the story is immediately undercut. It is self-consciously thematized and dissipated in the poignant ellipsis of the narration. The story of the couple's intimacy remains a secret, and Gurov does not have the words to talk about it. Back in Moscow he tries to tell his male friends about it: "I met a charming woman in Yalta," says Gurov. "This pork has a smell," answers a friend by way of response, in this way acknowledging the clichés of fragmentary social communication, a conventional communication in which a woman's charm and the smell of pork are interchangeable signifiers.[73]

In their first conversation, Gurov and Anna talk in clichés about boredom—it is boring to be on vacation, it is boring to be home. Moscow and the Crimea offer no escape, but only different sorts of commonplaces and other kinds of boredom. The story unfolds through the nonlinear criss-crossing of different spaces of confinement—the capital, a sea resort, a provincial town, escape from dull marital life to adultery, from unexpected love to commonsensical real life and back. It does not present a familiar narrative of escape from the triviality of daily existence, but offers only an escape or merely a detour from predictable narratives.

Poshlost' and vulgarity are reframed in the story. In the scene of their first amorous encounter, Anna's repentance of the sin of poshlost' and her clumsy tears disrupt Gurov's cynical scenario of a pleasant conventional affair. Her excessive affect makes their relationship embarrassing and illicit, because it is neither in sufficiently good taste nor in sufficiently bad taste, neither proper nor obscene. When Gurov goes to visit Anna Sergeievna, she looks like "a little, unremarkable woman lost in a provincial crowd, with a vulgar lorgnette in her hands." But here "vulgar" is transformed into a term of endearment. Anna's vulgar lorgnette is the poetic element of the story, that blemish or sign of imperfection that makes her lovable. Her provincial clumsiness and lack of artfulness offer a hope of escape from the stifling clichés of good taste and social convention.

In "A Lady with a Dog" Chekhov employs an unusually rich palette of tender greys, which color the "beautiful" grey eyes of Anna Sergeievna, her grey dress beloved by Gurov, and the pale lilac hues of the Black Sea at dusk. Poshlost' and poetry, poshlost' and love, are not always on opposite poles; in fact, poshlost', like love and poetry, has to be continuously redefined and reframed; the old-fashioned frames can acquire a charming aura while the institution of "good taste" can itself turn into a worn-out cliché. What some call poshlost' and vulgarity are part and parcel of the experience of the everyday, with its minor events and casual trifles, its little pleasures and small hurts. Poshlost' here has its tender charms; it is described from a lover's perspective and never reified. This charm in turn imbues poshlost' with an aura, giving it a poetic potential. After all, it is banal to have an affair with a married woman with grey eyes at a summer resort; it is even more banal to fall in love. Yet, to stay in love, at least for the duration of the story, is beyond banality.

Good Taste in Old Russia

Poshlost' leads us to examine the history of the Russian taste wars, from the early-nineteenth-century aristocratic preoccupation with *comme il faut* and its obsession with the beauty of gentlemen's fingernails, to the early-twentieth-century salon of Madame Poshlost' and the revolutionary dictatorship of taste, and finally to the battles against poshlost' in the 1960s and its cultural rehabilitation in the 1990s.

One of the features of the war on banality is the need to be un-common, that is, neither banal nor philistine, yet at the same time to reflect somehow the spirit of the common people. In the early nineteenth century one of the central concepts of aristocratic "good taste" was the French comme il faut. In French the phrase is not defined; one simply knows the correct way in which things should be done. "Not comme il faut" appears to be a predecessor of poshlost'. In his autobiography Lev Tolstoy affectionately and critically sums up his own adolescent view: the whole world for aristocratic boys was divided between people who were comme il faut and those who were not. The second category was subdivided between "those who were not properly comme il faut and the common people."[74] Comme il faut is an eclectic Russian aristocratic style that combines the self-fashioning of a Renaissance courtier with a gentleman's etiquette, here translated into Russian adolescent mythology in which fingernails happen to be a particularly important cultural fetish:

> My comme il faut consisted first and foremost of excellent French and, especially, the accent. The person who spoke bad French incited in me a feeling of hate. Why do you want to talk like us, when you can't?—I asked him mentally with a poisonous sneer. The second condition for the comme il faut were the nails, long, cleansed and pure, third was the ability to bow, dance and talk, and the fourth and very important one was an indifference to everything and a constant expression of a certain elegant and condescending boredom.[75]

The beauty of fingernails was by that time immortalized in Pushkin's verse, in his distancing yet sympathetic description of the Russian aristocratic dandy Eugene Onegin. "One can be an intelligent person, yet think about the beauty of the nails," Pushkin remarked wistfully. Tolstoy's autobiographical narration splits and intertwines two voices—that of an adolescent boy and that of a critical adult—one commenting upon the other and remembering his youthful prejudices with a gentle smile and light nostalgia. Comme il faut is both style and substance: it is enough to *be* comme il faut, and one does not need to *do* anything else. It is a form of communication based on exclusivity. In their small circle, comme-il-faut people understand each other without even using half-words; a mere movement of the lips suffices. Comme il faut has the perfect structure of a cultural myth, because the process of its self-fashioning is carefully veiled—one should never see how much work goes into it, and the initial aristocratic credentials are taken for granted. This way comme il faut remains a hermetic order that manifests itself in unspoken and seemingly ineffable naturalized conventions of aristocratic behavior and world view. Young Lev's ideal of comme il faut, Volodia, explained that girls by definition were not comme il faut, along with the majority of people whose nails are not so clean.

In retrospect, Tolstoy's autobiographical narrator sees himself as someone so embarrassingly not-comme il faut that he had to fight particularly hard for the purity of this principle. Tolstoy discloses a perfect mechanism of social snobbery: one boy, insecure in his command of the comme il faut, confronting his equally insecure peer who is perhaps a less skillful pretender. But the key issue to understanding the Russian conception of taste is the separation between people who are not comme il faut and the common people who are beyond, if not above, this distinction.[76]

In the mid-nineteenth century a new social group appeared on the Russian cultural scene: the intelligentsia. This group, composed mainly of people whose social background was mixed—provincial clergy and the lower strata of gentry and merchants—launched its counterattack. Ashamed of being too common and unable to be comme il faut in the traditional aristocratic sense, members of the Russian intelligentsia, and especially their most radical representatives, the nihilists, fought against poshlost' through a demonstrative disregard for polite behavior, social mores, and hygiene.

The desire to be different from the despised philistines included the desire to look different; hence the notorious costumes which the youths of the 1860s and 1870s showed off: plaids and gnarled walking sticks, short hair (for women) and hair to the shoulders (for men), dark glasses, Fra Diavolo hats and Polish caps.[77] If in the descriptions of their time male nihilists were at least occasionally presented ambiguously, women were almost always treated as caricatures: "Most *nigilistki* are usually very plain and exceedingly ungracious, so that they have no need to cultivate curt, awkward manners; they dress with no taste, and in impossibly filthy fashion, rarely wash their hands, never clean their nails, often wear glasses, always cut their hair and sometimes even shave it off."[78]

The *raznochinets intelligents* did not care very much about their nails and frequently bit them, but they inherited an aristocratic principle of distinction and a dream of spiritual superiority. They adopted a style of exclusive communication and shared a desire to belong to

a special community that would save the common people. Awkward-
ness and lack of social grace were turned into signs of authenticity
and were cultivated as a part of the new revolutionary self-fashioning.

Like many other Russian abstract nouns, including beauty, wisdom, and stupidity, poshlost' is grammatically feminine. In turn-of-
the-century culture bad taste often became synonymous with
feminine taste, which was connected to the growing number of
women writers, readers, and hostesses of literary salons. It was at that
time that the feminine gender of the Russian word poshlost' was
often used and abused in satirical critiques. In Sasha Cherny's poem
poshlost' was personified by a tacky goddess, a salon madame
dressed in lilac and yellow, painting watercolors of roses and sleeping
with her cabby:

Poshlost' (A Pastel)

Lilac corset and yellow bow on her bosom;
Eyes like navels—eyeless eyes.
Someone else's curls cling thick to her temples
And greasily hang down her sides.
. . . . .
In her salons *everyone,* the audacious crowd,
Having torn the skin off virginal ideas,
Clutch in their paws the unfeeling body
And zealously neigh like a herd of horses.

There they say eggs went up in price
And over the Neva a comet fell,—
Self-admiring, like mantlepiece Chinamen,
They nod to the beat of the gramophone's wail.
. . . . .
She sings, and paints a watercolor rose.
She follows fashions of all sorts
Saving up jokes and rumors, phrases, poses,
Corrupting the Muse, corrupting love.
. . . . .
The only ones not to know her are . . . who?
Of course: children, beasts, and common people.
The first when they don't look like grown-ups,
The last when away from their masters.

The portrait is ready. As I throw down my pen,
Please don't make a scene about my crassness:
When you paint a pig beside its shed—
No *belle Hélène* can appear on the canvas.[79]

Madame Poshlost' is presented as a grotesque, middle-aged, and sexually loose *nouvelle riche* who probably bought herself a title of nobility. She embodies all aspects of poshlost': sexuality, Western influences, and the mythology of social class. She is the guardian of a pseudo-artistic salon and of a hearth of hypocritical bourgeois domesticity with its tacky attributes: porcelain figurines, satin comforters, and the "howling" gramophone records. The proliferation of material objects of the impure urban domestic culture of the turn of the century goes hand-in-hand with the profanation of ideals. The major sin of Madame Poshlost' is her eclecticism; she mixes lilac and yellow, the works of the erotic writer Barkov and romances, watercolor roses and clichés about the political crisis. (The colors of poshlost' vary from text to text: from red and green, or red and yellowish in Chekhov's *The Three Sisters* to purple and yellow, and later to all shades of pink. The problem here is not so much with the colors themselves, but that they clash.)

Madame Poshlost' is an aesthetic and ethical prostitute, an allegorical bad woman, in contrast to the allegorical "good woman," the "virgin idea," and the Muse evoked in the poem. The operations of Madame Poshlost' are compared to rape and bestial cannibalism; she commits many acts of allegorical violence. However, in trying to pinpoint her entourage we notice an interesting circularity in the metaphors. In the poem the only elements exempt from poshlost' are "children, beasts, and common people." Bestiality is thus a feature of the poshlyi salon of Madame (at the end she is compared to a pig) and also a characteristic of the enemies of poshlost'. The antithesis of Madame Poshlost', the "belle Hélène," is only another not-so-virginal foreign cliché: a French-Greek figure of beauty, the ideal of antiquity appropriated by popular culture.[80] And the artist himself is hardly one of the "children, beasts, and common people" that are free from poshlost'. The new Pygmalion (or Pig-malion?) of Madame Poshlost' is implicated in her bestial salon scene and does not completely escape the dated charms of the goddess of bad taste.

Madame Poshlost' is the relative of many strange feminine figures of early-twentieth-century culture, both heroines and women writers. She is hardly a *belle dame sans merci*—rather, she is a *belle dame* without taste (and with an excess of mercy). She is kin to Alexander Blok's mythical "unknown woman," a Symbolist Muse steeped in the "mysterious poshlost'" of modern urban life.[81] It is perhaps this combination of mystery and poshlost', of poetic refinement and of the romantic commonplaces of popular gramophone romances about other evenings "smoky and blue," that made "To the Unknown Woman" among the most memorized and popular poems recited in the Soviet schools.

Madame Poshlost' also marred the reputation of many women writers. Women readers as well as women consumers of everyday artifacts had begun to play a prominent role in Russian society. Two popular female novelists of the early twentieth century, Charskaia and Anastasia Verbitskaia, were criticized for writing excessively emotional feminine prose; in addition, Verbitskaia was castigated for flirting with high culture and *belles lettres*. This is what made her poshlaia in the eyes of the critics—the pretense of writing great literature. Despite her enormous popularity and financial success, she was scorned both by critics of the socially conscious "people's intel- ligentsia" and by the modernists. Not only were popular women writers accused of vulgarity, but so were some modernist women poets. The "poetess" is a kind of nouvelle riche who lacks the genetic blue blood of the literary aristocracy.[82]

Although the common people are deemed to be free of poshlost', as soon as they stop conforming to the Russian intelligentsia's ideali- zation of them, they too fall victim to banality. The newly emergent Russian commercial culture, as well as the urban lower-class culture, produced sentimental romances, women's novels, *lubki* (early Rus- sian versions of comic books), and stories of an English Milord and Prince Bova. These productions, fitting neither the category of the great classical literature nor the idealized version of folklore, were condemned for their vulgarity and poshlost'. Jeffrey Brooks, in his pioneering work on the development of literacy and on popular artistic genres in Russia, collected a number of interesting responses to the popular books sold on the Nikolaevsky Market, a "sea of vulgarity, superstition, prejudice, and ignorance of all types." The message of *Milord Georg* was one of "extreme cynicism not covered by even the usual fig leaf of banal morality. The aim of life is debauch-

ery and riches."[83] Brooks convincingly demonstrates the existence of
an unlikely coalition of the Russian state, the Church, and the liberal
intelligentsia, united in their hostile attitudes toward "popular literature," attitudes which were later appropriated by the Bolsheviks.[84]

To the turn-of-the-century poets and intellectuals poshlost' appeared ubiquitous; it was found at home and in the public square, in
love and in death, among the common people and the intelligentsia.
Its pervasiveness appeared to many modernist writers as a sign of an
imminent apocalypse, and they often personified it in fantastic and
apocalyptic creatures. Alexander Blok in his prophetic essay-parable
"Timelessness" imagines an enormous symbolic spider of poshlost'
that spins his web in the corners of every home, protecting the "silence of poshlost'." This "invisible sticky spider inhabited the sacred
and peaceful place that was a symbol of Golden Age."[85] Time has
stopped. Behind the spiderweb lurks the figure of the wandering
horseman of the Russian apocalypse. Only a violent rupture, a revolt
or a revolution, can tear the webs of poshlost'. The twentieth century
brings poshlost' to the foreground of politics and makes it a chief
actor in the dramas of revolution and repression.

In 1928 the prominent Bolshevik Nikolai Bukharin (soon to be
persecuted by Stalin) wrote: "We are creating and will create a civilization in comparison with which the capitalist civilization will seem
like a vulgar street dance in comparison with the heroic symphonies
of Beethoven."[86] From this statement one might think that the Bolsheviks were fighting a taste war rather than a class war, or that the
two were inseparable. It is also surprising that one of the leaders of
the Bolshevik Revolution would denounce a popular street dance in
favor of a work of a nineteenth-century Romantic genius, and would
equate vulgar with popular. Bukharin's pronouncement voices the
early Soviet "dictatorship of taste" (to use a phrase from the 1920s),
as well as the traditional Russian intelligentsia's opposition to everything that it perceived to be ordinary, vulgar, and common. In fact,
disputes over taste characterize both the culture of old Russia and the
Soviet civilization. Taste wars reveal some fundamental paradoxes of
Russian cultural history.

In the early twentieth century a powerful attack on poshlost' came
from the artistic and political Left, particularly from the Futurists,
most of whom wholeheartedly embraced the October Revolution. In
their early 1914 manifesto, "A Slap in the Face of Public Taste," they
rebelled against "good taste" and "common sense," publicly derided

the great Russian classics, Pushkin and Tolstoy included, and proposed they be thrown overboard "from the ship of modernity."[87] The
early Futurists attacked the good taste of the liberal bourgeoisie, that
of the ascetic "people's intelligentsia," and that of the Russian Symbolists, targeted also on account of their "effeminate" manners.

Some five years later, the postrevolutionary and grown-up former
Futurists united in LEF (Left Front of Art) and gave up their eccentric
yellow and blue blouses for the "rational costumes" and black leather
jackets of the commissars. They ceased their anarchic rebellion
against good taste and common sense and joined in support of the
revolutionary dictatorship of taste, in a revolutionary community of
"good Bolshevik taste." Thus the Soviet history of taste follows its
Russian prerevolutionary model. In contrast to the well-known proverb, in Russia there are always disputes about taste—and taste, like
culture, can exist in the singular only. As we recall, the intelligentsia
of the 1840s and 1860s scorned the aristocratic principle of *comme
il faut,* so they did not bother to clean their nails but still insisted on
exclusivity, though in a new style. In the same way, the avant-garde
artists scorned the classical Russian tradition only to reproduce in the
radically new revolutionary style its unified and hierarchical structure.

The fundamental features of early Soviet self-fashioning are the
war against banality and the everyday, and the general persistence of
military rhetoric in artistic and everyday language. Poshlost' often
refers to reified domestic objects, as well as to sentimentalized human
relationships. For Mayakovsky the war on banality concerns especially two spheres of life—home-making and love-making. Sergei
Tretiakov announces a "battle of taste" regarding the everyday practices of Soviet citizens, their "psychological make-up." The battle
against poshlost', as Tretiakov stresses, is a battle against everything
that has become automatic:

> We will call byt or poshlost' (in the genetic sense of the word from
> *poshlo est',* that is, became established) . . . a way of feeling and
> acting that has become automatized in its reproducibility . . . Even
> the most powerful strokes of the revolution are incapable of break-
> ing this internal byt . . . In the objective sense, we will call byt that
> order of things that a person surrounds himself with, to which,
> independently of their usefulness, he transfers the fetishism of his
> sympathies and memories, and finally, becomes—literally—a slave
> of those things.[88]

Tretiakov distinguishes between consumers *(pri-obretateli)* and inventors *(izobretateli)*, between collectors of past and creators of the future. In the revolutionary discourse, a "thing" acquires negative connotations: it stands not for a thing *in* itself but *for* itself, a coziness for the sake of coziness, homeyness for the sake of homeyness and not for the sake of utility or revolutionary transformation. In his radical Marxist critique of fetishism and commodification, Tretiakov aspires to the radical defamiliarization of all conventions and habits.

In his play *The Bathhouse* Mayakovsky invents the hilarious Mr. Pont Kich (or Kitsch), listed in the cast of characters for the play as a generic "foreigner," a benign Monsieur Poshlost'.[89] Mr. Pont Kitsch is an Anglo-Saxon philatelist, a well-wisher, and a collector of foreign inventions. He speaks in a peculiar *transsensical* language, the generic Western tongue which translates into Russian absurdity. Mr. Kitsch is a mere voyeur of the Revolution, someone who turns revolutionary inventions into collectible gadgets. In retrospect he can be seen both as a parody of the acquisitive foreigner and a parody of the Russian construction of a paradigmatic Mr. West, a character from the Futurists' own playful poetic past.[90]

In the 1930s the avant-garde dream of the dictatorship of taste was superseded by the enforcement of the new Soviet culturalization. Socialist Realist culturalization means to ban not only counterrevolutionary poshlost' but also the satirical campaign ridiculing it. The Soviet comedy and satire of the 1920s—in the works of Zoshchenko, Il'f and Petrov, Olesha, Mayakovsky, and Erdman—which fed on the pleasures and horrors of banality, was deemed too negative. Exposing petit-bourgeois poshlost' in the 1930s became more dangerous than was living it in the 1920s: many warriors against banality were exterminated. The new "merry" Soviet men and women supposedly overcame and survived not only banality but also the campaign against it. The mid-1930s might have seemed like a period of temporary stabilization of everyday life (the arrests, camps, and victims of collectivization remained outside the limits of Socialist Realist transparent visibility). In the postwar Soviet Union the battle against acquisitiveness grew increasingly unpopular, and the domestic idyll was permitted to enter the pantheon of genres of Socialist Realist painting.

In the 1960s the invective against poshlost' is revived as a form of cultural critique of Stalinism and all the items of philistine postwar taste. At that time poshlost' and byt are frequently used interchangeably. As the Khrushchev thaw sets in, love returns, unattached to

Stakhanovite labor or the decadent exoticism of pop songs from the 1950s. The poets and artists of the thaw wish to cleanse the romantic discourse on love and revolution of the slime of Stalinist poshlost'.[91] Evgenii Yevtushenko proudly declares in the poem addressed to his beloved: "I have two loves in the world, revolution and you," and the poet asks both of them to forgive him for minor infidelities.[92]

A decade later the antifetishistic campaigns of the 1960s against love seats and crystal ware seem outmoded, and so do declarations of love to the revolution. The more sincere declarations of love are now in foreign languages—in Beatles' songs and in the albums of the popular French chansonniers, from Yves Montand to Salvatore Adamo and Joe Dassin. In the 1970s artifacts from the West become the fetish and the desirable black market commodities. Foreign articles and clothing enter Soviet everyday life. There is a great fascination for all kinds of foreign wrappings—the plastic disposable containers of Finlandia cheeses are kept in communal or private kitchens and cherished. Especially popular are plastic shopping bags with foreign logos; they circulate on the black market almost as a form of hard currency. Foreign words enter black-market slang and colloquial Russian. The black marketeers, in fact, begin to fabricate foreign logos and reproduce them on Russian-made T-shirts. The idea of "disposable objects" is completely foreign to Russian and Soviet culture, where objects, especially foreign ones, are so difficult to get; moreover, the memory of getting them often includes some great adventure, risky business, or narrow escape that turns the objects into personal souvenirs, worth preserving for this reason alone. By the time of Brezhnev's "stagnation" the word "poshlost'" seems to have gone full circle; by then the discussion of the banality of life itself began to appear banal and outdated.

Perestroika starts with a recovery of history and in its wake comes a recovery of the history of poshlost' and kitsch. Many art objects of perestroika turn into self-conscious or unselfconscious celebrations of the great carnival of kitsch. The very choice of political metaphors— Gorbachev's "reconstruction" versus Brezhnev's "stagnation"— seems to reproduce the old battle against the daily grind and poshlost'. The similarity is all the more uncanny because the word "perestroika" was used in the late 1920s in a Party ukaz "for perestroika of byt." Thus political metaphors do not escape the fate of poetic metaphors: they are invented, repeated, turned into clichés, and then undone, only to recur in new contexts. The intellectual history of Soviet Russia can be read as a history of changing definitions of poshlost'. Today's everyday artifact can turn into tomorrow's counterrevolutionary kitsch, while tomorrow's revolutionary enthusiasm becomes kitsch the day after tomorrow. In a similar vein, yesterday commercial culture was viewed with suspicion, while today it is the difficult art of "high culture" that might not pass the commercial competition.

The moralizing tone of the nineteenth-century intelligentsia and its fin-de-siècle apocalyptic premonitions about poshlost' were heard anew in response to the recent wave of Westernization.[93] Post-Soviet Russia returned to a fetishistic cult of tsarist memorabilia. In the summer of 1993 many museums mounted exhibits of various objects from the tsars' daily life—from the Fabergé collection in the Hermitage to the Treasures of Executed Monarchs in the museum in Pushkin. If in the USSR "every stone that knew Lenin" was cherished, now it is every stone (usually a rather precious stone) that "knew the tsar." Perhaps this popular obsession with tsarist objects will become the latest object of cultural critique.

I am afraid I cannot offer a final cure for poshlost'; its epidemic has been too frequently misdiagnosed and the moral invective against it can acquire a familiar banal ring. Perhaps it is not necessary to define poshlost' more precisely but rather to identify certain mechanisms of kitschification that deafen the faculty of critical thinking, sensual perception, surprise, and sympathy. The war against poshlost' helped to defamiliarize clichés and conventions, but at the same time it may have fostered a kind of moral snobism that frequently stops the chain of questioning with the assertion of its own impeccable taste. ("Snob," incidentally—or perhaps not incidentally—is another one of those travesty-concepts linked to the discourse on taste, art, and commonplace. Its initial use referred to a cobbler, "a person of the lower classes," but later the word came to signify something different—"a person who is convinced of and flaunts his social superiority."[94]

Meshchanstvo: Middle Class, Middlebrow

"No you wouldn't catch me on this word: I am not against meshchanstvo as a class. My salute is to all people of all classes," writes

Vladimir Mayakovsky.[95] It is not by chance that this cautious apology is parenthetical in a poem ("On Trash") that trashes postrevolutionary nouveaux riches. In fact, one would be hard put to catch the poet out: throughout Russian and Soviet history it is impossible to disentangle meshchanstvo as a neutral, legal, or descriptive term from a Russian cultural myth of inevitable philistinism of the middle class. The word *meshchane* comes from *mesto* (place), originates in Poland and the western Ukraine in the seventeenth century, and refers to the lower economic bracket of urban dwellers, such as peddlers, servants, and artisans. Meshchane are close to petit-bourgeois; the cultural war between meshchanstvo and intelligentsia informs all of modern Russian intellectual history. Like the Romantic poet who defines himself as against the "mob" but exists in a relationship of unhealthy dependency on it, so the Russian intelligentsia needs to fight meshchanstvo to construct its own identity. Vera Dunham points out that both meshchanstvo and intelligentsia are irreducible to economic classes and function instead as "modal personalities" and cultural myths.[96] The words are hardly neutral in contemporary Russian: they are perceived as value judgments.

The meshchane and intelligentsia developed their cultural identities after the Petrine reforms, which allowed for more social mobility and laid the foundation for Russian modernization. They are the two groups that undermine the feudal and aristocratic structures of the Russian society. Yet the intelligentsia, in a peculiar inferiority-superiority complex, sees itself as a spiritual heir to the aristocratic tradition. It is aristocratic in spirit and poor in means. Meshchanstvo, however, neither aristocracy nor peasantry, undermines the intelligentsia's romanticized ideal of the common people. Though they are quite common, representatives of meshchanstvo are considered a perversion and profanation of true Russian folk.

Meshchanstvo and intelligentsia are siblings in enmity—too close to each other socially, yet each alien to the old components of Russian society, the aristocracy and the peasantry. *Intelligentsia,* a word that came from German into Russian, and then in its Russian version immigrated into other Western European languages, reflects once more the influence of German Romanticism and the idealist philosophy on Russian self-fashioning and illustrates the cross-cultural adventures of national(ist) vocabulary.[97] Since the cultural sphere is one of the few areas where subversion of the patrimonial state is possible, and since literature plays a central role in the making of the Russian identity, the intelligentsia is perceived as the only dynamic force in nineteenth-century Russian culture. It is a spiritual heir to the old Russian tradition and the self-appointed voice of the nation.

A Russian middle class was perceived as a contradiction in terms by many intelligentsia critics. The very concepts of *middle* and *class* are problematic in Russian society, and so is the tendency to translate social into spiritual. When traveling Russian philosopher Alexander Herzen first observed the Western middle class, he found it contemptible. In his ironic description, middle-class ideals in Western Europe consisted of "a piece of chicken in the cabbage soup of every little man . . . a little house with not very big windows with a view of the street, school for the son, a dress for the daughter, a worker for the hard chores, indeed *havre de grâce.*"[98]

From the beginning this petit-bourgeois piece of chicken in the soup has the bad taste of poshlost'. (A simple vegetarian cabbage soup shared by the members of the utopian peasant commune of his dreams would not need chicken to taste good.) For a Russian intellectual, art and spirituality matter more than a piece of chicken in the soup; hunger is valued higher than self-complacency with a full stomach, spiritual homelessness and poverty are more important than a conventional mediocre home. Herzen observes how the revolutionary bourgeoisie in France and England turned into a self-complacent postrevolutionary caste of philistines. He was among the first to translate the Western European conception of the middle class into the Russian mythical category of meshchanstvo, making it a negative evaluation. In the nineteenth century both Slavophiles and Westernizers criticized the middle class not only for being capitalist but also for being radically non-Russian. Middle-class values—everyday life, a preoccupation with privacy, domestic survival—are not included in the intelligentsia's conception of Russian culture and identity. When Maxim Gorky attempts to present a hero from *meshchanstvo* in his play with the direct title *The Petit-Bourgeois* (*Meshchane*, 1902), he provokes a major cultural confrontation with representatives of the modernist intelligentsia of 1905–1908.[99] Dmitrii Filosofov and, especially, Dmitrii Merezhkovsky see the appearance of meshchanstvo as the sign of imminent apocalypse, the coming of the final phase of Western civilization.[100] Moreover, Merezhkovsky accuses Gorky and even Chekhov of meshchanstvo because they deny the values of a truly Russian "religious society." By the end of the nineteenth century, however, most of the Russian writers were accused of meshchanstvo. This accusation is one of the worst cultural insults, but the word is rarely used in reference to the actual social group. In his counterattack Gorky accuses Merezhkovsky, Nekrasov, Turgenev, Dostoevsky, and Tolstoy of "preaching humility" misguiding the people, and therefore unmasking their own conservative meshchanstvo.[101] As conflicting as the referents of the word are, one thing remains constant: the term meshchanstvo is negative. As in the Russian children's game "third-man out," the third term always complicates the matter. The middle is never "golden" in the Russian cultural context.

If for prerevolutionary intelligentsia meshchanstvo often appears as a perversion of the folk spirit, for the postrevolutionary left-wing intelligentsia it betrays the ideals of the revolutionary proletariat. Mayakovsky spends more time in poetic fights with "bad workers" (that is, those who show the slightest interest in private acquisitions and are hence considered "bourgeoisified") than against the bourgeoisie itself. Bad workers are worse than class enemies; they profane the ideal of the revolutionary class. Mayakovsky's meshchane are the workers and former peasants who embraced prerevolutionary poshlost'.

Mayakovsky's later poems parody the tastes of postrevolutionary meshchanstvo, but they also reveal how the rhetoric against it can be manipulated. This is especially true for the Soviet lover's discourse, which in Mayakovsky's view is particularly vulnerable. (We may remember that a Russian lover's discourse is always in danger of falling into poshlost'.) Mayakovsky satirizes the postrevolutionary romances and the hypocritical male discourse of "free love" practiced by a former worker, Ivan, now an importantly Frenchified "electrician Jean," who tells his naïve girlfriend Marusia, "it is terrible meshchanstvo to protect your innocence."[102] In the poems "Marusia Poisoned Herself" and "Love," meshchanstvo and poshlost' are closely linked to feminine sexuality and the loss of virginity, both literal and metaphorical. But this is a no-win situation: it can be meshchanstvo to protect innocence and poshlost' not to protect it. In both cases, the woman seems to lose.

In Mayakovsky's later works it is unclear what is more dangerous, meshchanstvo or the war against it, which appears to be appropriated by new Soviet parvenus in a kind of devilish vicious circle. In Maya-kovsky's play of the late 1920s, *The Bedbug*, the programmatic satire on the Soviet petit-bourgeois genus "obyvatelis vulgaris" (the *oby-vatel* is a man of byt, a sort of kitschman), also presents a problematic depiction of the communist utopia, which was supposed to be the radical "other" of everyday banality as dreamed by the revolutionar-ies. It turns out that utopia itself is made of clichés. The scientists of the future in *The Bedbug* and the "phosphoric woman" in *The Bathhouse* speak a sanitized and "disinfected" language of puritani-cal moralism and revolutionary didacticism, deprived of any poetic inventiveness. The reification of revolutionary ideals and the bureau-cratization of revolutionary discourse take center stage, even for revo-lutionary poets. By the 1930s the war against meshchanstvo is like Don Quixote's battle against windmills; although the social class has been wiped out, certain philistine ideals have entered the official Stalinist discourse.

The critique of meshchanstvo turns full circle from Chekhov to Andrei Platonov—from its incipience in Chekhov to its physical dis-appearance or complete transformation in Platonov. In both cases it is embodied in the female figure. In Chekhov's *Three Sisters*, Natasha, Andrei's fiancée and later his wife, is condescendingly called *mesh-chanka* by his sisters; she wears a vulgarly bright yellow skirt and a red blouse, and later a green belt with a pink dress. Natasha appalls the sisters, who come from educated gentry, with her lack of taste and her obvious sexual appeal.[103] But the combination of pink and green is more than a merely aesthetic assault; poshlost' and meshchanstvo go beyond matters of style and taste. Natasha proves to be the immanent threat in the play, a female impersonation of that new force that is going to displace the endearingly helpless sisters, these gentle and idealistic dreamers. In Platonov's *Fro* (1930), written some thirty years later, the meshchanka figure is delineated after the violent cam-paign against meshchanstvo in the 1920s. The heroine of the story, Fro, catches her poshlyi reflection in the mirror of the hairdresser's shop—her nineteenth-century hairdo, her outmoded intense tender-ness—and later she confesses to her father, the aging train conductor, that she "misses her husband, although she is not a meshchanka" (or maybe this only shows that she is one).[104] The father responds: "What kind of meshchanka are you! There are none of them left now, they are all dead. To become a meshchanka you have to live longer

and study more . . . Meshchanki were good women."[105] Platonov
defamiliarizes the term (a stereotypical insult by the late 1920s) and
returns to a literal rather than a metaphorical use of the word, in
reference not to the mythical petit-bourgeois enemy but to a specific
prerevolutionary social group that has vanished. While in Chekhov's
Three Sisters the arrival of meshchanstvo is anticipated with fear, in
Platonov's *Fro* its departure is contemplated with some nostalgia that
does not preclude but only contributes to the writer's intense and
tender utopian vision.

In the 1960s the conflict between intelligentsia and meshchanstvo
is slightly modified; now it is the battle between the romantic and the
meshchanin. "Romantic" is the 1960s more gentle version of the
revolutionary of the 1920s. Occasionally the meshchanin and the
romantic even sing the same songs, but the meshchanin sings with
"smoked salmon and shishkebab" on the side.[106] The petit-bourgeois
flora and fauna remain the same—rubber plants, yellow canaries, and
gramophone records. In Soviet descriptions of the Cuban revolution
the enemies of Fidel Castro are portrayed as meshchanstvo who sing
"poshlyi gramophone songs."[107] Emigré writer Felix Roziner remembers a tragicomic episode from his own life. When in the late 1950s
he invited one of his university friends to his wedding, the friend
replied that he would come and would bring as a present a yellow
canary in a cage and a gramophone. The implication was that marriage was the most philistine thing to do. Felix was insulted and
promised to throw his friend, together with his allegorical canary,
down the stairs. The friend was a serious romantic; he never showed
up for the wedding and never got married, although he fathered a
child out of wedlock.

The mythical wars between meshchane and intelligentsia have obscured their actual relationship. The misunderstanding concerns the
political orientation of the Russian would-be middle class and its
relation to the central power. In the second part of the nineteenth
century a large part of the intelligentsia allied itself with politically
radical forces, and the battle against meshchanstvo (perceived as
traditional, conservative, and conformist) and its poshlyi way of life
was a battle for the revolutionary future of Russia.[108] Yet the historic
meshchanstvo as a social sector hardly presented any threat to revolution and reform; unlike the middle class in Western Europe, the
Russian lower middle class sympathized with radical political move-

ments; in other words, especially in the early twentieth century, it followed the intelligentsia's ideals.[109] Moreover, the central—although often hidden—agenda for the Russian and later the Soviet intelligentsia was not the relation to the mythical meshchanstvo but to the state, whether the absolutist monarchy or the absolute power of the Communist Party. As S. Frederick Starr points out, the classical Russian *intelligent* conceives society "as an artistic or scientific abstraction."[110] Indeed, in the twentieth century the revolutionary war between the intelligentsia and meshchanstvo acquired many tragic and paradoxical twists. Part of the Russian and Soviet revolutionary intelligentsia ended up biting its own tail, supporting and creating a power that led to its annihilation; artists and poets who dissented from both the power and the old intelligentsia ideals were killed, while many members of the Soviet intellectual elite found a new patron in Soviet power and provided ideals of culture and "culturalization" for the new Soviet common people.

The war against poshlost' is often fought either by the nouveaux riches or against the nouveaux riches, or both. The spiritual new rich (the Russian intelligentsia) contend against the materialist new rich (meshchanstvo) in the name of a certain kind of purity—of the past or of the future, in art or in life. In the Russian context, of course, nouveaux riches cannot be regarded in economic terms, because in comparison with their Western European counterparts they are far from rich. Besides, in the Russian cultural narrative the new rich would likely be considered poor in spirit.

In the age of perestroika many elements of this narrative were reversed; as the blank spots in history got filled, many traditional underdogs were rehabilitated. Yet nobody was proud to reclaim the designation of meshchanstvo. The new entrepreneurs aspired to be the "new merchants" and recreated their flamboyant traditionalism in pseudo-Russian style. The merchants had been both wealthier and more spectacular than meshchanstvo, a class that seemed too ordinary for the post-Soviet elite. The "little man," the piece of chicken in the cabbage soup, a private home, decent schooling and clothing for the children, were valued low in the chaotic post-Soviet "stock market" of values (the stock market is a favorite new metaphor of the 1990s). Unlike most of the other social (or antisocial) groups—peasants, workers, gentry, intelligentsia, merchants or lumpen proletariat, bohemians, marginals, criminals, and "blessed fools," who had enjoyed at least their fifteen minutes of fame in one of the competing ideologies of the nineteenth or twentieth century—meshchanstvo remained the mythical scapegoat and the unremarkable, common underdog of Russian cultural history.

Private Life and Russian Soul

In his essay "Moscow" (1927) Walter Benjamin made a provocative and laconic statement: "Bolshevism has abolished private life."[111] He believed the Soviet regime meant to eliminate private life along with private property. For the Bolsheviks "private" was politically dangerous and deprived of social meaning. While it might appear rather obvious that from their point of view the "private individual" was ideologically incorrect, it is remarkable to discover that the Russian intellectual tradition also holds little respect for what is described as "Western, bourgeois" idea of privacy. The closest to the word "privacy" is the concept of *chastnaia zhizn'*—literally: particular (partial) life.[112] Private or personal life is hardly featured in any prerevolutionary dictionary. Moreover, the examples offered for "personal" reveal a certain bias: "An egoist prefers personal good to the common good."[113] Hence Russian personal life seems rather to fit a concept of publicly sanctioned guilt and of a heightened sense of duty.

"Private life" is often synonymous not with "real life" or authentic existence but with foreign, inauthentic behavior. The history of Russian private life remains unwritten, and it is certainly beyond the scope of this study. Yet I would like to raise the question why such a task never appealed to Russian writers, intellectuals, and critics and suggest a few recurrent motifs in the debate on privacy that contributed to the oppositional myth of the Russian soul. Privacy and aesthetics, culture and survival—such issues are intimately linked in the Russian context. In my sketchy mythological description I will discuss Russian homelessness and housekeeping, the connections between spiritual and artistic aspirations and state power, and the discovery of the "Russian soul" in the second part of the nineteenth century. In the Soviet period I will explore both the creation of the model Soviet personality, from the new Adam of the avant-garde artists to the Pioneer hero and the Soviet Oedipus, and the mechanisms of survival during Stalinism and the post-Stalinist thaw. At that time model personalities are redefined and defied and the new rituals affirm an alternative "I" and an alternative "we" of the imagined community of friends. Still, the private in the post-Stalinist decades, while not delimited by personal or property rights, is reconstituted in a different manner—in the minor æsthetic pursuits of communal-apartment dwellers and their personal collections of souvenirs, by means of poetic escapes, obsessive scribbling, and a few unofficial guitar songs shared with friends in the crowded kitchen.

In the 1990s, at the time of privatization and of new reforms (most of which did not yet get a chance to be properly implemented), the critique of the West and the discussion of Russian soul is revived. Some are also thinking of "Eurasian soul," an image wrought by the Russian émigrés of the 1920s–1950s as they dreamed of a new "ideocratic" utopia on the Eurasian continent. The Eurasian theory gives a new justification to reconstructing the borders of the lost Soviet Union with its center in Moscow. The philosophers of the Russian idea and Eurasian theorists are a big hit on the Moscow book market. In 1993 one could buy Berdiaev's and Dostoevsky's philosophical writings, the collection of the Eurasians and Oswald Spengler's *Decline of the West*, right in front of the Lenin Museum in Red Square. Often read out of context, or not read at all but paraphrased and chanted, these ideas are quickly becoming a new ideology that promises to provide some utopian comfort at a time of crisis. So the history of the debates on Russian model personalities and resistence to them acquires new urgency.

The opposition between *private* life and *Russian* life was developed by cross-cultural travelers, Russians going to Europe and European visitors to Russia; they observed the differences in everyday existence and proceeded to justify, glorify, or deplore them in terms that are themselves products of cross-cultural hybridization. But all such observations acquired mythological status when the cultural difference was translated into cultural superiority and patriotism—the general lack of "private life" becomes a sign of Russian chosenness; or conversely, travelers to the West criticize the democratic culture for its soullessness.

Travelers' accounts are particularly interesting because they often combine personal and national self-fashioning; the journey abroad is a kind of ritual, a border-crossing in many senses of the word. Peter the Great insisted that the apprenticeship abroad was part of the education of newly Europeanized Russian gentry; since that time every journey of a Russian nobleman to Europe provokes a reflection on the fate of Russia. Those reflections are frequently written in the form of letters for one's own countrymen, hence they are didactic as much as therapeutic. For instance, Russian playwright Denis Fonvizin traveled to Western Europe in the 1770s and 1780s and wrote many letters and essays complaining about the inauthenticity of European existence. In a letter to his sister he writes: "In general I will tell you that I am very displeased with the moral life of the Parisian French . . . Everyone here lives for himself. Friendship, kinship, honor, gratitude—all this is considered a mere chimera. Be polite, i.e. do not contradict anyone, be amiable, i.e. lie, whatever comes to mind—those are two rules to be *un homme charmant.*"[114]

Fonvizin's "Frenchman" uncannily resembles the Russian dictionary's definition of the egoist we have seen above, written a century later. The French *homme charmant* exists for himself and for the superficial theater of social life. Though he may be a straw man of Fonvizin's imagination, he will embody the foreigner or the enemy when juxtaposed against the Russian conception of a human being. Besides lacking humaneness, the French also "have no reason." (It is ironic, perhaps, that in Russia the French, the self-proclaimed founders of enlightened rationalism, "lack reason," while the Germans, who flatter themselves for having the language best suited to philosophy (according to Hegel), are called *nemtsy*—literally, "the dumb ones," that is, those who do not speak Russian.) In a distinctly Russian aristocratic fashion the traveler also laments the dearth of obedient and obliging servants like those in Russia.[115] In his view, even the servants of Europe are men for themselves, corrupted by the notion of *hommes charmants.* The servants would be the last ones entitled to the private life.

While Denis Fonvizin found unnaturalness, hypocrisy, and lack of humaneness in France and Germany, the Marquis de Custine was struck by the Russian "lack of human dignity" and the artificiality of their everyday behavior. St. Petersburg's high society of the time of Nicholas I is compared in his book to the Hoffmanesque dehumanized people-automatons that participate in a well-orchestrated and brilliant autocratic spectacle. The Russians identify themselves with their duties to the Church, the state, and the bureaucracy; a Russian does not possess an autonomous personal identity independent of his social and religious role. In describing the interior of the Russian aristocratic house, Custine notes the contradiction between the show of richness, the imperial magnificence, and "the untidiness of domestic life, a lack of private space and a profound natural disorder that reminds one of Asia."[116] What Russian Slavophile philosophers would later call "messianic homelessness" appears here as bad housekeeping. What shocks Custine most is that the bed, the most sacred and privately cherished object of French furniture, is the least used in Russia. He remarks that the "bed" does not exist in Russia in a same sense that it exists in "the countries where civilization dates a while back."[117] The Russian aristocratic house he describes has places for sleeping: wooden benches where the elderly, sickly count falls asleep, and pillows on the floor for male servants to nap, and a place behind the screen where female servants spend the night. Those are separated by a curtain from the "bed for display" *(un lit de parade)*, a luxury object that one shows off for the foreign guests but which one does not use. This Russian "bed for display" is a kind of Platonic bed, existing more as an ideal form than as a practical piece of furniture. The Russian obsession with keeping appearances over keeping "human dignity" is reflected in the many flimsy partitions that separate the magnificent public interiors of aristocratic palaces from their domestic interiors. Alas, the Marquis failed to discover the Russian sleeping beauty and her Russian soul in the interiors of the enchanted imperial palace.

To be sure, Fonvizin's account of European life and Custine's *Letters from Russia* are unreliable texts, both in terms of historical research and of balanced cultural judgment. Fonvizin writes a didactic text for Russian imitators of Europe, while Custine produces an antimonarchist satirical pamphlet. Yet they reproduce some common places in the cross-cultural mythologies of Russia and the West, and read the same philosopher of nature—Rousseau—in a strikingly different manner. This only confirms that conceptions of authentic and theatrical behavior, of natural and unnatural, change after crossing the border. One country's polarities of nature and culture, private and public, do not clearly translate into other languages. Petr Chaadaev, one of the first Russian émigrés (he returned home only to be declared a madman), develops the theory that homelessness and orphanage are fundamental features of the Russian fate: "We Russians, like illegitimate children, come to this world without patrimony, without any links with people who lived on the earth before us . . . Our memories go no further back than yesterday; we are as it were, strangers to ourselves."[118] In this letter Chaadaev echoes some travelers from the West like Bonald, who considered the Russian character to be intrinsically nomadic and compared Muscovite houses to Scythian chariots—chariots without wheels.[119] Osip Mandelshtam called Chaadaev one of the first private men in Russia. He uses the French word "privatier" with respect to Chaadaev and puts it in quotation marks.[120] And as if stressing the foreign character of the words *chastnyi* and *privatier* to the Russian tradition, Mandelshtam explains that Chaadaev's personality lacked individualist meaning; it did not belong to him as a person but was "part of a cultural and spiritual tradition."[121] Yet this "tradition" was truly cross-cultural and heterogeneous, a combination of French Catholic anti-Enlightenment philosophy and Russian literary imagination. Chaadaev, who moved from external exile in France to internal exile in Russia, is one of the most uncommon individuals in the Russian philosophical tradition. The idea of "transcendental homelessness" comes to the Western reader more directly from Georg Lukács, who regards it as a fundamental sign of international modernity. For Chaadaev it is an inherent feature of the *Russian* rather than the *modern* tradition; but with one important distinction: "Russian homelessness" is not the result of a loss of home and roots, as the case can be made for European modernity. Rather, it is a permanent condition due to Russia's geographical position between Europe and Asia, a fact that does not foster but hinders modernization.

Chaadaev's reflections stirred up his contemporaries and laid a foundation for thinking about Russian home and community. What appeared as a lack of roots, of home and of cultural legitimacy, in his first philosophical letter, is later reinterpreted by Slavophile philosophers Ivan Kireevsky and Alexei Khomiakov as Russian superior fate. Russian "homelessness" is revalued as a different kind of community and communion based on freedom and love and not on individualism. The Slavophiles rejected Chaadaev's social critique; their "free community" of those who share the Russian homeless spirit happily coexisted with absolute monarchy and absence of rights. Chaadaev himself resisted this idea of Russia's national superiority. In response to Khomiakov he writes: "No, a thousand times no. This is not how we loved our motherland in our youth . . . we desired her well-being,

good institutions, and sometimes dared to wish it some more freedom
. . . but we never thought of her as the most powerful or happy
country in the world. It never occurred to us that Russia personified
an abstract principle . . . that she has an ostensible mission to incorporate all Slavic people and in this way to renew humankind."[122]
Slavophilic nationalism was for him an abstract idea, a deception, an
untruth: "Thank God, I always loved my fatherland for its own sake
and not for my own. Thank God, I have never contributed, neither
in verse nor in prose, to the seduction of my fatherland from its true
road. Thank God, I never accepted abstract theories for the good of
my motherland."[123]

Yet the critique of European individualism is not limited to Slavophiles. During his stay in Paris in 1862, another exile, Alexander
Herzen, wrote a polemical letter to Ivan Turgenev. It contained a
detailed critique of European petit-bourgeois domesticity and the
middle-class conception of the individual who cares only about his
little house and that "piece of chicken" in his soup. Art, in Herzen's
opinion, cannot survive this cozy domestic self-complacency of "limited mediocrity" and vulgarity.[124] Suddenly, only a few paragraphs
later, he describes his great pleasure at finding a nice private apartment in Paris:

> The wing of the house was not too big, not too rich, but the position
> of the rooms, furniture, everything pointed at *another* conception of
> comfort. Near the living room there was a tiny room, completely
> apart, near the bedroom, a study with bookshelves and a writing
> desk. I walked through the rooms and it seemed to me that after
> long wandering I found again a human habitat, *un chez-soi*, and not
> a hotel room with a number, not the human herd.[125]

Is this the trap of a wandering émigré who suddenly succumbs to
the seduction of privacy while self-consciously seeking a different
kind of haven, the unsafe one, that of permanent spiritual exiles and
nomads? Why is it that here the individual "human habitat" is contrasted to the contemptible "human herd" rather than to the ideal
commune? Moreover, from this description it appears that art is not
opposed to privacy but the two exist side by side, like a bedroom and
a cozy study with writing desk and bookshelves in the new apartment. Herzen the displaced traveler is happy to discover *un chez-soi*.
The French expression itself brings together self and home and em-

phasizes the comfort of privacy as self-sufficiency. The home of the Russian thinker in exile is the place where the contradiction between public and private is enacted; his tastes as a public man are different from his private tastes, his own desire for home is influenced by Western conceptions of privacy, even if only the privacy of an exile. Why is it that the French *un chez-soi* does not translate well into Russian?

While all human beings have inner lives, private life is a recent cultural phenomenon, a kind of cultural luxury. Sociologists and historians offer us a narrative that echoes the travelers' accounts. In ancient Greek the word for a private person was "idiot," which referred to a layman and also to an ignorant man. The European revolution of the concept of privacy reveals a shift from civic man to inward man.[126] In Roman law "private" is defined negatively, simply referring to things that the individual may do "without failing of the duties required of a man holding public office."[127] The valorization of the private/public opposition shifts greatly through history. "Private" signifies both an exemption from the public and the realm of domesticity. Like "home" in Freud's *heimlich/unheimlich* paradigm, privacy has two sides: it designates both a realm of affectionate intimacy and a realm of secrecy, concealment, and suspicion.[128] The metamorphosis of the private is directly related to the development of the concept of the self. In this respect, "private" is uncanny in many ways, especially in its historical and cross-cultural variations: it can signify deprivation, the lack of a person's public role, and, in a different context, it can refer to the essential element of personhood.

If in Plato's *Republic* the souls are "housed" in the state and not in the individual habitat, in Kant's formulation the self and human identity are defined by the private home, the only refuge from the excesses of the state or of the revolutionary *coup d'état*. The new conception of self and the development of privacy are the result of changes in the European cultural mentality between 1500 and 1800, as well as of the development of a legal system, particularly the property laws. These include a new attitude toward one's own body and the bodies of others, changes in religious practices, increasing secularization of everyday life, and the spread of literacy. What one discovers in the course of that time is a certain way of being alone, of composing narratives of self, diaries, letters, and autobiographies in a secular rather than religious fashion, as well as a preoccupation with home and taste.[129] The flourishing of the private in Western Europe is the result of two sociopolitical factors. The first was the "deprivatization" of the public sphere, that is, a gradual abolition of feudal duties resulting in the development of a strong state. The second, according to Philippe Ariès, was the change in the forms of sociability and conviviality—from those in which the "public and private are confounded to one" to those in which they are distinct and the private tends to subsume the public.

According to Louis Dumont, individualism—in two senses of the word, as attention to "an empirical subject" and as valorization of a "moral being, independent, autonomous, and thus (essentially) non-social"—is the distinctive feature of modern ideology. Its opposite is holism, the ideology that privileges social totality and neglects or subordinates the human individual.[130] Individualism as developed particularly in eighteenth-century French philosophy, as well as in the English and American tradition from the seventeenth to the nineteenth century, is connected to the development of Protestantism and the ideas of equality, liberty, universal humanity (French or Anglo-American style), and property; in the early modern period, the relation between an individual and material objects begins to prevail over relations between people. The home, in this respect, is the most important "thing" that protects and defines the individual.

In Russia the umbilical cord between the state and its servants was cut rather late. The vagaries of Russian history and the close ties between state and property did not encourage the cultivation of privacy. Late-nineteenth-century Russian legal historians made much of the fact that there was no word for "person" in the old Russian codexes of laws, in which "person" *(lico)* referred actually to a denial of personal dignity and a kind of slavery.[131] In contrast to the laws of Novgorod and Pskov, the Muscovian legal tradition did not pay attention to the rights of the servants of the state. Moreover, the 1649 Code of Laws does not recognize the value of a human being as such; it lacks the concept of a person who could inflict or suffer from insult or dishonor. Everyone, including the clergy, is described according to their occupation and place in the state hierarchy. While professional associations, guilds, and unions protected their members under analogous circumstances in Western Europe, in Russia they did not have any rights. In Peter the Great's decree "On Recognizing Fools" *(duraki),* fools are described as people who might have inheritance and gentry origins, but are of "no use to the state." In this definition, fool in early eighteenth-century Russia, like idiot in ancient Greek, comes closest to the private individual. Private life appears as a dangerous joke, a fool's trick that the state should watch carefully. The decree lifting the nobility's obligatory service to the state was passed only in 1762, a century before the abolition of serfdom. The separation of public and private was safely in the hands of the state for a much longer period of time than in the countries of Western Europe. At the time of Peter the Third and Catherine the Great the nobles were encouraged to study—in order to avoid "the wrath of the monarch." Hence the permission to be cultured came from the monarch and went hand in hand with the liberation from obligatory service.[132] Until the end of the nineteenth century, the concept of "human rights" was of no particular relevance in Russia. The laws of inheritance were such that parents had virtually unlimited power over their offspring, and husbands over their wives. Peasants did not have full rights; nor did certain non-Russian ethnic groups, including Poles, Germans, and Jews. These groups had very limited rights to acquire land, and Jews did not have freedom of movement either and lived in the Pale of Settlement. Very few groups among the population, therefore, were in any position to develop a taste for the private.

For historical reasons, then, in nineteenth-century Russia it was the educated nobility, not the middle class, that created the sophisticated cultural life celebrated in literature. A variety of methods for the Russian nobleman's personal self-fashioning came into being. (The women of nobility, as both Lidiia Ginzburg and Iurii Lotman remark, did not have the same choice of self-fashioning, and in this respect they were more like peasants or people of lower classes.)[133] Among the new types were the sensitive and virtuous man, the intellectual messiah and romantic rebel, the rational man, and the "man without rhetoric." But even among the intellectual gentry the individual often fashions himself as the people's savior, whether he is understood by people or abandoned by them. A striking discrepancy exists between the collective aspiration of a class and an individual's self-stylization as communal savior.

In Dumont's view, to speak about the complete victory of individualism was an impossibility, even in the European context: "on the one hand, it is omnipotent, and on the other hand, it is perpetually and irrevocably haunted by its contrary."[134] The encounter between traditional culture and the dominant modern ideology of individualism has produced strange and hybrid cases of "acculturation." Some intellectual circles in Germany and in Russia rebelled against modern ideology and its conception of the private individual as a model for humanity. They proposed collective, national versions of individualism: the *Volk* in Germany and *narod* in Russia. Although there were two Russian versions of the "people's spirit" *(narodnost')*, neither one was created by the "common people." The first was part of the official monarchic doctrine of "autocracy, orthodoxy, and people's spirit" developed by an adviser to Nicholas I, S. Uvarov, who took it directly from Western models and even described it in French. Here "people's spirit" stands for state national policy. The Slavophile version of the people's community proclaimed it to be above and beyond politics; yet it entirely supported the *status quo* of the absolute monarchy.

Dostoevsky's travel account, "Winter Notes on Summer Impressions," offers a critique of the profane trinity of Western individualism—"liberté, égalité, fraternité." He goes on to describe Paris, in the tradition of Fonvizin, as the capital of a people "who have no reason" (in contrast to its description as "the capital of the nineteenth century," the way it was viewed by Baudelaire and Benjamin):

> *Liberté, égalité, fraternité.* Very good, what is liberté? Freedom. What freedom? Equal freedom for everyone to do what they wish within the limits of the law? When can one do what one wishes? When one has a million. Does freedom give everyone a million? No. A man without a million is not the one who does what he wishes but the one with whom everyone else does what they wish . . . As for this equality in the face of the law, the way it is presented now, every Frenchman should take it as a personal insult. What is left? Brotherhood. This is the most curious part . . . It turned out that in the nature of the French and Westerners in general no brotherhood could be found. What could be found is only the personal element of an isolated individual *(osobniak)*, an increased sense of defending oneself, defining oneself, selling oneself.[135]

The persona of the narrator-Dostoevsky has a lot in common with his bitterly self-contradictory creation—"the underground man." Yet in this text the writer avoids fictional framings, or rather, he makes himself, Feodor Dostoevsky, into the "Russian personality" par excellence. In his novels Dostoevsky explores torments and paradoxes

of personal freedom, limits of human dignity and humiliation, offering us a range of eccentric individual characters and novelistic dialogues. In his journalism, the dialogue is driven by the rhetoric of
persuasion and a single point of view. Here individual particularity
and individual rights matter less than the idea of true brotherhood.
The "I" has to sacrifice itself to society and "not merely not demand
his rights, but on the contrary, give them up unconditionally for
society."[136] Dostoevsky stresses that what he seeks is not "deperson-
alization" but "personality in the highest sense, much more developed and higher than in the West . . . Completely self-conscious and
voluntary sacrifice of one's entire self for the sake of society is a sign
of the highest development of personality." This appears to be a
paradox, a vicious circle of never-ending self-sacrifices that do not
improve human life but promote the idea of an inhuman "life elsewhere." It is self-sacrifice for its own sake, the perpetuation of self-
annihilation. Dostoevsky's brotherhood is perhaps even more
unrealizable than the French bourgeois *fraternité,* at least in this
world; it is a brotherhood of the dead. His freedom appears to be a
freedom *from* one thing only—the "bourgeois, private self"—and *for*
one thing—self-sacrifice. Dostoevsky insists that this is not his personal poetic conception but a "law of nature." (A popular Soviet
song of the 1950s about the freedom of "not having a million," seems
unwittingly to paraphrase Dostoevsky. "Would you like to have a
million?" ironically insinuates the singer. "No," he answers, echoing
the supposed answer of the Soviet people. "Would you like to go to
the Moon?" "Yes." This is perhaps a somewhat far-fetched example
of another dream of "life elsewhere," a hundred years after Dostoevsky's "Notes.")

In this view Russia contributes to the world not "enlightenment"
but illumination *(ozarenie),* not material abundance but spiritual
communality, not individuality but personality, not "individual freedom" but liberation of the soul. This is Russia's messianic role. The
major cultural opposition in Russia is not between private and public
but rather between material and spiritual existence, between byt and
bytie.

In her essay "The Russian Point of View" Virginia Woolf confesses
her own tendency to fall into commonplaces when speaking of Russian writers. Yet those commonplaces may reveal cultural myths and
cross-cultural differences better than many analytical statements. The

author focuses on the foreignness of Russian literature to the English-speaking reader. In Victorian fiction, for example, the story of a general's love affair would begin with his house, with the surroundings, social manners, and conventions of class. In Russian literature, says Woolf, writers as distinct as Dostoevsky, Tolstoy, and Chekhov center on the story of the soul: "These stories are always showing us some affectation, pose, insincerity—some woman has got into a false relationship; some man has been perverted by the inhumanity of his circumstances—the soul is ill; the soul is cured; the soul is not cured. Those are the emphatic points of the story."[137] Russian heroes, from Woolf's estranged point of view, appear as if they "have lost their clothes in some terrible catastrophe," which enables them to speak for the whole of humanity. In her discussion, which is not devoid of Russian exoticism, an interesting opposition emerges in Victorian literature between "social theatricality" (with all the elaborate costumes and manners) and "sincerity," determined by the consciousness of some apocalypse in the past or in the future, in reality or in the imagination. The other contrast is between life in the house and its surroundings and the "homeless life" of the soul—a contrast posed in Russian literature itself. The mythical and mystified Russian soul—the product of Russian fiction and Western interpretations and of a peculiar two-way love-hate between Russia and the West—confronts the Western conception of the private life. After all, it is the "inner life" that is important, not the "private life." Hence "Russian soul" and "private life" are incompatible.

The concept of "Russian soul" in itself is not a particularly Russian idea. At the turn of the nineteenth century historian Nikolai Karamzin speaks about national pride in Russian history, but the immortal soul that he glorifies is "human" rather than Russian. The soul is "nationalized" in the second half of the century. It was divined with the help of the German Romantics, particularly Herder and Schelling, as they were creatively "misread" on the Russian soil. Often the German writers were not read at all—creatively or otherwise, in the original or in translation—but absorbed from the retelling of others and summaries in popular literary magazines. The idea of the Russian soul developed directly in response to the German *Geist* and has something of an Oedipal relation to it (of resentment, rather than murder). Afterward, it was celebrated by many foreign travelers, from Marquis de Vogüé on. Soul is opposed to Enlightened

Reason as well as to cultivation of the body. It is a Psyche without psychology, or to rephrase it, its psychology could be literary but never scientific. Russian literature is famous in the West for its psychologism, but this might be another Western misreading. Dostoevsky wrote: "I am called a psychologist. Not true. I am only a realist in a higher sense." And later Mikhail Bakhtin said about Dostoevsky that he saw in psychology "a reification of human soul that is humiliating."[138] Perhaps it is not by chance that "idiot" (in ancient Greek, we recall, the term for the private individual), is the title of Dostoevsky's novel. Dostoevsky's "idiot" embodies neither solely mental deficiency nor privacy, neither disease nor dailiness, but the suffering and wanderings of the soul.

The nineteenth-century conceptions of the personality and the Russian soul challenge various European understandings of self and society and at the same time reveal a peculiar Russian-European hybrid. The discourse on the Russian soul, like the discourse on the German folk and domestic bliss in the *Heimat,* presupposes a certain degree of racial purity.[139] The Russian soul is inseparable from Russian blood. But is this not a contradiction in terms? In Dostoevsky's universe Germans, Jews, and Poles are deprived of the soul, but this unlikely combination of people makes a truly monstrous "other" of the Russians. A curious coincidence: those deprived of legal rights in the empire become conveniently deprived of soul. Dostoevsky, like his great twentieth-century admirer Berdiaev, also condemns any expression of national or religious sentiment in other nations: the former ridicules French patriotism and the latter criticizes "Judaic messianism" as less "universal" and more narrowly "national" than Russian messianism—the only "spiritually correct," so to speak, messianism in the world.[140] Moreover, "Russian" comes to stand for the true universal humanity. No other nation knew how to be universal the way Russians did: "The Russian people is not a people; it is humanity."[141] For Dostoevsky the embodiment of the Russian soul is Pushkin, in whom the Russian soul has found its home in Russian literature; the poet is at once a model human being and a model Russian. Artistic pursuits in the highest sense of the word take the place of the private pursuits. Culture is the only available sphere of self-fashioning, social climbing, and rebellion. Pushkin is uniquely qualified to be the "Russian superman and universal man" who could resolve all European contradiction and save the Russian soul from

European *Angst*. In short, Russians are universally human, while very few non-Russians could claim the gift of humanity at all. Instead, they appear as soulless scapegoats for Russian ills.

In some way the idea of the Russian soul is reductive even in relation to Russian literature and culture; it does not encompass their richness, originality, and diversity. Moreover, even the writers who wished to dissociate themselves from Slavophilic mythologies, from Pushkin to Mandelshtam, could never completely escape such soulful cultural interpretations. Robert Belknap offers an insightful description of what has become synonymous with "Dostoevskian" and "the Russian soul":

> What Dostoevsky learned from Hoffmann and Gothic novels, Edgar Allan Poe offered in a compressed, intensified and highly psychological form, which also derived heavily from Hoffmann . . . the exploration of the perverse, of abnormal mental states, the enunciation of the emotions more intense than those of the ordinary folk—as well as doubles, hallucinations, extraordinary holy figures, helpless women of great birth and beauty, flashing often fearsome hypnotic eyes, dark stairways and secret places in threatening buildings and a host of other elements that de Vogué and other Westerners have tended through ignorance or a need for alien excellence to call archetypically and exotically Russian.[142]

The Russian soul is here an uncanny creation of a foreign ghost-story writer and the Russian muse; it inhabits the haunted house of European Romanticism and predicts its fall to be much more spectacular than that of the house of Usher.

But that soul did not die with the end of the nineteenth century; it was reborn in the writings of twentieth-century émigrés and foreigners, together with the myths of utopian community. "The Russian soul," writes Berdiaev, "does not like to settle down in one place; is not a petit-bourgeois *(meshchanskaia)* soul, not a local soul. In the soul of the Russian folk there is an infinite quest, a quest for the invisible city of Kitezh, the invisible home."[143] (Kitezh is the site of a folkloric Russian utopia.) For Berdiaev, a former Hegelian Marxist, spiritual and social utopias are clearly linked. The aim of these missions is to transcend the everyday and to construct or imagine a utopia somewhere in heaven or on earth. In the symbolic rewriting of Russian history in the mid-nineteenth century certain historical communities acquire mythical significance; certain historical facts

turn into symbolic, myth-generating events and their historical specificity is erased. The mythical ideal Russian community *par excellence* is the peasant commune, which embodies "Russian
communitarianism, the chorus element, and the union of love and
freedom, without any external guarantees."[144] The peasant commune
was supposed to be an example of *sobornost'*, spiritual gathering and
community, which is a Russian untranslatable antipode to the Western concept of the individual and identity. Sobornost', the place of
communal spirituality, from the word *sobor*—literally, meeting and
cathedral—is opposed to authority and formal attributes of spirituality and power. A cathedral or a religious institution has no monopoly
over the spirit, but the true cathedral is where the spirit rules.[145]
Sobornost' is radically anti-iconographic, antirhetorical, and anticonventional. Love and freedom are not decreed; they are not defined in
relation to language or to convention. There are no formal attributes
of truth of spirituality. Sobornost' and true spirituality can only *be*
but not *mean;* they can be intuited mystically but not read or interpreted. In this understanding, the true community, like a symbol,
transcends language and iconography.

Berdiaev as well as Dostoevsky and Khomiakov before him contrast Western society with Russian community and Western civilization with Russian culture, which is based on "democracy of the true
spirituality." Civilization, writes Berdiaev, is bourgeois by nature in
the most spiritual sense of the word. The essence of what is bourgeois
is precisely the civilized kingdom of this world: the worldly craving
for power and for the enjoyment of life. "The spirit of civilization is
a bourgeois spirit; it attaches itself to ephemeral and transient things;
it does not like eternity."[146] Private life is simply too bourgeois to be
worth discussing. In Berdiaev's description of the Russian communality, German philosophical metaphors (mostly from Hegel and
Nietzsche) and Biblical imagery merge in the rhythmical, incantatory
style of a preacher. Nowhere in this text is the reader allowed to
doubt, to reflect, to raise a question, perhaps to look for the source
of a quote. The text reproduces the same totality it describes—or to
use Berdiaev's own word, "totalitarianism"—of the Russian intelligentsia.[147] The allegedly anti-authoritarian rebellion of the philosophers of Russian sobor offers a form of mystical authoritarianism.
We hear only one voice in Berdiaev, his own, and this single, highly
individualized voice speaks in the name of an anti-individualist community. The truth about sobor is beyond interpretation since it is

beyond language; it can be revealed only through the charismatic genius of the Russian philosopher. Berdiaev asks the reader to convert, not to converse, to have a spiritual communion (authored and authorized by Berdiaev), not a communication.

From a less romantic viewpoint, the peasant commune, as many historians agreed, was hardly a voluntary communion of soul-mates but a form of organization by means of which the state could control the peasant. The incantatory discourse covers up the role of the absolutist state. The use of the peasant commune to exemplify the community of soul-mates is ethically problematic; it internalizes and naturalizes absolutist forms of state control, making it a part of the people's inner life.[148] In the discussions of the peasant commune, the emphasis on true spiritual culture and sobornost' of the Russian folk often obscures the diversity of cultural practices, of actual associations and forms of social and domestic behavior. Peasants' voices did not contribute much to the idea of sobornost' and true communality (since they were not very grounded in German Romanticism). Nor do we hear the voices of the middle class (often ethnically mixed and not purely Russian), the class wedged between the tsar and the people, the aristocracy and the peasants. They contributed greatly to Russian history but remained foreign and external to the history of the Russian idea.

Marxism in Russia, the country described as the "weakest link in the capitalist chain," fed on many communitarian myths. While shifting the emphasis from peasant to worker, from the country to the city, from agriculture to industry, from Russian to international (or "supernational," Berdiaev's word), Russian Marxists preserved the utopian messianism and the strong critique of individualism characteristic of the believers in the Russian idea. Hence the ideal "proletarian" of Russian Marxists was not too different from the ideal communitarian peasant (both were quite distant from the average Russian worker or peasant).[149] The iconography of Soviet culture owes as much to Russian Christian utopianism as it does to Western Marxism.

From New Adam to New Oedipus

In 1920 Alexander Bogdanov, the author of the socialist utopian novel *Red Star* (1908), a former "God-builder" and a Bolshevik, proclaimed that the new principles for the organization of life should be "collectivism and monism." Such collectivism is the opposite of individual diversity or "bourgeois pluralism." It calls for a "monistic fusion" of art, politics, and the everyday, achieved in a single revolutionary sweep: "Collectivism illuminates the depiction not only of human life but also of the life of nature: nature as a field of collective labor."[150] In 1921 Bogdanov abandoned his direct involvement with politics and aesthetics and returned to medicine, but he never abandoned his utopian vision. He became director of the Institute of Blood Transfusion, which to him represented the ultimate syncretic fusion of science and dream. In 1928 Bogdanov died while conducting one of his experiments in blood transfusion upon himself—only a few years after Sergei Esenin committed suicide by opening up his veins and writing his suicide note in verse and in blood. Bogdanov's was another kind of writing in blood; it cemented the revolutionary collectivity and violently overcame the boundaries between the self and the other, between art and life.

Although the Soviet ideal person was the opposite of the Russian personality on the grounds of religious idealism, the constructs were structurally similar: self-sacrificial, anti-individualist, and ascetic. After the Revolution a political and aesthetic repertoire of images developed for the self-fashioning of the new Soviet men and women. The ideal of the comrade served both sexes and meant both to be equally virile, while it rejected "bourgeois psychology"; not surprisingly, the creation of the new person prefigures the destruction of psychoanalysis in Russia, which had flourished earlier in the century.[151] V. N. Voloshinov, a member of Bakhtin's circle, outlined a strong critique of Freudian psychoanalysis. In his view social needs are much more important than sexual desires, and a person is seen as a product of "everyday ideology" more than of his or her "private" and individual unconscious: "The individual consciousness not only cannot be used to explain anything; but on the contrary, it is itself in need of explanation from the vantage point of the social, ideological medium."[152] Voloshinov sees the emphasis on sexuality as an expression of Western "bourgeois individualism," which, predictably, leads to absurdity, decadence, and other dead ends. The conflict Freud described as an individual's internal conflict of consciousness and the unconscious should be located on the level of "everyday ideology" of a particular society, with its contradictions between "official" and nonofficial discourses. The new Soviet primal scene is that of a collective (and rather unerotic) intercourse, and there is no mirror in a fanciful *fin-de-siècle* frame in which a plump mama's boy reflects himself. In Soviet Russia social consciousness takes over the individual unconscious and the dreamwork takes place on a larger national level, but it uses similar mechanisms of displacement and condensation, repression and denial. Perhaps the problem with psychoanalysis was that it was too strong an ideology in its own right, and as such it was individualistic and transnational. The Freudian pantheon, with Narcissus, Rat Man, and Wolf Man, has different heroes than does the new Soviet pantheon, which starts with the New Adam of the avant-gardists and goes on to what I would call the New Oedipus of the Socialist Realists—Pavlik Morozov, the Pioneer hero.

The Russian New Person was born in the nineteenth century in the ascetic imagination of the Social Democrats and perpetuated in Nikolai Chernyshevsky's novel *What Is to Be Done?* (It was Lenin's favorite book and a blueprint for revolutionary self-fashioning.)[153] After the Revolution, however, the new person becomes progressively depersonalized and less individuated; what is needed at that time are not only exemplary revolutionaries and heroes but "little people-builders of socialism," or, in Stalin's time, the "nuts and bolts of the system."[154] Hence the refashioning of personality follows two conflicting models: on the one hand, there is a new antipsychological Adam born out of revolutionary avant-garde creativity and Dziga Vertov's associative montage, and on the other hand, there is the new anonymous Soviet citizen mass-produced by bureaucratic and authoritarian de-individuation, a process that follows prescriptive rules and rules out creative choices. The resulting models are not the same; they are often antagonists, but occasionally they appear as uncanny doubles. Dziga Vertov writes: "I will create a man more perfect than Adam. From one person I take hands, the strongest and most agile ones, from the other I take legs, the most slender and quick, from the third person I take a head, the most beautiful and expressive—and I create a new perfect person with the help of montage."[155] Of course, the "cutting" here is merely a cinematic metaphor. Nothing hurts; instead, the process displaces and cures by estrangement any emotional or physical pain. This new Adam is not a purely Russian revolutionary dream but a creature of the avant-garde Bible throughout the world.

By the mid-1920s the Soviet press replaces such artistic conceptions by pedagogical ones that are more in line with the practical needs of education in the country. The pedagogical ideal is not a fantastic new Adam or Eve[156] but a reformed orphan, the former homeless hooligan-*besprizornik,* a child of the Civil War turned into an exemplary builder of communism. The orphanage or camp of *besprizorniks,* a confined space with full-time instruction and paramilitary discipline as described in the Soviet collective Bildungsroman *Republic Shkid,* or later in *Pedagogical Poem,* turns into a model socialist republic.[157] Pedagogy in general is one of the most important revolutionary and postrevolutionary disciplines. The Soviet people are treated a bit like children by their stern but loving teachers, who help them to eliminate, as an early theorist of the Young Pioneer movement put it, "childlike mysticism, fantasy-making, individualism, and chaos."[158] (Incidentally, this Soviet pedagogue began as a psychoanalyst.) If in the 1920s the discourse of communality is sharply directed against the family and in favor of collective camaraderie, in the 1930s the family metaphor is back, with Stalin in the roles of lover, father, husband, and grandfather of the people. The nuclear family is encouraged again (to correct the "leftist excesses" of free love) and occasionally reminded to ensure the supervision of its straying members, those who are insufficiently dedicated to the larger-than-life Soviet patriarchy, with Stalin at the head and Pavlik Morozov, the hero-pioneer and kolkhoz-builder, as his most faithful son.

The story takes place in the 1930s at the time of collectivization in the countryside. Young Pioneer Pavlik Morozov informs on his natural father, accusing him of being a *kulak* (rich peasant). He acts for the sake of the Motherland and is later killed by the enemies of the people. This is the Soviet version of the Oedipal myth par excellence—only secrets, blindness, and the metaphysical conversation with the Sphinx are lacking. Blindness is not a part of the Socialist Realist commonplace; the emphasis here is on didactic transparency, not on the riddle of vision and visibility. In the time of glasnost' the popular journal *Ogonek* published new documentary evidence claiming that the boy was manipulated by his natural mother, who was jealous of the father, who happened to be not even a kulak but an impoverished *seredniak* ("middle" peasant, just barely above the poverty level). This retelling shows that the story of the hero-pioneer Pavlik Morozov was only a tragic family romance in the most traditional sense, a story of private obsessions rather than a didactic Soviet fairy tale. Ironically, the piece in *Ogonek* is as timely and mythological as was the legend of the young pioneer, since in the 1990s the mythology of private life is more important than that of heroic collectivity.

Besides the hero-pioneer there were also heroes and heroines of labor, Stakhanovites and explorers of the North Pole, heroes of the Great Patriotic War and great leaders. The great leaders were allowed to have private lives but only as a special privilege that they, in their natural modesty, choose to forgo. The leaders' private life was also a great source of secrecy and that gave them, in the words of Dostoevsky's Grand Inquisitor, "mystery and authority." The Soviet citizens were encouraged reverently to eavesdrop on the private life of the leaders; thus Lenin's and Stalin's study rooms, for instance, were objects of mass fascination and were frequently depicted in paintings. The survivors of Stalin's time remember that there was always one window lit in the Kremlin to show that "Stalin is working." And the cordial *babushki* on the street used to sigh, full of empathy and maternal care, for the long hours that the great leader put in for the people.

As for Stalin's subjects, they hardly became model Soviet personalities. In the memoirs written from the 1960s to the 1980s survivors of Stalinism meditate on the fate of the individual and the role of Russian and Soviet intelligentsia. Nadezhda Mandelshtam presents an anatomy of compromise during the Stalin years. Mandelshtam rereads Dostoevsky's *Diary of a Writer* after the war and engages in a dialogue with him about personality, the individual, and the fate of the nation. In her view, the disease of the twentieth century is "the shrinking of personality," but the reason for it is hardly bourgeois individualism. In Stalinist Russia two types of nonpersons emerged— the ones who lived in a torpor, with the single thought of "how to survive the burden of times" (a group in which she includes herself), and the egocentrists who thought only to save themselves and "are ready to do anything for an instance of pleasure."[159] In contrast to Dostoevsky's, Mandelshtam's "egocentrist" is of distinctly Soviet origin, and the loss of personality is a result of state power and totalitarianism, not of the national spirit. In her view, the Dostoevskian national idea and messianic individualism could lead to paranoic isolation from the world, and that was the Russian experience in the twentieth century. The homelessness she and her husband experienced was, unfortunately, not a poetic metaphor. "I" could be taken away as well as one's home or even a room in the densely populated communal apartment: "the 'I,' shrunk and destroyed, sought refuge anywhere it could find it, conscious of its worthlessness and lack of a housing permit."[160]

Lidiia Ginzburg, cultural critic and a disciple of the Formalists in the 1920s, elucidates further the mechanisms of survival during the war and the epoch of Stalinist terror and the degrees of compromise and betrayal.[161] A survivor herself, she does not assume a self-righteous pose of absolute moral authority but rather that of a witness and a lucid analyst. In her view,

> people operated through mechanisms of adaptation, justification, and growing indifference—only for some people these mechanisms worked with interruptions, instances of human decency. Among those who functioned or "coincided" with the regime were honest believers, the self-hypnotized, and the cynically resigned. In the years of Stalin's terror the "untruth" resided not in the general ideological worldview, but often in the intonation, in the ostensible public display of one's agreement with the regime.

This excessive display of allegiance and collaboration was a public display of eliminated private life and of absolute coincidence between inner thoughts and official ideology. At the end of her notes, written in 1980, Ginzburg meditates on the Soviet defense mechanisms and the breaks in the system: "In the course of life all kinds of defense mechanisms continued to function. They comfortably enveloped us, so that we would not scream of horror. We do not see the full picture of the lived life, only a part of it. And this part adapts to us or we adapt ourselves to it. And now at times, I experience retrospective horror. The 'abyss of humiliation' opens in front of me. How did we walk into this abyss, step by step, not missing anything . . . ?"[162]

Reinvention of Privacy and the Community of Friends in the 1960s

At the time of Khrushchev's thaw, the personal intonation described by Lidiia Ginzburg acquired a particular significance in public life. In reaction to both the new Adam and the new Oedipus, an alternative mythology of self-fashioning emerged in which the hero was romantic or intelligent and aspired to old-fashioned values of moral integrity. Although the 1960s returned in many ways to the revolutionary and very mildly avant-garde discourse of the 1920s (mildly, because most of the artworks and texts remained unavailable), yet this return was in many ways revisionist, particularly in the understanding of self and private life. The official collective was rewritten as an unofficial association of friends, a rather casual community of transient soul mates. Occasionally one of the soul mates would report on another one, occasionally the other one would be called to the KGB, but as the Soviet anecdote has it, a great progress was made in Brezhnev's time— the ten-year prison-sentence joke was reduced to only three years. In some ways this imagined community of friends ironically flaunted its own fragility. By the late 1960s privacy began to be seen as the only honorable and uncompromising response to the system of public compromise. Privacy was sought not as an escape but rather as a way of carving an alternative space and of personalizing and deideologizing (to use the favorite term of perestroika intellectuals) the official maps of everyday life. The songs of the popular bard of the time, Bulat Okudzhava, celebrated each insignificant incident of daily life, the streets of childhood, the last trolleybus, ephemeral loves. One of his songs celebrates ordinary life on Arbat Street, one of the old Moscow streets that became his vocation, his fatherland, and even his religion.[163] This Arbat religion consists only of minor everyday epiphanies on the street corners. The bards of the thaw did not try to invent a new language as did the revolutionary poets of the 1920s; instead, they rediscovered a *private intonation,* the private colloquial language that became the eclectic poetic slang of the 1960s intelligentsia. Many songs were about a momentary solitude and sadness, a feeling of urban alienation or nostalgia, still worth celebrating. The songs were not simply about solitude but about *a right* to solitude, a right to experience private sadness and to sing of private emotions. Most of the Soviet people at that time lived in the overcrowded communal apartments, lonely perhaps but rarely alone, hence the moments of self-conscious alienation and solitude were cherished. Privacy was carved through unofficial everyday artistic practices. (It was only some fifteen years earlier, in the late 1940s and early 1950s, that poets and writers, including Zoshchenko and Akhmatova, were criticized for being too lyrical and personal.) After the events of 1968 in Prague a very few members of the thaw generation became dissidents, and their private lives became literally equated with the political underground. The majority limited themselves to gentle subversion and minor private retreats from the public li(f)e.

In the 1990s the words of "Oh Arbat, my Arbat, you are my fatherland" would have very different connotations, because Arbat has become the first commercial street of Moscow where totalitarian kitsch is for sale. Arbat Street of the 1960s is gone the way of its older predecessor, but the former Kalinin Avenue, named after one of the prominent members of Stalin's government, is now renamed New Arbat. Now that the prefix "post" has become excessively fashionable—in the post-Soviet, postcommunist, postmodern era—many untranslatable words entered Russian in their stylized, markedly foreign form: *mental'nost'*, *identichnost'*, *manadzher*, *sponsor*, and so on. The words "communal" and "collective" are extremely unpopular. The new metaphor of post-Soviet communality is "cooperative" or "joint venture." Before, there was no word for privacy in Russian; now, there is privatization. If in the Soviet past private life was not brought out in public, now there is a newspaper called *Private Life (Chastnaia Zhizn')* that specializes in personal ads, cries of loneliness, and searches for Western husbands and wives. A woman reader wrote a teasing couplet in response to the newspaper's verse contest, which reflects all the ambiguities and paradoxes of the new and still untranslatable (or at least unprecedented in any Western language) post-Soviet byt: "What is to be done? I don't despair. I have no personal life but I have a 'Private Life'." Here the quotation marks around "private life" point to the name of the newspaper and a new cliché of post-Soviet language, but not yet the "property" of those Russian citizens still deprived of private life.

Truth, Sincerity, Affectation

Here is a Soviet joke about the cultural adventures of truth:

A man comes to the newsstand and asks: "Could you give me *Truth* please?"
—"There is no *Truth* left, all we have is *Labor*," the salesman answers.[164]

Now the joke appears outmoded since there is no *Labor* left either. As for the newspaper *Truth* or *Pravda,* it became the voice of the National-Communist opposition and, as such, it is readily available in the the post-Soviet Metro, between the former Revolution Square Station and the former Marx Avenue. But the devaluation of the word for truth—pravda—only stimulates the search for a *truer* truth in different words. In Russian there are two words for truth—pravda and *istina*—and no word for authenticity. Pravda evokes justice, fairness, and righteousness; istina derives from "is" *(est')*, and means that it *is* a kind of truth and faithfulness to being. In the Orthodox saying, "pravda comes from the heaven, istina comes from the earth,"[165] but the two words often sometimes reverse their meaning. By the nineteenth century pravda is the more colloquial term, while istina belongs to the literary language. Russian proverbs and folk sayings, as well as the Soviet anecdotes, are ambiguous when it comes to truth. (They only discuss pravda, never istina, which belongs to a different kind of talk.) On the one hand, there are warnings for truth-seekers: "truth is good but happiness is better,"[166] or "if you tell the truth, you give yourself trouble"; and "every Pavel has his own truth"; or, on the grim side, "there was truth at Peter and Paul's." This last "truth" does not refer to the evangelical doctrine but rather to confession under torture in the infamous prison at the Peter and Paul fortress in St. Petersburg.[167] On the other hand, pravda is also heroically celebrated: "truth does not burn in fire and does not drown in the water," or "Varvara is my aunt, but truth is my sister." Yet this common ambiguity about truth from Russian oral culture is rarely echoed in the writings of the Russian intelligentsia. In this respect Russian writers and intellectuals are unfaithful to the Russian folk tradition; many of them considered truth to be much better than happiness. They searched for the essential istina, the word that does not rhyme easily.[168] One feature, however, remains the same—truth has to be "Russian." In the proverbs found in Dal's dictionary, "Russian truth" is positively qualified, as opposed to "Gypsy truth" or "Greek truth" ("If a Greek is telling the truth, keep your ears open").[169] The affirmation of Russian truth and truthful behavior is one of the important cultural obsessions inherent in the intelligentsia's discourse on Russian identity since the nineteenth century. It is closely linked to the relationship between Russia and the West and the attitudes toward Westernized conventions, rules and laws of behavior, conceptions of legality and the legal system, and boundaries between social and antisocial, lawful and unlawful, private and public. Truthful behavior is frequently seen as sincere behavior, defined in opposition to Western conventional manners. The Russian word *iskrennost'* suggests kinship, proximity, closeness; it may be related to the word for "root"—*koren'*—making Russian sincerity appear more "radical."[170] This nuance could underlie different conceptions of interpersonal space, different rituals of friendship and cordiality— more touching, kissing, crying, and sighing—which are frequently beyond the threshold of personal tolerance of the respectable foreign tourist. The search for *pravda* and *istina* has produced many unconventional expressions as well as ritualized rebellions.

"Private life" in Russian is not opposed to public life, but rather to inner life. The private realm is an exotic land for the Russian cultural imagination; it was not discovered on inward journeys, however, but on trips abroad, mostly westward. The private sphere is the theater of a major comedy of cross-cultural errors: European private behavior appears affected and theatrical to the Russian travelers, while Russian everyday life strikes the foreign visitor as unnatural and excessive, full of Dostoevskian "scandal" scenes. Russian playwright Denis Fonvizin, who traveled to Western Europe in the 1770s and 1780s, wrote that the private homes and streets in Germany are so clean that it seems "like an affectation."[171] (The lack of dirt seems to reveal a lack of sincerity, humaneness, and truthfulness. Cleanliness per se is not the problem: it is the ostentation of cleanliness. Not being a Protestant, he fails to see the elimination of dirt as a virtue.) The same criticism comes up again in his description of Parisian urban life. Instead of "amusement and fun" he decries a life of "stupid affectation" and "lie without clemency."[172] Affectation, the word used to criticize the excess of Western theatricality, is of French origin, as if it were necessary to use a Western word to describe Western theatricality. Fonvizin's ideal of "natural behavior" is not purely native. It is not accidental that one frustrated purpose of his travels was to find Jean-Jacques Rousseau, whom the Russian writer greatly admired and whose many pronouncements on conventionality he translated into Russian.

Iurii Lotman offers a semiotic explanation of such cross-cultural differences. A "neutral middle-class" or European behavior became sharply semiotized when it was transferred to Russia at the time of Peter the Great, and the image of European life was "replicated in a ritualized play-acting of European life."[173] The areas of "nonspecialized," "natural," and nonritualistic behavior became the areas where teaching was most needed. In the time of Peter the Great young men from the new elite began to travel to Europe, where they were struck by the "privateness of the European life."[174] Thus Petr Tolstoy in his diary represents Venice of the early eighteenth century as a place of individual freedom where "everyone acts according to his will, each as he wishes." But once the Russian noblemen began to behave in a more European manner, they had "a feeling of being forever on stage." The theatricalization of everyday behavior turns into one of the main sources of critical parody in the early nineteenth century. It is then that the issue of taste, treated as a sign of Europeanization and superficial civility, is frequently contrasted with true spirituality, more important than a mere veneer of foreign politeness.

Yet it turns out that truly national behavior is even more difficult to learn than unnatural foreign manners. Not only those who followed Western European fashions were ridiculed, portrayed as untrue and insincere, or accused of affectation. Some fifty years after Fonvizin's travels the Slavophiles proposed a return to pre-Petrine Russian dress. Ivan Aksakov, a philosopher of the conservative Slavophile utopia, grew a beard and began to wear a garment he called a traditional Russian peasant coat. Contemporaries ironically remarked that he looked "like a Persian."[175] It is hard to understand how the Russian spirit could be affirmed through the change of national costume. This sort of national self-fashioning does not necessarily lead to natural behavior. On the contrary, the return to origins looks like a masquerade; instead of looking French one looks Persian—or, even worse, one ends up looking like an exotic Oriental, as featured prominently in Western European cultural imagination, this time in an incomparable, distinctly Russian fashion. Good taste in dress is as fragile as Russian cultural identity, and the fashioning of cultural purity is riddled with contradictions and paradoxical designs.

Protestant cultures, especially in nineteenth-century United States, have their own traditions of antitheatricality. There theatricality is connected to the public sphere and is contrasted to authenticity and privacy. American sociologist Richard Sennett deplores the "fall of the public man," particularly striking in contemporary American society, and looks with a kind of nostalgia to Parisian society of the nineteenth century and its highly developed social theatricality and taste for public life. Sennett challenges the privileging of authenticity.

He shows how throughout European history the metaphor of *thea-trum mundi* is progressively devalued: "As the imbalance between public and intimate life has grown greater, people have become less expressive. With the emphasis on psychological authenticity people have become inartistic in daily life . . . They arrive at the hypothesis that theatricality has a special hostile relation to intimacy . . . theatricality has an equally special, friendly relationship to public life."[176]

In the Russian context the concepts of "authenticity" and "theatricality" have a different history and their opposition is of a different order. Authenticity is connected to authorship, to a legal authentication. It is irrelevant if not negatively valorized in the Russian intellectual tradition which developed under an absolute monarchy with little interest in democratic legal culture. Theatricality or conventionality is opposed to truthfulness in both its variants, as manifest in the writings of Dostoevsky and Tolstoy. Russian literature offers us many heroes who ostentatiously defy the norms of European good taste and can be tongue-tied, uneloquent, clumsy—all of which only reaffirms their authenticity, as if language itself were already compromised, always endangered by poshlost'.[177]

Dostoevsky, in *Diary of a Writer*, criticizes the Western legal system of authentication, which is based on the paradoxical premise that a "lie is necessary for the truth." Dostoevsky presents a parody of the jury trial—or perhaps turns a jury trial as an institution into a parody. For Dostoevsky this is a mere spectacle, a "mechanistic method of exaggeration" and a cunning, artful game of lying. At the end he proposes his own self-consciously utopian, "angelic" Russian solution to the problem: "We might substitute this mechanism, this mechanistic method of uncovering the truth . . . simply by truth. The artificial exaggeration will disappear from both sides. Everything will appear sincere and truthful and not merely a game in uncovering truth. Neither a spectacle nor a game will take place on the stage but a lesson, a didactic example."[178]

This is the same anticonventional, antirhetorical, and antilegalistic stance we observed in the discussions of personality. Truth is the antithesis of rhetoric and game-playing. Significantly, however, in the search for simple truth the stage is not abolished, and the action itself is theatricalized. Dostoevsky's *Diary of a Writer* presents a spectacular morality play. (Before 1864 Russia had a primarily prosecutorial system, with no defense, and with confession frequently extorted under torture. The practice of defense was introduced only in 1864 together with jury trials, which did not become central to Russian legal practices. The authority of the prosecutor did not always contribute to the "uncovering of simple truth" and not all confessions were "sincere." But of course Dostoevsky speaks about utopia, not actual practices in Russia.)

The qualities Dostoevsky loved and regarded as uniquely Russian are "pure-heartedness" and sincerity. The question is, how does Russian sincerity compare to Western? Does it have a different history, or does it deny history all together? (The comparative study of sincerity is not yet an established scholarly discipline.)

Lionel Trilling began to reflect upon the moral history of sincerity in the European context. The English as well as the French words for it come from the Latin *sincerus*—without wax; the word used to refer to things, and only in the eighteenth century was it applied to persons.[179] According to Trilling, sincerity presupposes self-conscious reflection, the need to confirm one's own truthfulness to oneself. The commonplace of the epistolary genre, the inscription "sincerely yours," reflects an element of self-doubt and an effort to dispell it. "Authenticity" presupposes a less subjective relationship to the world, and it is celebrated in the postromantic era. The Russian word for sincerity, *iskrennost'*, suggests kinship rather than purity; it manifests itself in a number of familiar rituals that Russians deem sincere, but which foreigners could perceive as theatrical.

The Russian literary imagination is deeply concerned with sincerity. In Dostoevsky's novels, tongue-tied characters devoid of rhetorical and oratorical skills often appear as spokesmen for the authorial Russian truth. This includes Kirilov from *The Devils* and Count Myshkin from *The Idiot*. Such inarticulateness and social clumsiness are read as true and sincere. In "Winter Notes on Summer Impressions" Dostoevsky explicitly associates eloquence with French bourgeois civilization. Even nature, Dostoevsky writes scornfully, is for the Parisian bourgeoisie a mere pretext for linguistic clichés and nostalgia for lost eloquence. The French bourgeois makes nature itself appear unnatural, rhetorical, and constructed.[180] But Russian sincerity, as presented in the works of Dostoevsky, has its own commonplaces. The inarticulateness of his truthful characters is not without theater; these characters are often *exaggeratedly* antirhetorical, *grotesquely* tongue-tied. With their exaggerated gestures, they seem to prefigure the melodramatic heroes of the silent cinema. The drama of the first person in the fictional and nonfictional texts of Dostoevsky is a melodrama of sincerity in which the first-person voice tries to authenticate its truthfulness and pure-heartedness in the most exaggerated and occasionally scandalous declarations.

As another curious cross-cultural twist, in Dostoevsky's novels and travel accounts German characters are the principal carriers of a "mercantile civilization," while in their own conception of their national character Germans take pride in their special spirit of culture and sincerity. Nietzsche gives us an ironic description of it in *Beyond Good and Evil*: "The German loves 'sincerity' and 'uprightness.' How comforting it is to be sincere and upright . . . The German lets himself go looking the while with trustful blue empty German eyes—and foreigners immediately mistake him for his shirt."[181]

In the emotional realm Russian daily life is more ritualized and more theatrical. There is also more tolerance toward what would appear to Westerners to be excessively expressive behavior, an outpouring of emotions. This is a frequent European and American reaction to old Russian novels and to contemporary Russian films. Russian codes of sincere behavior are much more emotional and outwardly expressive than those of their Western counterparts. The "bruderschaft" rituals of collective vodka-drinking come to mind—the German expression is oddly useful to describe something that would appear to be unique to the Russian spirit (and spirits). The codes of emotionalism and intimacy found an outlet in Soviet diplomatic rituals, especially in the profuse kissing among the First Secretaries of the Communist Parties of the former Soviet Union and its former "fraternal socialist states": Stalin and Mao, Brezhnev and Honecker. These Russian-style brotherly kisses were followed by the Soviet-style comradely handshake, and constituted a remarkable semiotic ritual in the play of sincerity and Soviet "patronage" of the neighboring East European states. Now those snapshots of proverbial Russian cordiality and Soviet comradeship remain only on the ironic postcards sold in the former Eastern bloc countries for foreign tourists and émigrés.

The Russian word for "intimacy" is of foreign origin. "Intimacy" was decried in the 1920s and reemerged in the 1960s with positive overtones. In the 1960s, however, it usually refers to the intimacy within a group of true friends rather than the intimacy of a couple,

and the culture of friendly intimacy is opposed to the official collectivity, the Soviet family, and even the nuclear family. In the 1990s
nobody talks about a new intimacy, but there is a new sincerity,
voiced in the poetry of an ironic and estranged artist Dmitrii Prigov,
once a leader of the underground. Sincerity here is merely the voice
of an unfashionable provincial *intelligent* who read the journal
Ogonek and still desperately hopes to participate in the euphoric
public sphere of the first years of glasnost'! Prigov's new sincerity is
at once an act of defamiliarization and of unadmitted nostalgia for a
certain kind of pure-hearted and naïve first-person discourse that
escapes multiple narrative framings and scaffoldings; indeed, it is not
a discourse at all, but pure-heartedness itself—something that may
have never existed in its ideal pure form.

   Whatever its style, the Russian national mythology continues to
counterpoise its dramatic sincerity, pure-hearted (and pure-blooded),
against the self-conscious social theatricality characteristic of the civilized and mercantile West.

Kul'turnost': The Totalitarian Lacquer Box

In Soviet Russian the word "culture" acquired many suffixes and
derivatives: one could go to the Vocational School of Cultural Enlightenment or be a *kul'torg*—cultural organizer—and lead fellow
members of the Young Communists on a cultural outing to watch the
dioramas in the Museum of Revolution or the ballet *Spartakus* in the
Kirov Theater. The unwritten Soviet etiquette of *kul'turnost'* demanded that you bring a bouquet of yellow mimosas to your high-
school teacher on International Women's Day and a bottle of "Red
Moscow" perfume to your aunt. If you are cultured you drink a few
shots of vodka accompanied by pickles and pleasantries, but you do
not get drunk. Behind the glass doors of the cabinet with bookshelves
you keep the precious hardcover editions of the complete works of
James Fenimore Cooper, Jack London, Alexander Pushkin, and Alexander Dumas, and perhaps a new translation of *An American
Tragedy*. Why does kul'turnost' embrace so many diverse Soviet fashions, both imposed and internalized? What does it have to do with
our idea of culture and what roots do they share?

   In the last years of the Soviet Union a journalist observed: "The
unique Russian character is shaped by Russian bread lines, Russian
inefficiency, as well as Russian culture . . . a powerful word, which

has replaced everything—democracy, law, education, food."[182] It would be difficult to claim that the word "culture" is of Russian origin—it is a Latin word reinvented by the German Romantics—yet in Russia the word acquired many magic qualities and retained its status as an emblem of national identity for nearly one hundred and fifty years. In the nineteenth century culture is often synonymous with literature, and Russians are defined less by blood and by class than by being a unique community of readers of Russian literature.[183] According to Vissarion Belinsky, who masterminded the cult of literature in Russian society, "Our literature has created the morals of our society, has already educated several generations . . . has produced a sort of special class in society that differs from the 'middle estate' in that it consists not of the merchantry and commoners *(meshchanstvo)* alone but of people of all estates who have been drawn together through education, which, with us, centered exclusively in a love of literature."[184] These words and those of the perestroika journalist encompass the birth and twilight of the literature-centric and culture-centric Russian universe, from the intelligentsia's quasi-religious cult of culture to the avant-garde dreams of aesthetic transformation of the world, from the Soviet policy of mass culturalization to the dissent of underground art. The end of the culture-centric epoch does not necessarily signal the decline of the arts at the turn of the century, but only the decline of their central educational and ideological role in society. In Russia culture has been mostly defined in the singular and with a capital "C"; it has become a kind of civic religion that delimits an imagined community of spiritual refinement, a literary aristocracy of sorts. It is reflected in many contradictory phenomena: the flourishing of literature and the flourishing of censorship, the cult of the poet as a national hero and the extermination of poets. At the same time that Russian culture has helped to obliterate everyday life, it has helped people to survive it.

What began as a kind of supranational community of creative readers of Russian literature—the Russian intelligentsia that included people from different social groups and ethnicities within the Russian empire—late in the nineteenth century converged with the question of "pure Russian blood," a prerequisite of pure Russian spirit. (The most recent late twentieth-century instance is the ugly campaign against so-called Russian-speaking rather than real Russian writers, which in most cases refers to Russian Jews.)

From Ivan Kireevsky to Nikolai Berdiaev, Russian culture is viewed in opposition to European civilization, which is mercantile and "does not like eternity": it is the German Romantic idea posed against the French and English Enlightenment. Norbert Elias describes this opposition:

> The French and English concept of civilization can refer to political or economic, religious or technical, moral or social facts. The German concept of *Kultur* refers essentially to intellectual, artistic and religious facts . . . "Civilization" describes a process or at least the result of the process . . . The German concept of *Kultur* has a different relation to motion. The concept of *Kultur* delimits. To a certain extent, the concept of civilization plays down the national differences between peoples; it emphasizes what is common to all human beings or—in the view of its bearers—should be. In contrast, the German concept of *Kultur* places special stress on national differences and particular identity of the group.[185]

This polarization is problematic, however, in that the histories of both words themselves internalize this opposition. In other words, the history of the word "civilization" in French exposes the battle between true and false civilization, and the same applies to the idea of culture.[186] Thus no good or evil attaches to either "culture" or "civilization" as such; it depends entirely on the person speaking in the name of culture or civilization. Jean Starobinski writes that "civilization"—and I will add "culture" as well—have to be seen both as "threatening and threatened, persecutor and persecuted. It is no longer a safe haven for those who shelter beneath its roof."[187] Culture in the Russian context is this kind of a double-edged sword; it can be seen as a way of survival and of domination, of creating a community and of delimiting it, a way of dreaming of aesthetic emancipation and a way of taming those dreams.

After the abolition of serfdom in 1862, the young generation of the Russian intelligentsia launched a campaign for education and the spread of literacy among peasants; it was also a campaign for unity of the Great Russian national culture. Cultural consensus was seen as central to the Russian identity, defined at that time primarily through the great Russian literary classics of the nineteenth century, works in which one could never trace clear boundaries between literature, metaphysics, history, and religion. Russian high culture was supposed to become an all-people's culture, which entailed a didactic popularization of the texts of the Russian classics and, conversely, an attack on all other varieties of popular culture. Educators from the Russian intelligentsia tried to protect the Russian cultural identity against the generation of upcoming nouveaux riches from the peasantry and urban low classes, the pioneers of commercial mass culture. After the Revolution the period of cultural plurality was quickly followed by the abolition of all but state-sponsored culture. In the 1930s the old dream of the Russian intelligentsia, the dream of creating one united culture of all the people, came true, but with a tragic twist. The Socialist Realist all-people's culture was not what the members of the revolutionary intelligentsia could have imagined, not even in their wildest dreams.

It is in Stalin's time that the word "culture" acquired an important suffix, and the slogan of the 1920s "cultural revolution" turned into the advocacy of kul'turnost'. This term includes not only the new Soviet artistic canon but also manners, ways of behavior, and discerning taste in food and consumer goods. Culturalization is a way of translating ideology into the everyday; it is a kind of Stalinist "civilizing process" that taught Marxist-Leninist ideology together with table manners, mixing Stalin with Pushkin. Material possessions, crêpe-de-chine dresses, old-fashioned dinnerware, and household decorations were no longer regarded as petit-bourgeois; rather they were presented as legitimate awards for the heroes and heroines of labor, for the marching enthusiasts of the new Stalinist order. Moscow was proclaimed to be the premier Communist city of the future and the most "cultured city in the world." Moscow citizens were encouraged to discover new pleasures in rides in the Metro and walks in the Parks of Culture and Leisure, where they could taste delicious newly imported ice-cream. Culturalization offered a way of legitimating the formerly despised bourgeois concerns about status and possession; it both justified and disguised the new social hierarchies and privileges of the Stalinist elite.[188]

The aim of Socialist Realist mass culturalization was to synthesize—in a peculiar Hegelian-Marxist-Stalinist manner—the old opposition between culture and civilization, high and low art, public and private genres. While in the writings of European and American critics, including Clement Greenberg, Socialist Realism is seen as an equivalent of kitsch, in the Soviet context the term "kitsch" appears later and refers exclusively to Western mass culture. Indeed, Stalinist critics fought constantly for "true Soviet art" and against the "varnishing of reality." In other words, they engaged in their own war on bad taste, which is the equivalent of ideological incorrectness. The old opposition intelligentsia/meshchanstvo was revalued; in the wake of this process the modernist intelligentsia was either eliminated or assimilated, and many members of the new Soviet intelligentsia embraced the tastes and styles of what in the 1920s has been dubbed meshchanstvo.

The unified Socialist Realist culture did not have a unity of grand style. It was rather a kind of monstrous hybrid of various inconsistent elements from right and left: aristocratic and proletarian culture; radical avant-garde rhetoric and chaste Victorian morals of nineteenth-century realism; happy endings and stormy weather from popular fiction of the turn of the century; and "positive heroes" from the Russian classics and Slavic hagiographies. The only thing that was consistent and unified about it was its dependence on Soviet power.

Molotov's Tea Party

At a Moscow flea market I recently came across a unique gadget, a perfect fetish of Stalinist culturalization, which illustrates many paradoxes of the idea of unified culture. It is a traditional *Palekh* box representing Molotov and Stalin as folk-heroes on a black lacquered background. The palekh box is an example of the official reinvention of Russian national culture that began in the 1930s and also a sample of the everyday rituals of the Stalin era. Inside the box is a little visiting card that reads: "Mrs Molotov has the honor of inviting you for an afternoon tea on September 13 at 5 o'clock."[189] The writing is in the old-fashioned prerevolutionary hand—elegant, ceremonious, and refined. Afternoon tea *chez* Madame Molotov, the general and hero of the Civil War and the Great Patriotic War, is a perfectly exemplary ritual of the Stalinist *haut-monde,* the last aristocratic revival by the grand-style Soviet nouveaux riches. The box provides a rich insight into the everyday life of the Stalinist élite and embodies some quite old-fashioned ideals of culture and its Stalinist incarnation. Moreover, the lacquer box, a product of Stalinist arts and crafts, is exactly the kind of object that would have been trashed as kitsch in the 1920s, recovered in the 1930s, treated as a decorative art object

in the 1970s, and today become the best gift value for foreign guests:
a beautiful, well-packaged box of Russian exotica.

It might come as a surprise that the "traditional Russian" lacquer
box was in fact a very recent invention. After the Revolution the
craftsmen and icon painters organized themselves into the Artel of
Proletarian Art and began to use Russian icon painting techniques to
decorate traditional Japanese-style lacquer boxes. Maxim Gorky
called it "a little miracle of the revolution" and praised the transformation of the "craft into true artistic mastery."[190] The palekh makers
in turn followed the example of nineteenth-century *kustars*, who had
organized an industrialized production of Russian crafts for the
new middle class, nostalgic for premodern Russian ways and eager
to consume them in prefabricated (modern) packaging. This contributed to the creation of a pseudo-Russian style and to a national
revival. Much of the "folk art" was intended for international exhibitions abroad and was consumed by foreigners as Russian premodern picturesque objects. Hence there is a continuity between the
consumer culture at the turn of the nineteenth century and that of the
Stalin era.

When Walter Benjamin visited Moscow he was fascinated, not by
the future-oriented technology and the pace of progress, but by the
old-fashioned Russian toys and the black lacquer boxes from the
Museum of Popular Crafts:

> There are the heavy little boxes with scarlet interiors; on the outside
> on a gleamy black background, a picture . . . A *troika* with its three
> horses races through the night, or a girl in a sea-blue dress stands at
> night beside green flaring bushes, waiting for her lover. No night of
> terror is as dark as this durable lacquer myth in whose womb all
> that appears in it is enfolded. I saw a box with a picture of a seated
> woman selling cigarettes. Besides her stands a child who wants to
> take one. Pitch-black night here too . . . On the woman's apron is
> the word "Mosselprom." She is the Soviet Madonna with ciga-
> rettes.[191]

This exemplary Soviet allegorical artifact, with the dark background
and red interior, had a contemporary surface: the Mosselprom Madonna with cigarettes is the perfect salesgirl of Soviet ideology.

For Socialist Realist critics, blind to the black terror of the night,
these were examples of life-affirming and colorful popular art, at

once useful and decorative. Yet in the last years of Stalinism the lacquer box turned into a controversial object of ideology that represented the terror of Stalinist criticism. One of the key terms in Socialist Realist criticism, "the varnishing of reality," comes from the critical discussion of ideologically incorrect lacquer boxes, which we can dub "the critique of pure lacquer box."

In the early 1950s the boxes became a focus of the discussion of "people's culture," as well as of the critique of "the lack of conflict" *(bezkonfliktnost')*. Ideological correctness was at that time a complex balancing act. The boxes were supposed to reflect the Soviet "people's spirit" *(narodnost')* but not the "common people's spirit" *(prostonarodnost')*; to give examples of "refined artistic quality" *(tonkii artistizm)* but not of mannerism *(mann'erizm)*; to reflect taste *(vkus)* but not "pseudo-tastefulness" *(vkusovshchina)*. All the ambiguities of the Stalinist mimesis find their reflection on their lacquered surfaces:

. . . . The overcoming of some mistakes by certain Palekh painters consists not in the escape into naturalism, into mere copying *(kopirovka)*, or into a "light" stylization "à la Palekh." What is required is further study of reality, a development of the progressive tradition of Palekh arts, which consists of ideological wholeness *(ideinaia nasyshchennost')* of the works, their life-affirming spirit, festive brightness of coloring, and subtle artistry, along with great artistic taste, wise mastery of composition, expressive laconic drawing, and finally, attention to different kinds of decorative art.[192]

Everything that appeared in quotation marks in the criticism of the Stalin era was meant to be an insult; it parodied the words of the invisible enemy that was everywhere. In this case, the enemies were "naturalism" on the one hand and "stylization" on the other. The words "craft," "artifact," and "copy" tended to be negatively valorized in Stalinist criticism. While copying and reproduction were central to the Socialist Realist practice (as to most of the artistic practices in general), they were vehemently criticized in theory. While in the capitalist world craftsmen were "poor beggars deprived of rights," in Soviet Russia the "people's painters affirm their creative personality."[193] The artist was a "genius of the people," and despite the traditional nature of the work, artists were called "nature's treasures."

The lacquer boxes, miniatures, and small objects in general presented a great problem for the unified epic style of Socialist Realism. Its creative geniuses were urged to tackle new, ambitious subjects such as "The Battle of Stalingrad" or "Comrade Stalin Giving a Speech on the Meeting of Batumi Workers in 1902," all in the space of a small lacquer box. Critics instructed the miniature painters to learn from the epic styles of urban sculpture and to think further about the boxes' "architectonics" (the boxes' "plumpness" was criticized, perhaps for being incompatible with the modern age of physical culture). However, some modern genres such as photography were rejected. One critic denounced the use of photographs for portraiture on the lacquer boxes and appealed to the Palekh artists to make their lacquer miniatures in *plein air* and to use original models. The Stalin and Molotov boxes, however, were certainly not painted outdoors. "Art criticism" in Stalin's time was a peculiar balancing act, more about the art of survival than about art; the criticism could cost the artist his life, and the lack of criticism could cost the critic his job. Thus he usually had more training in ideology and the propaganda of culturalization than in art history. While some of the painters of the lacquer miniatures might have been forced to work in plein air, it was not the consistency of vision that mattered but the gusts of power and its whims. At the end, the "varnishing of reality" was not a critique of representation but rather a polishing up of that critique; it was an internal critique within the system.[194]

Having survived all the balancing acts of moribund Socialist Realism, the Molotov palekh box has now become a perfect totalitarian antique, a Stalinist *objet de* folk *art,* sold at the flea market together with the more expensive tsarist eggs. The addressee of this refined invitation for tea and the history of this Stalinist family souvenir remain unknown. Yet one doesn't have to discard the idea of culture together with the Molotov lacquer box. Nor should it be relegated to an exotic folk collection. In a sense, there are more ways of dreaming "world culture"—or, to paraphrase Osip Mandelshtam, of "longing for the world culture"—now then there ever were before, although this longing itself is becoming outmoded. Perhaps a Russian identity will develop that will not depend on a unified Russian culture: an identity that would acknowledge differences and paradoxes beyond polished-up picturesque reflections in pseudo-Russian style.

Soviet Songs: From Stalin's Fairy Tale to "Good-Bye, Amerika"

"And it's good to live, and life is good," wrote Vladimir Mayakovsky in the 1920s, just a few years before he committed suicide.[195] "Life has become merrier, life has become better," wrote another optimist, Joseph Stalin, in the late 1930s—the time of the great purges. In the 1960s the same optimistic message was delivered in a different style and in a foreign language: "c'est si bon," sang French singer-actor Yves Montand in a black turtleneck, one of the few left French intellectuals to visit the post-Stalinist Soviet Union, and the Soviet youth of the "thaw generation" sang along with him, "c'est si bon, c'est si bon." Nobody knew what exactly was "so good"; maybe it was just the tune, the tone of the voice, the accent, the informal ease of the black turtleneck.

This spirit of optimism pervades Soviet song from the 1930s through the 1960s. The songs conjured up the *perestroika* of byt, celebrated escapes from routine, and sometimes helped to survive actual everyday life. In the post-Stalin era they served as passwords for alternative communities. "The song helps us build and live, it is like a friend who leads us ahead / The one who marches through life with a song will never be defeated!" This popular song from one of the most celebrated musicals of the 1930s celebrates itself: it is self-referential, a mass song about the importance of mass singing. Stalinism was not merely a political system but also a mentality, a way of life and a grand totalitarian spectacle that needed to be continuously reenacted. The favored genres were no longer poetry or even the novel, but rather the arts of mass spectacle—film, ballet, and organized popular festivities. The move was toward a collectivization of the utopian vision, as in the words of the popular song entitled "The March of the Aviators":

> We were born to make fairy tales come true
> To conquer distances and space
> Reason gave us steel wings for arms
> And a flaming motor for a heart.
>
> And higher, and higher, and higher
> We aim the flight of our wings,
> And the hum of our propellers
> Spreads peace along our borders.

Our sharp gaze pierces every atom
Our every nerve is bold and resolute
And trust us: to any ultimatum
An answer will give our Air Fleet!

Here the romantic metaphor of the flaming heart is wedded to love for the machine; these cheerful humanoids with wings and motors in their chests are the product of Futurist and Constructivist imaginations. One is reminded of avant-garde ballets in which the dancers impersonated machine parts and made mechanical gestures instead of the undulating, organic movements of classical dance. The protagonist of the song is not an engineer of human hearts, a creative artist, or a modern Icarus. Nor is the pronoun Whitmanesque. It is rather a collective, patriotic "we," projected onto the millions of people who were supposed to fall in love with the song—and they did. The song has an amazing history that reveals a striking continuity between the art of the 1920s and the 1930s and kinship with other totalitarian cultures.[196] The song was written in 1920 by the little known team of poet B. German and composer D. Hait; it became popular in the 1930s and in 1933 was adopted as the official "March of the Aviators." It was translated into German and sung by the German communists, and later its catchy melody captured the imagination of the Nazis, who took the song for their own. After the words "and higher and higher and higher" they sang "Heil Hitler and dethrone the Jews" (this is particularly ironic because the authors of the song were Jewish). What it shows is how easily the words of a catchy patriotic tune can circulate from one totalitarian culture to another. The phrase "we were born to make fairy tales come true" became one of the central slogans of the time; it functioned like an advertising logo and was frequently recycled as a caption for paintings and for newspaper articles. These words were sung during the years of collectivization and hunger, of purges and war. The march was frequently performed on the radio to cheer up the Soviet youth while they performed heroic feats of labor. (My father, a Soviet émigré whose mother spent five years in a Stalinist labor camp, still occasionally hums his own version of the "March of the Aviators" as he washes dishes in his well-equipped American kitchen, with the TV on.)

According to the most popular song-writer of the 1930s, Lebedev Kumach, what people needed during those years was a song "with distinct patriotic character," a song-slogan, a "song-poster." The march, like the songs he composed for the "Stalinist musicals" of the 1930s, is, "from the musical point of view, . . . a cheerful march with robust rhythm; from the verbal point of view, it presents lines not connected by inner plot, lines patriotic in content . . . with lyrical tonality."[197] The lines of the song jump out to become edifying proverbs. The new Soviet song is not supposed to present a coherent narrative but to offer life-affirming punch lines and slogans.

A close reading of the song points out its elements of absurdity and incongruity. Among other things, the "flaming motor for heart" makes us apprehensive about the general success of this flight. But a mass song was not created to be read closely. The art of mass spectacle is not made for interpretation; indeed, it is extremely suspicious of interpretation and of any attempt at individual comprehension instead of shared experience. And one of those shared experiences is fear. The incantatory power of the song is only enhanced by the fear of interpretation internalized by the participants in the optimistic march.

The song was not made to be read but only to be memorized and repeated as an incantation of fairy-tale magic. This is a key issue in understanding the creation of the utopian commonplace of the Stalinist era. These clichés are not merely romantic or realistic. It is not the function of Socialist Realist art to promote a romantic alienation from old commonplaces or to perform a mimetic function, using commonplaces in the realist fashion to establish conventions of "verisimilitude" or simply to provide metonymical descriptions of the milieu. And by no means did Socialist Realist art intend to lay bare the rhetorical devices in the avant-garde manner by creating bold new metaphors. Rather, the commonplaces of Socialist Realist art, the slogans and punch lines, function collectively as a magic force that programmatically arouses a certain predictable emotional, even a behavioral, quasi-Pavlovian response. To understand the "March of the Aviators" it is necessary first of all to sing it in a crowd.

Boris Groys advances the paradoxical yet eye-opening argument that Stalinist art is not merely a return to academism and new conservatism but an even more radical continuation of the avant-garde project.[198] Avant-garde theorists and Russian Formalists regarded every new period in art in terms of how it managed to lay bare its modes of operation and devices, seeing art in terms of undoing, defamiliarizing, and critical negativity. Socialist Realist art does not simply, unselfconsciously, believe in the transparency of language, as did some of the realists of the nineteenth century. Rather, it self-consciously promotes the manipulation of consciousness, using the techniques that automatically secure specific emotional responses. Moreover, there is an ideological and theoretical justification for that radical self-conscious "automatization of consciousness," turning it into a collective unconscious, not in a Freudian or Jungian but in a Pavlovian sense. According to Groys, "Stalinist culture is very interested in different models of the formation of the unconscious, without exposing its mechanisms, as in the theories of Pavlov, or in Stanislavsky's method, which required the actor to enter the role so completely as to forget his identity."[199]

To read Socialist Realist texts as texts, revealing their strategies of manipulation, can yield important insights into the Stalinist cover-up. But it does not explain the magic spell of the totalitarian spectacle, and does not help us to comprehend how the absurd words of the songs could be made to sound true, even if only in the imagination. Stalinist magical commonplaces only become commonplaces when they are enacted in popular emotional rituals; they are hypothetical commonplaces that exist nowhere; they are omnipotent because circumscribed and guarded by fear. And there is no child who would innocently disclose them as the emperor's new clothes. This happy dénouement belongs in a foreign fairy tale.[200]

The new map of the Soviet Union at the time of Stalin's Constitution is also celebrated in a song:

Our country is the land of beauty,
Our country is the land of glee,
I don't know any other country
Where a man is so gloriously free.
From Moscow to the far away provinces
From the Southern rivers to the Northern seas
A man walks like a master
Of his boundless motherland.

But we will frown severely
If the enemy tries to break us
We love our country like our bride
We protect her like our caring mother.

A spring wind blows over our country
It gets more joyful and merrier to live
And nobody in the world
Knows how to love and laugh like us.[201]

The song comes from a celebrated musical, *The Circus,* beloved by
Stalin himself, a story of an American circus performer who falls in
love with a Russian. After realizing the greatness of Soviet interna-
tionalism and humanism, she decides to emigrate to the Soviet Union.
(The American star is played by Liubov' Orlova, the most famous
actress of the time, a Marlene Dietrich type.) In the film the song is
performed by the American star turned Soviet patriot during a mass
demonstration. According to the authors, the song was dedicated to
the new Constitution. Exuberant patriotism and subdued eroticism
go together in the film and in the song: the voice of the song is male;
the beloved country is *his* bride and mother (though the bride is the
vocalist). The patriotic language is naturalized; at first glance the song
appears quite innocuous, a song about nature rather than politics, in
the eternal spring of patriotic love and life-affirming laughter (not its
ironic or absurdist variety). The Socialist Realist iconography knew
only two seasons, spring and summer; winter and fall afflicted only
the decadent West. The boundless space of the motherland cannot be
found on any precise map. All more or less accurate maps of the
USSR disappear some time in the late 1920s to return only in 1990.
Before that time, the most accurate Soviet maps were produced by
the CIA and other foreign intelligence agencies. In Stalin's time, geography was perhaps the most political of all sciences: in the song the
multinational Soviet Union is presented as a completely unified country with Moscow as its geographical center and the center of ideological gravity. In this remapped and deterritorialized country the
spaces of terror, the camps, are hidden from view and absent from
the maps. Another utopian ideological map of the motherland is
created, that of a "land of beauty and a land of glee." Its best
architectural embodiment is the Stalinist subway system—the ideal
blueprint of Socialist Realist culture, with neoclassical columns, mosaic portraits of great poets and great leaders, and plenty of exotic
vegetation to adorn the Russian tropical utopia under the ground.

By the end of Stalin's epoch in the early 1950s more exotic maps
of the world were drawn. Alexander Vertinsky, the decadent Pierrot

figure of the 1910s, returned to the USSR after a long emigration, begging forgiveness for his bourgeois sins, yet bringing with him his old songs and melodies. The tango had come back—the only dance that was not prohibited—but the fox-trot and later rock-and-roll remained emblematic of "bourgeois decadence" and "the crisis of capitalism" until Stalin's death. Here is one of Vertinsky's not-so-revolutionary flights of fancy:

> In banana-lemon-yellow Singapore,
> Where the ocean is always stormy,
> You were singing and laughing in the storm
> And the storm was singing with you.[202]

This was a favorite song of urban teenagers, evoking memories of school dances in the 1950s, before schools were made coeducational: "When the fatigued sun says a tender farewell to the sea, / In this hour you told me that love is gone." These exotic songs about foreign seas were sung during the last wave of the great purges against cosmopolitans and Jewish doctors, the infamous "agents of world imperialism and Zionism."

The "thaw generation" launched its attack on the grand epic style of the Stalinist edifice and created melodies of its own. At that time a parody on the "March of the Aviators" circulated among the urban intelligentsia: instead of "we were born to make fairy tales come true" they sang "we were born to make Kafka come true." (In Russian, Kafka and *skazka* (fairy tale) is a near rhyme.)[203] Humor began to play an important part in de-Stalinization, but only some twenty-five years later, during glasnost', did Stalinist tragedy come back as a farce in the new experimental cinema. In the late 1950s and early 1960s the main tool in the war against Stalinist totalitarian kitsch was a new tone of voice—casual, lyrical, individual, frag-mented. Tone of voice, like sensibility, defies description and theoreti-cal paradigms. It is the tone of voice that disrupted the performance of the totalitarian musical without necessarily undermining all of its founding myths. Poets again returned to play a central role during the thaw: Yevtushenko, Akhmadulina, Rozhdestvensky, Voznesensky, the Soviet rough equivalents of the Beat Generation, and the bards Okudzhava and Vysotsky, who gave new songs to the first post-Sta-linist generation. A revolutionary change of tone during the time of the thaw helped to melt the frozen, reified clichés of Socialist Realism, as well as those of the more ordinary, contrived, and hypocritical realism. The change was not quite a "revolution in the poetic language": still, without revolutionizing the syntax, the new personal voices poetically undermined the totalitarian generalizations, corroding the optimistic aesthetics of the Grand March. The time of heroic epics had passed.

The 1960s mark the romantic reconquest and remapping of the lost Soviet continent: its secret Gulag regions and closed cities. A new breed of nomads celebrates hiking and camping trips and resists the daily grind, domesticity, and conformist stability. This nomadism is a part of the campaign against poshlost', now conducted in a softer tone of voice. The loves of the 1960s tend to be extramarital. They take place outdoors, the romantic affair between a geologist and a stewardess exemplifying the traveling eros of the time. The opening lines of Bella Akhmadulina's poem lyrically—if not ironically—summarize the romantic scene of the late 1950s: "Here are the girls: they want to love, / Here are boys: they want to go camping."[204] (The gender differences remain the same: Soviet boys leave home to explore the tundra and taiga, and Soviet girls—those who did not become stewardesses and geologists—sing wistful farewells and wait. This is a popular mythology of the 1960s nomadism.)

This new nomadism is reflected in one of the most popular guitar songs of the period, by Iurii Kukin. Like the songs of Vysotsky and Okudzhava, it was never officially released but was nevertheless known by thousands of young people. It circulated on unofficial (but not prohibited) tapes that were passed around among friends and friends of friends and formed part of an oral youth culture:

> You know it's strange, quite strange
> I guess I am a complete fool
> But I am leaving in search of the fog, just for the fog
> And there is nothing I can do about it.
>
> Others are caught up in daily chores
> Others run away in search for money,
> Away from hurt and from grief
> But I am leaving, I am going for the fog, just for the fog
> For the fog and for the smell of the taiga.
>
> My suitcases are packed for the road
> There is an aftertaste of sadness left,

And a few unpaid debts,
But I am leaving, I am going for the fog, just for the fog,
For the fog and the smell of the taiga.

Like the "March of the Aviators," this song too dreams of a journey, but this is a personal, not a collective flight. Instead of the collective *we* projected through loudspeakers into the *we* of the audience, this is a quiet voice, for a group of close friends bound together by this intimate intonation. The words could be sung by a virile romantic traveler and addressed to his casual beloved, who carefully packs his bags, pays his debts, and gently forgives his *Wanderlust*. The search for the fog is an individual romantic escape, both temporal and spatial, from the world of everyday chores. The hero seeks only the fog: only the immaterial, the evanescent and beautiful. And this fogginess is what makes the song poetic. The song is not about picaresque adventures in the taiga or the happiness of departure; instead, it brings back melancholy memories of everyday life, or at least of a certain everyday intimacy. It is the familiar fog of the time of the thaw that blurs but also outlines the shape of the imagined community of the youthful Soviet intelligentsia. In the 1970s the song about searching for the fog was rewritten, and its parodic version was very popular among the high-school crowd of my generation. Obviously the unbridled romanticism of the sixties had faded. The tundra and taiga of romantic escapades became commonplaces in their own right, partly officialized and partly ridiculed. The older generation's escapes from clichés became clichés themselves, and the moral zeal of the war against banality and meshchanstvo weakened when the thaw generation left center stage. In the seventies the song mostly circulates in its parodic version, "I am leaving for the money, just for the money / Only fools are now searching for the fog." In the 1970s, some of the lyrical intonations of the "tape-culture" songs were coopted to serve an official Komsomol romanticism. At that time the trips in search of fog were superseded by obligatory journeys to construction sites in Siberia. A particularly publicized Komsomol construction site of the early seventies was BAM, an abbreviation for Baikalo-Amursk Major Line, a railroad. The main construction site was close to the Chinese border, which served to strengthen the Soviet defense systems and military complex and to foster the development of the area. The Komsomol song goes something like this:

> The sky sings—BAM
> The sea sings—BAM
> BAM—is a heartbeat of the young.

The word BAM was so full of absurd and comic associations that we loved to hum it—bam bam bam, bam, bam, bam . . . In our ironic rendering BAM was not so much a "heartbeat of Russia," or a "heartbeat of the young," but an onomatopoeic sound, completely devoid of meaning. Bam, Bam, Bam—the noise of familiar clichés of the era of stagnation; it gave an enticing rhythm to the quintessential song of totalitarian decadence.

For the dissenting and critical urban teenagers of the early 1970s, the romanticism of the thaw generation—from campfire songs to poetic discourses on a bright communist future and true revolution— was in bad taste.

In the early 1970s the teenagers were more interested in journeys to the West in the "yellow submarine" than in the journey to the East. Here is a parodic rewriting of the celebrated Beatles journey.

> They have a yellow
> we have a red submarine
> red submarine, red submarine, red submarine.

It is a collective translation of the song, ironically patriotic and humorously cynical, which presents the point of view of an angry "ideologically correct" person "back in the USSR" singing the praises of the Soviet submarine industries to protect Soviet pride. It assumes the official hypocritical voice that divides the utopian collectivity of the submarine of our youth into "us" (those who prefer the red submarine) and "them" (the fellow-travelers from the West). But the colors easily reverse. The dream of the journey in a foreign submarine, though much mistranslated and misunderstood, survives to the present day.

In the new, much less unified 1970s youth culture, the imaginary topography of the Soviet Union is remapped again and so is the imaginary topography of the West. In Soviet eyes the West of the 1960s was immaterial, embodied in black-and-white portraits of Hemingway and Fidel Castro, optimistic songs of Yves Montand, and the long takes in Antonioni's movies with their suggestive empty spaces, wind, and free-floating characters who easily cross foreign borders and possess the luxury of silence and existential alienation, so exotic for a Soviet intelligentsia that grew up in overcrowded communal apartments. In the 1970s Russians imagined a Western cosmogony with "Jesus Christ Superstar" and "Lucy in the Sky with Diamonds," colored by the memories of semiforbidden rock "sessions" and collective listening to Beatles tapes purchased on the black market. This was the decade for serious study of foreign languages, and the urban intelligentsia sent their kids to so-called English or French schools. The topography of the West grew less impressionistic and more politicized under Brezhnev's renewal of the Cold War.

In the early 1990s the hit of the season was a rock song by the famous rock group Nautilus Pompilus.[205] It has a refrain in English with a Russian accent: "Good-bye Amerika—oh / . . . where I will never be." In the genre of the escape song the theme is to flee from the Russian daily grind into some kind of imaginary land, be it the foggy taiga or Amerika with a "K."

When all the songs are silent
The songs that I don't know
And in the sticky air
My last paper boat will call

Good bye Amerika—oh!
Where I have never been
Good bye forever
Take a banjo and play farewell to me.

Your washed out-jeans
Became too small for me
We were taught for so long
To love your forbidden fruits
Good bye, Amerika—oh
Where I will never be.

This song has as little to do with the USA as the Beatles' "Back in the USSR" had to do with the USSR. The "USSR" and "Amerika" of those two songs do not exist on any map; rather, they are specular images of each other—of the two mythical enemies of the Cold War. The "American" banjo of the contemporary Russian rock group is a mirror image of the "Russian" balalaika: both are seductive instruments of cultural exoticism. The song of homecoming (back to the USSR where the Ukrainian and Georgian girls keep the comrades warm) and the song of farewell (to Amerika) are interchangeable: in both cases they celebrate the country where "one has never been," which represents an alternative homeland of the youth counterculture. "Bye-bye, Amerika" is a farewell to the beloved Amerika of Soviet underground culture, a farewell to the old songs from those smuggled records acquired on the black market and to the adolescent paper boats and ironic red submarines that inspired many imaginary journeys. Amerika here stands not for the United States but for the mythical West of the Russian imagination. Now, when one can actually travel to the USA if one has the money, the old Amerika and the Wild West of the Beatles and the "capitalist evil empire" of the newspaper *Pravda*—the imaginary lands on the other side of the Cold War looking-glass—are no more. But the strange eclectic rhythm of Russian rock still incorporates jazz variations on gypsy potpourri, reminiscent of the old songs about *troika* bells, nights when the moon is full, and long roads to nowhere.

"Good-bye, Amerika" is a farewell to Soviet culture, both its distinctive conformism as well as its distinctive form of dissidence; it is also a farewell to the familiar counterculture that has become quickly "too tight" and rather mainstream, like those washed-out American jeans. "Good-bye, Amerika" is also "Good-bye, USSR"—no more comforting homecoming to the utopian fantasy land of one's youth.

2

Living in Common Places: The Communal Apartment

Family Romance and Communal Utopia

This is another version of the Soviet family romance; it could be entitled "In the Old Apartment." Instead of a portrait of Stalin there is a televisual image of Brezhnev, but no one listens. My parents are having foreign guests for the first time in their life in our room in the communal apartment. Our neighbors, Aunt Vera and Uncle Fedia, are home. (Russian children call their neighbors "aunt" and "uncle," as if they were members of one very extended family.) Uncle Fedia usually came home drunk, and if Aunt Vera refused to let him in, he would crash right in the middle of the long corridor—the central "thoroughfare" of the communal apartment—obstructing the entrance to our room. As a child, I would often play with peacefully reclining and heavily intoxicated Uncle Fedia, with his fingers and buttons, or tell him a story to which he probably did not have much to add. This time we were all in the room, listening to music to tone down the communal noises, and my mother was telling our foreign guests about the beauties of Leningrad: "you absolutely must go to the Hermitage, and then to Pushkin's apartment-museum, and of course to the Russian Museum." In the middle of the conversation, as the foreign guest was commenting on the riches of the Russian Museum, a little yellow stream slowly made its way through the door of the room. Smelly, embarrassing, intrusive, it formed a little puddle right in front of the dinner table.

No one seems to remember what happened afterwards. In the

From the window of the communal apartment (photo by Mark Shteinbok)

apartment Uncle Fedia and Aunt Vera were displaced by lonely Aunt Valia, who worked in a bread factory, and her mentally ill son Yura, and then by a couple of homonymic drunkards—Aunt Shura and Uncle Shura, who endearingly called themselves "Shurenkis." And if it were not for the benevolent foreign guest enjoying the beauties of the Soviet public places, and for my mother's deeply personal embarrassment, the story would not have been particularly exceptional. After all, as one of my Soviet friends remarked, some neighbors peed into each other's teapots. Yet this scene, with its precarious coziness of a family gathering, both intimate and public, with a mixture of ease and fear in the presence of foreigners and neighbors, remained in my mind as a memory of home. The family picture is thus framed by the inescapable stream of Uncle Fedia's urine, which so easily crossed the minimal boundaries of our communal privacy, embarrassing the fragile etiquette of communal propriety. (And it smells too much to turn it into a mere metaphor. This is something that is hard to domesticate.)

If there had been such a thing as a Soviet cultural unconscious, it would have been structured like a communal apartment—with flimsy partitions between public and private, between control and intoxication. The Soviet "family romance," now in melancholy twilight, was adulterated by the fluttering sound of a curious neighbor's slippers in the communal apartment, or by an inquisitive representative of the local Housing Committee. It was a romance with the collective, unfaithful to both communitarian mythologies and traditional family values.

The communal apartment was the cornerstone of the now disappearing Soviet civilization. It was a specifically Soviet form of urban living, a memory of a never implemented utopian communist design, an institution of social control, and the breeding ground of police informants between the 1920s and the 1980s. This is a place where many battles for reconstruction of daily life were launched and most of them were lost. Here the neighbors engaged in quite un-Marxist class struggles; "domestic trash" triumphed; and privacy was prohibited only to be reinvented again against all odds. *Kommunalka*—a term of endearment and deprecation—came into existence after postrevolutionary expropriation and resettlement of the private apartments in the urban centers. It consisted of all-purpose rooms (living rooms, bedrooms, and studies became a "decadent luxury") integrated with "places of communal use," a euphemistic expression for shared bathroom, corridor, and kitchen, spaces where hung schedules of communal duties and where endless complaints were exchanged among the fellow neighbors. The communal neighbors, most often complete strangers from different classes and social groups thrown together by the local Housing Committee, were joined in a premodern practice of "mutual responsibility." (Every communal apartment dweller is probably scarred for life by that symbolic "mutual responsibility"—a double bind of love and hatred, of envy and attachment, of secrecy and exhibitionism, of embarrassment and compromise.)

The communal apartment was not merely an outcome of the postrevolutionary housing crisis but also of a revolutionary experiment in living, an attempt to practice utopian ideologies and to destroy bourgeois banality. Hence this is a Soviet common place par excellence, which reveals all the paradoxes of the common place and of Soviet communality. The archeology of the communal apartment reveals what happens when utopian designs are put into practice, inhabited, and placed into history—individual and collective.

The communal apartment stands as a metaphor of the distinctive Soviet mentality. It was a favorite tragicomic setting for many Soviet jokes. Thus when Stalin was taken out of the mausoleum, people joked that Khrushchev had "resettled Lenin's communal apartment" (which in the post-Soviet time might be further "privatized").[1] More recently, the behavior of Russian national-patriots and members of the Russian Parliament was compared in the press to "communal apartment tactics" of boorish intimidation, conformism, and collective guilt.[2]

Actually, the communal apartment was conceived in Lenin's head. Only a few weeks after the October Revolution of 1917 Lenin drafted a plan to expropriate and resettle private apartments. This plan inspired many architectural projects of communal housing and new revolutionary topography. The "rich apartment" is defined by Lenin as "the apartment where the number of rooms equals or surpasses the number of residents who permanently inhabit this apartment."[3] A minimum living space of about 10 square meters per person and 13 square meters per family was established. In his memoirs Joseph Brodsky calls his family's living quarters, poetically and quite literally, "a room and a half."[4] What appears striking in Lenin's decree is that it suggests a different understanding of home and space than one is used to in Western Europe or in the United States. A person, or rather a statistical unit (in Lenin's expression, "the soul of the population"), was not entitled to a room or to a private space but only to a number of square meters. The space is divided mathematically or bureaucratically as if it were an abstract problem in geometry, not the real space of existing apartments. As a result, most of the apartments in the major cities were partitioned in an incredible and often unfunctional manner, creating strange spaces, long corridors, and so-called black entrances through labyrinthine inner courtyards.

The communal apartment is not to be confused with a kibbutz or merely an apartment with roommates. Since the late 1920s and especially during the Stalin years the communal apartment had become a major Soviet institution of social control and a form of constant surveillance. At that time the "separate apartment" became a sign of special privilege, or occasionally, of special luck. Only in the late 1950s was there a new revolution in Soviet daily life, consisting of resettlement out of communal apartments to outlying "micro-districts," where people were able to live in separate, albeit state-owned, apartments—many for the first time in their lives. The building blocks received the unflattering name of *Khrushchoby* (a combination of Khrushchev and slums. Ironically, in Brezhnev's time the older construction became an example of high quality). These bleak versions of "garden cities" still did not end the housing shortage. In the 1970s some people were allowed to purchase cooperative apartments in the outskirts; in some cases it took decades of waiting. But it took forty more years and the end of the Soviet Union to put an end to the communal apartment as a social institution.

My "thick description" of the communal apartment will include projects for collective living and utopian architectural house-communes, literary anti-utopias and tragicomedies of actual communal living, and personal observations of present-day communal apartments and the daily practices of their residents. An archeology of the communal apartment helps to uncover the ruins of Russian and Soviet communality and the once illegitimate private life. We will eavesdrop on the elusive private behavior of Soviet citizens behind the communal partitions and visit exhibits of ideologically incorrect domestic trash, precarious possessions that challenge many theoretical "systems of objects." The observation of the cultural ethnographer will be occasionally disrupted by memories of the communal apart-

ment survivor, frequently scolded by the neighbors for all her un-
fulfilled communal duties.

From the House-Commune to the Communal Apartment

The 1920s in Soviet Russia was a unique moment in history when
art-making and life-making intersected, and the country turned into
a creative laboratory of various conflicting utopian projects. "Utopia" in Russia was never perceived merely as a work of art; fictional
utopias were guides to life and blueprints for social change. Revolutionary architects dreamed of turning architecture into an arch-art
and more: into a material embodiment of the revolutionary superstructure, which would impose order on a chaotic world.[5] Since
Marx and Engels did not develop a specific blueprint of communist
life, it was necessary to go back to the utopians—More and Campan-
ella, Owen and Fourier—and to their various Cities of Sun and
Ikarias. They inspired a variety of projects for socialist cities that
would bring about the "socialist resettlement of mankind." A new
revolutionary (u)topography was going to alter radically the commonplaces of culture and the public and private spaces; in the avant-
garde designs not only the places themselves but the very way of
creating the space was to be revolutionized. Masters of photomontage, experimental film makers, and Formalist theorists dreamed of a
space created by a montage of perspectives, a truly revolutionary
prospect that would open new dimensions of living free from the
bourgeois realist illusion of three-dimensionality.[6]

   In the utopian map of the "land of the Soviets" House-Communes,
Palaces and Parks of Culture, Workers' Clubs and Artists' Labor
Collectives, and later also collective farms supplant old forms of
sociability in apartments and barracks, cafés and pubs. Walter Benjamin commented that together with "private life" and "petit-bourgeois homeliness" what disappeared in Russia were the cafés: "Free
trade, like the free intellect, was abolished."[7] The worker should
prefer the swimming pool. In fact a few postrevolutionary avant-
garde groups announced a war on cafés, salons, and cabarets, where
"the public demands frivolity and poshlost'."[8] The café relationships
are too intimate and too accidental, collective in an ideologically
incorrect manner, eccentric but in a wrong style, not classless but
déclassé (if not bourgeois). The café is a place for conversation, not

for conversion, a place for minor theatrical revolts, not for revolutions. Instead of the café the revolutionary artists wished to go out to the streets. The slogan of their day was: "Revolution carries the art of good taste from the palaces to the boulevards."[9] By the late 1920s the emphasis shifts from the unruly streets to the "organized outdoors" in the Parks of Culture and Rest and in sports stadiums. The "boulevard" that evokes the dynamism of the early avant-garde and its foreign accent gives way to the square, the place for parades and collective festivities. The Soviet park and the subway station compose the Soviet urban iconography. The Moscow Metro of the 1930s becomes a material embodiment of a new utopia—this one located not on the island of utopia but under the ground.

The house-commune was a kind of microcosm of the socialist city, and the city a microcosm of the "land of the Soviets" as a whole.[10] They were avant-garde matreshka-dolls, one inside the other, repeating the same utopian designs. One of the first projects proposed in 1918 borrowed its name directly from Fourier's Phalanstery.[11] Interestingly, some seventy-five years earlier Fourier's design inspired the Parisian Arcades—a site of mythical modernity par excellence, serving the passage of commerce and providing a display of commodities; a place where the modern urban *flaneur* catches his fragmentary illuminations during his leisurely walks.[12] The French utopian's idea proved adaptable enough to inspire the Soviet house-communes, which were meant to eradicate the commodity culture along with the leisurely strolls of the intellectual fellow-travelers. In this way the same utopian element characterizes both early capitalism and early socialism.[13]

The designs for new collectivity and new ways of living demanded a new language. The architectural writings of the time contain a whole series of neologisms: "block-commune," "dwelling space," "socialist settling," and so on. (Unfortunately, some of them later became part of Soviet bureaucratic jargon.) The word *apartment*, in fact, is rarely used. The central nucleus was the house-commune, a model of "socialism in one building" to use Richard Stites's expression. The house-commune would radically reconstruct the individualist bourgeois quarters, "defamiliarize" them in a literal sense of the word by subverting the structure of the bourgeois family and instituting the relationships of proletarian comradeship. In the house-commune kitchens and children were to be shared, to avoid the burdens of the bourgeois family. One of the slogans of the time was "Down with the dictatorship of the kitchen!" The individual kitchen was the symbolic space of the nuclear family and the cause of women's enslavement by the daily grind. (Although the "woman question" was widely debated in the first years after the Revolution, in practice the division of labor within the family in the communal as in the individual kitchen remained very traditional.)[14]

Although many house-communes were established in the countryside and in the cities during the 1920s, they did not become widespread and by the 1930s were abolished, together with other leftist excesses. Paradoxically, the few house-communes that were built in Moscow and Petrograd were never turned into communal apartments but became privileged housing for members of the intellectual elite. They offered more spacious and luxurious family housing than the partitioned communal rooms, and were inhabited by the architects and writers who later became part of Stalin's establishment. A few of those house-communes, like the famous House-Ship, an exemplary avant-garde project by Ginzburg, turned into a ruin of modernist architecture, with trees growing through the half-fallen balconies, revealing the poor quality of the Constructivist building materials.

Instead of building new "dwelling massifs" and "garden cities," in the late 1920s the government gave orders to reconstruct and partition already existing bourgeois quarters, renaming them with important designations like "dwelling comradeships" and "workers' communes." These were transitional communal arrangements later institutionalized as the communal apartments. The Soviet *kommunalka* shares more than a linguistic resemblance to the house-commune; it includes elements of revolutionary topography such as the communal kitchen and other places of communal use. Yet the topography of the communal apartment often also presented a peculiar superimposition of old and new hierarchies. In many cases, when the owner of the apartment did not leave the country, he or she and the family took the former master bedroom while the new neighbors took the dining room, study, guest rooms, and maids rooms. Occasionally the former servants of the apartment owner continued living in the same apartment, hence the old structure of the bourgeois household appeared transplanted into the communal apartment. (The survival of the domestic servants and nannies until the 1950s is a peculiar feature of Soviet everyday life that does not fit the ideological

self-image of the socialist system.[15]) In due course some Party enthu-
siast might inform on the "bourgeois class origins" of the former
owner of the apartment; he might be sent to a camp and his room
might be appropriated by ideologically correct neighbors, who would
continue employing the same servants and acquire new prestige in the
communal hierarchy.

While housing shortages, urban poverty, and various forms of
collective living were a part of Russian life before and after the
Revolution (recall Dostoevsky's heroes Makar Devushkin and Raskolnikov and their squalid St. Petersburgian quarters), collective living
was never a specific ideological institution. In the Soviet Union it did
become codified, and by the mid-1930s the communal apartment had
turned into a prominent Stalinist institution of social control. The
new laws enforced the passport system and *propiska*—resident permits that tied the individual to a specific place—and established new
privileges that allowed certain groups—Party apparatchiks or members of the intellectual elite that collaborated with the regime (and
were not arrested)—to have additional "living space." Under these
conditions the local bureaucrats of the Housing Committee (ZhEK)
acquired the power to "educate" Soviet men and women and became
an important local institution of Sovietization. Lidiia Ginzburg describes the Housing Committee as an "institution of denial of human
rights—rights to air, to toilet, to space."[16] The other important figure
in a Soviet communal apartment house was the janitor *(dvornik)*; this
official was also connected to the Housing Committee and to local
authorities. Janitors had usually moved to the city recently and were
given resident permits in exchange for performing a number of services—least of which was any actual yard cleaning. They informed,
supervised, drank with the members of the Housing Committees, and
occasionally swept the staircases.

During the Stalin years the communal apartment was both omni-
present and invisible. It was everywhere in daily life and nowhere in
its official representation. Only the idealized *New Apartment,* albeit
spoiled by the bourgeois rubber plant, appears in the painting of
1952. *Kommunalka* was a kind of mockery of ideal Soviet communality, but an ideal place to look for actual everyday ways of Soviet
communal living. It inspired writers and artists in the 1920s and later
in the 1980s but did not attract the imagination of the historians,
neither in Russia nor abroad.

Whereas the house-commune had been a microcosm of the ideal revolutionary universe, the communal apartment was an actual Soviet microcosm, a nonidealized image of Soviet society in miniature. The economic circumstances are not alone responsible for the transformation of a socialist idyll into a social farce. A more fundamental problem is that any utopia is a u-chronia; in other words, it assumes a certain atemporality, a cessation of the time-flow and an immutability of life.[17] What an architectural utopia does not take into account is history and narratives about inhabiting places. Thus the utopian Common Places turn into "places of communal use" in the apartment, a shabby stage for many scandals between the neighbors and a ruin of utopian communality.

Art and the Housing Crisis: Intellectuals in the Closet

Obscure Objects of Desire: Beds, Sofas, and Commodes

The builder of the Integral and loyal citizen of the Single State, D-503, hero of Evgenii Zamiatin's dystopian novel *We* (1920), inhabits an architecturally perfect house-commune with transparent walls; in such a house people live perpetually in public sight, bathing in light. Curtains are provided only in exchange for pink coupons during the "sexual days." The most incredible event in D-503's life is a visit to an "ancient house" with apartments in quotation marks:

> I opened the heavy, squeaky, opaque door in the gloomy, disorderly building (they call it "apartment" house) . . . White on top, dark blue walls, red, green, and orange covers of ancient books, yellow bronze—candelabra, the statue of Buddha, and the curves of furniture, contorted, not fitting any rules . . . We moved through the rooms with little baby beds (children then were also private property). And again rooms, the shining of mirrors, gloomy cupboards, unbearably bright sofas, a huge fireplace, a large bed of red wood. Our present-day glass—beautiful, transparent, eternal—existed only in the shape of the fragile little squares of the windows.[18]

Only from a futuristic perspective of the resident of a perfect house-commune can a fairly ordinary, if not banal, bourgeois interior of the turn of the century, with its minor excesses of orientalism, appear so radically strange. This is precisely the kind of interior that it was fashionable to criticize in the circles of the radical intelligentsia in Russia and in the West. It has all the obvious excesses—of privacy, fancy, and eclecticism. But in the permanent theocracy of good taste the low ceilings and fanciful curtains promise liberating surprises and erotic seduction to the inhabitant of the rationalist utopia, where the sky is a constant bright blue with hardly a single shapeless and unpredictable cloud to spoil the view.

The ancient, overcrowded, eclectic interior conceals illegitimate love-making, no pink coupon required. When D-503 experiences unbridled emotions toward I-33, he loses control over the interior; it seems to him that he disappears inside the huge cupboard and the darkness of private furniture. The builder of the Integral makes love not only to I-33 but also to the old-fashioned bourgeois interior, the archeological relic from prerevolutionary time, a forbidden zone.

It would not be an exaggeration to say that the major "private" passion in Soviet literature of the first postrevolutionary decade is a passion for dwelling space. Indeed, the identity crisis and the housing crisis are closely linked. The communal apartment became an important artistic topos in the late 1920s. In the literature and film of the 1920s "defamiliarization" is not simply a metaphor for a literary device but also a central thematic preoccupation: the break-up of families and the loss of homes. In postrevolutionary life defamiliarization has become a norm, and it is the familiar that can no longer be taken for granted. Love, hatred, even melancholy are all secondary passions—they usually translate into love of dwelling space (zhilploshchad'), hatred for those who have it, and melancholy for lost housing. Early on, when the communal apartment is not yet completely established as an institution, anxiety about communal living is already present. The quest for housing space and furniture appears to be the major driving force of plots in literature and films of the 1920s. The development of the plot often follows the adventures of commodes, beds, and sofas. The literature of communal living reveals the instability of relationships between people and things, as well as between the interior of the room and the inner self. While objects, commodes and sofas especially, are endowed with nearly superhuman powers, people are often objectified, deprived not only of individual psychology but also of artistic play and of their role in driving the plot. In many of these works the slogans and clichés of the Soviet language are woven into an ambivalent and humorous text, prescriptive paradigms are turned into narratives, class conflicts appear as clashes of discourses and styles of thinking. They provide comic relief from the lofty seriousness of the utopian design and collective pedagogies.

Mikhail Zoschenko's "What the Nightingale Sang About" (1927) is a prototypical communal apartment romance, an affair made possible by the housing crisis. The narration is estranged through the creation of an aspiring writer, Kolenkorov, who practices the outmoded genre of the sentimental tale under the critical guidance of the head of the literary club, Zoshchenko.[19] Many statements proclaimed in *Komsomol Truth* appear in Zoshchenko's stories as stylized opinions of the characters. "What the Nightingale Sang About" is the tale of Comrade Bylinkin who conveniently falls in love with Liza, a daughter of the landlady. In Bylinkin's eyes Liza is a perfect domestic woman, she possesses the "charming sloppiness and even untidiness of that Russian woman who gets out of bed in the morning and, without washing up, starts her domestic chores in her thick felt slippers."[20] She is certainly not "a doll-like madame, an invention of the bourgeois culture." At this time the communal apartment is not yet completely established, but the fear and anticipation of it are already there. Marriage promises a new coziness.[21]

After many walks outside, and some old-fashioned communal apartment flirting, Bylinkin proposes marriage to Liza, and the two begin to imagine their new nest. Liza dreams about a little dressing table near their bed which, in Bylinkin's view, is meshchanstvo. In turn, he has more ambitious plans and hopes to get Liza's mother's chest of drawers *(komod)*, which will provide true comfort to the newlyweds. But conflict over this unfortunate komod, a desirable petit-bourgeois commodity, creates a family scandal between Bylinkin and his future mother-in-law and tragically ends the romance. "The love boat has crashed against the daily grind," as Mayakovsky repeatedly claimed. Bylinkin moves into the new flat of Mrs. Ovchinnikov, who is also afraid of the housing crisis and who also has a young daughter, fated to become Bylinkin's lucky spouse.

Liza's mother's commode, a commodity par excellence, breaks both the romance and the romantic discourse of the novella. In spite of the unhappy ending, the love of commodes will persist in Soviet literature and life. The new communal men and women might be adulterous with their lovers and fiancés, but they are quite faithful in their attachment to their furniture.

A popular early Soviet film, *Bed and Sofa* (1927) (titled in Russian *Third Petit-Bourgeois Street, Tret'ia Meshchanskaia*, dir. Abram Romm), also portrays a communal romance built around furniture, this time the bed and sofa. The film portrays a peculiar love triangle between a young woman, her husband (the representative of the new Moscow proletariat), and his friend, a printer with whom he fought in the Civil War. The friend moves in with the couple because he simply has no other place to live. The film combines Eisenstein-like shots of Moscow public life that clash with the old-fashioned cluttered domestic space of Soviet youth. The script was written by Formalist Viktor Shklovsky; it was rumored that the plot was inspired by the unconventional living arrangements of Vladimir Mayakovsky, who cohabited with his beloved Lilia Brik and her husband, the poet's friend, editor and critic Osip Brik. In any case, in proper Formalist fashion, the plot is not determined by the psychology of the characters but rather by their structural position in relation to furniture—bed or sofa. The bed and the sofa in the film are like musical chairs—the husband and the friend change their positions and move from spousal bed to marginal sofa as the plot unfolds. It is appropriate that neither the English nor the Russian film title mentions any people; it is either the name of the street or the prominent objects of the household. Mario Praz begins his *Illustrated History of Interior Decoration* with the didactic poem "I Sing a Sofa," an object, "though humble, yet august and proud."[22] In postrevolutionary Russia sofas are rare luxuries, but odes to them are inconceivable. Moreover, sofas appear as suspect objects of petit-bourgeois comfort and coziness. Sleeping is, of course, a matter of ideology and has to be ideologically correct.[23] (Architect Konstantin Melnikov's project for a Laboratory of Sleep included an Institute for Changing the Form of Man that would supervise the sleepers.) The way the hero and the heroine sleep and what they dream of reveals not so much their unconscious but precisely its opposite—their revolutionary conscientiousness.

In the opening scene the heroine of the film, Ludmila, is portrayed as her husband may see her: almost like an object of furniture or a domestic pet. Her cinematic attributes are the cat and the mirror. At the end, from being the queen of a petit-bourgeois interior, Ludmila turns into a truly emancipated woman, a mistress of her own life. She decides to keep her child, move to the country, and work. Meanwhile

the two men are left alone, in their rather unusual male bonding over
a cup of tea with jam. Now the bed and sofa are theirs.

Iurii Olesha's novel *Envy,* written the same year as Romm's film
was made, also presents a hero who travels between different people's
beds and sofas.[24] He is an intellectual turned lumpenproletariat or
rather lumpen leisure class whose last name, Kavalerov, ironically
suggests the courtly male heros of the past—cavaliers *(kavalery)* and
caballeros andantes. Kavalerov's masculine pride, however, is subor-
dinate to housing and is challenged at every displacement; he is ready
to be a domestic fool or an affectionate slave for anyone who gives
him a home. Thus he is both infatuated with and envious of the
Soviet self-made man Babichev, who sings in his bathroom out of
sheer happiness of being, exuding masculine health and cheerful self-
complacency. At the end Kavalerov moves to the uncomfortable bed
of the middle-aged widow Anushka; but even this half of the bed is
not permanently his: he shares it with his soul-mate Ivan, another
homeless artist and the inventor of a useless magic machine. The
displaced intellectual prostitutes himself, sometimes literally and
sometimes metaphorically, to those who can house him and offer the
most transient illusion of belonging to the postrevolutionary common
place.

Laughing through Tears and Pacts with the Devil

In the satirical topography of the Soviet literature intellectuals are
spatially connected to the closet. Besides other suspicious closet activities, this is the place where they hide to read. The position of the
intellectual, somebody who falls in between revolutionary class categories, is ambiguous, and the narrative dependent upon him is fragile
and volatile. One of Zoshchenko's short stories, "The Summer
Break," describes such an intellectual, who uses up communal elec-
tricity by reading "who knows what" in the closet, occasionally even
cooking macaroni; his selfishness outrages his neighbors. He writes
this at a time when the Soviet intelligentsia is experiencing a major
catastrophe: many will be killed, some will go into hiding and hiber-
nation; and the few that escape the purges will join the Soviet elite
and enjoy warm toilets, polite neighbors or no neighbors at all, and
occasionally even bathrooms with a shower in the rooms of the

magnificent old-fashioned building of the House of Soviet Writers built in the imperial classical fashion.

Ilia Ilf and Eugene Petrov's satirical novel *The Golden Calf* (1931) offers us one of the first grotesque representations of the communal apartment, the "raven's haven," complete with voracious petit-bourgeois neighbors and a Soviet antihero and soon-to-be underdog, the intellectual.[25] The "raven's haven" is a battleground; neighbors unite in camps and blocs and periodically attack their unfortunate victims. When Sevriugin the hero-pilot flies to the North Pole to save a missing foreign expedition, his communal apartment neighbors enthusiastically expropriate his room and throw out all his personal belongings. Dunia occupies the room and puts in six beds which she rents out individually, and all the neighbors get together in a wild celebration with Russian folk dances. But the heroic aviator comes back and soon gets a new apartment from the government.

The true scapegoat of apartment 3 is the intellectual Vasisualii Lokhankin, who always forgets to switch off the light in the "places of communal use" and is finally dumped by his wife. Here the victim of love turned cruel in consequence of the housing crisis is a man, not a woman. He is, however, completely feminized; he does nothing but reflect upon the tragedy of liberal intelligentsia and write iambic farewells to his unfaithful wife.

Lokhankin is presented as a postrevolutionary Oblomov, with the chronic intellectual disease of inaction. He has turned into an obsolete piece of petit-bourgeois furniture.[26] The parody of the intellectual is one of the central elements of the novel. Lokhankin embodies several enemy figures of both intellectual and meshchanin targeted by two seemingly opposite campaigns: one was led by the left artists against the petite bourgeoisie, and the other was the official anti-intellectual campaign led by the government that in many cases ended in the extermination of the intellectuals (including the fighters against the bourgeoisie themselves). The mythology of the radical intelligentsia crosses over into the official Soviet mythology of anti-intellectualism. But perhaps the two only seem opposite and in fact they reveal a tragic attempt of the artistic intelligentsia of the left to "pass" for the Soviet establishment. Lokhankin could be seen as a product of intellectuals' self-hatred—something like, and metaphorically linked to, Jewish self-hatred.[27] Then again, are we to condemn a comic hero who did not finish high school, or put his authors on trial? It cannot

be helped that with the passage of time some of the comical characters have become less funny.[28]

Mikhail Bulgakov, a writer with personal experience of many Moscow communal dwellings, shows us another side of the Soviet class
struggle in which intellectuals and writers try hard to escape the
Soviet closet by employing mostly fantastic methods. To protect his
privacy and his right to eat "in the dining room and not in the
bedroom," Professor Preobrazhensky from "The Heart of the Dog"
performs an extraordinary experiment and brings to life a new creature, a new Soviet man with the heart of a dog, to occupy the room
that the Housing Committee threatened to expropriate. But this un-
grateful Soviet Frankenstein joins up with the Housing Committee to
threaten the professor himself—an allegory of the fate of the Russian
revolutionary intelligentsia that created its own destructive Franken-
steins.

The housing crisis acquires a metaphysical significance in Bulgakov,
and so does the contrast of home and pseudo-home. Among such
pseudo-homes are the madhouse, the camp, or the hospital, but also
the Griboedov House of Writers' Union, the comfortable apartment
of Margarita's conventional unloving marriage, and the new Soviet
communal apartment. According to Lotman, "a flat, and especially a
communal flat is a chaos masquerading as home and making a real
home impossible. The home and the communal flat are antipodes."[29]
"Home" becomes a nostalgic dream rather than specific living quarters of postrevolutionary Moscow; it combines memories of affectionate domesticity and spiritual freedom. However, the communal
anti-homes also have many alternative dimensions; with a little help
from the devil, Bulgakov's characters learn to carve imaginary spaces
in their communal apartments.

In *The Master and Margarita* the communal apartment turns into
the most fantastic place on earth—more fantastic than the palace of
Pontius Pilate. While some of Bulgakov's intellectuals refuse to sell
out to the Soviet establishment, they occasionally sell their souls to
the devil.[30] Satan's ball takes place in the "fifth dimension" of the
Moscow communal apartment. "For anyone who knows how to
handle the fifth dimension it's no problem to expand any place to any
size whatever—to the devil knows what size"—explains the devil's
assistant Korov'ev to Margarita before Satan's ball. Yet the devil
himself is surprised at the tricks of Moscow "apartment exchange"

and the expansion and divisibility of the dwelling space in the post-revolutionary capital. In all its multiple dimensions the reality of the communal apartment appears more fantastic than fiction; even the imaginary escapes from Soviet communality into the fifth dimension of fiction could not entirely escape the Soviet communal designs.[31]

Bulgakov's own novel was hidden in the fifth dimension of the writer's desk drawer and was not published until the early 1960s. At the time when the communal apartment became an established social institution in the 1930s, the satirical and tragicomic representations of Soviet communality ceased to have the right to exist. In the 1950s there was a new preoccupation with domestic interiors and the domestic things, which became very valuable as a result of postwar deprivation, but the tragicomedy of communal living is not to be found anywhere in art until the late 1970s, when the communal apartment turns into the nostalgic site of the conceptual artists' own totalitarian childhood.

No More Tears: The Soviet Cinderella

One of the last "epic" films of the era of stagnation, *Moscow Doesn't Believe in Tears*, looks back upon three decades of Soviet postwar history and sums up the housing passions for the last two decades of Soviet power, from the 1950s to the 1970s, in the context of mainstream Soviet mythology.

If the French Cinderella finds herself a prince, the Soviet Cinderella finds herself a working-class Mr. Right and a three-bedroom apartment. There is no fairy here and no crystal shoe, that suspicious object of bourgeois fetishism. Cinderella's own willpower and the magic of the cinema take on the fairy quality. *Moscow Doesn't Believe in Tears* is the story of Katia, a working girl from the provinces who becomes the director of a prominent factory and finally gains personal happiness. The film won an Oscar in the United States, perhaps because this is the closest that Soviet cinema came to Hollywood, in the way it put together realistic settings, popular mythologies of anti-intellectualism, and fairy-tale logic. The plot develops around various housing displacements, false identities acquired through other people's apartments, envy, love, imposture, and a final resolution of crises, including the housing crisis. While the anti-intellectualism of the film is definitely not in the closet, one of its working-class heroes turns out to be a closet 1960s intellectual, at least in his musical tastes.

This Cinderella of the era of Brezhnev's stagnation is a peculiar remake of the Stalinist Cinderella, a textile worker and heroine of labor from one of Stalin's favorite films—*Illuminated Road*. In both films the problems of everyday life are taken care of with the help of movie magic, and history is erased with the help of a single seamless cut.

The three heroines of *Moscow Doesn't Believe in Tears*, recently (in the late 1950s) arrived in the capital from the countryside, share a room in the Workers' Dormitory, a fact they often try to hide. One day Katia is offered a chance to take care of a professor's apartment in his absence. Her enterprising girlfriend, obsessed with improving their social status, decides to organize a party and invite all the eligible bachelors from the privileged intellectual elite, and the two girlfriends will pass for the professors' daughters. In this version of the Cinderella story the prince is a privileged member of the intelligentsia; in relation to him a working girl is merely a poor stepdaughter.

During the evening the girls meet the men of their dreams, but the moralistic logic of the fairy tale requires them to be Mr. Wrong types, because false pretenses cannot be rewarded. Thus Katia's new boyfriend, a TV journalist bearing the un-Russian name Roman, gets her pregnant but declines to marry her when he finds out that she is only a worker without a permanent residence in Moscow. Once things begin to look bad for Katia, a miracle takes place—a miracle of the sort that is only possible in the cinema. We see Katia crying herself to sleep in the student dorm, pregnant, preparing for the exams to the technological institute. Then—cut—she wakes up some fifteen years later in a large three-bedroom apartment of her own with a teenage daughter. Moreover, she is now director of the factory.

The cut appears nearly seamless, but in fact it erases all the problems that could have made the film polemically interesting. This "happy awakening" is taken straight from the Stalinist Cinderella story. But as is frequently the case, the three-bedroom apartment does not bring happiness, since Katia's private life is empty. The preoccupation with private life is a phenomenon of the 1970s, but this is a carefully constructed private life. Moreover, the housing passions are not yet completely quenched. Again as if by miracle, Katia meets a man on the train who mistakes her for a simple working girl or a technician. Once the romance begins he is a bit taken aback by her spacious living arrangements, and by realizing that she might have a higher social position than he does, since he continues to live in one room of a communal apartment. But after a couple of misunderstandings, a little help from their friends, and a series of fantastic discoveries, love and truth prevail and the lovers will certainly marry and live happily ever after in Katia's large apartment.

Despite occasional appealing acting and its emphasis on the private sphere, the film is strikingly old-fashioned in its unabashed anti-intellectualism and misrepresentations of Soviet power structures. Intellectuals rather than party officials occupy all the power positions and serve as objects of popular envy. Moreover, Khrushchev's thaw, presented from the point of view of sympathetic provincial newcomers to Moscow, is made out to be a superficial and pretentious affair of intellectuals, incomprehensible to the common people. The central device of the film, the cut that displaces the heroine from the communal student dorm and sweeps her into the private apartment, is a way of erasing history and reestablishing a mythical consciousness and fairy-tale logic.

This "private epic" of the era of stagnation culminates in the three-bedroom apartment, but that is hardly an element of realism. Only in the 1990s did the radical perestroika of life break down some partitions of the former communal apartments. The visitor can wander through those haunting spaces with ruins of the communal walls, hinges of former doors, and fantastic floral bas reliefs around the holes in the ceiling where the dim communal light hung, illuminating unusual finds for a cultural archeologist and bringing back uncanny memories of a Soviet homecoming.

Welcome to the Communal Apartment

"Black Entrance"

A few years before returning to Russia, I had my first dream of homecoming. In the dream I stand in front of my house and I try to enter it but I can't. I don't remember what the doorknob looked like.

Then somehow I manage to enter and quickly rush through the dark corridor fearing there is someone hiding behind the elevator

Entering the communal apartment (photo by Mark Shteinbok)

right near the door of the mysterious office named "Little Red Cor-
ner," the office of the Housing Committee, which seems to be forever
locked or forever in the middle of a meeting. I am scared of a familiar
ghost, a wicked stranger, a drunk man in the dark. I hear his resound-
ing laughter followed by his stinking, spitting threats: "Fuck your
mother in the mouth, you little bitch . . . Stinking ass." If I could only
twist my tongue to repeat the curses with pleasure and self-
confidence, if I could only forgo my shamefully proper intelligentsia
habits and linger on every guttural sound "kh," the drunkard would
stop laughing at me. I could enter my house fearlessly and give the
hallway stranger a wink of complicity. I could have been home by
now. My compressed lips are ready for the forceful "u" sound, my
throat is about to utter the guttural sound. But somehow, the air is
blocked, the sound freezes on my lips, and my obscenities remain
mute, harmless, unheard and unheard-of—defenseless.

The entrance that I have just failed to take used to be the main
entrance to the house. To enter the communal apartment requires a
long "rite of passage": in and out through a dark hallway with ruined
mosaics and pieces of beer bottles and across the interior yards full
of communal trash, with occasional graffiti and half-erased hop-

scotch on the asphalt. Visiting a Soviet home one is struck not only by a deep contrast between the public and private spheres, between official communality and the community of one's own inner circle, but also by that strange no-man's-land, the space that belongs to everybody and to nobody but that creates discomfort in both public and private existence. Since the communal restructuring of the building one rarely enters the old house from the front door; the front hallway is merely a space to cross.

The hallway occupies a special place in the Soviet mythical topography; it is a space of transition, a space of fear, the dark limit of the house. It could preserve traces of a building's former elegance: fragments of mosaics and ruined, not-so-classical pilasters with obscene graffiti scribbled all over. The hallways are usually inhabited by old drunks, local fools, youth gangs, and teenagers in love. Here all sorts of unofficial initiations take place. (In the romantic version we would imagine the last farewell kiss in the hallway, a little poem by Sergei Esenin, perhaps "Life's a lie, but with a charming sorrow" recited by one teenager to another, with the sound of benevolent laughter in the background, of a couple of slightly tipsy comrades, old war veterans with a bottle of Stolichnaya . . . For the darker side, we would have to picture all sorts of unreported crimes happening in the hallways—from rape to murder, committed in a state of total intoxication.

The Soviet bard Bulat Okudzhava dedicated a song to communal "black staircases" inhabited by black cats and ghosts of fear. The black entrance to the communal apartments leads to a dark corner of the Soviet unconscious. In the song the black cat that "never cries nor sings" embodies the suspicions of Stalin's times, the mutual fears and occasional tragic complicity of informants and victims who often inhabited the same communal apartment. The end of the song is a poetic reflection on the Soviet collective mentality. All it will take is "to put a new light bulb on the black staircase"—one collective illumination, metaphorically speaking, and then some of the dark fears can be eliminated. But somehow collective inaction conspires to keep the public spaces dark. The black staircase is a Soviet public site par excellence, a space that is everybody's and therefore nobody's responsibility; it is where the ghosts of collective fear are kept alive much longer than they needed to be. In Soviet Russia there was no interface between public and private, no space of conventional socialization, the space that is governed neither by the official decorum, like the Soviet subway, nor by the unwritten rules of intimacy that reign in the overcrowded domestic nooks. The space between is the space of alienation—the Soviet zone—the space on the outskirts of the Soviet topography.

My house, a typical old St. Petersburgian building partitioned into many communal apartments, was located on Bolshoi Avenue near the Karpovka River, which in the nineteenth century constituted the urban frontier. The building was rumored to have belonged to a wealthy St. Petersburg engineer, a nouveau riche with a non-Russian name and cosmopolitan, eclectic tastes. After the Revolution all the apartments—now communal property—were partitioned; only the ornamental front hallway reminds us of the past. As for the engineer, he was forever erased from history and from the well-kept list of house residents in the Building Committee Office. (It was rumored that he was a liberal. He even collaborated with the revolutionary government. But around 1926 he obtained a foreign passport and "went traveling." He may have died of consumption on the French Riviera with a little volume of Pushkin's poems in his hands. Perhaps he suffered a heart attack in a small Mexican village while making love to a beautiful member of the local Trotskyist group . . . I am glad he did not turn into an anonymous neighbor in the partitioned and subdivided apartment on the third floor, vanishing in the purges of 1937 or 1942.)

With the engineer's disappearance, the single narrative of the house becomes infinitely subdivided like the space inside; it bifurcates into the interrupted, aborted narratives of the countless neighbors in the communal apartments. The shabby façade of the house with its whimsical and eclectic bas reliefs of the turn of the century was an embarrassing reminder of the engineer's cosmopolitan tastes incompatible with the new Soviet style.

When I worked as a Leningrad tour guide, mostly for the Young Pioneers from provincial towns, I was supposed to take my tourists away from the Petersburg eclecticism to the harmonious classical ensembles on the squares around Neva, the monuments to Lenin with his hand outstretched and the revolutionary cruiser *Aurora*. (Leningrad in the Brezhnev era had a precise iconography immortalized on a series of official postcards, where even the clouds had Soviet classical shapes—not too fluffy and not too thin—and the sky had the proper blue of East German color film.) When the bus passed by my

house, I would inevitably recite the memorized lines from the
"Guide's Instruction Manual": "This building on the right with
strange beasts on the façade derives from foreign models, lacks classical proportions, and does not present any real architectural value."
Hence the obscenity of the entrance, the curses of the drunks, and the
"bad taste" of the façade marked the road to the communal apartment.

Communal Neighbors: Oral History and Class Struggles

Imagine entering one of the communal apartments in Leningrad/St.
Petersburg, not mine but the one across the street. We pass by the
back staircase and stop in front of the massive door with several
separate bells: "three rings for Petrov, two for Khaimovich, one for
Skripkina, four for Genalidze." This is the first affirmation of sepa-
rateness—if we don't have a separate door, at least we've got a
separate door bell; if not a separate kitchen, at least a separate gas
burner. If we share the same electric light, then each of us should have
a switch; even if it is completely irrational and inconvenient, we will
go all the way along the long corridor to our room in order to turn
on the lights in the toilet. In circumstances of extreme overcrowdedness and imposed collectivity there is an extreme—almost obsessive—
protection of minimal individual property. Just be sure to remember
how many times you have to ring the bell, and God forbid you ring
the wrong one! As you enter the communal corridor you hear the
flutter of slippers and the squeaking of the floors and you notice
many pairs of eyes scrutinizing you through half-opened doors. Some
look at you indifferently, others with suspicion or with basic self-de-
fensive hostility, just in case. When a guest comes to the apartment it
is everyone's business, a mini-event, a source of gossip and argument.
Please don't forget to clean your feet, right on the threshold of the
communal apartment—do it thoroughly and just a bit longer than
needed, otherwise you will violate the schedule of communal duties,
especially the time-table of corridor-cleaning, and bring a lot of communal misfortune to your host.

Meet the neighbors of this exemplary composite communal apartment: most of them come from my grandmother's large communal
flat, others come from shared Soviet folklore, perhaps not exactly the
way they really were, but the way they could have been. The collec-

tive of the communal apartment included an old woman named Glebovna, who claimed to have swept the floors of the Winter Palace, and had been a maid of the first owner of the apartment; she hid a little photograph of Tsar Nikolai II in the back of a drawer. There was Gertruda Genrikovna, a piano teacher of German descent, who was exiled during the war to a special camp for russified Germans in Kazakhstan and had nineteenth-century porcelain figurines representing all the nations of Great Russia; there was the former Stakhanovite and now drunkard Uncle Kolia, who occasionally watched TV with Gertruda Genrikovna; the old maid Aleksandra Ivanovna, a member of the intelligentsia with the manners of a governess and the complete works of Russian and French classics, and her retarded aunt, Raisa; there was Uncle Vasia, who walked down the hall half-naked, exuding the cheap eau-de-cologne "Red Moscow"; and finally, the sailor Nikita, who sailed abroad, brought Peruvian panties to his longtime fiancée Galia, and was promised a new cooperative apartment in the new year. Galia is the daughter of one of the first neighbors of my grandmother's, Aunt Klava, who left the village and went to Petrograd after the Revolution together with her friend Aleftina. Both became devoted Bolsheviks; Aleftina worked as an accountant in Smolny—briefly after the Revolution the headquarters of the Soviet government and later of the Leningrad Party Committee—and she used to enjoy special vacations in the Party sanatorium; Klava became a secretary of the local district Party organization, and was the communal apartment's authority on "ideological correctness." In the 1950s, during the purges of Jewish doctors, Aleftina stopped talking with my grandmother in the communal kitchen, while Klava publicly announced in the communal corridor in the presence of Aleftina and my grandmother that she never believed that all Jews were guilty "of using the blood of Christian children." After this authorial statement Aleftina got scared and just in case started to chat with my grandmother again, at least when Aunt Klava was there.

But this was more than thirty years ago, and now Klava's daughter Galia hangs her foreign underwear on Aleksandra Ivanovna's personal laundry line in the communal bathroom because she objects to Aleksandra's "imperialist attitude towards communal property." Nikita periodically screams at Gertruda Genrikovna, calling her "German swine" or a "kike" (she was not Jewish, but he said it just in case, since she had a non-Russian last name), and asks her what she was doing in 1941. Retarded Aunt Raisa spits on Uncle Kolia because she does not like the smell of alcohol.

One amazing version of Russia's oral history would show the whole country as a gigantic communal apartment with many mysteries and secrets. Old Glebovna tells stories of everyday life in the Russian Imperial court from the perspective of someone who swept the floors and the staircases—a cinematic perspective worthy of Eisenstein. But another story is that of the neighbor who informed on old Glebovna and her monarchist affections at the local Housing Committee meeting in 1937 and temporarily took over her shabby little room while she was taken away for investigation. Another neighbor, Elena, who moved away and gave her room to Galia, used to tell and retell this obsessive story: in 1938 she saw Fanny Kaplan, the woman who shot at Lenin, twenty years after her execution for her failed attempt to kill the great leader. The woman our neighbor saw wore a little jacket, the color of young grass . . . "no, it was more like the color of sea wave, and she was brutally treated by the guards on the ship but she behaved herself with the dignity of a true revolutionary . . . and there was blood on her aqua jacket."

Stories were told about war defectors and about Stalinist informers—in the 1950s and 1960s the former victims began to inform on the informers—and then in the 1970s a story circulated about Galia, and her illegitimate children fathered by a leader of a "developing country" studying in Russia. Then there were stories of the "new traitors," the victims of Zionist propaganda who tried to emigrate to Israel or to America. And now there are stories of the communal survivors and the *limitchik*—the new marginals of post-Soviet society who arrived in the city from the country for temporary jobs and live on limited permits and on the margins of urban communality. Thus in addition to being the site of class conflicts and kitchen wars, the communal apartment was a place of old-fashioned story-telling and myth-making, where the now-vanishing Soviet folklore was preserved and cherished.

Psychopathology of Soviet Everyday Life

Once I was asked what were my earliest memories of growing up in the same room with my parents. The first thing I remembered was the texture of the curtain (port'era) that partitioned our shared room.

The port'era *of my childhood was heavy and dark yellow, with an ornamental appliqué. I remember overhearing the voices of my parents and their friends and the songs of Okudzhava and Vysotsky, but most of all I remember the* port'era *itself. So much for the primal scenes.*

The partition is the central architectural feature of the communal apartment. Most of them are made of plywood and they mark the intersection of public and private spheres within the apartment. After the expropriation of property, the old rooms and hallways were partitioned and subdivided, creating weird angular spaces, with a window opening into a sunless back yard or without any windows. Every tenant exercised her imagination in inventing curtains and screens to delineate their minimum privacy. A plywood partition was so much flimsier than a wall, more a sign of division than a division itself. It let through all the noises, the snoring, the fragments of conversations, the footsteps of the neighbor, and everything else you can think of. The partition served not so much to preserve intimacy as to create an illusion that some intimacy was possible.

Secrecy is one of the most important ways of keeping the illusion of privacy. But secrecy in the communal apartment was a game of searching for alternative communalities. There used to be an unofficial children's game we played in the kindergarten, called "the game of burying secrets" which had nothing to do with the official collective "hide-and-seek" orchestrated by the teacher, a game in which there were no secrets and nothing particular to seek or to find. Our unofficial game consisted in a ritual burial of our little fetishes; the ceremony was performed by a group of close friends and hidden from the kindergarten authorities. The buried "secret" might be a piece of colored glass found in the trash, an old stamp, a piece of the glittering foil wrapping of chocolates, an old badge. The point is that something had to be hidden in order to be shared, to be a bond between friends, a perfect something to be exposed as a seal of another, unofficial, communality. This secrecy is not solitary; it has to be dramatized in public. As for the secret itself, the fetishized useless souvenir preserved only for the sake of the game, it parallels some styles of personal collecting in the communal apartments.

Games of secrets were played by adults in their attempts to establish an alternative community and communality, but not necessarily individual privacy. The places of communal use—kitchen, corridor, bathroom—were both the battlegrounds and the playgrounds for the communal neighbors. The use of the toilet, as the fictional and nonfictional accounts of communal life attest, was the most frequent ground for communal disagreement. Toilet paper, a rare commodity in the Soviet Union, was kept in the room and carried inconspicuously to the toilet. Next to the toilet were neatly cut up sheets of *Pravda*, to be read or put to another functional use. The figure of the intellectual in the closet—in the literal rather than literary sense—is prominently featured in many communal apartments. (The toilet was often occupied by some avid reader. The neighbors tried to be discreet, not lining up for the toilet but watching and eavesdropping through the half-opened doors of their rooms, planning when to make their strategic move. Sometimes, though, the wait went beyond the limits of their patience and they would bang ferociously on the door. And, of course, the neighbor who did not turn off the lights in the toilet was considered "an enemy of the people.") Until the 1970s very few apartments had bathrooms (usually separate from the toilet). And where there were bathtubs, they were used for much more important occupations than mere self-indulgent washing. When my mother was a secondary school student, she and the neighbor's daughter used to do their homework on a shelf put across the never-functioning bathtub. The bathtub became my mother's study, her only private space in the crowded apartment.

The communal kitchen hardly resembles the dream of the utopian architects: to be a place of women's liberation from the daily chores. The kitchen is not a communal meeting place, rather it is a place that exemplifies the kind of communality to be avoided. One of the recently interviewed communal apartment residents called it a "domestic Nagorno-Karabakh." Because communal life was endlessly bureaucratized according to schedules dictating in detail the use of each oven and sink, the potential for friction was unending. The burden of the communal interactions and negotiations rested entirely on women; the world of the communal kitchen has often been called matriarchal, but I would add that it has been matriarchal by necessity and not by choice.

In the 1960s an alternative "kitchen culture" emerged. The members of Moscow intelligentsia who happened to live in their own separate flats (in Leningrad this was more rare) started to have unofficial kitchen gatherings at their homes. The kitchen became a kind

of an informal salon for the culture of the 1960s, of the thaw generation. The most important issues were discussed in the overcrowded
kitchen, where people "really talked," flirted, and occasionally ate.[32]
The kitchen provided a perfect informal setting for the subtle, casual
but friendly intimacy that became a signature of that generation. The
kitchen gathering of the 1960s represents a different form of collectivity—it is neither utopian nor forced, like that of the communal
apartment. It was a company of friends, unofficial though not an-
tiofficial; in this collective the bonds of affection and friendship constituted its ideology. (But these friendships too were affected by the
cultural myths of the time.) The kitchen salon of the 1960s was where
grown-up children continued to bury their secrets and to celebrate
their shared escapes from the predictability of Soviet life.

The communal apartment is a perfect stage for displaying various
forms of theatricality of daily behavior. The main feature of communal interaction can be called "performance disruption." The communal intrusion into the intimate life of a couple is comically featured
in many Soviet literary works and films. Soviet sexologists consider
the lack of privacy and an internalized fear of interruption as one of
the major sources of sexual dissatisfaction and neurosis. Embarrassment is the most characteristic feature of communal life: it does not
happen in solitude. Embarrassment is the painful awareness of one's
loss of control in the presence of the others, the self-consciousness of
loss of confidence, and an exemplary trope of social theatricality.[33]
The word "embarrassment" initially referred to a physical obstruc-
tion of passage, and only since the eighteenth century has it been
applied in reference to people. In this respect the incident with Uncle
Fedia urinating in the communal corridor and violating the codes of
propriety and social etiquette in front of foreign guests is a typical
case of embarrassment, which my mother internalized as a kind of
personal shame. Embarrassment was so frequent it almost turned
into a ritual in itself. The consequences of ritual embarrassment
varied: it could lead to establishing communal tolerance, to making
a compromise of minimal plausible conviviality in the impossible
circumstances, or to continued intolerance and repressed anger.

The communal apartment as the minimal unit of Soviet communality can be both endearing and stifling. Russian "political folkways"
are said to have "a strong tendency to maintain stability, a kind of
closed equilibrium, risk avoidance, . . . the considerable freedom of

action and expression 'within the group,' the striving for unanimous final resolution of potential divisive issues."[34] In the communal apartment survival strategies flourished in a similar way. Many people internalized the imposed communality as a fact of life, a guarantee of stability and of peaceful stagnation.

On the stage of the communal apartment the chorus of conservative public opinion prevailed. The "intellectual" agreed not to read in the closet, the drunk slept in one special kitchen corner, the kids rode their bicycles in the communal corridor very very quietly, and Aunt Shura reported to the authorities only every other political joke, not all of them. The communal battlefield was also a field of compromise. Alcoholism, which became extremely widespread in Brezhnev's time, was tolerated as a fact of life. Indeed, social psychologist Alexander Etkind sees alcoholism as a metaphor for stagnation. (In Russian *zapoi*—the drunken binge—and *zastoi*—stagnation—rhyme.) There was no encouragement to act sober, to aim at specific accomplishment, to differ from the masses; intoxication was the best way to survive. "The best moments in the life of an alcoholic are not his sober achievements but the drunken union with his peers."[35] No wonder that Gorbachev's reforms began with a campaign against alcoholism.

In the communal apartment any manifestations of individualism or uncommon behavior were discouraged, as they had been in the old village commune. In addition to embarrassment, relationships were dominated by envy—the title of one of the first novels of Soviet cohabitation. In its opening scene the infantilized intellectual is listening to the "new man" singing in the shower. The phenomenon of envy, which is obviously not restricted to Soviet communal living, reveals a peculiar adolescent sensibility and a kind of "historical immaturity." It reflects "a survival of pre-industrial community relationships governed by 'zero-sum'" presupposition where each person's gain is regarded as the other's loss. In the words of leading Russian psychologist Igor Kon, "the dictatorship of envy disguised as social justice efficiently blocked the individual efforts to do better and to rise above the average"; it disclosed "a general mistrust of individual achievement and the fear of social differentiation."[36]

Yet the effect of imposed communality was often contradictory and paradoxical; people professed to hate any form of communal interaction yet they internalized the communal structures and later recall them with nostalgia. An elderly Russian woman now living in the

United States suffered all her life in the horrendous communal apartments. Now she complains of solitude: "At least if worse comes to
worst, even after peeing in your teapot they will still call an ambulance for you if you need it, or lend you a little bit of salt for your
cooking . . . it is this little rough-grained salt that I miss."

Interior Decoration

The campaign against "domestic trash" did not triumph in the majority of the communal apartments. Instead, as in Mayakovsky's play
entitled *The Rebellion of Things*, the so-called domestic trash rebelled
against the ideological purges and remained as the secret residue of
privacy that shielded people from imposed and internalized communality.

Ode to the Commode

Walter Benjamin wrote that "to live means to leave traces."[37] Perhaps
this is the best definition of the private—to leave traces for oneself
and for others, memory traces of which one cannot be deprived. A
Soviet room in the communal apartment reveals an obsession with
commemoration and preservation in the most ostensible fashion. The
minimum of privacy is not even a room but a corner in a room, a
hidden space behind the partition. The cherished object might be
something almost immaterial: a pen, a writing table, a letter in the
drawer, a sea shell, little fetishistic objects, embodiments of human
desires and aesthetic and ideological imperfections.

Let us enter the room of an aging widow, Liuba, who lives in
a communal apartment next door to my old house in Leningrad.
Although she has lived here for almost thirty years, her room was not
"reconstructed" in the sixties. It appears untouched by the recent
changes in taste and in ideology; instead, Aunt Liuba's room preserves a sense of a long duration of time of a certain domestic mentality that survives historical upheavals. It also illustrates almost
literally everything that was considered to be in bad taste from the
1920s to the 1970s, including the rubber plant.

Aunt Liuba's room (approximately 13 square meters) contains a
sideboard, a version of a commode made in the early 1960s, a bed,
a table, and an old-fashioned TV set. The television stands in the

center of the table on a Russian shawl like an altar of modern conveniences. The console is covered with a special golden velvety cloth that used to cover icons and later gramophones, all of which were treated with a special reverence. Aunt Liuba's room reminds us of traditional homes of peasants and meshchanstvo. In the central space of a Russian village home, which has been framed and idealized by the ethnographers so many times that it has become hard to imagine what it was really like, there was a stove, the symbol of an old Russian hearth, used for cooking and for sleeping during the cold nights. Right across from the stove there was another source of light and warmth, this one spiritual. It was the so-called red corner, where the icons were kept and the candles for the icons were lit. In the Soviet public spaces the "red corner" was turned into "Lenin's corner," still with a lot of red—the color of blood, the color of the Russian icons, the color of the Revolution. In the rooms of the communal apartment the functions of the stove and the red corner were taken up by the TV and the display shelf of the commode, where the most precious items were kept. The artificial light of the TV is reflected in the glass doors of the sideboard, casting bluish shadows upon the personal possessions.

The commode (called also *servant* or *bufet*) is the most important piece of furniture in the old-fashioned communal apartment room. It survived all the ideological purges—the campaign against domestic trash, the civil war on meshchanstvo, and literary irony. Perhaps a nostalgic poet from the former Soviet Union should write an elegy or even an "Ode to the Commode."

The genesis of the item is of great historical importance. It symbolizes bourgeois commodity and the conceptions of comfort, home, and interiority.[38] According to Mario Praz the commode was invented in the early eighteenth century, out of the "confluence of bourgeois and patrician tastes," and it contributed greatly to giving rooms "a more intimate character."[39] In mid-nineteenth century, as Walter Benjamin put it, "the private individual enters the stage of history."[40] In contrast, in the mid-1920s in Russia the private individual goes backstage. Yet the old and not so luxurious commode in the room of the communal apartment remains the site of personal pride, a display of one's externalized interior and of the desire for individuation.

Aunt Liuba has carefully arranged the objects on her sideboard. There is a big plastic apple brought from her native Belorussian

village, a Chinese thermos with bright floral ornaments, a naturalistic
porcelain dog, three bottles containing different glass flowers—daisies
and some exotic red flowers not without a touch of elegance—a
samovar, a set of folk-style Soviet-made porcelain cups. "You see, I
have it all here—it's my still life," she said proudly when I photo-
graphed her room. It is curious that she would use the artistic term
"still life" to describe it. (She called it *nature morte,* a term familiar
from the obligatory high-school excursions to the museum.) To her,
the display is obviously imbued with an aesthetic quality as much as
with personal memories. She almost never drinks from her beautiful
porcelain cups. They are precious objects of decoration, not for
everyday use. Indeed there is something pleasing and cheerful in the
brightness and unabashed eclecticism of the objects, in contrast to the
bleak uniformity of the communal corridors.

The still life appears to be removed from historical narrative and

Aunt Liuba's room in the communal apartment, Leningrad, 1990 (photo by
the author)

Aunt Liuba's "still life" (photo by the author)

Aunt Liuba's "still life": Detail (photo by the author)

from narrative as such; it reflects a conception of time as habit, repetition, and long-duration; it is, to use Norman Bryson's expression, "the sleep of culture."[41] But it is hard to imagine a still life in a culture where one major devastation follows the other—revolutions, wars, housing crises, famine, Stalin's purges—where habit, repetition, and everyday stability are so difficult to sustain. In Russia one can only speak about nostalgia for a still life, for a sustaining everyday materiality in the face of continuing crises. Liuba's collection of Soviet ready-mades, objects of trivial private utopias and of mass aesthetics, framed by the glass of the commode as if it were a museum exhibit, is a kind of monument to that desire for a still life, for a life that does not rush anywhere in a whirlpool of uncontrollable change.

In Aunt Liuba's room ornaments clash: the carpet with its oriental motifs, the standard roses on the wallpaper, the bright country flowers on the tablecloth, the big polka dots on the pillow covers, and the geometrical decoration of the modern blanket on the bed. Obviously she did not choose them to match; she simply collected what she could get and tried to imbue it all with warmth and vitality, recreating distant images of the village home and prerevolutionary images of cozy merchants' dwellings whose covers, napkins, and laces gave the feeling of "completeness and personal touch" that Benjamin decries in bourgeois interiors.

Liuba's room is full of flowers: Soviet roses on the wall; exotic red glass flowers and simple plastic daisies on the shelf, and stylized golden and yellow daisies painted on the porcelain objects, and even red floral patterns on the wooden *khokhloma* spoon. Obviously, many of the objects themselves are ideological artifacts and products of cultural myths. For instance, the little busts of Pushkin, Tchaikovsky, and other great Russian geniuses that have persistently decorated apartments from the late nineteenth century to now represent the popular prestige of high culture. The glass flowers are cultural hybrids, impure flowers of degraded *art nouveau* and low-brow urban culture, artifacts that annoy intellectual ethnographers in search of authentic popular culture. The porcelain cups and plates come from the Leningrad porcelain factory, a former imperial factory. Its designers changed the tsarist insignia, Victorian roses, and floral *chinoiseries* for more democratic and folkloristic national motifs. And what could be more national and expressive of "simple folk taste" than daisies, the flowers of the field! The daisies on Aunt Liuba's porcelain, however, are stylized, abstract 1960s daisies.

Next door to Aunt Liuba lives a documentary filmmaker, Olia, with her twelve-year-old daughter. Her room too is overcrowded with personal memorabilia: portraits of Pushkin in the bookcase, reproductions of Hindu goddesses, sea corals, calendars with Soviet actresses in foreign black lingerie, images of prerevolutionary St. Petersburg. There is the usual clash of ornaments and conflicting styles. Olia is not happy with my taking pictures in her room: "Do you think I like all these pictures torn out of old journals and calendars? I have to cover the holes in the wall. Do you think I like this wallpaper? But how can I change it?" Indeed, who can afford here to have "good taste"?

In the rooms of the intelligentsia one finds similar "still lives" of personal memorabilia. Instead of cupboards and chests of drawers, there are bookcases built to occupy the whole wall, designed in a modern and functional fashion and made in the so-called developed Socialist countries like Hungary or Yugoslavia. These shelves seem to lack the fetishistic quality of the other pieces of furniture, having none of the ornamental details of the commodes. However, the bookcases themselves became fetishes of the intelligentsia and items of social status. The bookshelves display many hard-to-get hardcovers and collected works of foreign authors that are the mark of belonging to the intelligentsia. Yet the most important space here is the space between the folding glass doors on the bookshelf for the display of one's most personal objects—postcards, baby pictures, portraits of a bearded Hemingway or Vysotsky with or without a cigar, snapshots of faraway friends, toys or souvenirs from Crimea or Susdal, envelopes with foreign stamps, loose pages from old books, dated newspaper clippings. This narrow, nearly one-dimensional space behind the glass of the bookcase reflects the image of the resident; it is his or her carefully arranged interface with the world. The narrative of treasured objects cannot be easily reconstructed by the outsider: it is nonlinear, full of blank spots, oddly meaningful banalities, and minor obsessions. This life history is not a biography but rather a biographical legend, a story of inner life externally fashioned, a story of what really matters, what leaves traces and survives the drudgery of dailiness. Often it is also a story of travels, real or imaginary—of journeys to exotic places, of escapes into wishful thinking. In the 1960s and early 1970s, when traveling abroad was nearly impossible, Soviet citizens engaged in "virtual travels" through the popular television program "The Club of Cine-Travelers" (a Soviet version of "National

Private exhibit with Alexander Pushkin (photo by Mark Shteinbok)

Private exhibit with popular bard Bulat Okudzhava (photo by Mark Shteinbok)

Geographic"), or through collecting foreign stamps and pictures of Western writers, artists, and intellectuals.

The objects on personal display on the bookshelves are not completely individual: some unwritten law tells everyone when Hemingway is out and Vysotsky is in, when Pasternak is out and Solzhenitsyn is in. Then Solzhenitsyn himself is out and in his place reigns exotic and apolitical Nefertiti, the beautiful queen of ancient Egypt. The reproduction is from the traveling exhibit "The Treasures of Tutankhamen," to which hardly anyone could purchase tickets. Now side by side with Nefertiti there is a picture of a half-dressed foreign pin-up girl with a non-Russian smile, which seems to supplant the political and poetic heroes of the past and present.

The private memorabilia are steeped in cultural myths; they are separated from the dominant discourses by a mere plywood partition. But in that space the elements of those myths can be reconstructed in a creative personal collage; it doesn't matter that it lacks aesthetic unity. The objects/souvenirs are the minimal repositories of personal memory. Both priceless and cheap, conspicuous and private, they make us question certain commonplaces of the commodity theory.

Poverty of Sociology and the Aesthetics of Survival

Pierre Bourdieu begins his chapter "Social Critique of the Judgment of Taste" with an epigraph from Alain Besançon's *The Russian in the Nineteenth Century:* "And we do not know whether cultural life can survive the disappearance of domestic servants."[42] The sociologist goes on to analyze the French "aristocracy of culture," subordinating the "delights of art" to a class-based construction of taste. Yet the seamless passage from the epigraph to the main body of the text glosses over the fact that Russian cultural life survived not only the disappearance of the servants but even the rise and disappearance of a variety of sociological approaches to art and to everyday living. Bourdieu contrasts the "popular" movement to translate art into daily life with the "aristocratic" movement to "confer aesthetic status on objects that are banal or even common." In his view, "Popular taste applies the scheme of ethos which pertains in the ordinary circumstances of life to legitimate the works of art, and so performs a systematic reduction of the things of art to the things of life."[43]

Yet as some of the Russian examples demonstrate, the opposition between aesthetics and ethics, disinterestedness and empathy, elite and popular, does not function so neatly. In fact, popular aesthetic is often escapist and fantastic rather than entirely realistic; or rather, the elements of fantasy and verisimilitude in it tend to interact in a complex and ambiguous manner, as they do in the folk tales or science-fiction movies. Moreover, popular tastes are eclectic—together with urban middle-brow culture they often preserve a trace of peasant prerealist or slightly primitive sensibility (which should not be exaggerated, to avoid falling into the trap of folk exoticism). Popular tastes frequently incline to bright colors and fantastic ornaments. In Russia the culture of icons—their spiritual and also their pictorial and ornamental qualities—influenced both popular tastes and the taste of the avant-garde elite. Bourdieu takes two reductive steps: reducing popular culture to ethical projection and equating ethical projection with realistic representation.

In the everyday, especially in the highly politicized and semioticized Soviet everyday, the aesthetic and the ethical are indistinguishable in the ordinary micropractices. Moreover, it can become unethical to deny the aesthetic experience of the impoverished residents of the communal apartment.

The personal domestic objects of Aunt Liuba are difficult to categorize: they are too useless for both use-value and exchange-value theories, not authentically primitive or exotic enough for "transgressive" modern theories, too trivial and banal—in a nonfatal manner—to be turned into a simulacrum à la Baudrillard. The fetishistic aspect of these objects is not sufficiently perverse to make interesting psychoanalytical reading.[44] In other words, these objects are impure and outmoded on all grounds.

In Soviet Russia, the experience of material scarcity for the majority of the population and the official critique of bourgeois commodities (combined with thinly disguised social inequalities) endows private objects with a different cultural significance. While in Western Europe the critique of commodity is a marginal oppositional discourse, in Soviet Russia it is the mainstream. At the time of the campaign against domestic trash, Osip Mandelshtam made the cultivation of "domestic object" the cornerstone of his poetics of remembrance and his "nostalgia for world culture." Mandelshtam's autobiographical novella, *The Egyptian Stamp* (1928), opens with a toast to lost domesticity: "I propose to you, my family, a coat of arms; a glass of boiled water. In Petersburg's boiled water, with its rubbery aftertaste, I drink to my unsuccessful domestic immortality. The centrifugal force of time has scattered our Viennese chairs and the Dutch plates with little blue flowers."[45]

The same centrifugal force disperses the domestic objects and shatters the "I" of the hero. The fate of the things is parallel to the fate of persons. Those Viennese chairs and Dutch plates with little blue flowers exist in the past perfect or future indefinite of literature; lost domestic objects that can only be recovered through art. The poet has to be "a good house-sitter."[46]

Of course, the artifact on display in the communal apartment is less the trace of world culture than a mass-reproduced object. Yet it is aesthetically commemorated. Aunt Liuba's perfectly functional porcelain cups are made useless, and therefore beautiful. These cups and glass flowers have something in common with Mandelshtam's Viennese chairs and Dutch plates; they partake of the same aesthetics of survival.[47]

In her book *The Body in Pain* Elaine Scarry talks about the object in a world that is always in danger of being "unmade," where materiality is fragile and not to be taken for granted.[48] The object is treated not as a commodity or fetish but as an artifact, a product of human creativity that helps to make the world and undo the suffering. It is this conception of the object that is particularly suited for Soviet circumstances. There, the artifact is a personal souvenir and a souvenir of privacy itself; it is an object displaced from a common into an individual history. The owner of the souvenir becomes the author, who reinvents the use of the object and makes it memorable. As Susan Stewart points out, the tragedy of the souvenir is the death of memory, the nightmare of the "unmarked grave."[49] It is another way of describing the impossibility of "leaving traces."

The objects in the personal display cases of the communal apartments are neither bare essentials nor merely objects of status and conspicuous consumption. If they do represent a need, it is first and foremost an aesthetic need, a desire for beauty met with minimal available means, or the aesthetic "domestication" of the hostile outside world. They are not about defamiliarization, but rather about inhabiting estranged ideological designs.

The Ruins of Utopia

Communal Apartment as Conceptual Art

As a postscript to the discussion of precarious objects and marginalized domesticity, I will examine the communal apartment as a conceptual installation and the artist's dream and nightmare, as it appears in the works of Ilia Kabakov. He is one of the founding fathers of Moscow Conceptualism, the last movement of Soviet underground art. Kabakov says that he is interested in the "metaphysics of the commonplace"; his installations look like emptied theatrical sets of Soviet everyday life, labyrinths of communal apartments in art.

In Kabakov's work word and image could not be separated; he uses a rebus-like language of Soviet found objects. His conceptual communal apartments commemorate all the imagined spaces carved in the Soviet homes, from Bulgakov, Zoshchenko, and Mandelshtam to Aunt Liuba and the intelligentsia of the 1960s. They also house the

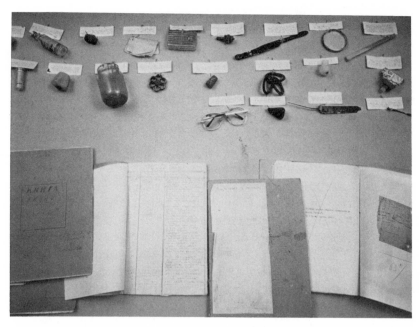

Ilia Kabakov, "The Man Who Never Threw Anything Away," 1988

ruins of avant-garde utopia, among them Kasimir Malevich's white square.

One of the installations, entitled "Sixteen Strings," has sixteen laundry lines strung in an imaginary communal kitchen. From the lines hang bits of trash, fragments of everyday things, wrappings, and useless bric-a-brac, and to each of the found objects corresponds a "found phrase," a fragment from endless communal conversations, often an emphatic exclamation, a demand, a complaint, a plea addressed to a displaced neighbor. With Walter Benjamin in mind, this work can be called a ruin of the communal apartment or a museum of traces—of fragmented public and private lives. In Kabakov's communal apartments ordinary chores are occasionally interrupted by fantastic happenings. Here, the artist could vanish in the white space of the canvas, and the aliens could arrive from outer space to disrupt the meeting of the Housing Committee just when it was denouncing his untidiness. Some of the apartments look like catacombs discovered in a not-so-distant future, after some disaster that may not be fantastic.

Most of Kabakov's communal dwellings and albums of communal neighbors have an empty room, a white wall or a white page. Kabakov cherishes emptiness and silence as metaphysical limits of collective control as well as of his own artistic power to organize fragments and labyrinths. Bakhtin distinguished between two Russian words for silence—*tishina* and *molchanie,* one referring to the silence of the world, where nothing makes sounds, and the other to the silence of people, where nobody speaks. Kabakov's emptiness is a spatial correspondence to those two silences; it contains the silence of voices and the silence of things. Yet this emptiness, the blank space and white page, are not entirely empty of cultural traces. This mystical escape into emptiness is reminiscent of the poetic self-effacement proposed by Stéphane Mallarmé in the 1880s and practiced by Malevich in the 1920s in his numerous paintings of white on white. But Malevich would never have dreamed of placing his white square on the walls of the communal apartment. Kabakov did. In one of his conceptual communal apartments it is rumored that the neighbor called "artist Kabakov" went mad, threw his dirty clothes all over the place, transgressed communal propriety, and escaped naked. According to another rumor, he disappeared into the white space on the canvas that he was painting for the local Housing Committee. Indeed, it seems that the fantastic disappearance in the fourth dimension and the white space on the canvas is the only conceivable way out of the overcrowded communal labyrinths and the burden of communal duties. Russian and Soviet metaphysics depend on the housing crisis. Kabakov's flight into the white of the canvas does not escape the myths of the Soviet culture and of European modernism.

Some of Kabakov's work was presented in the Museum of Modern Art, in the exhibition appropriately entitled "Dislocations." It is uncanny to see Kabakov's happening in the communal apartment placed (displaced) in the Museum of Modern Art and framed by the pure white museum walls. This is not the virginal whiteness of the avant-garde utopia, but the conventional whiteness of commercial modernism. But then again, one should not feel nostalgia for the purity of avant-garde escapes. In fact, Kabakov's art opens the stage for a clash of styles, alien and cross-cultural encounters, and reflections on utopias: white against white, against white (multiple layers of white paint: never a tautology).

Kabakov populates his communal apartment with eccentric neighbors. Their images are never painted but their private collections are exhibited for us. Among them there are many trash-collectors, graphomaniacs, and untalented artists: the "man who collected the opinions of the others," the "man who never threw anything away," the "composer who combines music with things and images," and even the "person who describes his life through characters." They are artistic impostors who nevertheless constantly search for a minimal aesthetic experience in the communal drudgery. One of such characters is a collector who saves postcards, albums, candy wrappers, and notices with trivial demands and messages. The narrator suggests that the haphazard items and accidental notices the collector obsessively tries to organize might suggest a "new order":

> It seemed to me that in some terrible way, some kind of, how shall I say it, idea of Communality, was expressed in them [the collector's notices], that very same thing which surrounded us all in our common overcrowded apartments. Didn't a certain anticipated and fulfilled dream sound in them, a dream which was ultimately about a rhythmic silence and harmony, about the merging of everything into a certain harmonious figure, it's unimportant what kind of figure: a flower, a star or a pyramid, full of agonizing contradictions which closely surround us. Wasn't that an image of some happy

Utopia into which the daily and hourly witches' Sabbath ringing all around us was to turn?[50]

The idea of utopia has gone full circle. First, the revolutionary utopian designs were "degraded" into the petty intrigues of the communal apartment neighbors and the overcrowdedness of haphazard, impure objects. And then, at the twilight of the Soviet communality, those useless, fragmentary, and imperfect objects can be magically reassembled into a new utopian harmony by the amateur collector, as imagined by the ironic artist and a metaphysician of commonplaces. But this new order is neither a serious revolutionary utopia nor a theoretical blueprint for collective practice. It is only the kitschy dream of an "untalented artist," no less and no more than that.

The End of the Communal Apartment

By the late 1980s a few completely dilapidated communal apartments had been taken over by artists. But suddenly—almost like in downtown Manhattan—they began to be reconquered by newly emerging shady cooperatives and businesses, branches of heretical Buddhist sects prospering in Russia, or some mysterious astrologists anonymous. After the adoption of the 1991 law allowing for privatization of domestic property, a new wave of "gentrification" of the communal apartments began; it turned out to be one of the most intricate exercises for the emerging post-Soviet legal culture. The law inevitably got tangled in the unpredictable (or rather very predictable but never legally accountable) webs of Soviet everyday practices.[51] The privatization policy met with a lot of popular criticism, however, some of it the result of seventy years of building communism, and some the continuation of old Russian folkways and particular attitudes toward property and privacy. A friend reports a conversation on the trolley in 1991: "They are going to give out vouchers; we are going to privatize!"—To which his comrade replies, "Don't use such words in the presence of women." An aging schoolteacher wrote a letter of complaint to the journal *Ogonek*, describing how she was ostracized by the other dwellers of her apartment block when she decided to privatize her one-room standard apartment. She was called "NEP woman, capitalist, and private property owner"—insults that, in Stalin's time, could have deprived people of the rights of citizenship. In popular slang privatization is ironically called *prikhvatization* (grab-what-you-can, from *prikhvatit'*, to grab).

Here is a story about privatization. Our heroine is newly rich: a young woman who works as a financial director for an international "joint venture." She falls in love with an old and fairly dilapidated Moscow communal apartment with bay windows and a neoclassical façade. She would need to pay each communal apartment neighbor a significant fee and also to offer each one a satisfactory place in another apartment. Moreover, she would have to deal with the surviving Soviet bureaucrats of the Housing Committee, an old institution of control that is now becoming obsolete. There are still many Soviet atavisms in law, especially in bureaucratic practice. One of them is the requirement of the resident permit, which now functions as a kind of permit for bribery, or what can be described as the unwritten sanctioning of state bureaucracy racketeering. In this privatization story of one of the communal apartments on Arbat Street, the apparatchik from the Housing Committee demanded a bribe of no less than $20,000 (more, probably, than a year's income for all the residents of the building put together). When the bribe was declined, threatening phone calls and other practices of harassment began. The harassment ceased only when the aspiring owner of the building came back accompanied by the prime minister's wife.[52] The Housing Committee members still understand best the language of the old system of power, protection, and favoritism.

The would-be buyer said that in the eyes of many communal apartment members she took on the role of the former government and offered them what the government always promised but never delivered—apartments of their own. She had to follow all the old rules, overcome attitudes of dependency and entitlement, and fight against the new structures of the shadow economy. Furthermore, the work of resettling a communal collective turned out be more personal than professional; she had to provide psychological as well as financial assistance. The new owner of the apartment had to become a part of that collective, entering the old communal structures of mutual responsibility and becoming responsible for the future of former neighbors. These were the first experiences of the post-Soviet "lawful practices" of domestic privatization. On the one hand, a few brave members of the post-Soviet elite mobilized superhuman efforts to overcome the old Soviet bureaucracy and achieve their dream of a

Western-style private dwelling; on the other hand, though, the great number of former communal apartment dwellers, taught by both the long tradition of subsistence economy and the recent experience of unstable political power, learned that they might survive capitalism but not necessarily inhabit it or make it work for them. Russian privatization follows a crooked path between new and untested democratic laws and old practices of bureaucracy and bribery (which had many precedents and unwritten rules). According to the official statistics of 1993, on the Russian territory 30 million people continued to live in the communal apartment.[53] So the communal apartment ceased to be a primary institution of social control, but it still remains a necessity of life in post-Soviet Russia.

A Homecoming, 1991

Ten years after I left the USSR, I went to visit the house where I had lived in Leningrad. The main entrance was blocked, and on the broken glass door an outdated poster advertised a "video-salon" featuring *Rambo II, Emmanuelle,* and a Brazilian soap opera, *The Slave Isaura Part IV.* The house at 79 Bolshoi Avenue looked the same, but that first impression was disappointing and unevocative. This house was not my home but an impostor, a look-alike, which imitated the "original" so literally as to be uninteresting. "What is happening here?" I asked an elderly woman standing on the street where there used to be a bus stop. "Repairs," she answered. (*Remont* was the first word Walter Benjamin learned on his travels in Russia, when everything seemed to be in the process of being repaired.) "When did it start?" "About ten years ago, or earlier."

So I failed to enter my house through the front door and had to sneak in through the broken wooden fence on the other side of the yard. This altered my narrative of entrance and made the yard look different. I was surrounded by heaps of trash, telephone wires, pieces of old furniture, worn-out slippers (that might have belonged to Uncle Fedia), the pages of a 1979 calendar, mysterious schedules and graphics—all fragments of perfect organization whose purpose was now entirely lost, along with pieces of a broken record by a once-popular French singer of the 1960s. Oh, I think I know the song: "Tombait la neige / Tu ne viendrais pas ce soir / Tombait la neige / Tout est blanc de désespoir."

Climbing through the trash, I made my way upstairs. The apartment looked uncanny. Some of the partitions had been taken off, and the whole framework of our interpersonal and communal interactions was broken. All the wrong doors, which once were locked and hidden behind the wallpaper to keep separate entrances for the neighbors, were open. The communal kitchen, our apartment forum, seemed to have shrunk in size, and so had our interminable corridor, where the communal telephone was located. As a teenager I used to conduct my personal conversations here using elaborate codes and suggestive hints to irritate curious Aunt Shura, who was eavesdropping tactfully behind a half-opened door. The apartment looked like a stage set, and my whole trip seemed predictable and obvious. It was not the space itself, not the house, but the way of inhabiting it that had made it home, and that was forever lost. But a few insignificant things remained: silly white squares on our yellow wallpaper and the floral bas relief on the ceiling, the last remainder of the "decadent" tastes of the first owner of the house. Suddenly I noticed something painted on the wallpaper—a window frame, with a vase of flowers and an open book on the sill, and an empty center. It had been painted by my friend some twelve years ago around a glossy poster of a faraway Mediterranean country; something that I would now consider to be tourist kitsch. The dark room did not have a window and we used to joke that this was our "window to Europe." It was at a difficult time when we were trying to emigrate to what then appeared as a mythical West, but often thought that the escape from the communal apartment would be virtually impossible. Now the poster was gone, a foreign or pseudo-foreign commodity, probably stolen by a local drunkard, only the dream-frame had somehow remained to evoke us and our communal neighbors.

I looked through a cracked kitchen window into the yard: black balconies with holes were still precariously attached to the building and a few uprooted plants continued to inhabit them. An old lonely drunk wandered into the gaping hole of the back entrance, which used to be an unofficial gathering place of the local youth. He stopped to urinate near the skeleton of the old staircase. I took just a few snapshots of the apartment and the yard: the balconies, the trash, the floral bas reliefs. In the center of the yard there was an old truck, looking like it could be from the 1940s, inscribed with the single word DEATH. I thought it would make a good picture, but I decided never to show it to my parents. They had spent most of their adult life in this apartment. However, when I came back and told them that our old house on Petrogradskaia is in repairs, they seemed remarkably indifferent, as if far removed from my somewhat artificial search for memories.

"We heard they were making a movie in the yard. Lenfilm, I think. And they brought an old and rusty truck in. It must have been something about the war and the Leningrad blockade."

"No, no, it was a film about a poet Daniil Kharms who wrote about a man who went to the forest one day and never came back. And then Daniil Kharms left his house one day in 1937 to buy a pack of cigarettes and never came back . . ."

3

Writing Common Places: Graphomania

Graphomania is a disease, say the psychiatrists, an incurable, malignant urge to produce verses, plays, novels, in defiance of the whole world. What talent, what genius, please tell me, what genius has not suffered from this noble disease? And any graphomaniac—note well—the smallest, the lousiest old graphomaniac in the depths of his weak heart believes in his own genius. And who knows, who can say in advance? Surely Shakespeare or Pushkin were graphomaniacs too, genius graphomaniacs . . . They were simply lucky. And if they hadn't been lucky, if they hadn't been published, what then?
> —Abram Tertz, "Graphomaniacs"

Graphomania. The Mania not to create a form, but to impose one's self on others. The most grotesque version of the will to power.
> —Milan Kundera, *Sixty-Three Words*

One can never embrace the unembraceable.
> —Koz'ma Prutkov

History of the Literary Disease

Graphomania (literally, writing mania) is a literary disease, an uncontrollable obsession to write and to be a writer. It is a unique epidemic, a complication of Great Literature. Its grave side effects include feverish plagiarism, genius-envy, and a sadomasochistic relationship with the reader. The graphomaniac is a permanent resident of common places, a kitschman or kitschwoman of letters. The relationship between a genius and a graphomaniac is something like love-hatred, or an unhealthy codependency. The virus of graphomania is widespread, and, as the history of Russian and Soviet literature shows, it is hardly curable.

Graphomania will be regarded here as a broad cultural phenomenon and as a critical trope. It refers to any practice of writing perceived as unhealthy in its own time, whether excessively prolific, excessively banal, ideologically incorrect, or culturally improper. The history of graphomania illuminates the tenuous relation between the art of writing in the singular, and the arts of writing in the plural; between *literature,* which in some cultures constitutes the core of national identity, and everyday writing, which could jeopardize it.

Graphomania is not only about writing banalities and worn-out commonplaces, but also about violating the etiquette of literary behavior. A graphomaniac is someone whose literary behavior is in bad taste, who practices inferior forms of literary communication or styles of self-presentation. Literary behavior is the practice of writing in relation to the existing literary institutions.[1] Boris Eikhenbaum distinguishes between a theatrical and a domestic life of literature, as manifest in the changing forms of literary communication—from the album poems of "an aristocratic poet-dilettante" to the published works of a professional writer and, later in the 1920s, to the newspaper articles on current events written by journalists.[2] What makes a "bad writer" could be an excessive "domestication" of literary communication or a preposterous theatricality that is inappropriate in a given historical moment. Graphomania, more than a private sickness, is a public threat; it dramatizes the tension between writing and publishing (or not publishing), between writing and the presentation of the self.

Graphomania is about handling literary commonplaces clumsily and inappropriately, and about excess: writing too much, plagiarizing too much, behaving too much like a writer. This excess in writerly practice can be pathetic and parodic, embarrassing and revealing. It can function as a way of self-affirmation and self-fashioning as a writer and a figure of powerful cultural prestige; it can also turn into a self-defeating attempt at aesthetic emancipation. Graphomania poses the problem of the boundaries of literature, of the relationship between writing and the making of the self. The history of graphomania reveals an amplitude of nuances in attitudes toward the common-place, ranging from parody to imitation and from estrangement to engagement.

In Russia literature has always been a matter of primary political and national importance. In the cityscape the monuments to the poets rival the monuments to the tsars and party leaders. Moreover, it is not by chance that many of the recent Soviet party leaders, including the organizers of the August 1991 coup, were established writers who wrote under pseudonyms. Thus Brezhnev composed a lengthy trilogy of memoirs; Andropov, once head of the KGB and briefly the head of the Soviet state, indulged in detective fiction; and Yazov, one of the members of the infamous Emergency Committee, was a poet, as was Lukianov, the president of the last Supreme Soviet, who wrote lyrical poems under the pseudonym "Osenev" (Autumnal). The prestige of literature makes the confrontation between genius and graphoma-niac, a legitimate pretender to the throne of Russian letters and an impostor, particularly urgent. The bad writer, victim of mockery and self-mockery, is one of the most pathetic heroes of the Russian cul-tural mythology. But the difference between the graphomaniac and the genius is not always clear.

American dictionaries do not even have an entry on graphomania; this particular mania seems not to be part of the "American heri-tage." Conversely, in the Soviet Union and other Eastern and Central European countries there was an explicit preoccupation, if not an obsession, with the concept.[3] Although the practice of obsessive writ-ing goes far back in history, its dangers become acutely perceived in the early modern period, particularly with the advent of Romanti-cism, when the written word acquires a new sanctity as the mark of genius and the stamp of artistic originality. The critique of obsessive writing coincides also with the spread of literacy among much of the population. One might think in this connection about the many servants and "lady-scribblers" of eighteenth-century English novels, writing endlessly in search of their own voices. Graphomania was diagnosed toward the end of the nineteenth century, a period of medicalization of cultural and artistic phenomena. Max Nordau calls it a disease of degeneracy or decadence, a psycholinguistic disorder that can manifest itself as an "epistolary mania" characterized by the urge to write erotic letters in a style that overuses metaphors. The graphomaniac is afflicted with an insatiable desire to write, while having nothing to write about except his or her own mental and moral ailments.[4] The juxtaposition of "mental" and "moral" is very revealing: for some turn-of-the-century doctors like Nordau, with their own scientific manias, any nonutilitarian kind of writing, whatever its artistic quality, verges on psychic disorder. According to this particular theory of degeneration, any writer is a sick man or a hysterical woman, always on the brink of graphomania. In contrast, Russian and Eastern and Central European graphomania is not a medical but a cultural illness. Graphomania is used as a necessary discriminatory term to preserve a healthy canon of national literature.

Not only is the concept of bad writing problematic: "mania" is even more complicated. In Greek it signifies divine inspiration, ecstasy, and madness. In Socrates' second speech on love Plato laments that in his own "modern times" mania has been misunderstood. It is a "splendid thing," "a gift of the gods," and "a sign of divine guidance." Moreover, the true poet cannot exist without "the Muses' madness (mania) in his soul"; he cannot depend solely on "art" (techne, technique).[5] In fact, the medicalization of mania in contemporary European languages is in itself a revelatory usage. If we play with linguistic potential, we might imagine that had the word "graphomaniac" emerged in a different historical moment, it could have signified a divinely guided poet. In this fantastic conjecture, genius and graphomaniac could have exchanged roles.

This little linguistic game points at the crucial instability of the diagnosis of graphomania. The syndrome crosses the borders of both aesthetics and pathology, of private obsessions and public harassments. It is an important cultural symptom that points at the changing historical status of writing and at the growing prestige of literature. One could try to distinguish—in a desperate if not maniacal attempt at classification—between graphomania in quotation marks and graphomania without quotation marks, or to describe the practitioners according to the predominant root of the two that make up "graphomania": whether it is love of writing or obsession that drives the author, a passion for scribbling or the will to power. (The first kind can be provisionally called "graphophiliacs" and the second, "scribblomaniacs.")

Milan Kundera and Andrei Sinyavsky present alternative descriptions of graphomania East and West. Kundera, in *The Book of Laughter and Forgetting*, writes about the Western mania of writing and of publishing countless books about oneself in countries "with a radical absence of significant social change . . . where nothing really happens" (that is, Western Europe of the late 1970s): "If general isolation causes graphomania, mass graphomania itself reinforces and aggravates the feeling of general isolation. The invention of print originally promoted mutual understanding. In the era of graphomania the writing of books has the opposite effect: everyone surrounds himself with his own writings, as the wall of mirrors cuts off all voices from without."[6]

The purpose of such writing is not to communicate with others but to prevent any kind of human communication; it is a form of self-advertisement, a continuous composition of the self and its individual variations. Kundera reports his encounter with a taxi driver in Paris who suffered from insomnia and spent all his nights writing the book of his life—and not by way of a family chronicle for his grandchildren (they "don't give a damn"). "Graphomania is not a desire to write letters, diaries, or family chronicles (to write for oneself, or for one's immediate family); it is a desire to write books (to have a public of unknown readers). In this sense, the taxi driver and Goethe share the same passion. What distinguishes Goethe from the taxi driver is the result of the passion, not the passion itself."[7]

According to Andrei Sinyavsky, a writer and famous dissident of the 1960s, it is state censorship that encourages graphomania, since it gives the unpublished writer the chance to be an "unrecognized genius" and a victim of totalitarianism. In the story "Graphomaniacs," the president of the club of graphomaniacs, Galkin, explains this point:

> We live in a remarkable country. Everybody writes and writes, even schoolchildren and pensioners . . . A general popular inclination towards elegant literary expression. And do you know what we have to thank for it? Censorship! It is our mother, it is the dear one who caressed us all. Abroad it is simpler. Some lord publishes a little book of *vers-libre,* and it is at once evident that it's shit. Nobody reads it, nobody buys it, and the lord will occupy himself with some useful labor, energetics, stomatology . . . But we live our whole lives in pleasant ignorance, we amuse ourselves with hopes . . . The state itself, devil take it, gives you the right—invaluable right!—to consider yourself an unrecognized genius.[8]

Although these two exiles, one from Czechoslovakia and the other from Soviet Russia, write about graphomania from different angles, the fact that this is of concern to them reveals how deeply they value the high literary culture.

The contemporary émigré writer Sasha Sokolov complained that in "local [American] language the good old title 'graphomaniac' in our [Russian] understanding does not exist."[9] In the eighteenth and nineteenth centuries English, French, and German writers make many satirical references to "poetasters" and "poetesses"—all kinds of impure poets with various suffixes, the marks of graphomania. But such satires have become unpopular (with the exception, perhaps, of Jorge Luis Borges), and the word "graphomania" itself has become obsolete. The stock figure of "bad writer" hardly exists in contemporary Western mythology, where we might find a ham actor, a bad cop, a fake cowboy, an amateur gangster, or a rock musician who plagiarizes songs and lip-synchs to someone else's soundtrack. Graphomania yielded to video-mania; the obsession with writing is an anachronism, an exotic disease like Spanish influenza.

The persistence and survival of Russian graphomania tells us a great deal about the deep-seated national belief in art and in the possibility of aesthetic emancipation against all odds. In the Russian literary tradition the graphomaniac is the alter ego of every great Russian classic. Many writers invest a good deal of inspiration in creating a prototypical figure of the bad writer, and take a deliberate delight in writing bad poetry or bad prose in the name of the fictitious graphomaniac. Here I will present a gallery of illustrious graphomaniacs that offer an alternative history of Russian literature, from its Golden Age to its Silver Age, and finally to the electronic age of post-glasnost'. Graphomania cannot be diagnosed in abstract; in order to write about graphomania, one has to create the figure of a graphomaniac, to dramatize the disease. Creating the parodic character of a bad writer is a way of exorcizing the demons of language and guarding against the invisible seduction of commonplaces and conventionality. Many writers created pseudonyms that turned into literary legends; at the same time, many fictional graphomaniacs acquired a real-life following. Graphomania complicates the relationship between author and character, between the author and his multiple personae and pseudonyms, the fictional and semi-fictional selves that incarnate Romantic geniuses and graphomaniacs. In the twentieth century, self-inflicted graphomania offers a unique insight into the Russian and Soviet avant-garde tradition, while the never-acknowledged graphomania of the writers of the generation after the avant-garde helps to shed some light on the experience of Socialist Realism and the ethical and aesthetic compromises of the writers.

Despite all the diversity, one feature of graphomania remains constant; it is an embarrassment to literary institutions. An as-yet-unwritten comparative history of graphomania in different cultures would be a most revealing history of the interaction between literature and politics. The embarrassment of writing can be made harmless by the official establishment. It might be dismissed by laughter, coopted, or violently destroyed. The graphomaniac can be both a conformist and an outcast.

My incomplete but representative gallery of graphomaniacs includes nineteenth-century Russia's most prolific author, Count Khvostov; the Romantic poet Lensky from Pushkin's *Eugene Onegin*; Dostoevsky's pathetic and sympathetic letter-writer Makar Devushkin from *Poor Folk*; the violent author of moral fables and epigrams, Captain Lebiadkin, from *The Possessed*; the most famous nineteenth-century graphomaniac, Koz'ma Prutkov, a literary persona created by Alexei Tolstoy and his cousins; the lady-scribblers, including Chekhov's housewives and Nabokov's poetess-psychiatrist Liza Pnin-Wind; the idealized folk singer and mail-carrier Strelka from Stalin's favorite film, *Volga, Volga*; the last avant-garde poets and ironic subversive graphomaniacs, Oleinikov and Kharms, who paid with their lives for their literary games; Socialist Realist writers; the heralds of glasnost', and the members of Abram Tertz's club of graphomaniacs. The last two examples are a nostalgic Russian émigrée, part-time receptionist, and graduate student of Romanticism, and the post-Soviet taxi driver who shared his oeuvre with me during our memorable ride in the summer of 1991.

The Forgotten Classics

One of the first widely parodied bad writers, both in his texts and in real life, was Count Khvostov, whose work bridged the eighteenth and nineteenth centuries. His contemporaries nicknamed him "Grafov" (the Russian for "count" is *graf*), which might be regarded as a

double pun on Khvostov's ostentatious aristocratism and on his graphomania *avant la lettre*, so to speak.[10] This author of odes for all
occasions was far more prolific and lived much longer than most of
the Russian writers of the nineteenth century. Count Khvostov is an
anachronism: an eighteenth-century gentleman opting for the prestige
of a Romantic poet. He adopted the eighteenth-century custom of
sending literary works to friends and swamped them with his writings. He kept a circle of panegyrists to whom he paid daily allow-
ances and upon whom he occasionally bestowed professorial
positions. He sent his marble bust to the sailors of the Kronstadt, and
distributed his portraits all over Russia.[11] Khvostov is better known
as the satirical protagonist of the many epigrams written by the poets
of Pushkin's generation, for whom he personified "sublime stupidity."
It often seems that if Count Khvostov had not existed, he would have
to be invented. He lives in the history of Russian literature as a
literary personality, a real but also mythical ancestor of many
fictional graphomaniacs. Count Khvostov became ridiculous because
he exceeded the literary etiquette of the time and abused the poetic
commonplaces.

   Pushkin, acclaimed as the founder of the Russian literary language,
is also one of the first poets to confront seriously the problem of the
commonplace and cliché. If Baudelaire merely dreamed about "inventing a banality," Pushkin virtually did just that: he introduced
many expressions into Russian which became "expressions of national
wisdom" and the commonplaces of more-or-less educated Russians.

   In *Eugene Onegin* Pushkin created a figure of a mediocre practitioner of romantic clichés in art and life—Lensky, one of the first "failed
poets" of Russian literature. Lensky is also the first to suffer the tragic
fate that became uncannily paradigmatic for many actual nineteenth-
and twentieth-century poets as they committed suicide, were killed in
duels, or were murdered for political reasons. Lensky's portrait is
made up of romantic clichés; he has beautiful dark curls, dreams of
freedom, harbors a charming naïveté in his heart and passion in his
soul. He writes poetry and admires Kant, and also blond Russian
beauties whom the narrator does not even bother to describe since
they can be found in any romantic novel. Lensky's banality appears
innocuous, if not charming, yet it is partly responsible for his death.
Lensky's senseless death in a duel is the result of a conspiracy of
different social and aesthetic clichés, of noble behavior and of roman-

tic self-fashioning, which perpetuate a seamless relationship between literature and life.

The night before the duel Lensky composes an elegy, a confession in the first person that is full of of romantic commonplaces:

> Where, o where have you gone,
> Golden days of my spring?
> What does the coming day prepare for me?
> In vain does my gaze try to seize it
> In the deep darkness it hides.
> There's no need, the law of fate is just.
> Whether I fall, pierced by an arrow,
> Or whether it flies past,
> All is good: the determined hour of dream and vigil approaches;
> Even the day of cares is blessed,
> Blessed even the approach of darkness![12]

Lensky's elegy combines lines and references from Karamzin, Goethe, Baratynsky, Kuchelbekker, and Zhukovsky.[13] "This is what we call 'romanticism,' although I don't see much of it here,"—the narrator ironically comments in one of his digressive parentheses. Lensky's elegy reflects the paradoxical romantic attitudes toward clichés: a denunciation of the common language of the mob combined with an unacknowledged debt to the commonplaces of Romanticism. At the same time, the anticipation of death and the farewell to the beloved in Lensky's elegy turn out to be more than "literary facts": his romantic commonplaces anticipate his actual fate. As Lensky wishes to make those romantic conventions into conventions of verisimilitude, he ends up living out his own—or rather his creatively plagiarized—poetic tropes. Lensky's death is the outcome of a nonironic attitude toward romantic banalities.

Pushkin places Lensky's conventionally poetic text within an everyday prosaic context: the young man, tired after his all-night poetic wake, falls asleep on the word "ideal." The scene of romantic inspiration turns into a comic scene of everyday writing. Lensky is described as a charming contradiction that undermines his single style of romantic self-fashioning. He is a learned poet and "an endearing ignoramus in the matters of heart"; his worldly pose masks his innocence. Lensky is not a reified parody: the narrator does not keep him at a constant level of ironic distance from himself. The narrator's attitude toward Lensky, as well as toward the romantic clichés, shifts. At the last, Pushkin incorporates Lensky's elegy into his text; he assimilates it to the rhythm and meter of his own strophe. And the parody is aimed not so much at Lensky's poetry as at his self-styliza-tion as a poet.

At the end of the chapter the narrator, a chatty confessional impos-tor and one of Pushkin's literary alter egos, returns to the motifs of Lensky's elegy and brings in some autobiographical facts from Pushkin's life. In his own final elegiac stanza, he combines self-con-scious play with poetic commonplaces, such as the conventional rhymes of *mladost'* (youth) and *sladost'* (sweetness) alongside some wistful reflections on life. We are invited to reexamine the banalities about fleeting youth and its ideals and, along with the author, to reinhabit their tragic triviality. Near the end of this chapter, Pushkin moves toward a realistic reinvention of banality. There is in Pushkin's writings a nostalgia for certain nonromantic (and non-poshlye) com-mon ways that would lead to common happiness. Pushkin quotes Chateaubriand often ("there is no happiness but in the common ways"), sometimes appropriating the words as his own in letters to the friend of his youth, or else giving them to his fictional heroines. However, common ways do not offer an easy linear narrative of happiness, but only a crossroads. Iurii Lotman points to the ambigu-ity of the "common routes" in Pushkin: "The image of the common ways appears to double, vacillating between the healthy prose of life and trivial (poshlaia) routine, and correspondingly, the rebellion against them at times takes the shape of romantic egoism, and at other times appears as a natural human need of freedom."[14]

The pursuit of common happiness—"common" here not in the sense of "shared," but in the sense of "ordinary"—unlike some other plots and projects of Pushkin's did not become a common topos in Russian literature, dominated as that was by the search for redemp-tive suffering.

At the end of his long poem Pushkin expresses a desire to write prose. If Pushkin-the-poet engenders a romantic poet-graphomaniac obsessed with being a poet both in love and in life, Pushkin the prose-writer creates a series of figures of prose-writer-ventriloquists who record stories heard from others, like Ivan Belkin, author of the celebrated *Belkin Tales,* or like the unnamed author of *History of the Village of Goriukhino.*[15] The Goriukhino chronicler is enamored not so much of literature as of the glamorous and glorious figure of the *litterateur.* He comes from a background of impoverished gentry, and his literary education amounts to the tutoring of the local sexton, three months at a boarding school, and avid readings of N. G. Kurganov's *Newest Primer,* a popular eighteenth-century compendium that contains elementary information on every subject, from astrology to grammar, popular proverbs, occasional salacious anecdotes, and moral tales. The gentleman from Goriukhino makes himself a notebook with the firm resolution to cover its pages with whatever he can come up with—a perfect recipe for graphomania, agony over white pages in pursuit of glory. He moves from genre to genre, from one half-mastered convention to semi-ignorance of another. Starting with an epic poem about the Viking Prince Riurik and quitting at the third line, he switches to tragedy (though still about Riurik), then attempts a ballad, only to fail again. Finally he finds himself writing history: "To be a judge, a witness and a prophet of centuries and people seemed to me the highest position available for a writer."[16] Instead of writing the history of the world (which would be plagiarism, since that had already been done), he decides to write the history of his native village, Goriukhino, a kind of microcosm of Russian life.

Writing the village history, which is a record of local anecdotes, oral mythology, and written documents—a microhistory as compared to the history of the Russian empire or something equally "noble and glorious"—presents a problem of genre. This generic hesitation between fiction and history, which is at the very core of Pushkin's "prose writing," is humorously played out in the narrator's unfinished "History." (The Russian word "history" is used for both story and history, and in this case this ambiguity needs to be preserved.) Curiously, Pushkin's semiliterate graphomaniac tells some actual episodes from the history of the Pushkins' family village. It is as if the *History of the Village of Goriukhino* can be justified and turned into a writerly project only with the help of humor and fiction. This hesitation of genre, and of the prose writer's self-fashioning, is characteristic of Pushkin's later writings involving history, which result in "double texts" of history and fiction, such as *The Captain's Daughter* and the *History of the Pugachev Rebellion,* for example.[17]

The chronicler of the *History of the Village of Goriukhino* gives us several portraits of village *litterateurs,* since in Goriukhino "sciences, arts and poetry were blossoming since ancient times." One of the local figures presented is Archip the Bald, whose works "in their tenderness are not inferior to Virgil's eclogues, and in the beauty of imagination are superior to the idylls of Mr. Sumarokov. Although in the whimsicality of the verse they are second to the most recent products of our muses, they are equal to them in wit and fancy."[18] If Archip the Bald is a folkloric bard, Terentii is a more modern figure; he is called a *grammotei*, someone versed in letters and in grammar (often the only person who could read and write in the Russian village). Terentii, however, excels in various graphological arts—he can write beautifully with both his right and left hands, and at the time of his death was practicing writing with his right foot. Terentii is not only a respected village scribe known for his composition of letters, papers, and passport applications, but also an obsessive graphologist. Or perhaps he is a pure graphomaniac in the literal sense of the word—obsessed with any kind of writing, physical, bureaucratic, and personal. Terentii promises to play a prominent role in the story, but since the tale is unfinished, his role in it remains a mystery.

The repertoire of cultural roles given to the "great national genius" Alexander Pushkin throughout the nineteenth and early twentieth centuries is much narrower than Pushkin's own repertoire of writers and poets, ventriloquists and impersonators, romantic sufferers and semi-ignorant literati, geniuses and graphomaniacs. Pushkin's cultural fate was the fate of a quasi-romantic poet, a larger-than-life monument to the Russian national spirit, and occasionally a classical example of national kitsch.[19] Pushkin has been reified as a statue—a fate he was so much afraid of. In Moscow the celebrated Pushkin monument by Opekushin has moved through the cityscape, following the ideological whims of the Soviet authorities. Any twentieth-century poet who wishes to talk or walk with Pushkin has first to wrestle with his overpowering monument.

Yet Pushkin's uncanonical, apocryphal doubles have proliferated throughout Russian culture. First there was the "pseudo-Pushkin," the author of many light poems and epigrams which, in most cases, the real poet never wrote. Pushkin turned into a name for collective authorship. By the twentieth century Abram Tertz calls him "Pushkinshulluer," a kind of Chaplinesque character, a figure from the Russian comic theater who, among other magic tricks, has a real knack for rhyming. Tertz's Pushkin is a somewhat heretical and sacrilegious character, yet in his fantastic "strolls with Pushkin" Tertz, better than anyone else, manages to recover the aesthetic play that is at the core of Pushkin's texts.[20] Galkin, from the story "Graphomaniacs," claims that Tolstoy and Chekhov were genius graphomaniacs. Kundera likewise claims that the graphomaniac and the great writer go through the same adventures of writing. "Poetry has to be somewhat silly" *(glupovata),* wrote Pushkin. Contemporaries often parodied this line by changing "poetry" to "the poet," and ridiculing "silly poets." But the trap of Pushkin's line lies in its resistance to paraphrase; it resists the creation of a monodrama of the national poet. Pushkin, then, is the first genius graphomaniac who excelled in the Protean art of shifting from sympathy to irony, from dense literariness to frivolous casualness.

Dostoevsky: Graphomania between Good and Evil

Dostoevsky offers us a broad spectrum of graphomaniacs and creators-impostors, from a sympathetic little copyist to the devil himself. A poor clerk and obsessive letter writer, Makar Devushkin is perhaps one of the most sympathetic graphomaniacs in Russian literature. For Makar letter-writing is a means of communication with his beloved Varvara, but also his only mode of self-realization. Throughout his letters he continuously flirts with the idea of becoming a writer or even a poet, the author of a book of verses. He dreams that all the duchesses and countesses will recognize him as he strolls on Nevsky Avenue, so that he might even have to replace his old worn-out boots to preserve his writer's dignity. Letters offer him an ample opportunity to improve his literary style.

Literary style preoccupies Makar Devushkin almost as much as Varvara's response; at times he seems to write letters for himself and to himself, barely preserving the conventional epistolary dialogue. The writerly ambition is entirely absent from the letters of his addressee, Varvara, although it is she who gives Makar the works of Pushkin and Gogol and seems to have a more refined literary taste.

Several heroes of Balzac and Flaubert are represented as failed poets; for instance, Lucien de Rubempré from *Les Illusions perdues* and even Frédéric from *L'Education sentimentale,* but the main aspiration of French nineteenth-century heroes and anti-heroes is social climbing. This is very uncommon in the Russian tradition. The little man in nineteenth-century Russian literature can only aspire to be a writer; a Balzacian social climbing is hardly possible. Social mobility is not a prominent feature of Russian life, but in the second part of the nineteenth century there is more freedom for imaginary self-fashioning by lower-class urban dwellers, as well as for the new Russian intelligentsia. Writing provides the cheapest access to cultural prestige. The making of the self, which for some is equivalent to the remaking of the world, is possible chiefly through the work of fiction. Likewise, in Russian culture the practice of literature tends to be perceived as the practice of a secular form of spirituality that can promise a kind of rebirth or aesthetic emancipation, creating the perfect conditions for graphomania.

In this respect letters are of particular interest. The epistolary genre is borderline between *belles lettres* and everyday writing; letters move in and out of literature, reflecting the changing conceptions of literariness and the shifting boundaries of literature.[21] What makes Dostoevsky a "great writer," in Belinsky's evaluation, and what makes Makar Devushkin a potential graphomaniac, is only a matter of novelistic framing.

For Makar Devushkin, writing letters is a way of endowing with meaning his everyday experiences and ordinary pleasures, like taking a walk with Varvara on the islands, or sending her a little package of caramels bought with his last thirty kopeks, as well as dealing with the daily humiliations from his landlady or from his fellow-clerks. The ending of *Poor Folk* is a pathetic cry for communication, a plea to continue writing at any cost:

> Dearest, dearest one! But you must write me one more letter telling me everything . . . Otherwise it will be the last letter, my heavenly angel, but it is impossible for it to be the last letter. It can't be so suddenly, just like that, the very last one. But no, I'll write, and you write too . . . I am starting to get some style into my writing. Oh, my darling, what has style got to do with it? I don't even know what I am writing. I have no idea, I don't know anything, and I'm not reading over it, not correcting my style, and I am writing just for the sake of writing, just for the sake of writing more to you . . . My precious, my darling, my dearest![22]

The last lines of Devushkin's letter are full of desperate contradictions: he both knows and does not wish to acknowledge that this is

his last letter. The letter ends and begins with the same address to
Varvara, as if wishing to begin perpetually again, to defy closure and
the break in communication. Even in the last lines he cannot entirely
give up his obsession with literary style: he is both proud and
ashamed of it. He is writing, at once, "for the sake of writing" and
"for the sake of writing more to [Varvara]." The two claims are
contradictory and complementary.

Devushkin's writing endows him with dignity and gives style and
sense to his daily pursuits. His is a kind of existential graphomania,
potentially an emancipatory practice. Aesthetic emancipation, a way
of distancing himself from experience and reflecting upon it, is the
only freedom he can hope for. In those letters he is indeed the author
of his own life and not a pawn or a minor character in somebody
else's game.

Devushkin's relationship with literature is that of love-hatred. On
the one hand, he admiringly calls it a "delicacy" *(ob'edenie)* and
exalts the life of a writer. On the other hand, Devushkin is afraid of
being used by literature and by writers who can make a "lampoon"
of his life. He fears becoming a voiceless character in a prosaic tale
without any uplifting potential. Dostoevsky's irony consists of his
attempt to confront Makar Devushkin with his literary ancestors, the
little men of Pushkin and Gogol. Devushkin immediately identifies
with Pushkin's Samson Vyrin and Gogol's Akaky Akakievich. The
publication of Pushkin's "The Station Master" and Gogol's "The
Overcoat" is perceived by Devushkin as his own public humiliation:
"they'll write a lampoon on you, and your whole public and private
life is thrown open to literature—it's all published, read, mocked, and
gossiped about." He does not see any purpose in it: "What's good
about it? It's just an empty example from vile, everyday life."[23] These
books seem to violate his private space, the space in which he can
compose his personal letters, dream, and develop his own literary
style.

Dostoevsky seems to realize that writing *about* "poor folk" does
not necessarily mean writing *for* them. Indeed, Devushkin prefers
popular romantic stories of overwhelming passions: edifying, occasionally risqué, and always neatly balanced with a happy ending. He
opts for the literature of escape and diversion from the everyday over
the great Russian literary tradition. *Poor Folk* is one of the few
sympathetic (even if somewhat ironic, on the part of Dostoevsky)

attempts of a major Russian writer to include popular mass fiction within his work. The novel tells the story of Ermak and Zuleika, a romantic version of an old Russian legend dating back to the time of the conquest of Siberia in the sixteenth century, and talks about a Western-style novel by Rataziaev, entitled *Italian Passions*. Rataziaev is one of Dostoevsky's many bad writers. If Makar Devushkin is obsessed with writing for the sake of writing and personal survival, Rataziaev is a fashionable graphomaniac, accepted in the second-rate literary salon of the Countess N. and published. Rataziaev is also a modern personage, extremely efficient and prolific, interested in new means of mass communication and print, such as book illustrations. This early kitsch writer consciously and successfully composes for popular tastes. Graphomania in Dostoevsky is a ubiquitous disease to which any Russian is prone, whether poor clerk, member of the nobility, or even murderer.

Another evil graphomaniac in Dostoevsky is the violent, treacherous drunkard Captain Lebiadkin, from *The Possessed*. He has writerly ambitions and composes moral fables about spiders, odes to governesses, and love poems. Here is a typical example of Lebiadkin's oeuvre: "Once upon a time there was a cockroach, / A cockroach from childhood / And then he fell into a glass / Full of fly poison . . . / The cockroach took up space, / The flies started to cry out, / 'Our glass is very full,' / They shouted out to Jupiter. / But while their shouting was going on, / Nikifor came along, / An ex-treme-ly noble old man."[24]

Lebiadkin's heroic cockroach, together with the "buzzing bug" *(zhuk zhuzhzhal)* from Pushkin's *Eugene Onegin* (which makes only a brief cameo appearance in the novel in one line), are prominent insects from the nineteenth-century literary canon that inspired an avant-garde and absurdist following in the twentieth century.

In Dostoevsky's later works the positive characters tend to be the opposite of graphomaniacs: inarticulate, tongue-tied, clumsy. Such are Shatov and Kirilov in *The Possessed*, Count Myshkin in *The Idiot*, and Aliosha Karamazov. In the Dostoevskian universe there is something sinful in the writerly obsession; the gift of words is a treacherous gift that can be too easily profaned. Dostoevsky tries to exorcise bad writers from his own text, as if purifying himself from his own writerly indiscretions through parody. According to Nabokov (another writer who proliferated the images of graphoma-

niacs in his texts), Dostoevsky himself often succumbed to the disease
of bad writing, not so much when he tried to describe evil as when
he tried to describe the good.

Dostoevsky is both a self-conscious pioneer of the "banality of
evil" and an unselfconscious prophet of the "banality of the good."
Possibly it is his predilection for the melodramatic staging of metaphysical conflicts that plunges him into the depths of poshlost'. This
is the central issue in Nabokov's ironic and aristocratically modernist critique of Dostoevsky. In *Crime and Punishment* (VII, 4),
Nabokov finds a "glorified cliché" which in his opinion makes "the
whole Dostoevskian edifice crumble ethically and aesthetically." It is
the scene of Sonia and Raskolnikov reading the Bible, which Dostoevsky presents as "the murderer and the harlot reading the eternal
book." In this description, Nabokov's ironic tone turns into ethical
indignation:

> "The murderer and the harlot" and "the eternal book"—what a
> triangle . . . I suggest that neither a true artist nor a true moralist—
> neither a good Christian nor a good philosopher—neither a poet nor
> a sociologist—should have placed, side by side, in one breath, in one
> gust of false eloquence, a killer together with whom?—a poor street-
> walker, bending their completely different heads over that holy
> book. The Christian God, as understood by those who believe in the
> Christian God, has pardoned the harlot nineteen centuries ago. The
> killer, on the other hand, must be first of all examined medically.
> The two are on completely different levels. The inhuman and idiotic
> crime of Raskolnikov cannot be even remotely compared to the
> plight of a girl who impairs human dignity by selling her body. The
> murderer and the harlot reading the eternal book—what nonsense.
> There is no rhetorical link between a filthy murderer, and this
> unfortunate girl. There is only the conventional link of the Gothic
> novel and the sentimental novel. It is a shoddy literary trick, not a
> masterpiece of pathos and piety.[25]

Nabokov's moral indignation is crucial to our archeology of common places. Melodrama has been defined as "a set of dramatic conventions" that presents a certain code of the apprehension of ethics
in "a heightened spectacular form."[26] In the nineteenth century melodrama turns into an "expressionism of moral imagination." Melodrama provides an incestuous and scandalous connection between

the realist novel of the nineteenth century and sentimental and Gothic popular fiction. In the Russian cultural imagination there is more tolerance for melodramatic modes; the subsequent reaction against melodrama is much less pronounced and comes much later than in the West. Moreover, since literature never aimed at and never was forced to assume a cultural autonomy, it performed the functions of philosophy, religion, and political agitation. Melodrama, then, became the perfect vehicle for a diversity of conflicts, with heightened spectacular special effects that elicited immediate response on the part of the audience.

In his discussion of Dostoevsky, Nabokov wishes to distinguish between "sentimental" and "sensitive." "Sentimental" is a "non-artistic exaggeration of familiar emotion, meant to provoke automatically traditional compassion in the reader." "Traditional" and "automatic" are used here as synonyms; in other words, Nabokov is not idealizing "traditional" but seeing it as a realm of clichés both emotional and artistic. In Nabokov's view the aesthetic is parallel to the ethical; Dostoevsky's flaw, therefore, is his occasional artistic deafness that leads to moral blindness. To a large extent owing to Dostoevsky, Russian ethics became inseparable from melodrama, which, since Dostoevsky, became a privileged genre for the theater of the "Russian soul." In reading Dostoevsky today it is often difficult to discern when clichés of melodrama pass for the depth of emotion or of metaphysics, and when genuine insights into the human psyche are obfuscated for us because of our fear of melodrama. He is a master of melodrama who elevated the genre to philosophical depth; at the same time, he set an unfortunate convention for Russian philosophy as well as for the philosophy of Russianness, with their spectacular and predictable dramas of good and evil embodied in Russia and the West, Russians and foreigners. In Dostoevsky's works the staging of the eternal "cursed questions" of Russian boys inescapably demands melodrama.

It is not by chance that a derivative from Dostoevsky's name became a Russian expression: *Dostoevskishchina* ("Dostoevskianism"), which refers to a heightened melodramatic ambiance. *Dostoevskishchina* is a reduction to absurdity, or a reduction to cliché, of Dostoevsky's novelistic universe. Unfortunately, it is the banal prophet of apocalypse that has become a hero of the early years of perestroika and of the new brand of Russian nationalism. It is not the "dialogi-

cal" Dostoevsky who is reread but the melodramatic one; not the
ludic master of the banality of evil, a master-puppeteer of trivial
devils and doubles, but the master-metaphysician and prophet of
Russian salvation. But perhaps this is merely one of his personae, a
graphomaniac, a distorted double of the great novelist. Is he just a
trivial ghost, like Ivan's devil, or is he indeed more powerful than the
novelist himself?

Graphomania under a Pseudonym: Koz'ma Prutkov

Perhaps the most celebrated and prolific graphomaniac of the nineteenth century is Koz'ma Prutkov, a little man with huge political and
literary ambitions. He is a self-proclaimed genius author of many
plays, fables, poems, and aphorisms, including ballads about old
Armenians and the Don Cossacks, "letters from Korinthus" (from
"ancient Greek"), a Spanish *romancero* about the siege of Pamba,
lyric poems "as if from Heine," Slavophilic dedications, and most
important, the famous "Project for the Introduction of Unanimous
Thinking in Russia." His ambition is not limited to the desire to
rewrite the history of world art; he wishes to change life itself.
Koz'ma, however, is not a member of the liberal intelligentsia but a
radical conservative.

   This literary personality was created by a group of witty and
free-thinking young writers: Alexei K. Tolstoy and his cousins, the
Zhemchuzhnikov brothers. In the early 1850s they begin to publish
the works of their "genius friend" Koz'ma Prutkov in the journal *The
Contemporary*. This personage was destined to have a long literary
career, and his fame has survived much longer than that of his
authors—strong proof of the graphomaniac's vitality. In fact, in 1913
there was a huge celebration of the fiftieth anniversary of Prutkov's
death, perhaps more sumptuous than the celebration of the fiftieth
anniversary of Alexei K. Tolstoy's death.

   Koz'ma Prutkov turned into a banal Frankenstein who haunted its
creators with a monstrous liveliness. The Prutkov phenomenon is a
rare, although not unique, instance of the creation of a literary or
parodic personality that acquires a life of its own. Several writers of
the time began to publish under the hospitable name "Prutkov," and
so many new works were attributed to Koz'ma that his creators had
to fight against false attribution. They fell victim to a vicious circle of

authorship in trying to preserve the "originality and purity" of their celebrated master of banality. The Zhemchuzhnikov brothers wrote numerous letters to the editors of *The Contemporary* explaining exactly which works belonged to Prutkov, and denouncing Nekrasov, Dobroliubov, Panaev, and others for trying to pass their work as his. "Prutkov" offered a seductive form of authorship, a justification for light forms of graphomania, self-indulgent practices of wit, social parody, and gratuitous writerly fun.

Koz'ma Prutkov is one of the most avid collectors of commonplaces, ranging from official bureaucratic banalities to poetic gems. (Prutkov liked to call them "aphorisms.") In one sentence he sums up Kant's theory of the sublime: "One cannot embrace the unembraceable," or in an alternative version—"spit into the eye of the one who will tell you that you can embrace the unembraceable."[27] Then he offers his description of Romantic genius: "Genius is like a hill looming above the plain." Or consider certain proto-surrealistic pronouncements, such as: "If you read 'buffalo' on the cage of an elephant, you should not believe your own eyes." (This particular gem of wisdom is a reversal of "Ceci n'est pas une pipe" scribed under the picture of a pipe on René Magritte's famous painting representing a pipe.) There are also general observations on the human condition: "Wisdom is like turtle soup—it is not accessible to everyone"; or "Some people are like sausages—what you stuff them with, they carry inside themselves." Analogy and tautology are Prutkov's favorite devices. Occasionally his phrases are moralistic and prescriptive—like the secret-police command "Beware!"—or bureaucratically authoritarian—"If you have a fountain—shut it down. Let the fountain rest."[28]

Koz'ma merges literary and political banalities. He writes in "officialese," the language of official ukazes, bureaucratic procedures, and judicial clichés. The copyist's language is turned into a literary language. Prutkov redeems Akaky Akakievich's silence and Makar Devushkin's timid attempts at improving his literary style with enormous self-complacency. Prutkov's writing applies the official *(kazennyi)* language to what passes for Russian folk wisdom, mixing old Russian proverbs advocating conformity and obedience with the official ideology of "autocracy, orthodoxy, and the people's spirit." "Everything human is foreign to him," write his creators about Koz'ma, who occasionally sounds like the voice of the bureaucratic

machine, a kind of imaginary nineteenth-century computer programmed to pronounce officially approved commonplaces. This language of *kazennye poshlosti* will be parodied again in the twentieth
century in its new version, the Soviet officialese.[29]

Prutkov insists, however, that his works should not be read as
parodies but rather as "imitations." He claims to have analyzed the
works of all the successful poets and synthesized them in his own
writing. This is Prutkov's theory of artistic mimesis: to imitate, not
nature, but its successful imitations by other artists.

The relation between parody and imitation in Prutkov's reiterations
of artistic clichés and conventions is quite intriguing. Parody, in Tynianov's view, requires the presence of the parodied material; it is a kind
of dialogue with another text.[30] At times in Prutkov's translation of
the masterpieces the parodied text was clearly present, as was quite
obvious to his educated contemporaries. Other poems, especially the
aphorisms, are simply worn-out expressions of Russian cultural
myths, proverbial statements that perpetuate the existing order of
things. Irony is never inscribed within Prutkov's texts: rather, irony
results from the reader's interaction with the text. The reader is
invited to be an accomplice of the multiple *double-entendres* of the
creators of Koz'ma Prutkov. Yet Prutkov's masterpieces are irreducible to mere parodies. Consider the poem "Junger Schmidt":

> The leaf fades. The summer is passing.
> The hoar-frost is silver . . .
> Junger Schmidt wants to shoot himself with his pistol.
> Wait, mad one, once again
> The foliage will revive!
> Junger Schmidt! My word of honor,
> The summer will return![31]

Amidst all the appropriate nature clichés—from autumnal melancholia to silver wintry delights—Junger Schmidt, a Werther look-
alike, is contemplating suicide. The poet attempts to cheer him up
while misplacing accents, violating meter, and giving the most con-
vincing and circular of all arguments, that of nature's circularity:
"Junger Schmidt, take my word for it, the summer will return!" This
poem is beyond parody and imitation: it includes an indescribable
little something, a kind of naïve writerly excess—the sheer pleasures
of rhyming, playing, and mixing styles. It has the inimitable naïveté

and sloppy good-naturedness of the great Russian genius Prutkov. Perhaps these pearls of genial absurdity and pleasures of the text, this silly and mischievous letting-go in the writing, is what constitutes the immortal signature of Prutkov. The mask of the self-complacent graphomaniac gave his creators a certain degree of unconventional freedom of play they may never have allowed themselves under their own names, liberating them from some of the more serious diseases of literary authorship. (One wonders in this respect about the historical plays of Alexei Tolstoy, which imitate the style of the times. Are they to be regarded as parodies, occasional inadvertent imitations of Koz'ma?)

Koz'ma's closest foreign relatives are Flaubert's loony civil servants Bouvard and Pécuchet. (Incidentally, the two Russian words listed in Bouvard and Pécuchet's *Dictionary of Received Ideas* seem to come directly from Prutkov's work: these are "knout" and "ukaze." The knout is described as "a word that troubles the Russians," while ukaze is a good word to use to "trouble the government."[32] Prutkov, for his part, gives a good assessment of the relationship between Russia and the West (which seems to be quite topical now): "Why do Russians wish to stay abroad while foreigners never wish to stay in Russia?—Because they already live abroad." Bouvard and Pécuchet, Koz'ma's direct contemporaries, are clerks, practitioners of the bureaucratic officialese of the French bourgeoisie, and spokesmen of its self-complacent cultural mythology. Their most original undertaking consists of putting together an encyclopedia of nineteenth-century knowledge, *The Dictionary of Received Ideas*. Like Koz'ma's creators, Flaubert does not interfere in Bouvard and Pécuchet's oeuvre and does not betray his ironies in occasional italics. He lets them utter their stupidities without an explicit parodic structure. There is a striking difference between Koz'ma, the aspiring literary genius, and his French cousins, who lack any literary ambitions. Bouvard and Pécuchet are scientific or pseudo-scientific graphomaniacs and encyclopedomaniacs. In fact, they look rather condescendingly upon the whole literary enterprise. Compare the following entries in the *Dictionary of Received Ideas:* "Literature: occupation of the idle" and "Art—it leads to the hospital . . . What good does it serve? since it's being replaced by machines that make things better and faster."[33] The comparison offers an insight into comparative graphomania: whereas in Russia the obsession with writing is primarily literary, in France, the writerly obsession, at least in this case, has more moral and scientific aspirations.

Nabokov's Others: The Lady-Scribbler and The Amateur Psychiatrist

In the second part of the nineteenth century some of the most celebrated and ridiculed graphomaniacs are women novelists and decadent poetesses. They are scorned without the ambiguity that characterizes the treatment of their male counterparts—the irony that threatens the boundaries between genius and graphomaniac, between *belles lettres* and the obsessive writing of commonplaces. Female graphomaniacs are satirized as irredeemably bad writers caught in the labyrinth of melodramatic commonplaces. In this case there is a unanimity among Russian, European, and American writers. Additionally, male graphomaniacs often scorn female ones. Bouvard and Pécuchet, for instance, in their entrance on "artiste" write, "the woman artist—can't be anything but a whore."[34]

Chekhov's stories are populated by obsessive women writers. Mrs. Turkina in "Ionych" writes countless novels that start with the inevitable description of a frosty day and then talk about, say, a young, beautiful, philanthropic countess who organizes schools and hospitals in the village and falls in love with a wandering artist. The author composes every day and reads to a circle of friends in a kind of obligatory social ritual in the provincial high society: she writes "about the things that never happen in life," offering her listeners an hour of pleasant and comfortable boredom or even an escape. She does not aspire to publish, since she "does not need money."[35] Mrs. Turkina would qualify as a graphomaniac only literally—she writes prolifically and obsessively, but on the other hand she has no "will to power," no desire to become a writer. She is a prototypical "woman-scribbler" whose writing is confined to the domestic sphere. It is nothing but charming social entertainment for her privileged houseguests. The moment a woman writer has larger inspirations, she is in danger of being reduced to a scribbling housewife, a literary prostitute who trivializes her feminine nature.

Hence Russian women writers in the nineteenth century always straddled the fences between public and private, high and popular genres. At the turn of the century, and particularly after the 1905

Revolution, women wrote a number of best sellers. The most celebrated woman writer of the time was Anastasia Verbitskaia, the
author of *The Spirit of the Time, The Keys to Happiness,* and *The
Yoke of Love.* Verbitskaia created a scandal, not only because of her
multiple descriptions of wild ecstasies in fashionable Nietzschean-
George Sandian rhetoric, but also because of her ambition for and
flirtation with *belles lettres.*[36] Verbitskaia's popularity, testifying to a
new urban reading public, threatened the division between high and
low culture and jeopardized the conception of the unified people's
culture dreamed by the traditional Russian intelligentsia.

One of the funniest though quite offensive caricatures of the poet-
ess-graphomaniac is Vladimir Nabokov's Liza Bogolepov (a.k.a.
Pnin/Wind—she changed husbands often), the poetess *fatale.* She is
the beloved of the absent-minded Russian *intelligent* Pnin, who has
been transplanted into a bizarre American soil. Liza is described as
an "émigrée rhymesterette" who "wrote after Akhmatova: lackadai-
sical little lyrics tiptoed in more or less anapestic tetrameter and sat
down rather heavily with a wistful sigh: 'I have no precious gems /
Besides my eyes. / But there is a rose tenderer still / Than my pink
lips.' / And the quiet youth said: / 'Your heart is tenderer than
everything else . . .' / And I dropped my gaze."[37]

This is one of the examples of poetry in her collection *Dry Lips.*
Liza is a zealous epigone of Anna Akhmatova, whose much-praised
laconism, elegance of verse, and poetic reticence inexplicably provoke
Liza's logorrhea. The narrator, a professor of Russian literature, tells
Liza that her poetry is bad and recommends that she stop writing—
advice she obviously does not take. Liza is described as "one of those
women who combine healthy good looks with hysterical sloppiness;
lyrical outbursts with a very practical and a very commonplace mind;
a vile temper with sentimentality."[38] While Pnin and his father are
distinctly Chekhovian characters, Liza reminds us of her more or less
healthy, and more or less hysterical, namesakes, the many Lizas and
Lises in Dostoevsky. Liza has a streak of vulgarity that makes her so
lovable and so *fatale* for poor Pnin; she is his "lady with a dog" and
poetry (Anna's vulgar lorgnette and gray eyes are subtly reflected in
Liza).

In this character the literary and medical implications of the term
"graphomania" are brought together. Liza is both an amateur poet
and an amateur psychiatrist, practicing something called "psycho-

dramatics." Bad poetry and psychiatry are perhaps the two worst
evils for Nabokov—evils with which the writer flirts continuously
and which inspire many of his artistic works. The narrator, in his
own words, is fond of "rambling comparisons"; he compares Liza to
the Easter rabbit, involved in "lyrical ovipositing, laying eggs all over
the place . . . and in those green and mauve poems about the child
she wanted to bear, and the lovers she wanted to have, and St.
Petersburg (courtesy Anna Akhmatova)."[39] The "Easter-rabbit"
model of literary production is obviously gendered and would hardly
apply to Nabokov's other failed poets and artists, like Victor's art
teacher in the same novel. Liza, as the narrator tries to convey to us,
is simply a bad girl and a bad mother (and a bad *literary* mother).
She is the wife, successively, of a literary scholar and a psychiatrist,
men who practice her own failed talents; and she is mother to the
genius son Viktor, and he, of course, is beyond her "commonplace
mind." Liza is presented as a banal Russian heroine who should have
never tried to be an author herself. In this case feminine graphomania
is a transgression not so much of literary as of womanly etiquette.
Liza Pnin cannot even hope to be an "unrecognized genius" in the
Nabokovian universe because there are no rules of proper literary
behavior for a woman writer.

Paradoxically, the narrator's "rambling comparisons" occasionally
lead him to lyrical outbursts of his own, which do not parody but
rather imitate those of Liza. The comparisons of her eyes to different
precious stones (be it moist aquamarine or sapphire) and other commonplaces in the description of her almost flawless, although not
"well-groomed," beauty seem to follow Liza's poetic similes. Besides,
Liza is not a mere extra in the story of the unfortunate professor Pnin
and the teenage talent Viktor; in fact she is the romantic trigger of
the plot, and the narrator is deeply dependent on her charming vulgarity—and particularly on her graphomania, which he lovingly recreates. It shows again how difficult it is to frame the obsession with
writing, to sustain it and limit it to the fictional character, to estrange
the mask of the graphomaniac from one's writerly self.

The Genius of the People and the Conceptual Police

The avant-garde presented a major challenge to the literary environment and literary etiquette. Its activists in prerevolutionary Russia

and in Europe assumed the personae of the graphomaniac and hoo-
ligan who indulged in bad behavior and turned cultural conventions
upside down to discover how "language was made."[40] Some ten years
after the Russian Revolution many avant-garde metaphors and slogans that proclaimed the "death of the bourgeois writer" came to life,
occasionally jeopardizing the existence of the slogan creators themselves. Avant-garde "life-building" was taken literally and turned into
bureaucratic and ideological "rules of conduct," as well as rules of
writing. On the one hand, the official Socialist Realist canon can be
seen as institutionalized graphomania, a form of premodern writing
of commonplaces, a neoclassicism of sorts, with a number of watered-down realistic devices and some equally watered-down revolutionary clichés. On the other hand, the practice of self-conscious
graphomania, with its multiple personae, pseudonyms, and narrator-
ventriloquists, is regarded with great suspicion as "ideologically incorrect" because it does not allow the readers to pin down the
writer's intentions, allegiances, and beliefs or allow the guardians of
culture to safeguard the literary canon. Moreover, the borders between literary and literal are easily transgressed and the actual writers
who practiced graphomania as a literary device—Zoshchenko, Oleinikov, Kharms, and later Andrei Sinyavsky—ended up being censored, killed, or put on trial. During the Sinyavsky-Daniel trial in
1962, Sinyavsky insisted that the opinions expressed in his book
should be read merely as the statements expressed by his characters,
and that the "free indirect discourse" used in his text is not his own
point of view but only a literary device. It turned out, however, that
no indirection was allowed to go free and the price of the metaphor
was imprisonment. This is why in the decades of the 1970s and 1980s
the conceptual artists and writers of the late Soviet underground such
as Kabakov, Sorokin, Prigov, and others considered that the practice
of graphomania as a literary device was the only honest artistic
practice. Speaking in quotations was the only way of speaking sincerely, thereby estranging and questioning the possibility of sincerity
in the highly compromised society of the era of stagnation. By the
1990s the heroic graphomaniacs of the 1920s and 1930s are published again and sold out in the bookstores, while their faithful conceptual followers, now above ground, occasionally lament their heroic
past when censorship was not simply a critical metaphor.

In the 1920s Mikhail Zoshchenko created a rogues' gallery of bad

writers, one competing with the other. They were the folkloric character Nazar Sinebriukhov (Nazar the Blue-Bellied, honorary grand-
son of Gogol's Rudyi Panko); Michel Siniagin, an "unknown and
unremarkable" lyric poet famous for his poems "Ladies, Ladies,"
"Storm," and "Petals and Forget-Me-Nots," inspired by Blok and
Nadson; and Kolenkorov, author of sentimental novellas full of insignificant quotidian trivia he harps on in the midst of the Revolution.[41]
In fact, all of Zoshchenko's stories may be said to have been written
by this or that graphomaniac, as they offer more or less edifying
examples of bad writing caught up in the "trivial petit-bourgeois
details of everyday living." Instead of composing "Lives of Remarkable Men" (a famous Soviet series of biographies), Zoshchenko
writes the biographies and works of infamous, unremarkable graphomaniacs.

Four prefaces to the different editions of I. V. Kolenkorov's *Sentimental Novellas* between 1927 and 1929 demonstrate a kind of
buffoonery of authorship and the changing literary climate in Soviet
Russia. In the first one, signed by Kolenkorov himself, he confesses
that his tales deal with a "little man," an *obyvatel*, in all his unattrac-
tiveness. The second and third prefaces are signed by the anonymous
critics K. Ch. and S. L., who claim that Kolenkorov belongs to the
right wing of the "fellow travelers" (writers who were always under
suspicion by the Party), but that he is in the process of "perestroika."
With the help of the creative writing teacher of a literary club, Mikhail Zoshchenko, Kolenkorov might soon become a major representative of the "natural school."[42] In the third preface the critic S. L.
emphasizes that the teacher (Zoshchenko) did not receive any hono-
rarium from Kolenkorov, and that the "sentimental notes, nagging,
and ideological vacillations from one side to another" have nothing
to do with the writing instructor. In the preface of 1929, actually
signed by Zoshchenko, the writer makes a final confession:

> Due to previous misunderstandings, the writer informs the critics
> that the character from whose point of view these stories are told
> is, so to speak, an imaginary character. He is that average intellec-
> tual type who happens to live at the turning point of an era. Neu-
> rasthenia, ideological vacillation, major contradictions and
> melancholy—we have had to provide our "promoted worker," I. V.
> Kolenkorov, with these.[43]

Here the author states explicitly that a graphomaniac is a graphomaniac and a literary device is a literary device. The time for literary
playfulness is over or almost over, and the games with ideologically
unstable graphomaniacs are life-threatening. Yet the explicitness here
also borders on parody. The author tells the same ironic truths and
brings forth the same ideologically correct clichés about overcoming
"major contradictions, melancholia, and ideological vacillations" as
in the other prefaces. Moreover, when naming the "writer Mikhail
Zoshchenko, brother and son of the same unhealthy people," it seems
Zoshchenko himself is made into a fictional character; he is only a
slightly more ironic but no less vacillating writer at the turning point
of history.

"Kolenkorov" the character is a pretext for an explicit satire on
"unreconstructed" fellow-travelers; it is, however, also a self-defen-
sive mask in the postrevolutionary literary theater, from which ambiguity and other literary devices were gradually being eliminated. The
sentimental graphomaniac, the ideologically vacillating fellow-traveler is an uncanny double of the writer, someone he wishes to estrange and yet, at the same time, someone he cannot do without. The
relationship between the author and his beloved graphomaniacs is
that of a causal, everyday acquaintance: Siniagin happened to have
stolen the author's monkey-fur coat, while Kolenkorov was one of his
students in the literary club.

Kolenkorov's *Sentimental Novellas* expose the "ideological vacillations" noted in the preface, and shift among various clichés. The
genre of the sentimental novella, an anachronism in this epoch of
revolutionary upheavals, dates back to Karamzin's "Poor Liza" and
blossoms in popular literature of the nineteenth century. If, at its
birth, the sentimental novella was a reaction to the classical hierarchy
of styles, then the postrevolutionary sentimental novella, depicting
small individual turmoils, subtly undermines the new revolutionary
hierarchy favoring heroic epics, in which the common good perpetually struggles against the common evil. As a petit-bourgeois relic and
a reaction against revolutionary utopias, the postrevolutionary sentimental novella is at once anachronistic and antifuturistic; it is a
repository of old clichés of individual self-expression and of a new
revolutionary common language that is on the verge of official reification.

"What the Nightingale Sang" is a communal apartment romance, the love story of Liza and Comrade Bylinkin, which ends badly, at least for Liza. ("Bylinkin" is another great name for a graphomaniac; it is a cross between *bylina*—a short epic tale, a common oral genre in ancient Russia—and *pylinka*—a speck of dust.)

Liza nearly makes a poet out of Bylinkin. He writes a poem entitled "To Her and to That One," which he submits to the paper *Dictatorship of Labor*. Yet comrade Bylinkin does not choose the difficult path of the poet, because he is more "inclined toward Americanization," meaning that he is a practical man and does not put his "crazy ideas on paper." (This proves again that graphomania, even in the view of its native practitioners, is a Russian disease that weakens as one moves westward.) In other words, Bylinkin is a failed graphomaniac (strange, but such a thing is possible) who ends up preferring life to literature.

An argument over furniture breaks the romance and breaks up the romantic discourse of the novella. The title, "What the Nightingale Sang," comes directly from one of Bylinkin and Liza's conversations in the heyday of their romance:

> It was in full swing, at the highest moment of their feeling, that Bylinkin and his beloved went to the countryside and wandered in the woods till the night. And there, listening to the bugs buzzing and the nightingale singing, they stood for a long time in immobile poses. And then Lizochka, wringing her hands, would repeatedly ask:
> "Vasia, what do you think, what does the nightingale sing?"
> And Vasia Bylinkin would respond with restraint:
> "He wants to guzzle, that's why he sings."
> And only afterwards, when Bylinkin learned more about maiden psychology, did he respond with more Romantic vagueness and more details. He supposed that the bird sang about some future, beautiful life.[44]

Here the nightingale, the most quoted bird in Western culture, is more like a parrot or would-be graphomaniac that can be heard to sing about anything, from trivial romance to bright communal future. This paragraph humorously stages all the lovers' clichés of the time. Liza takes the rules of romantic courtship seriously, although both she and her lover remain unskilled in petit-bourgeois romancing. The amateurish theatricality of the scene is heightened by the melodramatic gestures of the two lovers, which invoke nineteenth-century

Romantic novellas and silent movies: Liza wrings her hands and the two lovers assume "immobile poses." The discussion about nightingales is rather unskillfully and mechanically tacked onto the end of the story, which intensifies the comic effect: the characters of the Soviet sentimental novella are amateurish romantic lovers, and their bard, the postrevolutionary graphomaniac Kolenkorov, is an amateur moralist.

The precarious Soviet author of sentimental novellas at the time of revolutionary upheavals and postrevolutionary conformism searches for his own happy ending, the romantic dream of a communist utopia: "The author thinks the same about some future excellent life in some three hundred years, or maybe less . . . But if even then life is bad, the author, with a cold and empty heart, would agree to consider himself a superfluous figure against the background of newly rising life. And then he could end under the tram."[45]

This confession is prophetic. Only some five years later, in 1925, Kolenkorov is killed off by the creative writing teacher of the literary club, Zoshchenko, who begins to fear for his own life. If Kolenkorov did not die under the tram, another graphomaniac and official writer did. It was Berlioz, from Mikhail Bulgakov's *The Master and Margarita,* written in the 1930s but not published until the 1960s.

The last heroic graphomaniacs of Stalin's time were created by the last avant-garde group in Soviet Russia, the OBERIU, consisting of Daniil Kharms, Alexander Vvedensky, Nikolai Zabolotsky, and the poets and writers who were close to them, especially Nikolai Oleinikov. They were Zoshchenko's poetic counterparts. Kharms, Vvedensky, and Oleinikov were killed in Stalin's camps in the late 1930s. The OBERIU, which existed from 1925 to 1935, was a modernist anachronism in the atmosphere of consolidating Socialist Realism and the Stalinist codification of the commonplace, to which the poets' response was black humor. Nikolai Oleinikov declared Koz'ma Prutkov to be his literary forebear. He proudly continued the nineteenth-century tradition of bad writing and was especially fond of its literary insects. One of the poems, entitled "Cockroach," uses these lines from Lebiadkin's poem as an epigraph: "'The Cockroach: A cockroach fell into a glass.'—Dostoevsky."[46]

For Oleinikov and Kharms, Koz'ma Prutkov was one of the few venerated literary classics. In fact Kharms used such literary geniuses as Pushkin and Gogol for his absurdist characters, stumbling over each other like a circus juggler's colorful balls. In Kharms's playground Pushkin and Gogol can easily take the place of Koshkin and Myshkin (Catman and Ratman). In one of Kharms's anecdotes from Pushkin's life, the well-known romantic poet Zhukovsky actually catches Pushkin in one of his moments of inspired graphomania and calls him "poetaster."

Oleinikov also creates for himself the literary persona of a graphomaniac: Makar the Ferocious (Makar Svirepyi, after Maxim Gorky—Maxim the Bitter—although Gorky's pseudonym is both romantic and serious). Makar the Ferocious was the author of many fables, odes, and poems written on private social occasions. Many poems are humorous dedications to the women friends—such as "An Epistle Scourging the Wearing of Clothes," "A Poem to the Typist on the Occasion of Buying a Cape," and "An Address to the Actress of One of the Theaters"; or mock moral tales like "A True Story That Happened to the Author—An Epistle Scourging Debauchery." These poems recreate the old tradition of "domestic poetry" popular in Pushkin's circle, written for private occasions and for friends. In fact he continues the tradition of that famous poshly madrigal of Pushkin's—the banal madrigal—in which we encounter one of the first usages of the word "poshly." In Oleinikov's rewriting, however, these madrigals are hardly conventional; they become subversive once taken out of the etiquette of the high aristocratic society of the early nineteenth century and displaced into the drab Soviet everyday, in which everything private is considered to be deprived of collective significance and to be socially dangerous. Poems of circumstances are quite common in the 1930s, but those circumstances are exclusively political and social. It is as if Oleinikov, through those humorous poems, sought to create a society of playful friends to defy the official collectivity.

Oleinikov's poems again bring up the issue of parody or imitation, as in Koz'ma Prutkov's dilemma. Furthermore, would it resolve the problem if we did call them "parodies"? Oleinikov's contemporaries, including Kornei Chukovsky, considered him to be a "poet of genius," yet his only surviving legacy consists of the poems written by the fictional graphomaniac Makar the Ferocious. Should we continue to look for redeeming masterpieces written by an "authentic" Oleinikov, the Oleinikov without a pseudonym, the genius of the avant-garde?

Lev Losev writes that "Oleinikov is the Zoshchenko of poetry: the foundation of his poetics is not 'transense' but 'skaz.'"[47] In other words, Oleinikov's poetry does not attempt to go beyond the referential meaning of language into the utopian realm of pure signifiers, as in the poetry of Khlebnikov; rather, it plunges into the everyday theatricality of postrevolutionary language. *Skaz* is a term introduced by Boris Eikhenbaum in his discussion of Gogol to suggest the presence of a narrator-character, which colors the story. Oleinikov's persona is that of a somewhat old-fashioned, even anachronistic graphomaniac who evokes eighteenth- and nineteenth-century urbanities and social uses of writing in polite society. The pose of an outmoded and playful scribbler who occasionally reduces to absurdity the very conventions he practices and constantly places the linguistic commonplaces in quotation marks seems to be the only honest stance for the poet to take in the era of imminent purges and growing conformism.[48]

Daniil Kharms dedicated a friendly epistle to Oleinikov:

> Conductor of numbers, mean mocker of friendship,
> What have you gotten pensive about? Or are you defaming the
> world again?
> Homer is poshly to you, and Goethe a stupid sinner,
> Dante is ridiculed by you.
> Only Bunin is your idol.[49]

Kharms's epistle is written in a traditional meter and is both humorous and elegiac. To use the word "poshliak" in relation to Homer indicates that even the great epic fathers of Western literary tradition were not spared in Oleinikov's poetic play. Oleinikov's was a radical, heroic graphomania: the relentless estranging of banality and the playful yet faithful practicing of everyday genres of writing constituted a defiant challenge to the official literary and social canons.

In 1935 an informer wrote that Oleinikov's poems about flies and cockroaches, and especially his children's tales, "trivialize" the heroic Soviet past, and that therefore his books should be confiscated and destroyed.[50] The author followed the fate of his books; Oleinikov's and Kharms's practice of ironic graphomania cost them their lives. Kharms and Oleinikov were arrested and died in Stalin's camps in the period between 1940 and 1942. Literary insects—the Stalinesque cockroach with the huge moustache from Mandelshtam's notorious epigram, for which he was put in the camps, and the absurdist cockroach of Oleinikov, the carrier of a noble tradition of graphomania—threatened to contaminate the optimistic spirit of the Socialist Realist utopia with a dose of satire and black humor.

All-People's Graphomania: From Stalinist Musicals to the Literary Clubs of the Thaw

Socialist Realism redefined and "corrected" the concept of graphomania. The 1930s developed the idea of the "genius of the people," which was a part of the Stalinist folkloric revival.[51] The people (narod, in its most abstract definition), not the individual writers, are the source of genius, but only if their talents are channeled in the right direction. Everyone is encouraged to be an artist, to write and compose in an effort to reveal his or her great patriotic talent. As the slogan in the Lenin years proclaimed, under socialism every cook (kukharka) will take a turn to rule the state. During the Stalin era every cook was told to produce culture as well. But, in practice, only a few specially designated top chefs were given the recipes for stardom.

One of Stalin's favorite films, which he saw a hundred times (without exaggeration) was Volga, Volga, directed by Grigorii Alexandrov. On one level the film is a "joyful and life-affirming" love story between the classical musician Aliosha, who likes Wagner and Beethoven and the mail-carrier Strelka, a would-be folk poet and singer, played by the leading lady of Stalinist cinema, Liubov' Orlova, a Soviet Marlene Dietrich. Despite the intrigues of Byvalov the village bureaucrat, who wishes to steal Strelka's song in order to go to Moscow himself and participate in the people's celebration, the story reaches a happy ending in a glorious march to the new Communist Moscow. ("Byvalov" is linked to "obyvatel," which in this context refers to someone who trivializes Soviet laws and regulations.) In the words of the director, the film is dedicated to "the people's creativity"; it testifies to the "genius of the people," which can also be described as mass graphomania.[52] The bureaucrat's attempt to plagiarize the people's creativity is publicly exposed and satirized. The film reflects the Stalinist campaign for Russian folklore, or rather the official reinvention of Russian folklore.This highly programmatic version of the people's culture rejects bourgeois foreign classical music as well as the petty bourgeois popular music of the 1920s—the "gramophone romances" and other urban songs, tango and jazz, all signs of Western decadence (patriotic Russian classical composers, especially Tchaikovsky and Glinka, Stalin's favorites, are of course a part of the people's culture).

For students of graphomania, the most interesting feature of this film is that its own authorship seems to echo the drama and mystery of authorship that it tells. In fact, as Maya Turovskaya has shown, one of the scriptwriters of the film was made into a ghost writer as his name was erased from the film credits for political reasons.[53] This was Nikolai Erdman, a celebrated poet and playwright close to the Moscow avant garde, who at the time the film came out was in exile. He wrote the play *Suicide* and numerous film scripts, and was known in private circles as the author of many imitations of popular genres, Odessa romances, tangos, and poems for special occasions.[54] How are we to read his script for this most popular of Socialist Realist comedies? Is it a parody, a work of the ironic graphomaniac writing in Socialist Realist style? Perhaps it really was Erdman's exaggeration of the devices and his explicit rather than moderately realistic use of the official programmatic commonplaces, formulated in his characteristically sharp and humorous language, that made *Volga, Volga* an exemplary Soviet comedy of the thirties. Would Stalin have seen *Volga, Volga* a hundred times had it been the work of a mediocre Socialist Realist, say Vladimir Radostin (*radost* means "joy")?

Obviously it is impossible to reduce Socialist Realism to a mere parody, a skillful manipulation of official clichés by coy former avantgarde artists. In fact many artists and writers were forced to write official works, including Zoshchenko himself, who produced a series of "stories about Lenin" for children of preschool age under his own name. The new seriousness, even in the most "joyful and lifeaffirming" genres, precluded the theater of language that allowed graphomaniacs to procreate, defamiliarize, and combat the growing dominance of the official bureaucratese.

Abram Tertz's 1960 story "Graphomaniacs" stages the conflicts among many literary myths and recapitulates the history of the disease of graphomania and its aesthetic and political complications in the Russian-Soviet context.[55] Tertz continues the tradition of Zoshchenko and Oleinikov, writing the story from the point of view of a graphomaniac. Moreover, this is graphomaniac's autobiographical tale. The main character is an unrecognized Socialist Realist genius, Pavel Straustin, author of the unpublished novel "In Search of Joy." He lives with his wife, Zoia, once as devoted and passionate as the heroine of his novel, but now an aging, sloppy, and tired woman "exhausted by female diseases." Their precocious son Pavlik is a baby-graphomaniac and writes his own stories about various fantastic creatures whenever he is able to get hold of a pencil. The jealousy between father and son is humorously played out throughout the story. Straustin's son is his father's uncanny double, but it is unclear to the father whether his son is mirroring his genius or his graphomania, further confusing the two.[56]

One day Straustin encounters the prolific and insidious poet Galkin, who would impose his poems on any victim in sight and has published nineteen volumes of poetry. Galkin brings Straustin to a club of graphomaniacs. Its members include retired army colonels, old women in Chekhovian pince-nez, young neophytes with Pushkinian whiskers writing in the manner of Esenin, a botany teacher, the author of a book in the shape of a sea urchin that opens like an accordion and offers "a synthesis of poetry, painting and sculpture." There is also a woman playwright, the ex-wife of a well-known gay violinist, who talks about herself exclusively in the male gender, criticizes the top bureaucracy, and is not published "exclusively for political reasons"; finally, there is a young poet-sailor "smelling of alcohol, prison, and suicide."[57] Galkin, the self-conscious president of the club of graphomaniacs, is a relic from the 1920s and 1930s, an anachronistic epigone of the avant garde, a stepson of Oleinikov and the other experimental poets. On the whole, the graphomaniacs certainly present a much more colorful and diverse group than the official Soviet writers of the 1950s who produce their homogeneous, bleak, banal descriptions of Soviet joy.

One sentence circulates through the text of "Graphomaniacs" as a kind of *objet trouvé*—found, disowned, and found again. It offers a unique insight into the graphomaniac's writing process as well as his process of gradual self-knowledge.

"It was hot and stifling. Pushkin Boulevard was dry. In the air one could feel the breath of the coming storm." I will end the novel *In Search for Joy* with this line. I will definitely include it right into the page proofs. The approaching storm enlivens the landscape and resounds with the event: a light allusion to the revolution and to my Vadim's love for Tatiana Krechet.[58]

The story opens with the hero experiencing a moment of romantic inspiration on Pushkin Boulevard; he meditates on nature and nature descriptions. "In the air one could feel the breath of the coming storm" is used in quotation marks; this is not a casual remark on the weather but a great poetic find, an appropriate closure for his Socialist Realist novel that describes the love of the revolutionary hero for Tatiana, whose blond hair reflects the color of the ripe wheat. The line would fit well in Straustin's would-be Socialist Realist novel; it is a wonderful example of how Socialist Realist description both "naturalizes" and transforms, in a supposedly "revolutionary manner," one of the chief conventions of nineteenth-century realism: a truthful description of nature. The sentence, in Straustin's view, communicates the pathos of anticipation, of future storms and of their rejuvenating powers. Straustin's poetic intuition leads him to discover an exemplary commonplace that didactically condenses the historical transformations of realism and romanticism into a glorious revolutionary apotheosis. Yet Straustin is unaware of another approaching storm that would forever transform his literary career—a storm of revelations about graphomania.

The line about the coming storm appears again in a scene of almost transensical collective delirium among the graphomaniacs. According to Galkin, a writer must let himself go, not seek to express himself but *efface* himself in language, and only then he might be able to come up with "the world's most exact synonym." Here Galkin formulates the main foundation of modernist aesthetics: giving oneself over to language, creatively erasing oneself. It is his version of Mallarmé's famous lines about the "elocutionary disappearance of the poet in the text," and of the Russian avant-garde's idea of the poet-ventriloquist or poet-producer. When the graphomaniacs collectively voice a babble of literary conventions and clichés, Straustin distinctly hears his literary pearl: "in the air one felt the breath of the coming storm." He thereupon claims that his unpublished oeuvre has been collectively plagiarized and turned into clichés by the Socialist Realist classics Fedin, Fadeev, Sholokhov, Paustovsky and others. It is unclear, however, who is plagiarizing whom: Straustin, the established Soviet classics, or the grotesque members of the Galkin club? And how does one distinguish between plagiarism, parody, and imitation? Thus one trivial line about the coming storm, first used without quotation marks, acquires multiple qualifiers. From an unselfconscious commonplace it turns into a parody on Socialist Realism and its nature-loving pathos, which weds a restrained romantic impetus to revolutionary teleology. In the end Galkin proclaims that the line is nothing but a worn-out cliché of no significance whatsoever. Ultimately the product of graphomania does not matter so much as the aspirations, desires, and obsessions that motivate it. Galkin, the unpublished author of a graphomaniac manifesto, insists it is the originality of failure that makes the graphomaniac an embodiment of human and aesthetic self-consciousness. As for Straustin, the storm resulting from his beautiful sentence makes him recognize his own graphomania.

The drama of the story is not the war between genius and graphomaniac, but between different kinds and styles of graphomania: antiestablishment versus the official establishment, self-conscious versus unselfconscious, avant-gardist playful self-effacement versus Socialist Realist conformism.

The obsession with writing also extends to an obsession with the writer's prestige. In the story the Socialist Realist writers and the barely surviving writers and epigones of the generation of the 1920s can at least agree on their common envy of the Russian classics. "Graphomaniacs" exposes the grand kitschification of the great classics of the nineteenth century turned into Socialist Realist monuments, joyfully greeting the young generations on the streets of the new Communist Moscow. Even the nails of Leo Tolstoy and the tubercular spit of Chekhov are reified into aesthetic objects.

But some elements of the myth of a great writer's self-fashioning apply across the spectrum: to Russian classics, modernist epigones, and unrecognized Socialist Realist geniuses alike. One of these elements is the perpetual struggle between the writer and his byt; the opposition of art and life, or, more precisely in this case, of art and wife. Galkin tells Straustin that if he is to belong to the community of writers/graphomaniacs, he has to choose between his art and his family, personified by his wife in her not-so-tidy stockings, frying not-so-fresh cutlets. This is not surprising, as "good" and "bad" writers' wives have their own mythology in Russian and Soviet culture—from Natal'ia Goncharova-Pushkina-Lansakaia, one of the *femmes fatales* of Russian literary history, to Nadezhda Mandelshtam, the poet's self-sacrificial wife, the preserver of memory and a writer herself.

"Graphomaniacs" explores many paradoxes in the incestuous relationships between the commonplace and artistic invention, between unrecognized genius and graphomaniac, between the canonized Russian classic and the new Soviet writer. The title is repeated in the last line of the story: "'Graphomaniacs' (from the stories of my life)." Hence the story about a visit to the club of graphomaniacs is also a story about writing a story about the graphomaniacs, a writing that promises, to a resentful would-be Socialist Realist enmeshed in the mire of Soviet everyday life, a spark of new inspiration. It turns out, however, that even the idea of writing about graphomania is not so original: it was suggested to Straustin by Galkin. So are we reading a story *about* graphomaniacs, or a story *by* the graphomaniac Galkin and his ventriloquist Straustin? Or else a story by the ironic, pseudonymous Abram Tertz? It becomes more and more difficult to see where graphomania ends and healthy writing begins. As the story unfolds, the conflict between genius and graphomaniac turns hazy, like the spring air awaiting the proverbial storm. Perhaps this Manichaean duel, fought throughout Russian and Soviet culture with melodramatic passion, has been strongly exaggerated by writers and critics alike.

Glasnost', Graphomania, and Popular Culture

The early period of glasnost' encouraged a variety of graphomania and logorrhea—from numerous letters to the newspapers to memoirs, "true stories," opinions, and revelations of wide political range. The years of silencing created a great need for speaking up and being heard, and the gradual lifting of censorship allowed for broader possibilities for publication. It became possible to write without thinking of the censor as one's first reader and without elaborating a subtext in the "Aesopian language" of allusions, metaphors, and anecdotes. But can Russian literature survive double-speak? Some poets claimed that the Aesopian language was the quintessential literary language and raised questions about the role of art under democracy.

A few years ago, in the journal *The Art of Cinema,* a debate was launched about "mass culture," and in broader terms, about culture

in the singular and cultures in the plural.[59] What provoked the discussion was the publication of Tatiana Anokhina's (this may be a
pseudonym) novella "Izabella Bedford," a text that could have been
written by a member of Galkin's club. In fact, initially her work was
rejected by the editors with the insulting comment: "graphomania."
Like Strelka from *Volga, Volga,* Tatiana Anokhina works in the post
office in the town of Toliattii; in her own words, writing, reading,
and watching movies are her way of "self-knowledge," of "freedom
from society and its bustle." So if she is to be called a graphomaniac,
she is the old-fashioned, idealistic type of a graphomaniac, for whom
writing and reading are the sources of emancipation from everyday
drudgery through the imagination. Her heroes and heroines bear
foreign names, but the reality appears to be surprisingly Soviet.

"Izabella Bedford," written in the early 1980s, is a tale of an escape
trip from the depressing everyday of the Soviet provinces into the
land of polite and smiling "humane people," written from the point
of view of a Soviet provincial woman with a foreign name. One day
Izabella Bedford decides to quit her job and leaves on an old bus with
her little son Tomas. Until then she led a life of Soviet mass culture,
whose particulars include popular therapeutic tests (drawing the head
of Beethoven before going to bed), yoga exercises, mental appeals for
help to the spirit of the popular actor Andrei Mironov, and condem-
nation of the United States' imperialist nuclear build-up. (She even
dreams of transforming nuclear waste into a heap of rose petals.)
"Izabella Bedford" is a perfect example of "women's writing": its
main characters are women, and it is written by a woman and perhaps for women (if it is written for the public at all), although there
is no love story here. It is the antithesis of Hemingway's world of
"men without women," being a world of women with children and
almost without men. Here is what Izabella is taking with her on the
road, all her "bare essentials of existence":

> On the second day her flu ended, on the third day she was fired from
> her job, on the third day she put a big yellow bus in a good spot
> under the windows of the house . . . In it she had quite a large
> library, consisting for now of the works of Stevenson, Dumas, Jules
> Verne, Defoe, Pushkin, the writings of the ancient Greek authors, as
> well as the biographies of famous composers, scholars, artists, phi-
> losophers . . . Izabella gathered some warm clothing for herself and
> for her son Tomas, something that is especially important when

traveling. In one place she set up a good refrigerator. She acquired a magic tape recorder with tapes of old classical music and modern cosmic music, took optical tools from the magnifying glass to the telescope that magnifies things two hundred times . . . and even wished to have an original laser revolver for self-defense.[60]

Izabella's yellow bus is at once a magic means of escape, like Jules Verne's *Nautilus* or the Beatles' yellow submarine, and a rare repository of Soviet mass culture. At first glance it strikes us that her bus library is not particularly Soviet (the only Russian writer mentioned is Pushkin). What is Soviet about it is the arrangement of books and the cult of high culture popularized in mass series like the "Lives of Great Men." The fascination for all things exotic and foreign in the story is unrelated to contemporary Western popular artifacts—no McDonald's and Coca Cola here (not yet). This foreign land is from the popular fiction of Dumas, Walter Scott, and Jules Verne, who ranked very high on the Soviet black market in the early 1980s. It is a rare example of surviving nineteenth-century popular urban culture, frozen in the Soviet provinces. "Izabella Bedford" shows that mass culture can furnish powerful aesthetic experiences to an individual viewer and reader. At the same time, it reveals how old-fashioned the Soviet mass culture of the 1980s used to be, and how these nineteenth-century classics and novelettes coexisted with propaganda slogans from current Soviet papers, songs from TV musicals, and comedies. Interestingly, the editors of the *The Art of Cinema* called the story an example of an alternative underground culture—one that is not engaged in experimenting with representation and that does not claim any subversive or avant-garde status.[61] This evaluation might be the beginning of an interesting rethinking of the old official clichés, "people's culture" and "people's creativity." The novella also suggests that a spontaneous product of mass culture might be different from the mass culture as it is dogmatically programmed by the commercial establishments, the way it is done in the United States.

Anokhina's tale is not prescriptive; it is surprising in its juxtaposition of high and popular culture, and of unselfconscious Soviet commonplaces with primitive and striking poetic finds. It presents an urgent aesthetic drive as the only means of personal spiritual emancipation, and writing as an almost existential necessity. These tales of narrow escapes in an old-fashioned yellow bus reveal a lot about the

Soviet scene of writing without a room of one's own. At the same
time, even after the publication of "Izabella Bedford," Tatiana Anokhina refused to behave like a writer. When asked repeatedly to appear
on a television program on the problems of popular culture, she
politely refused, as if fearing that modern electronic media would
interfere with her private creative world.

The Last Policeman of the Literary Empire: Dmitrii Prigov

At the end of the cultural euphoria produced by glasnost', the hero
of Moscow conceptualism, Dmitrii Prigov, warned about an approaching catastrophe—a "global catastrophe," namely, the disappearance of a "socio-cultural mentality" defined by the cult of great
letters and the "Russian Imperial spirit." This catastrophe affects the
followers of the Slavophiles and of liberal Westernizers alike, since
both are products of the imperial and culture-centric mentality. In his
"Wishes of Good Health to You, Gentlemen-Writers," which is not
deprived of some hellish Dostoevskian and Nietzschean ambiguities,
Prigov ironically suggests that the "writers fighting for Europeanization of Russia, that is, as we know a priori, the writers possessed by
quite noble and progressive impulses . . . are digging their own grave,
or if you wish are cutting that beautiful century-old branch on which
they sit; and as a result they will confront the complete disappearance
of Russian literature as an even remotely significant socio-cultural
phenomenon."[62] The end of the Russian literary empire, in which the
writer was a kind of ideal, could be the end of "everything sacred,"
the death of the Russian god of sorts. "Thus Spake Dmitrii Prigov,"
or was it his literary persona and double, the celebrated graphomaniac Dmitrii Aleksanych, the everyman of late Soviet letters? Is the
heroic graphomaniac nostalgic for the cultural empire that he himself
helped to trivialize?

Prigov often reflects on the myth of the poet in Russian culture;
that is, of someone who is regarded as Russia's second government
and the conscience of the nation:

> I, for one, am an ordinary poet
> And just because of our Russian fate
> I have to be the conscience of nation
> But how to do that if I don't have any conscience

Maybe I have a few poems, but no conscience
So what's there to do?[63]

Prigov both parodies and cherishes the Russian poetic myth. His intonations are colloquial and almost naive; his everyday language seems to water down poetic metaphors, slogans, literary common- places. Prigov often breaks poetic rhythms—not in an avant-garde fashion but in an ordinary fashion, as if he was simply interrupted by outside noise and chaos of daily routine so that his poetic line re- mained imperfect and unfinished like a conversation in which the poet and his addressee suddenly lost interest. This broken line is Prigov's poetic signature.

A hero of Moscow underground culture since the late 1970s, Dmitrii Prigov was a veteran of the club of conceptualists, not gra- phomaniacs, but there is a close relationship between those two exclusive clubs. Prigov's semifictional incarnation Dmitrii Alek- sanych, the author of "strong poems" and "weak poems," of banal reflections and of dedications to The Lonely Policeman, could have been a younger member of Galkin's club. In the 1970s many of the best artists and writers turned into self-reflexive graphomaniacs, es- tranging the commonplaces of the stagnant Soviet cultural text as if to deprive this text of meaning and turn it into a series of recycled signs. Prigov was one of the most authoritarian conceptual authors— someone who reified his own signature, even if he meant it ironi- cally.[64] For more than a decade Prigov was engaged in intense conceptual self-fashioning and life-creation. In his case, the everyman Dmitrii Aleksanych took over Dmitrii Prigov himself; in meeting the poet in person it is never clear who is speaking and whether it matters who is speaking. As a fellow conceptual poet Lev Rubinstein re- marked, "Prigov works not so much for the text, as for the image of Dmitrii Aleksanych."[65] It is a case of vampirism: Dmitrii Aleksanych has sucked the literary blood of his author.

Since the 1980s Dmitrii Aleksanych has continued the classical themes of his illustrious graphomaniac predecessors—from Koz'ma Prutkov to Oleinikov. The great imperial literary culture that Prigov the critic frequently recalls with nostalgia is recreated in his work through the themes of graphomania. The insects that crawled from Pushkin to Dostoevsky to Oleinikov play a special role in his poetics. Prigov created a cycle of poems about "cockroach-machia" (tarakanomakhiia):

It is raining, the cockroach and myself
Sit near the wet window,
And look ahead, where from the fog
The country of our dream raises
As it were in a mist from beyond
I say somewhat voluptuously
Hey, hairy one, let's fly away
I can't, I can only
Run
Okay, run, run . . .[66]

The poem, from the cycle of "strong poems," uses lines from
Pushkin's *The Bronze Horseman,* Peter the Great's reflections on the
newly built imperial capital, and images from Gorky's romantic prose
poems about flights into the "country of one's dream." Moreover,
insectomania is clearly part and parcel of conceptual graphomania. A
fellow conceptual poet compared the author himself to a spider
which spins an infinite thread: "he is Arachne, not Parca."[67] The
author makes his own web of favorite quotations, but he also plots
his exit out of the conceptual mind-games and intertextual virtuosi-
ties. At the end Dmitrii Aleksanych seems to give up the poetic effort.
Like a kind nanny, he just lets his childlike lines play. Prigov is the
advocate of the "new sincerity." It is, of course, sincerity in quotation
marks, but occasionally it breaks through them. Yet this sincerity can
be achieved only after the poet has traveled through the conceptual
webs and paid his dues to the club of graphomaniacs. The critical
conceit of the purely intellectual nature of conceptualism, of its attempt at a radical emptying of meaning and divorcing the signifier
and the signified, tends to overlook this peculiar pathos of sincerity
that manifests itself in the broken lines at the end of many of Prigov's
poems. This "new sincerity" takes the place of the old one from the
first-person lyrical narratives of the 1960s, which had compromised
itself beyond repair.

   One of the most "sincere" heroes in Prigov's universe is the lonely
Policeman:

   In the buffet of the House of Writers
   Policeman drinks beer
   He drinks it in his usual manner
   Without even looking at the writers

But they, they look at him
Around him everything is light and empty
And all their different arts
Mean nothing in front of him

He represents Life
That appears as Duty
Life is short, Art is long
And Life wins in the fight.[68]

Prigov's Policeman is the last romantic hero of Russian literature; he is not a poet (yet he cannot abandon the House of Writers completely, perhaps because the beer there is particularly tasty). The figure of the Policeman is reminiscent of the children's stories of the 1960s about kind Uncle Stepa-Policeman who fixes things for Soviet children. (Uncle Stepa stories became more unpopular as the children grew up and found the real-life policemen working for the KGB.) Prigov's lonely Policeman is the last poet-in-life, a guardian angel of the old literature-centric universe. At times Prigov's Policeman is almost a Soviet or a Symbolist hero, accompanied by his urban bride Ambulance, all dressed in white. "Policeman" is a hybrid character—something of an aging Uncle Stepa, a bit of a white horseman of the apocalypse, and with an air of a Russian "rebel without a cause." He is also a visionary who dreams of a utopia when he himself will become obsolete:

Policeman walks in the park
In late autumn
And over his covered head
The sky is a pale arch

And the future, not a lie
Appears between the alleys
When his profession will disappear
Among conscientious people

When his uniform will not be needed
Neither his belt nor his revolver
When all people will be brothers
And everyone a Policeman.[69]

The not-lie is the closest the poet can come to truth and sincerity. The Policeman's utopia is self-effacing on all levels—in his dream

world there will be no need for policemen, nor for Dmitrii Aleksanych, nor for Prigov himself. The dream of a world where all
people will be brothers is a Russian and Soviet banality made sincere
through conceptual estrangement and nostalgia.

After all, the great conceptualist poet and heroic graphomaniac
belong to the "country of his dreams" and to its heroic imperial
cultural past. Glasnost' broke the prestigious webs of cultural underground; with the abolition of censorship and disappearance of real
policemen (in the 1990s their function was taken over by "body-
guards") the conceptual Policeman also becomes obsolete, though
not in the way dreamed in his utopian poem. Post-Soviet intellectuals
are fascinated by the image of the apocalypse: the end of the millennium, the end of the Soviet and Russian empire, the end of great
literature, the end of the Club of Conceptual Graphomania, hence the
catastrophe. Dmitrii Aleksanych Prigov remains one of the "last of
the Mohicans," the ironic martyr of the great empire of Russian
letters.

One does hope that literature will survive the empire, even if the
writer ceases to be an exemplary model of the Russian personality.
As for the Russian catastrophe, this commonplace of the Russian
philosophy may gradually disappear together with the empire. Is it
possible that the alternative to the apocalyptic "Russian dream" is
not the "American dream" but a different kind of postimperial thinking? At this difficult time of transition, why not dream about something less than catastrophic, however utopian this might seem?

As the Russian graphomaniac turns into an extinct (or at least
endangered) species, one begins to feel nostalgic about the loss and
wish for the continuation of some kind of pure, unadulterated love
for writing (without the will to power) and mania for self-fashioning.
In short, graphomania without a Club of Graphomaniacs, graphomania outside the empire, graphomania without police, graphomania
for its own sake. One hypothetical aspirant is a self-effacing bilingual
graphomaniac and émigrée of the past wave. Her pen name is Anya
Krasivaya (Anya the Beautiful). She is not a conceptual poetess but
only a part-time receptionist and a graduate student in Romanticism.
While working at the office computer and politely putting her clients
on hold, Anya dreams of a purely "altruistic" graphomania, an obsession with writing minus the obsession with becoming a writer. This

is a fragment from Anya's unfinished draft, "d'inachevé," as Koz'ma Prutkov used to put it:

> Pure graphomania is not a disease but a form of therapy, not a talking but a writing cure, a way of following up one's doddles till the very end of the line. Graphomania is a dream of a leisure, of digressive parentheses and long convoluted sentences addressed to "my dearest friend," a dream of endless epistolary romances with ornate letters, like the branches of the trees in an overgrown English garden, or of the E-MAIL affairs of the heart that enact the rhythmical pleasure of pushing soft computer buttons with intervals of delightful boredom. And you continue writing while your plane takes off for a long transatlantic journey, you continue writing in the conditions of comfortable weightlessness over a glass of fat-free orange juice as the videotaped flight attendant explains THE EMERGENCY PROCEDURES, and you continue writing hoping that somewhere somehow there is an EXIT.[70]

A Taxi Ride with a Graphomaniac

During my last trip to Russia my scholarly pursuit of graphomania ended in an incident of personal embarrassment: myself, a voluntary scholar of graphomania, was turned into a graphomaniac's guinea pig. It happened when I met a new post-Soviet poet, the only one who can afford to be one: the taxi driver, that mythical hero of the new Russia already immortalized in the film *Taxi Blues* (a Russian-French co-production).

Once I was taking a taxi in Moscow at 1:30 AM and was trying to act as natural and as native as possible. The taxi driver, a handsome young man with a gold tooth and Eseninian blond curls, was listening to a song on tape.

"Just listen to this," he said. "Have you ever heard anything so gorgeous?"

"It has very nice rhythm," I said cautiously.

He started to drum the beat with his left hand. "Now, pay attention to the words . . . it's the work of a genius."

"Just a little bit of kindness," sang a male voice on the tape, "just a little bit of kindness."

"This is my greatest work," he said.

When we listened to the song for the second time, I praised the words.

"This song has very kind words," I said.

"Yes, I'm really fond of it," he responded.

When he turned on the song for the third time, I started to run out of compliments.

"It is a very good song," I said. "Do you write songs?"

"Yes," he said. "This is my second record, my twenty-fifth song exactly."

"Oh," I said politely.

The fourth time, I began to really like the song and to tap the beat with my right foot. "A little bit of kindness, yes, you know that's exactly what we all need . . . a little bit of kindness . . . a little bit of kindness . . . a little bit of kindness."

On this happy note I was home. This is a true story.

4

Postcommunism, Postmodernism

The End of the Soviet World: From the Barricades to the Bazaar

In the summer of 1989 I went back to Leningrad, after an absence of nine years. My friends asked the usual question: "How long are you staying?"

"Two weeks," I said.

"I'm afraid you'll only be able to stay one week."

"Why?" I asked.

"Next week we're expecting the end of the world."

I knew then that I was in Russia, a country where nobody observes small-talk conventions. In July 1991, when I visited the Soviet Union again, that apocalyptic mood seemed to have passed, yet only ten days after my departure the much-awaited disaster, so proverbial that no one believed in it any longer, finally happened. On the morning of August 19 I watched CNN in Boston. On the screen news of Hurricane Bob—one of the most swift-moving and unpredictable hurricanes in New England history—alternated with images of tanks in Red Square. Apocalyptic *fin-de-siècle* commonplaces proliferated in the headlines: "The End of the Era," "Catastrophe," "Fear for the Future." As Mikhail Gorbachev was reported "ousted from power" by his own men and Boris Yeltsin was climbing the tank, Hurricane Bob blew by and "left millions of New Englanders without power."[1] As Soviet tanks were reported "storming television and radio stations" and blocking land access to harbors, the New England vaca-

The monument to Khrushchev and the shadow of the photographer (photo by the author)

tioners clad in their bathing suits "were riding out the storm." In fact, "vacation interruptus" seemed to be the major traumatic trope of the season; Bush and Gorbachev, New Englanders and Russians, were forced to take a break from their vacations. "Emergency measures" were taken in both countries. Stores ran out of candles.

As the tanks drove down Moscow streets I, too, experienced a "shortage of power." This time I knew I was in the United States, where disasters are characterized as "natural." In American media lingo the clichéd expression "power shortage" has no political, social, or metaphysical connotations. It refers merely to practical inconveniences: for instance, one can no longer watch TV.

While two "states of emergency," two disasters—natural in the United States and political in the Soviet Union—were competing for television time, the natural and political clichés started to cross the borders almost as rapidly as the new means of communication. In Brighton, Massachusetts, where many Soviet émigrés live, people rushed out to stock up on groceries, and no one could tell whether they worried about the power shortages or shortages in the Soviet Union. Meanwhile, in barricaded Moscow, the only program still televised was that of the ubiquitous CNN, transmitting to Russia via satellite as part of the peaceful gesture of the end of the cold war. And CNN, which for Russians was the only source of information about Russian events, masterfully intercut the images of Yeltsin on top of a tank with the threatening announcements of Hurricane Bob and advice on emergency measures. The rumor spread on the barricades that a horrendous destructive hurricane was raving from Florida to Siberia and would soon reach its peak. In the commercial breaks the optimistic and comforting messages about "home, kids, and fun" were lost, and Hurricane Bob turned into an ominous apocalyptic hero approaching Moscow with its final destruction. While Vice President Yanaev was only a banal fictional devil unable to "possess" the country, the true hero was Bob, the pale horseman of the apocalypse with an American first name.

Natural and political disasters illuminate the disasters of interpretation. Obviously, neither of the two potential fin-de-siècle catastrophes brought with them the end of the world. Yet the August 1991 coup d'état became the watershed of an era: it precipitated the end of the Soviet Union and of the Russian cultural empire with its common cultural text, shared double-entendres, and mythical status of the intelligentsia, which remained unquestioned until the end of glasnost'. After the coup everything referring to Russian life carried the prefix "post"—post-Soviet, post-glasnost'. These Russian post's are superimposed on the foreign ones: posttotalitarian, postmodern, postcolonial, postindustrial, and so on. Do these prefixes overlap?

The August 1991 coup was turned into televised spectacle and benefited from a system of global communication. But some Muscovites and Leningradians who did not have access to CNN had to figure out what had happened by watching Soviet TV and guessing what was not shown. A friend of mine was awakened by her mother, who told her that tanks were coming to Moscow. My friend thought at first that it was a bad joke, a banal example of Soviet paranoia. She turned on the TV. All the channels were transmitting the ballet *Swan Lake*. It was then that she realized that something terrible had occurred. (Similarly, during the massacre in Timisoara the Romanian TV transmitted folk dances.) *Swan Lake*, a dull spectacle of classical goodness, deemed safe and the least upsetting both for the Soviet people and for the members of the Emergency Committee, brought back the old commonplaces of stagnation that had been silently naturalized and internalized by people. Here the ballet performance of *Swan Lake* has to be understood not as an autonomous work of art but as a Soviet media spectacle. *Swan Lake*, a story of the victory of good over evil conveniently personified by white and black swans, is an icon of Russian and Soviet traditionalism. It preserves an air of tsarist luxury and nostalgia for classical art, old-fashioned virtuosity, and order. It was one of Stalin's favorite ballets; in Brezhnev's time it assumed the high style of developed socialism and became the most desirable Soviet commodity for the West, a kind of an official package of nostalgic Russian exotica.[2] (Recently *Swan Lake* has been performed in Boston to raise funds for post-Soviet Russia.) On the day of the coup the ritual of performing the great Russian ballet in the place of all the glasnost' programs, and the familiar restrained tone of the TV announcers, with measured intervals of official gloom and official optimism, made people experience again the time of Brezhnev's stagnation and recover the old practices of reading official texts between the lines and between the elegant classical leaps of little swan skirts.

The style of the coup lacked the old Stalinist, KGB brutality; rather, it was a mild Brezhnevite compromise with an old Soviet-style pretense at legality. The Emergency Committee hoped to appeal to public inertia, to regain the miraculous power of the meaningless discourse of the Brezhnev era with its few buzz words, appeals to the Soviet people, and promises of better food, the words secured by the presence of the tanks. In the end it turned out that the style of high Brezhnevism no longer framed Soviet politics, and that the postwar Soviet cultural myths of "people" and power, cemented by mutually compromising favors and fears, had become denaturalized in the past five years. In the Committee's speech the Soviet clichés were used together with the apocalyptic rhetoric of Russian nationalist right: a mythical enemy was disrupting law and order and making the country "ungovernable," bringing it to the edge of complete chaos. However, the bleak and uninspired language, lack of humor, and lack of energy made the manifesto of the Emergency Committee a sort of parody on Soviet discourse and its decadence. The anchorman on Soviet TV who read the speech of the Emergency Committee kept stumbling over the clichés, mixing them up and making quasi-Freudian slips of cultural unconsciousness: instead of "continuing" *(prodolzhenie)* the reforms he announced their "overcoming" *(preodolenie);* instead of warning about the danger of bloodshed *(krovoprolitie)* he warned about the danger of "bloodpolitics" *(krovopolitika).*

In the alternative Russian press, officially forbidden by the Emergency Committee, subversive language games and the self-conscious ironic play with clichés began the next day, aiming at necessary comic relief and distance from the new rulers. The newspaper *Smena* started the humorous competition to come up with the best deciphering of the abbreviation for the State Emergency Committee (GKChP in Russian) and since the response was overwhelming the newspaper jokingly concluded "our apologies to those who couldn't reach us in time; we have to wait for another coup and then we will announce a new competition."[3] When Gorbachev was invited to support the activities of the Emergency Committee, he allegedly responded: "What shitheads you all are." Whether Gorbachev actually used these words does not matter; what is important is the gross violation of "good taste" and official style, which appeared authentic and signifying. It was a mark of his resistance to the old Brezhnevite clichés and the assertion of the eclectic discourse of glasnost'.

Meanwhile, at CNN it was business as usual. On the one hand,

220   POSTCOMMUNISM, POSTMODERNISM

some brave Western reporters were at the Moscow barricades, bringing images back to the Russians, and as some participants testify, assuring them that communication with the outside world was not broken, that the world was watching. On the other hand, for the foreign viewers the events were conveniently framed by a bright new logo—"crisis in the Soviet Union"—and on the bottom of the image, simultaneous with the documentary footage, the screen broadcast information about stocks, which was the way the Soviet crisis was made relevant to some Americans. Images of Russian soldiers on tanks alternated with images of American body builders and "Soloflex" exercise machines, which help to eroticize the strong men and their paramilitary paraphernalia to make them look more "healthy and natural." In this way the spectators were receiving a nonlinear multiple narrative; between the lines of the tanks, as between the lines of the text, commercials offered us another, more "natural" drama with a happy ending, a *Bildungsroman* of personal improvement.[4]

In the view of Jean Baudrillard, the most popular postmodern theorist among contemporary Russian intellectuals, in an age of media culture the "disruptive event" can no longer happen. "The war would not take place," wrote Baudrillard in his essay in *Liberation* a week before the Gulf War.[5] The condition of simulation makes it particularly difficult to think about historical change, crisis, disaster, or catastrophe. According to Baudrillard, in an era of TV domination we always live already *après coup* or "after the orgy"—for we live in the age of global indifference, with a permanent power shortage.

Catastrophe (from *cata*, "over," and *strephein*, "to turn"), an overturning, originated in the theater and not in nature, and referred to the dénouement in a classical Greek tragedy.[6] Because a catastrophe disrupts the everyday flow of existence, it can effect a radical paradigm shift; those who have experienced it could claim a privileged access to the elusive and ephemeral "real" of the human existence. Yet the actual experience of catastrophe is superseded by its memory, its everyday effects and traces; the radical character of the catastrophic is quickly assimilated for the sake of survival of both the human species and the media.

The aftermaths of the coup bring forward the connections between postcommunism and postmodernism, as well as the paradoxical effects of global communication and cross-cultural misreadings. Did the coup reveal that history indeed has turned into a simulacrum, or, on the contrary, did it show that postmodernist irony is not incompatible with political action?[7]

This question was posed right after the coup to a group of young Russian "postmodern" artists and art historians who went to the barricades. Their no less postmodern interviewer observed that they "did not go to the miraculously open international airport and leave the country like good yuppies but instead went out to the streets."[8] "What the hell did you go to the barricades for?"—was the first question. Here is the answer of Viktor Misiano, a curator of contemporary avant-garde art and a postmodern critic:

> The experience was "pure art," and a gigantic performance. The most striking metaphor of the events was the barricade near the subway called "Barricade Station." Our barricade was built on top of the barricades of the monument to the Revolution of 1905. It was built in such a way that it did not defend anything. But from the semantic point of view there was a great contradiction in cultural symbols, since the new revolution was defended in the name of ideals inimical to those of the old revolution. This was a typical postmodern revolution. By the way, during the coup I was writing the article "Art and Politics" so I was interested in the events from a professional point of view. And I was not alone there on the streets. Everyone was there. It is no secret that had the coup succeeded both the racketeers and the avant-garde artists would have been the victims.[9]

It appears as if the building of the barricades was only another kind of Moscow party. Yet when I pressed Viktor during our meeting to speak beyond his professional interest in art and politics, he confessed that there were two moments of authenticity. The first was when he saw Gorbachev on TV reading the text given to him by his captors, and the former Soviet leader looked aged and scared; even his intonation—again it's the intonation, and not the message—betrayed his fear. And the second moment of authenticity was when the people on the symbolic barricades heard shots and started to run, only to realize that they were running precisely in the direction of the tanks and that they were in fact surrounded. Perhaps irony and fear, aesthetic self-reflexivity and disruptive experiences, can go hand in hand. There is often no time to choose between them.

The artist Konstantin Zvezdochetov, who in fact had been arrested by the KGB and called to serve in the Army only some five or six years earlier, confessed that he was "a sentimental kind of guy" and that he had "dreamed of that experience all [his] life."[10] The experience was to him at once "carnival and corrida." One of the most amazing ironies of the coup's aesthetics was that the Russian flag which flew over the Moscow White House during the events of the coup—the tri-color, as opposed to the blood-colored Soviet flag—was actually made by Konstantin Zvezdochetov and Andrei Filippov for their new artistic installation. Zvezdochetov took the flag with him when he went to the barricades to the Russian White House on August 19 to protect him from the wind, and was happy to donate it for a good cause. This pragmatic political use of an aesthetic object, an object that itself mimes a political symbol, goes against the grain of both contemporary American conceptions of pop art and the new conservative outlook that guards against the "defamation of the American flag." It would be hard to imagine Jasper Johns's American flag flying over the White House in Washington.

The experience of the coup had some aesthetic *trompe-l'oeil* effects. On the day before the events, the Soviet TV showed an adaptation of *The One Who Doesn't Return,* Alexander Kabakov's apocalyptic science-fiction novel which predicts a victorious military coup in the mid-1990s. But occasionally life only pretends to imitate art and in fact cheats on it. The apocalypse that would certainly have made for a stunning aesthetic dénouement did not take place; the coup did not succeed. Even the most ironic intellectuals may lose their distance, as well as the internalized conscience of a perpetual simulation that it is not in their power to affect. Many people told me that the events of the failed coup became a kind of cathartic experience, a celebration of loss of fear, a redemption of the years of silence and anger. Others reported that it was a kind of carnival, with lots of free food delivered by the new cooperative restaurants, with music and tanks—and nobody was completely sure which side those tanks were on at any particular moment.

So did the coup really take place? Ironically, in the Russian context this Baudrillardian question could be posed only if the coup had succeeded. In other words, had the coup succeeded one could have said that it had never happened, that it was merely a restoration of order and not a disruptive event. But at that moment "fatal banality" did not triumph; everyday behavior changed, and people rejected the new clichés of responses to power. In the moment of extremity, the cathartic theatricality of the events effected a crucial "power shortage" in the internalized structure of the vicious circle of simulations. The potential catastrophe, or at least the disruptive event, disrupted narcissistic theorizing and certain kinds of self-generating intellectual paradoxes.

And what can be better than a failed catastrophe or disaster with a happy ending! The Soviet coup was a late-twentieth-century coup—the quickest of the failed Russian revolutions. The apocalypse turned into a petty, badly organized, and unspectacular melodrama that failed not only in its military tactics and strategies but also in its style. But after the coup everyday life returned to being much less spectacular than the coup itself. It subsided into that untranslatable Russian *byt* that people do not know how to survive. Some ironic Russian journalists have suggested that the abolition of the Soviet Union was a theatrical necessity: people who participated in building the barricades began to be bored and disenchanted with their daily grind, and the new exciting risky event was uplifting for their imagination. So in the Russian case, perhaps, the problem is not that people always live "already after the coup," but that they live always in anticipation of a coup that would relieve their unspectacular *dailiness*.

In the midst of this historical change Russian postmodern theory flourished. Some ex-Soviet writers, exhibiting a peculiar patriotic zeal, declared that Russians in fact invented postmodernism, particularly its apocalyptic branch, and were the first to live through the era of "fatal banality" and simulacra later described by Baudrillard. In this view, Socialist Realism is seen as a kind of postmodernism *avant la lettre* that came literally after the official destruction of Russian modernism, but inherited some of its utopian claims.[11] The era of Brezhnev's stagnation was its final decadent stage. In Russia, therefore, postmodern simulation was experienced in daily life much before it was theorized in the West. Many late-Soviet postmodern artists and critics, in a classically Russian totalizing gesture, propose one single truly postmodern master narrative radiating from Moscow.

It is not by chance that in Russia postmodernism had been primarily connected to Baudrillard; his authoritarian voice and totalizing apocalyptic vision, exemplified in the very choice of quasi-religious metaphors, and his reduction of everyday culture to fatal banality are much more appealing to a Russian thinker than the experimental indeterminacy and attention to singularity, to hybrid impure cultures and diversity of voices, that were explored by many Western philosophers and artists. For them, postmodernism exists only in multiple versions; perhaps as a playful, antinationalist, cosmopolitan, and dystopian artistic dream. (In this case, Socialist Realism would certainly not qualify.) As for Baudrillard, he plays directly into Russian apocalyptic thinking, in both its traditional and postmodern versions; he is read together with Berdiaev and Dostoevsky and interpreted through them. Russian postmodernist theory looks more like a variation on Russian mythology, a late-twentieth-century encounter between Russian and Western thinking.

One feature of postmodern culture is particularly relevant to post-Soviet situation: the loss of the master narrative. Its disappearance could be both liberating and frightening.[12] The 1991 August coup d'état was a heroic and comic dénouement to the grand Soviet narrative as well as to the main narrative of sovietology. It left a perception of loss of Soviet communality and of the unified Soviet cultural text, but there is no clear agreement as to what exactly constituted this cultural text in the first place and, in the second, what part of it had ceased to exist. Further, the question remains whether this loss of a Soviet master narrative, which produced a distinct kind of conformism as well as a distinct form of dissidence, is to be unconditionally celebrated or partially mourned. Did the demise of this narrative signify the elimination of hypocrisy and double-speak? Or was it the loss of a certain kind of idealism that ended up compromising all ideals? What is to be done with a catastrophic narrative that links the future and the past and perpetually escapes the everyday? In Russia it is often easier to imagine time "after the future" and "beyond history" than to describe and confront the present.

Visiting Russia two years after the coup, in 1993, I was struck by the altered perception of time. In response to snowballing historical changes and hyperinflation, as well as vertiginous changes of language and much less change in daily life, people began to live exclusively in the present. The humorous saying of the day was the famous pronouncement supposedly made by Lenin on the eve of the October Revolution: "yesterday was too early, tomorrow too late—hence this evening." People seem to live by this principle, adapting to the unimaginable economic changes and living again in some state of historical simulation, often penniless but never humorless. In the field of art and ideas new waves were followed by newer waves, postmodernism was already outmoded and so was liberalism. Everything appears to be a fad or a fashion—life, art, history. I do not attempt to follow this accelerated rhythm, trying to catch the latest wave. Instead, in hope of suspending the catastrophic narrative, and to avoid the vertigo of already excessive new labels, I will follow the route of common places and their unconventional rewriting.

The loss of a master narrative manifests itself in the changing cityscape, in falling monuments and rising dolls. Similar shifts of cultural boundaries can be found in the art and culture of glasnost' and post-glasnost', which no longer belong solely to the intelligentsia but are shared with new entrepreneurs, the mythical descendants of the old Russian merchants. From the "restructured" maps of post-Soviet Russia and the displays of kitsch sold on Arbat Street, we will turn to the "works of art" and examine how Soviet history is presented through the history of kitsch—from the old cult of Stalin to the new cult of the nude—and how everyday mythologies are recovered in the works of some women artists, writers, and film makers. The new cultural diversity produces inevitable paradoxes: while the "high art" of cinema, experimental fiction, and conceptualism replays the history of kitsch and recovers everyday life, the galleries of the new merchants make a scandal out of art and life, and the born-again commercial culture aspires again to the good taste of old and new Russia, developing reverently its own mythical history in pseudo-Russian style. Finally, in the 1990s, "culture" in the traditional Russian as well as official Soviet and underground dissident sense is in a deep crisis. The demise of censorship was followed by the demise of readership, and the new economic realities further devalued the role of culture. From the hindsight of the 1990s perestroika appears as the "golden age" of Russian art and the glorious twilight of the Russian intelligentsia.

Glasnost' Streetwalking: Fallen Monuments and Rising Dolls

The most striking event of glasnost' was the return of street life. The food line was no longer the only forum for voicing public opinion. The squares and bazaars, the open-air discussion clubs and the kiosks displaying everything from the *Manual of Theosophy* to the *Secrets of Sex,* from the complete works of Tolstoy to cotton panties made

The dog of the mayor of Moscow inspecting the head of the former head of
the KGB, Felix Dzerzhinsky (photo by Mark Shteinbok)

in Turkey, offer a plethora of street entertainment. Street music ranges from prisoners' romances to Beatles imitations, from great performances by unemployed members of the orchestra to accordion tunes played by war veterans. Window shopping becomes exciting again—not so much for what is displayed in the window of an old state store, but rather for what is displayed outside, on the window sill, by the amateur salesmen. An old joke from Brezhnev's time went like this: a man asks the salesgirl: "Don't you have meat?" "You must be in the wrong store," she answers. "Here we don't have fish. Across the street is where they don't have meat." In the glasnost' window with a cheerful sign in Brezhnevite style saying "Meat, Fish, Canned Food" there is no food at all but rather clothes, wine, and sneakers, while outside they sell souvenirs and Marlboro cigarettes. Those objects represent a perverse mirror image of the old Soviet consumerism and all the predictable repressed desires of the unified culture. There is—and there has always been—a perfect incongruence between the store sign and the objects on display, an incongruence that no longer surprises anyone; on the contrary, it is the correspondence between the two that would appear suspicious and strange. The shop window superimposes numerous reflections: old signs, new consumer items, and the city crowds.

During his visit to Moscow in 1927 Walter Benjamin wrote that the one human species which has become endangered in postrevolutionary Moscow is the free-floating wanderer and cultural observer, a *flaneur*, who is at once inside and outside the crowd, alienated while engaged, engaged, but not too much; he is only a "fellow-traveler." Benjamin's own account of the life in Moscow is the last attempt of a foreign *flaneur* to describe Moscow, to record the fleeing Present, and to collect material evidence without yielding to predictable ideological narratives. Benjamin writes, in a letter to Martin Buber: "I want to write a description of Moscow at the present moment in which 'all factuality is already theory' and which will thereby refrain from any deductive abstraction, from any prognostication, and even within certain limits from any judgment."[13] He wishes to collect facts that are not statistical or scientific, but unfinished and imperfect slices of life, material fragments, ephemeral collages of the Present. He believes this to be the most honest critical exercise in times of confusion. By the early 1930s the fact-collector could no longer travel in Russia; street life had become more ideologized, covered by the grids of official narratives that cut through the city like the utopian lines of Stalin's Metro, the most efficient in the world.

Now, sixty-five years after Benjamin's visit, the *flaneur* is born again. In Brezhnev's time the choice was either to conform or to dissent, either to marginalize oneself or to internalize the impossibility of marginality. Crossing borders back and forth, in both a literal and a metaphorical sense, was hardly possible. But at present many imaginary maps of the city coexist once again and one can wander around, sometimes appearing native, other times speaking with a mild foreign accent in both English and Russian, occasionally threatened by taxi drivers, capricious and omnipotent rulers of new urban communication.

Glasnost' marked not the end of history but its rediscovery and its passionate rewriting. The first thing that was voluntarily abandoned at the time of early glasnost' was the attempt to build a utopia. Glasnost' was not an ideology of newness. The ideology of the new was associated in the Russian context with the revolutionary avant-garde, or rather with its Bolshevik, and later Stalinist, appropriation; any utopian discourse of a new world order and building new life from a *tabula rasa* appeared passé. Glasnost' promoted the reappropriation of history. This way of creating the future through reinventing the past often goes hand in hand with an inability to capture and comprehend the present. The commonplaces of glasnost'—both in a literal sense as urban public sites and in a rhetorical sense as the clichés of language—look like a bizarre conglomeration of imperial ruins. Beheaded Communist leaders and other totalitarian antiques lie or stand next to cheap Western gadgets and expensive Russian artifacts made for tourist consumption. There is still, in present-day Russia, a great urge to find a single, all-embracing narrative—national, religious, historic, political, or aesthetic—to recover the single dramatic plot with devils and angels, black and white swans, hangmen and victims, that would explain Russia's Past, Present, and Future. Yet as Russian history shows, authorial narratives could easily become self-fulfilling prophecies. Perhaps now is the time to wander around the "restructuring" cities and renamed streets, collecting the ephemeral slices of life, incongruous and incomplete, contradictory and illuminating, letting them speak for themselves.

In the Gorbachev period the future-oriented ideology of the avant-garde and Socialist Realism was replaced by a backward glance of commemoration. The past in contemporary Russia has turned into a kind of future perfect, or future imperfect (both are clear deviations from Russian grammar). During my first visit to what still was the Soviet Union, in 1989, I could not keep track of the anniversaries: within three days, there was the 750th anniversary of Alexander Nevsky's victory, a commemoration of the rebellion of the Left Socialist Revolutionaries against the monopoly of Bolshevik power, and the day of Devout Vladimir, the holiday of the Old Believers. There was great confusion about what was to be comˉnemorated and what was to be forgotten. One had a distinct sense that people were living out history, but it was less clear what the true Russian history should look like. Should it be presented as the history of the great Russian state, as a suppressed history of the Orthodox Church, or as the history of resistance to Bolsheviks? History appeared to be rewritten every day. On TV shows the age of glasnost' was compared to the "rule of two powers" after the February Revolution in 1917 and also to the "time of confusion" after the death of Ivan the Terrible in the seventeenth century, when there was no clear power in the country and a series of pretenders tried to assume the Russian throne. The present needed a precedent, some historical way of explaining it. Streets were renamed with disorienting swiftness, usually returning to their pre-Soviet names, and there was great uncertainty as to which holidays were to be celebrated and which erased (the general tendency is to celebrate more, not less). The confusion is reminiscent of the time right after the Revolution, when the frenzy of renaming was taking place for the first time. So the renaming is not new, but it is a redemptive reenactment of a revolutionary ritual turned into a popular carnival.

    In 1991, on St. Isaak Square in Leningrad, I was greeted by a large sign in English, "Welcome to St. Petersburg! McGrory Stores." For a moment I thought it was an advertisement for vacations in Florida, but obviously this was not the case. When it was decided that Leningrad (Petrograd and St. Petersburg in the past) would return "to its original name," there was a debate as to what the original or authentic name of the city really was. Alexander Solzhenitsyn suggested to go beyond the historical name St. Petersburg (given the city by its founder, Peter the Great) to the Russian source of the original name: Sviato-Petrograd (this would be a literal translation into a nonexistent language, a purified Slavonic Russian, of St. Petersburg). This was a gesture characteristic of the nationalist, mythical, and corrective rewriting of history.[14] This schizophrenia of language, which might be regarded as therapeutic, occurs all the time. The Soviet clichés are rejected in favor of an eclectic mix made up of euphonic-sounding prerevolutionary words, contemporary American business jargon, and the songs from the "tape culture" of the 1960s. The fashionable word of the 1991 season was "stock market" (birzha). Not only is everyone opening his or her own "stock market," which is now very fashionable, but the image of the stock market embraces all spheres of life. The newspapers have sections labeled "stock market of news" (birzha novostei), or "a stock market of ideas," or even "a stock market of intellectual property." This is the latest dictate of fashion: the outmoded word "intellectual" is surrounded on both sides by the new words "stock market" and "property."

Public sites were also subjected to transformations. After the coup Russia witnessed again the fantastic spectacle of moving and flying monuments. Lenin was strangled by the neck in Tallin; in Kiev he was caged and taken off his pedestal and all that remained were his bronze boots standing alone, like a Magritte picture. The toppling of the statue of Felix Dzerzhinsky, the so-called Iron Felix, turned into a public celebration.[15] The celebrated émigré cellist Rostropovich, who returned to Russia during the coup, suggested that a statue to Alexander Solzhenitsyn be put in his place, and someone on the street proposed Jesus Christ instead. Tatyana Tolstaya, writing in Moscow News, claimed that everyone, herself included, was touched by "the pathos of iconoclasm and vandalism."[16] And everyone had specific favorite candidates for toppling. She proposed to pull down the gigantic statue to Mother Russia, because it insults every mother as well as Russia.

The iconoclastic destruction of monuments goes hand in hand with a nostalgia for new idols.[17] New memorials appear all the time but they tend to avoid the kind of figurative, grandiose representation that seems to have compromised itself. Dzerzhinsky Square reflects this strange dialectic of monumentality; the old monument to Dzerzhinsky stood in the center of the square in front of the Lubianka building—the headquarters of KGB—cheek by jowl with a new modernist monument to the revolutionary poet Vladimir Mayakovsky, who used to live in the apartment next door (it is also where he committed suicide). The Mayakovsky monument, the poet's oversized

On the pedestal: The toppled monument to Dzerzhinsky now lies in the grass
across the street from Moscow's Gorky Park (photo by Mark Shteinbok)

bold head, stands in front of the little-visited Mayakovsky museum; it is the last pre-glasnost' monument in the city that pays its dues to the ironic avant-gardism of the Moscow architects of the 1970s, who were mostly resigned to being architects "on paper," rarely allowed to realize their whimsical and dreamlike projects. (The relationship between Dzerzhinsky and Mayakovsky, the revolutionary hero and founder of the KGB and the revolutionary poet who both supported and suffered from the revolutionary order, deserves a special study.)

The third memorial in the square was erected not by architects but by the people: it is a memorial to the victims of the KGB, adorned with flowers, red banners, and names. Similar kinds of spontaneous popular memorials of different generations appear all over the city. On Arbat Street there is a memorial dedicated to Viktor Tsoi, the popular rock singer of early perestroika who died in a car accident. The memorial is a wall covered with graffiti, dedications, and inscriptions, as well as tapes of Tsoi and his photograph (surprisingly, not yet stolen). It brings to mind the grave of Jim Morrison. The other site of popular commemoration is the house of Mikhail Bulgakov, where according to the legend lived the celebrated character from this novel, the kind devil Woland. The house embodies Soviet political and aesthetic history: once the house of the well-known publisher Peguit, after the Revolution it was turned into one of the first communal houses in Moscow, the house of the revolutionary communes where alternative lifestyles blossomed. According to legend, the woman who called herself Fanny Kaplan lived here briefly, the anarchist and Socialist Revolutionary who attempted to shoot Lenin in August of 1918. Or perhaps in the popular imagination Fanny Kaplan and Woland joined together in one ghost. The haunted house of Bulgakov was reinhabited by young people in the 1980s, and its black entrance was covered by new graffiti celebrating the heroes of Bulgakov's fantastic novel. Now people are trying to collect funds for opening a Bulgakov museum in the house, and meanwhile the old and decrepit communal apartments are inhabited by the Soviet homeless. Bulgakov's house is a haunted house of postrevolutionary Soviet history. Perhaps a few years hence the abandoned, graffiti-spattered yard of Bulgakov's house will be cleaned up and turned into a newly planted sculpture garden, in which a bronze witch Margarita from Bulgakov's novel will fly around an equestrian statue of Fanny Kaplan.

But the principal monument to glasnost' is McDonald's. The Pushkin monument, which was already turned around in Stalin's time to face the main thoroughfare of new Moscow, now faces a two-hour line to McDonald's. The "great genius of the Russian letters" contemplates a distant, huge "M"—not for nearby Marx Avenue. The McDonald's in Moscow is like a monument to the Western world in miniature: it contains a model Big Ben and Eiffel Tower under a brightly painted Californian sky, with windsurfers on the horizon. To the left of Pushkin's monument is the headquarters of the *Moscow News,* which in the late 1980s was a center for all the unofficial press. There one could purchase—at triple the price—everything from Baltic Independence papers to *Sexual Anecdotes* to a paper called *Anti-Soviet Truth (Anti-Sovetskaia Pravda),* published by one man in 1990–91. Its front page featured portraits of Marx, Lenin, and Nicholas II, and a collage of cultural symbols, including the Soviet star, the Nazi swastika, and the British cross. In 1991 *The Anti-Soviet Truth* truthfully reflected the confusion of signs; the editor, the sole writer and censor of the text, played the role of fool in the liberating political carnival. In 1991 the editorial office of the *Moscow News* had a major fire, and although it was rebuilt, the place has lost its urban significance. In 1992 people had become oversaturated with Moscow and other news and, instead of global events, discussed the food shortages and the intrigues of the TV soap operas.

Between 1988 and 1992 Arbat Street was Moscow's prime commercial street, a monument to the newly born Soviet market economy (which has more to do with the marketplace than with the economy). Here one could purchase matreshka dolls with Gorbachev or Jesus Christ faces or any other touristic images of Russianness, such as Russian landscapes with churches and birch trees; there were oil-painted blondes in black shawls with naked breasts, reproductions of works like Raphael's *Sistine Madonna* and Rembrandt's *Danae* (the painting that has been recently vandalized in the Hermitage), and pink stuffed pussy cats. Here is what Benjamin saw on sale on Arbat Street:

There is the Mother of God with three hands. She is half-naked. From the navel rises a strong well-formed hand. At right and left the two others spread in the gesture of blessing. This threesome of hands is deemed a symbol of the Holy Trinity. There is another

A bird's-eye view of Arbat Street, 1991 (photo by Mark Shteinbok)

devotional picture of the Mother of God that shows her with open belly; clouds come from it instead of entrails; in their midst dances the Christ child holding a violin in his hand. Since the sale of icons is considered a branch of the paper and picture trade, these booths with pictures of saints stand next to those with paper goods, so that they are always flanked by portraits of Lenin, like a prisoner between two policemen.[18]

The objects for sale on Arbat during the glasnost' era were similar; there were many different saints and some of the same portraits of Lenin; these are sold for a higher price if they are revolutionary antiques from 1926 or 1966. But their status has changed; now it seems that it is Lenin who is flanked by the Orthodox saints, the Holy Virgin, and Jesus Christ; they surround the dethroned Party leader like new spiritual policemen. Religious images no longer have to be hidden. By 1993 Arbat has become gentrified and once again cleared of the street vendors; the hard-currency cappuccino places, souvenir boutiques, and antique stores supplanted the anarchic salesmen and their precarious kiosks that made the street famous during the glasnost' days.

The toys sold on Arbat are not for children's consumption: children prefer Ninja Turtles or some Russian version of Superman 3 made in Turkey or China. The toys on display here are no longer merely playful exemptions from totalitarian mythology; rather they play with this mythology and mock it. The matreshka dolls and the chess sets replay history on a different scale. They are parodic yet faithful guardians of the Soviet cultural text. The matreshka personages, like commedia dell'arte masks, picture only the leaders who captivated the popular imagination. Thus Malenkov, Andropov, and Chernenko, who were too quick to leave their Party leadership, are excluded. First there were matreshkas with Gorbachev enclosing Brezhnev, Khrushchev, Stalin, and little Lenin last. Raisa Gorbacheva had her brief moment of fame underneath her husband but was quickly supplanted by Yeltsin. In the summer of 1991, right before the coup, I was given a present that became symbolic. A woman engineer (who during the time of glasnost' took up the more profitable trade of matreshka-painting) gave me a set of dolls in which Gorbachev was still the top doll, and a little smaller Yeltsin, painted in red, was still unfinished. Only a week later there were plenty of top Yeltsin dolls on Arbat Street for sale to the stranded foreigners, while Yeltsin himself was on top of the barricade.

Postcommunist toys, 1991 (photo by Mark Shteinbok)

Literary matreshkas follow the same designs as the political ones, though they are not necessarily ranked chronologically but mythologically. Pushkin, the "sun of Russian poetry," is frequently the one to enclose his literary brothers and sons, who include Lermontov, Tolstoy, Dostoevsky, and either baby Gorky or even baby Solzhenitsyn. Thus matreshkas reproduce a common cultural text memorized by heart in Soviet high schools. In the choice of principal political and cultural protagonists matreshkas faithfully follow their public prototypes, the monuments on the city streets and squares. These days monarchist matreshkas are also in popular demand. Ivan the Terrible and Peter the Great hide inside Nicholas II, adorned by a picturesque moustache.

The original matreshkas are female, yet except for one set with Raisa Gorbacheva, I have not seen any female protagonists of Russian literature and history immortalized on matreshkas—no Catherine the Second and, for more obvious reasons, no Tsvetaeva or Akhmatova either. They are beyond the accepted repertoire of the Soviet commedia dell'arte.

Are matreshka dolls objects of art, craft, or kitsch? If kitsch, is it self-conscious, playful kitsch, or a self-complacent kind? The matreshka—the most Russian of all dolls—in fact originated in Japan. The first matreshka in the Russian style had two authors: the painter Maliutin and the toymaker Zvezdochkin. It was designed in the workshop "Children's Education" in the 1890s, when folk art had become fashionable among the urban elite. Such crafts were usually made by *kustars* for international exhibitions, and they reappeared later, in stylized versions, when some artists of the Russian avant garde rediscovered the bright "popular" color of the Russian icons and traditional folkloric ornaments against the bleak grey-brown-green palette of the nineteenth-century realist painters. The matreshka is at the core of a changing discourse on what is "popular" in Russian culture, like one definition nestled inside another. Only certain types of dolls and village crafts were chosen to represent an authentic people's culture, while the other kinds were regarded as too impure, too unprofessional, or else were simply overlooked by the artists and arbiters of artistic taste. At first, the primitive shape and bright ornamentality of the matreshka attracted the avant-garde artists of prerevolutionary times. Later, the peasant-looking artifacts were supplanted by more industrial-looking technological images. In the early Stalin years of the 1930s, matreshkas were back in style standing for the official people's culture. Forgotten in the 1950s and 1960s, surviving only in remote villages or on the stuffed shelves of the communal apartments, matreshkas made their triumphant return in the 1970s as exemplary embodiments of Russian-ness for the West. (Stalin created a perfect commercial package of Russian-Soviet people's culture that still sells very well in the West.) Today, there is a direct relationship between the growing number of matreshkas and the diminishing number of monuments. Cultural scales and hierarchies are changing, as the imperial Soviet monumentality finds its ironic reflection in the minor commercial arts, and the intimidating public statues find their comical reflection in ironic ordinary objects and toys. Now that political and aesthetic dramas are played out in the everyday realm, the war of the monuments like that in Eisenstein's *October*, takes place in the marketplace of toys.

The matreshkas displayed on Arbat are ironic and cheerful dolls; they laugh at the Russian folk culture packaged for the foreign tourists and at the same time testify to the art of bright ornamentation and to people's inventiveness. The more conservative dolls imitate traditional Russian matreshka style; others appear in more stylized avant-gardish versions or in the guise of political cartoons, while some are merely tacky quick jobs for easy money-making. Matreshkas are made by unemployed artists, students, black-marketeers, or even former engineers who can no longer make a living. Matreshkas are in a way the authentic artifacts of the impure and eclectic commercial culture of Gorbachev's time.

For Walter Benjamin the Russian folk toys were nostalgic artifacts—triply nostalgic, in their evocation of childhood, of village life, and of the vanishing pretechnological era of craftsmanship. He endowed Russian dolls with a special aura; as survivors of both the bourgeois institution of art and of Soviet ideologization, they were historical anachronisms at a time of futuristic utopias and Soviet Fordism-Leninism. Sixty-five years later, the toys too become ideologized and, in the postutopian climate of glasnost' and post-glasnost', they are comic artifacts with which adults play at politics and the new commercialism. These toys too have an aura—an aura of history of ideological manipulations and of many paradises lost: the paradise of childhood, of totalitarian infantilism, and of pure folk spirit.

My tour of contemporary Russian commonplaces is a bit like walking along Arbat in search of the ultimate matreshka doll that would hide and cover up the imperfections of the other ones. But I would be afraid to look into her perfect, starry eyes.

Stalin's Cinematic Charisma, or History as Kitsch

"Cinema is an art of illusion," wrote Stalin, "yet it dictates its laws to life itself."[19] In the last years of his life Stalin turned into a film critic, a kind of postmodernist *avant la lettre*, who reflects upon the lively powers of artistic illusion. In the early years of glasnost' Stalin himself became a cinematic fetish, and the denunciation of totalitarianism turned into one of the critical master narratives.[20] For a brief period many Soviet directors believed again that the cinema would be the "most important art" that would dictate its illusions to life.

The new clichés of glasnost' cinema were summarized in this image: a nude girl sitting in front of a portrait of Stalin smoking marijuana. The three taboos of Brezhnev's time—nudity, representation of Stalinism, and drugs—had been eagerly lifted, occasionally to excess. Before becoming merely a middle doll of a large matreshka with Nikita Khrushchev on top and Vladimir Lenin inside, Stalin had been

the most seductive villain of the Gorbachev period. The search for
lost Soviet history was accompanied by the search for artistic expression. This led to the emergence of an eclectic, surrealist cinema with
Stalin as its kitschy devil, as well as to the flourishing of the documentary genre. Yet the exhilarating recovery of archival footage led
to a reconsideration of the status of "documentary" in the Soviet
context, since much unshelved documentary footage appeared staged
and camouflaged. So while early glasnost' documentaries aimed at
filling the "white spots" of Soviet history, the provocative and controversial documentaries of the late 1980s, such as *I Served in Stalin's
Bodyguard* (1989) and *Stalin Is with Us?* (1989), highlighted the
relation between fact and fiction and discovered new, ironic, and
absurdist uses of ideological montage. By the 1990s the cinematic
representation of Stalinism had become more self-referential, a reflection on both the making and the unmaking of the cinematic illusion
and on the early discourses of glasnost', which have quickly receded
into history. Recent films, such as *The Abyss* (1992), which presents
scenes from the life of the Stalinist elite and makes a "retro" re-crea-
tion of the Stalinist grand style, bring together two fashionable
"post"s: post-totalitarianism and postmodernism. The *tableaux vi-
vants* of totalitarian nostalgia made in post-Soviet Russia reveal a
nostalgia for the grand style of the masterpieces of European cinema
along with regret for the vanishing cultural importance of cinema
itself. So Stalin in late Soviet and post-Soviet cinema is a truly postmodern hero, subject to demystification and remythologization, to
documentary exposure and fictional recreation, moving back and
forth between irony and nostalgia. The Stalin treatment reflects recent
changes in the conceptions of history and art and their diminishing
role in the post-glasnost' period.

   In the late 1980s Soviet life became more interesting than art; going
out on the streets was more exciting than going to the movies. By the
end of glasnost', however, people seem to have become overburdened
by the onslaught of historical revelations (the implication of which in
many cases remained undigested), and after the coup the most popular spectacle was a TV soap-opera serial made in Brazil or Mexico a
decade ago that provided mass therapy for the historical traumas.
Old-fashioned Latin American soap operas did not "dictate their laws
to life" but disclose escapist and survival strategies. Hence visual
fascination with Stalin and the totalitarian "grand epoch" was re-

placed by a much less critical cult of Don Alonso and Dona Mariana, occasionally disrupted by an emergence of some forgotten member of the late tsar's family. Yet the charisma of totalitarian spectacle colored a brief euphoric twilight of Soviet cinema, one of the first arts to confront Soviet history and embody the aesthetics of this time of confusion.

The subtitle of Semion Aranovich's film *I Served in Stalin's Bodyguard* is "An Experiment in Documentary Mythology." Documentary mythology might sound like an oxymoron, but only if one differentiates the historical from the mythological consciousness and considers the documentary to be a factual representation devoid of myth and mystification. In Russian the word *istoriia* is used for both "story" and "history." In the Russian tradition since the eighteenth century fictional and nonfictional histories were equally respectable, since history was written by major writers and poets, not by professional historians.[21] Hence the critique of positivist historiography launched by the new historians in the American context would hardly apply to the Russian situation, where the ties between historiography and literature have never been severed. The same may be said for the relationship between documentary and myth.

The cult of personality and the cult of the leader are among the central cultural myths that require some critical documentation. Roland Barthes considers the Soviet Stalinist myth to be the chief "myth on the left."[22] In fact, this myth is not so modern and not so "left"; the cult of personality is an old Russian version of the ancient Roman cult of emperors, which later developed into the cult of the Russian tsar, "the little father of the people" *(batiushka)* and the savior of his people from apocalypse and disorder. It has been argued that the apocalyptic structure is fundamental for Russian Orthodox beliefs and Russian Marxist thinking alike, as both are predicated on the construction of a "paradise on earth," and both rest on an inescapable opposition between a strong, centralized order (the rule of the great Orthodox tsar, or the dictatorship of the Communist Party and its leader) and chaos, anarchy, and the end of the world—nothing in between.[23]

I Served in Stalin's Bodyguard, the first film in Aranovich's trilogy about Stalinism that includes *I Served in Stalin's Nomenclatura* (1990) and *The Great Concert of the People* (1991), documents the naturalization of the cult of personality. The film centers around an uncensored confession from, or rather conversation with, a dedicated Stalinist and also a charming "little civil servant" Alexei Rybin, who was one of Stalin's inner circle.[24] His activities combine art and politics: he served in Stalin's bodyguard and was responsible for mining the Bolshoi Theater during the war, but now he works in the local House of Young Pioneers, where he teaches music together with patriotic marching—"to get a better sense of rhythm." Rybin tells us heartfelt stories about Stalin's love for borscht, porridge, and dried fruit, his affection for the common people, and his extraordinary knowledge of *solfeggio* and cinema. The great leader was a folkloric hero, modest but stern, strict but fair, tough but loving. The viewer is forced by Rybin's account into the uncomfortable position of actually experiencing Stalin's personal charisma. Rybin's face is shot mostly in close-ups, looking almost straight into the camera, so that we become uncertain whether we are listening to him, or he is inspecting us with his well-trained eyes.

Unlike most Soviet documentaries, *I Served in Stalin's Bodyguard* does not have an omniscient voice-over to provide a unifying narration and a central point of view. The way it is made questions the authorial structure of communication, and the film does not join those open denunciations of Stalinism which by now have acquired a familiar, almost official ring. Aranovich's poetic montage often does not contradict Rybin, but rather appears to illustrate his words in an almost childishly naïve manner with rare archival footage from Stalin's time. (When asked why he chose not to comment on the Rybin story, Aranovich remarked that he promised that to Rybin. One thinks of the film maker Claude Lanzmann, who also promised the former Nazis he interviewed that he would not put them into *Shoah,* but later admitted that he did not feel ethically obligated toward them; most viewers of the film congratulate him on this decision.) The relation between image and text in the film, as well as that between the documentary footage of the 1930s and Rybin's narrative of the 1980s, is quite complex. Moving away from Eisenstein's "ideological montage," it is based on a reduction to absurdity. The iconographic sequence of Stalin waving to his people from the tribune of the mausoleum is uncannily repeated several times in silence, which makes this symbolic gesture of father-savior and great leader of the people appear mechanical and ridiculous. Stalin is deprived of his aura: he looks like a marionette whose strings are pulled by another director, a marionette that is no longer in charge of the terrifying spectacle. This kind of cinematic disempowerment is very subtly accomplished throughout the film. Absurdity is more capable of killing the aura of the great leader of the people than a direct political invective.

Rybin himself is a charismatic character engaged in self-fashioning as well as in the fashioning of history. He presents himself as a naïve but dedicated people's servant, a "little man" surrounded by a crowd of "well-wishers" (a euphemism for informers) who helped him "do his work." With his accordion as prop, he is an arbiter of art and politics, voicing opinions about the Bolshoi Theater singers and their performances in the competition for the best "Voroshilov Shooter." He is a little mirror of the charismatic dictator. And he has his own double: he tells us that he has lived under two names, Rybin and Lebedev: one name for his private life and another for "the well-wishers"; frequently even his wife confused them. He is a great story-teller, a man of details that give his tale a charming specificity, a "human touch."

Rybin-Lebedev is a guardian of Stalinist kul'turnost' and Socialist Realist beauty. He is obsessed by minor imperfections such as a little dust in the Bolshoi Theater or any other uncontrollable and elusive blemish that could spoil a great spectacle produced in the grand Stalinist style. Milan Kundera writes that every "imperfect" human element is construed in a totalitarian society as a blemish.[25] A blemish is a seemingly insignificant detail that hinders seamless representation and embarrasses the Stalinist "age of idyll." Blemishes point at erasures in private and in collective memory, turn a totalitarian icon into a narrative, and inject history into the iconic and mythical image. The poetics of blemish is one of the central devices operating in the film. Rybin's story attempts to erase all the blemishes, but they reappear in the flow of details and are subtly foregrounded in the film. For the filmmaker it is precisely those details, those uncodifiable imperfections, that are of extreme importance. The film zooms in on the seams and erasures of history. The poetics of blemish is a different way of thinking about the position of the glasnost' artist vis-à-vis the totalitarian commonplaces based on estrangement and engagement.

The history of the title of another documentary entitled *Stalin Is with Us?* illustrates one of the last Soviet attempts to erase the blemish, this time not for the sake of totalitarian beauty but for the sake

History as kitsch: A still from the film *Stalin Is with Us?* (courtesy of Kinocenter, Moscow)

of the beauty of glasnost'. The initial title proposed by director Shakhverdiev was the simply affirmative "Stalin Is with Us." The question mark is a creative addition of the Vice President of Goskino (State Film Agency) who told the filmmaker that without the question mark the film would not be released, because it "undermined the achievements of glasnost'."[26] The censor of the early years of glasnost' prescribed ambiguity, an authorial ambiguity in the spirit of glasnost'. The story is one of the last incidents of the paradoxical censorship in Gorbachev's time. According to Shakhverdiev this incident only proves that the answer to the gently imposed question is in the affirmative: yes, Stalin is still with us.

The film deals explicitly with the aesthetization of politics manifest in the carefully orchestrated Stalinist marches and songs, as well as in the militarization of art, especially in the scenes of the chorus of Red Army veterans. The Stalinists, here too presented without a directorial voice-over, appear human, all-too-human.[27] The schoolteacher Kornienkova, shown in a cozy domestic scene feeding birds, quietly tells the story of her life and her lifetime love for one person only—the one with "little devils in his eyes." Her love for Stalin is very personal and almost mystical, the way women mystics spoke about Jesus Christ. And the camera forces us to look at Stalin's monument through her loving eyes. One of the most amazing scenes takes place in a park, when Kornienkova affectionately brushes away dry autumnal leaves from the buried Stalin monument. It is as if she were trying to remove all the blemishes from the dear monumental face. We see the close-up of Stalin's head, with his blind stone eyes, framed by the leaves on the ground.

The film offers a rare insight into the phenomenon of historical nostalgia. Instead of showing the Stalin era as historical past, the film construes it as a mythical time which can be evoked and recreated through old rituals of emotional bondage between people and their leader. "Tyranny is terrible. Tyranny is wonderful. It depends on how you look at it," says the director.[28] What these aging Stalinists lament is the loss of a totalitarian world view that helps to keep all nuts and bolts in place: an ideological and aesthetic system that offered a clear "road to life." "Before, there were songs about the leader," says one of the old Stalinists, "now nobody writes songs about the leaders." This is a yearning for the joyful Socialist Realist march of their youth, together with thousands of other athletic citizens of the new world.

The paradox of kitsch cannot be unveiled by the observer's distancing himself from it, or then one is in danger of turning into an unselfconscious and self-righteous practitioner of kitschy idealism. In these films totalitarian kitsch is not merely reified and ironically erased as another kind of aesthetic blemish; it is presented as an important kind of aesthetic and living experience that has to be reenacted by readers and viewers in order to be revised later.

Yet there is a major difference in the two directors' approaches. Aranovich avoids any verbal commentary on Rybin and does not incorporate any alternative point of view into the film. In Shakhverdiev's film the prisoner Chekal, who has a tatoo of Stalin on his chest, narrates the parable of a visceral link between Stalinism, socialism, and prison: "All our life is rationed. Not a step to the left or to the right . . . We march in lines. We live modestly but joyfully. In one word, this is socialism, the Stalinist kind of socialism. In prison we have true socialism in miniature." These powerful words are intercut with images of prisoners marching and flocks of sheep pasturing in the mountains. Stalinism is with us so long as a certain kind of socialism persists. The documentary turns into an explicit allegory. This is also the point of the scenes showing a hypnotist practicing his art on contemporary young men and women. Under hypnosis they confess lies, as in the time of trials, and call black white and white black. Stalinism as mass hypnosis is the conclusion the viewer is invited to reach. Unfortunately, the old cultural myths are not dispelled as easily and quickly as hypnosis in the show. In fact, hardly anyone within the culture has the privilege of an absolutely clear sight.

Two 1992 films about Stalinist charisma, *The Abyss* and *The Inner Circle* (dir. Andron Konchalovsky), one made in Russia and another in Hollywood, export Stalinist mythology into the international marketplace. Both search for totalitarian *temps perdu* and for cinematic esperanto that would need no translation. In the case of *Abyss* it is the language of the European classics of Bertolucci, Fassbinder, and Visconti, and in the case of *Inner Circle* it is the language of Hollywood with a familiar Russian accent, a kind of Russki-Hollywoodski jargon. Both films use documentary material within a fictional frame, but for different purposes. *The Inner Circle,* a story of another little Stalinist, the "great leader's" personal film projectionist, was made in Hollywood primarily for American audiences; here the documentary footage (archival photographs of Stalin's inner circle collected by the director) is employed to authenticate the fiction, to confer upon it the status of "a true story," Hollywood style. The American actors speak with well-rehearsed Russian accents. Konchalovsky wished to avoid cinematic and historic complexity and chose instead to "formulate the story in an essentially emotional register, because emotions are universal—fear, love, loss, pain."[29] His universal language is a language of Russian soul-searching emotionalism punctuated by Hollywood syntax. The result of this cross-cultural exchange is not postmodern eclecticism or "poetics of blemish," but an impressive, although fairly conventional, genre film.[30]

Like *The Inner Circle, The Abyss* begins with documentary footage of the 1930s, but here that is not intended to lend authenticity to the fictional drama but to reveal the stylized nature of all Stalinist documentaries. The film is not about seduced "little men" but about the *dolce vita* of the Stalinist elite, and unlike *Inner Circle* it has no happy ending and yields no catharsis. Most of the figures of Stalin's inner circle are shot at the end of the film together with their beautiful horses. The Stalinist epoch looks like a festive, perpetual holiday, a show of life that has indeed become "better and merrier." In no rush to demystify, the director engages in something like a remythification, a mythical recreation, with parades of athletes, triumphant marches, white suits and red roses, happy songs, and celebrations of healthy youth and romance. The film brilliantly recreates the Stalinist topography, from the Golden Fountain at the Exhibition of National Economic Achievements (VDNKh) to the marble baths in the apartments of the elite, to the new Moscow Metro with its colorful mosaics, frescos, and marbles. The film proliferates mirrors and reflecting surfaces where new, beautiful Soviet men and women can see themselves. The historical time is self-consciously violated in an atemporal, mythical space of the Stalinist Grand Style.

It is difficult to say what the plot is. Like many Soviet films of the previous period the film cuts across genres, incorporating elements of decadent thriller and stylized melodrama. Its glamorous characters include, in addition to Stalin's generals, a pregnant commissar, a fallen noblewoman tragically in love with a simple worker who resembles an idealized Eisensteinian sailor, a rapist-tenor courting a ballerina, and so on. (No glasnost' or post-glasnost' art film can escape a certain kind of cruel and stylized sexuality à la Fassbinder,

Lynch, or Bertolucci.) There is also the obligatory young genius-poet who reflects on the "nothingness and the abyss that everyone fears" and gives the title to the film. On the whole, the film has a chilling aura of calculated detachment, brilliantly accomplished by celebrated cameraman Vadim Iusov, who worked with Tarkovsky and other well-known directors.

To show the Stalinist epoch in an aesthetic, "retro" style has an undeniable element of cultural *épatage*.[31] Yet the film's antecedents are neither Soviet nor Russian, but foreign: not Stalin's favorite Soviet classics by Alexandrov or Pyr'ev but Visconti's *The Damned*, a film about "fascinating fascism," and Bertolucci's *The Conformist*. While other Soviet films turned Stalin into an easy grotesque, a ridiculous marionette, and conducted playful exorcisms of kitsch symbols and carnivalesque demystifications, *The Abyss* offers a nostalgic recreation of myths that evoke the aesthetic appeal and fascination of totalitarian culture.

Ultimately, the film is about what I would call totalitarian nostalgia in its peculiar 1990s version. This is primarily an aesthetic nostalgia for the last grand style in the twentieth century—the Stalinist Empire Style—and even more, a "nostalgia for world culture." In this case, it is a longing to participate in world cinema together with all the beloved Western idols of the Russian directors: Visconti, Bertolucci, and Fassbinder, and now Greenaway and Lynch. This is happening at a time when the post-Soviet cinema in general, not only the art films, is becoming an elite cinema, often against the will of the directors. (Russian films are practically unavailable to domestic audiences and are shown only in the movie clubs, Houses of Cinema, or during special film festivals. Movie theaters across the country show almost exclusively third-rate American films.) New films made in Russia and in the former Soviet republics have to survive a balancing act between the old Soviet ideology and mentality, the demands of art, and new commercial imperatives. And the directors who are elite by choice wish to belong to the mythical *cinémateque* of a utopian European Common Home. This longing to belong to a European culture has little to do with Stalinism as such. It is rather a desire for the freedom to manipulate cultural myths and tell decadent fairy tales against all the moral and commercial odds.

In the summer of 1992, while the historic constitutional trial of the Communist Party of the Soviet Union was taking place, the majority of citizens of the former Soviet Union preferred to watch an old Mexican soap opera called *The Rich Also Cry*. This soap opera does not represent history as kitsch; in fact, there is hardly any history in it at all. The señores and señoras are rich, not *nouveaux riches*, and many have Stalinesque moustaches. But those moustaches do not appear as a parody or as a cultural sign referring to the totalitarian epoch, and the audience sighs with relief—the moustache might only be a moustache. At best it reminds the audiences of another popular hero of everybody's Soviet childhood: D'Artagnan, of *The Three Musketeers*, a favorite for three generations of Soviet teenagers, mine included. As the monuments to the founders of the Soviet Union began to crumble, the new entrepreneurs began to collect money for a monument to the now-aging star of the soap opera *The Rich Also Cry*, Verónica Castro. When Ms. Castro visited Russia, she received much more popular and official recognition than did the Secretary General of the United Nations, or the Grand Duchess Maria and her son, the head and heir of the Russian imperial dynasty. And rumor has it that the residents of then break-away republics Lithuania and Moldova begged their governments not to boycott Moscow TV channels. Some said that even the bloody fighting in the Caucasus stopped for forty minutes so the members of the warring factions could cry with the Mexican rich.[32] When one of the heroines of the show died, women in Vladikavkas held a funeral ceremony for her and did not go to work. That year many baby girls were named Mariana and Verónica, just as after the Revolution they were named Vilena (V. I. Lenin), Marlena (Marx/Lenin), or Oktiabrina. It is interesting that the most popular spectacle of mass culture in the post-Soviet era is a Mexican soap opera, rather than the new Russian films depicting the dark side of contemporary society *(chernukha)*—sex, drugs, and violence—or the American action movies that monopolize U.S. movie theaters (they are too fast-moving and too action-oriented for the post-Soviet audiences). If movie producers used to favor the Americanization of popular culture, Russian audiences clearly prefer "Latinamericanization."[33] The particular heightened treatment of emotions and the melodramatic staging of ethical dilemmas characteristic of Spanish and Latin American popular movies seem to have a strong appeal for Russian viewers. Neither Russian nor American, the heroes of *The Rich Also Cry* have more in common with the romances of Alexander Dumas, Walter Scott, or the forgotten American Captain Main Reed and his Mexican *femme fatale* Isidora Co-varrubio de los Llanos. *The Rich Also Cry,* besides having the obvious charm of a sad but beautiful fairy tale (with Juan the Handsome in the place of Ivan the Fool), also makes a nostalgic appeal to another and less visible level of popular culture: the teenage culture. Their foreign romantic heroes and heroines seem to exist in another historic (or ahistoric) romantic dimension of outmoded nineteenth-century popular novels. During the Stalin era such novels were considered quite innocuous; they passed the censors and were published along-side the Russian classics.

So cultural myths do not die as quickly as do popular and intellec-tual fashions, and neither do certain conceptions of history and its endings. One would hope that the best films from the former USSR will continue to play with charismatic images and to expose historic myth-making, without iconoclasm and with a good dose of humor. As the rich on TV continue to cry, the poor, surviving cinema-goers could also laugh.

The Discreet Charms of Bad Taste

In the Soviet film *Assa* (1988), a cross between a Soviet *Godfather* and an old-fashioned Russian romantic story, the hero makes a pro-vocative statement: "This is banal but original." Russia has always been a country of oxymorons and this is perhaps the one that best characterizes the art and life of glasnost'. In contemporary Russia, banality and originality are indeed co-dependent. Bad taste and every-thing that throughout the twentieth century had been considered improper—not avant-garde enough or not correctly realist, exces-sively feminine or uncouth, counterrevolutionary or petit-bourgeois—now exudes its discreet charm. In the age of Gorbachev the petit-bourgeois poshlost' of the time of the 1920s, the totalitarian kitsch of high Stalinism in the 1930s, the middlebrow art of the 1950s, and the neomodernist euphoria of the 1960s are all occasions for nostalgia and explosive laughter. In the new aesthetics of late Soviet art, reflections on history and reflections on kitsch, banality, and bad taste go together.

"Eclecticism" was a bad word until the 1980s. First regarded as a degradation of the great classical style of the Russian empire, it was later seen as a sign of bourgeois decadence. In the 1930s and 1950s "eclecticism" in style was considered to be a crime, a kind of "cosmopolitan conspiracy." In the 1980s, as an act of aesthetic revenge, eclecticism became a single concept that united many film directors, artists, and writers. Eclecticism came to be regarded as an antiutopian gesture, a subversion of the grand styles of the past. The aesthetic collage, with many absurdist intercalations, is more characteristic for this period than either the Eisensteinian ideological montage or the seamless cuts of Brezhnev's cinema, exemplified, among others, in *Moscow Doesn't Believe in Tears*. The early cinema of glasnost' rebels against the cynical slickness of the era of stagnation, with its carefully circumscribed half-truths and bland metaphors. A number of films, such as *Zerro grad*, *Prishvin's Paper Eyes*, and *Side Whiskers* (dir. Yuri Mamin), use elements of the carnivalesque and attempt a kind of cultural purification through laughter. Those films can be compared in spirit with the Czech and Hungarian New Wave of the 1960s; they mark the rebirth of the Soviet comedy.

The cinema of glasnost' and after pioneered many postmodern devices; the very economics of its existence were in some ways illusionary and postmodern. Even in the 1990s, when the prestige of the newly liberated medium proved short-lived, the number of films made in Russia has increased at least ten times.[34] The art of post–Soviet cinema consists in defying the cruel rules of the economic market and maintaining the illusion of cultural relevance, in the hope that some day it will regain the importance it had during the first years of glasnost'. Indeed, in the late 1980s, the cinema taught lessons of cultural liberation in its heroic and comic mode.

The glasnost' films by Sergei Soloviev can be called an "encyclopedia of Soviet kitsch" (to paraphrase Belinsky's "encyclopedia of Russian life," referring to Pushkin's *Eugene Onegin*). They feature the eclecticism and make self-conscious use of kitsch. Soloviev's "perestroika trilogy," which includes *Assa* (1988), *The Black Rose* (1990), and *The House under the Starry Sky* (1991), became a glasnost' classic. Soloviev, an exemplary film maker of Gorbachev's era, began in the epoch of the thaw with a series of poetic films about Soviet teenagers. He then attempted to make a leap of faith from the gentle skepticism of the 1960s and 1970s to the playful but radical defiance of the youth culture prevalent in the late 1980s. He was one of the first established directors to make a film in the uncertain transitional time of the mid-1980s that would bridge the gap between the counterculture and the official culture. That attempt resulted in the widely popular *Assa*, first member of the trilogy, which features many cultural heroes of the 1980s and 1990s, including Stanislav Govorukhin (later director of pro-monarchist pseudo-documentaries, *The Russia That We Have Lost*) as a Soviet Godfather, and Viktor Tsoi (leader of the rock band Kino, an idol of the new generation), playing himself. The central character in the film, a young nonconformist rock musician, was played by the painter Afrika, now fashionable in New York and Saint Petersburg, whom the director virtually saved from imprisonment by giving him this role. Soloviev wished to bridge the generation gap and the cultural hierarchies and make truly popular yet artistically honest films. That aspiration was the first to go in the time of post-glasnost', and the last film of Soloviev's perestroika trilogy was virtually unseen by Russian audiences. Hence, *The Black Rose* turned out to be one of the last of the auteur films which, for a short time, enjoyed the status of cult movie among the established intellectuals and teenagers alike.[35]

Soloviev proclaimed with ironic seriousness that his trilogy belongs to the genre of "romantic cretinism," which therefore captures the very chemistry of contemporary Soviet life.[36] The films invite us to explore the connection between "cretinism" and "romanticism," between self-conscious and involuntary uses of kitsch in late Soviet cinema, between poshlost' and irony.

Black Rose Is an Emblem of Sadness, Red Rose Is an Emblem of Love (the film's full title) presents an eclectic collage of narratives, images, and cultural references. A beautiful, playful, and irresponsible woman-child, daughter of an elite party official and a ballerina, has an affair with a married fashion model and eventually gets pregnant. Alexandra decides to keep the baby, causing much family embarrassment, and is saved by a noble and pure orphan teenage boy, a descendant of the aristocratic Russian family Lobanov, who proposes to marry her and save her honor. Mitia has a great-grandfather, a Decembrist, as well as a rich grandfather in Cannes (another cinematic hint, perhaps), who happened to die and leave the boy a few million dollars. At the end of the film Mitia goes through the ceremony of Orthodox baptism which is presented both humorously and seriously, and—at least in a dream—he gets to live out some of his teenage fantasies of long sea voyages and escapes. But the romantic story is only one of the plots. Mitia lives in a dilapidated communal apartment in the old part of Arbat with his neighbor Tolik, a *limita*, a perestroika-struck, blessed fool. (*Limita* is the name for someone who lives in Moscow illegally, without an official residence permit.) Tolik wakes up every morning to a tape of the shot of the revolutionary cruiser *Aurora* and the detailed physiological description of Stalin's death. Until the end of the film it is unclear whether he is "mad or just pretends to be," and the distinction between the two is difficult to draw. Tolik is half Chaadaev's "philosopher in a robe" and half Gogol's madman. Other residents include a lonely general and his drinking partner, a leader of a developing African country, both made obsolete by perestroika. Interspersed in the plot are jokes about Stalin's constipation, Tolik's dreams of changing the letters on Lenin's mausoleum from LENIN to TOLIK, provocative subtitles addressing the audience, and even a few fleeting appearances by Jesus Christ.

Black Rose is densely packed with various references to popular and high culture, literary quotations, and cultural clichés, interwoven throughout the fragmentary and explosive structure of the film. Soviet history appears as a montage of kitsch signs. The many examples of the self-conscious use of the totalitarian kitsch of the Stalinist period include the cruiser *Aurora* and images of Stalin. There is also Gorbachevian kitsch, with a programmatic new glasnost-speak and glasnost' T-shirts bought in the West. The title song, a leitmotif of the young heroine, is an example of the so-called petit-bourgeois poshlost', the effeminate culture of gramophone romance, from the 1920s to the 1960s.[37] Alexandra's black lace garments and military trinkets, along with her S&M relationship with her father (aestheticized almost à la David Lynch), make Soloviev a pioneer of "camp" attitudes in Soviet cinema.

Soloviev self-consciously employs elements of melodrama and explicitly refers to "Dostoevskianism" *(Dostoevskishchina)*, which can be defined as the kitschification of Dostoevsky, or as a highlighting of the already present elements of kitsch in Dostoevsky's writings. Russian culture has a higher tolerance of what in the West would be considered sentimental excess; in general, more frequent and more expressive elements of melodrama are acceptable in what is considered high culture. (The American viewer generally feels that Russian films are too long, too sentimental, and with too much talk. This is not because melodrama is absent from American culture and American movies, but because the Russian conventions of melodrama are more old-fashioned, more in line with nineteenth-century literature, while the American ones are more slick and succinct, dating from the Hollywood cinema of the 1930s.

The ironic stance of the director has its limits. He desires to give the public antidotes to poshlost', both on the level of the characters and in the comic or carnivalesque and subversive elements of the film's structure. The two main "anti-poshlye" characters are young Mitia Lobanov and Alexandra, the teenage couple. The grown-ups seem to have lost the capacity to resist poshlost'. In this respect, the film reflects upon the contemporary Russian crisis of parenthood and of the relationship between fathers and sons or fathers and daughters. Alexandra turns into a typical Russian heroine. For the director she embodies "the wandering of the ideal in the real." (Every Soviet intellectual must be an amateur metaphysician—this feature is one that has not yet been sufficiently satirized. From a playful woman-child, Alexandra's character develops toward cliché. The pregnant girl in glasses is a cross between a pregnant Lolita in Kubrik's film and Tolstoy's Natasha Rostova in a perestroika T-shirt. At the end she is further idealized and trivialized, transformed into a Christmas Virgin Mary, through Mitia's loving eyes. He sees Alexandra through the waters of baptism that are poured over him by the priest. The scene with the falling water and the blurred image of Alexandra as Madonna with child has elements of so-called Tarkovskianism—that is, using elements of Tarkovsky's cinema as mere stylistic clichés.[38]

It is too bad that in the version of the film made for foreign distribution many absurd interpolated episodes, including Stalin's constipation, have been cut to preserve a more coherent narrative. This is unfortunate because the film, which, for better or for worse, still does not fit the conventions of Hollywood narrative and would hardly make a box-office hit in the United States, loses some of its charm in the cut version. To my mind the most powerful antidote to Soviet poshlost' is to be found precisely in the childish pranks of the film, not in the romantic teenage heroes.

If in Clement Greenberg's definition kitsch imitates the effects of art, here we see art meditating on the history and effects of poshlost' and kitsch. They are ironically redefined and turned into a cultural sign. In a recent interview, while discussing his latest film, *The House under the Starry Sky,* Soloviev mentions David Lynch as one of his inspirations. Yet Soloviev's film hardly resembles its American post-modern counterpart's work. It participates in many cinematic genres and clichés but lacks that recognizable archetypal genre structure characteristic of David Lynch—that of the "boy-next-door-coming-of-age adventure" *(Blue Velvet)*, or that of the classical road movie *(Wild at Heart)*. While the ex-Soviet cinema flirts with the Hollywood cinematic genre system, these experiments are much less interesting than the native hybrids. (In any case, a Russian film made in Hollywood genre is still doomed to be perceived as a foreign film by the American audiences. And after all, there is nothing wrong with foreign films.)

Stylistically, Soloviev's films possess many elements of Western postmodernism. However, postmodernism is not postmodernism, is not postmodernism. His *Black Rose* offers to the audience an eclectic Russian bouquet with some withered aristocratic flowers, some subversive "flowers of evil," and many sharp thorns of black humor on the red rose of poshlost'.

Trashy Jewels of Women Artists

Tatyana Tolstaya

As history comes to be equated with the history of kitsch, and the past appears either as a mythical elegiac fiction or a map of kitsch signs, everyday life moves to the foreground of the Russian cultural imagination. In the post-Soviet cultural recycling the boundaries of culture, kitsch, and art shift rapidly, and the new cultural diversity undermines the traditional Russian prestige of high culture. Artists and writers of the 1970s and 1980s had their own privileged sites of the everyday: for Ilia Kabakov it is the communal apartment; for the writer Vladimir Sorokin, the perpetual Soviet queue standing for nothing in particular, just for its own sake; for Benedikt Erofeev, it is Moscow's public transportation system, which can transport one to the limit of one's senses. Conceptual artists Elena Elagina and Igor Makarevich explore Soviet daycare and nursery schools and hospitals, revisit school textbooks and popular journals. In the work of some women artists, writers, and film makers, everyday culture is not merely treated with a conceptual scalpel but is brought to bear on and to undermine conceptions of banality, kitsch, and bad taste or what was frequently perceived as aesthetic effeminacy.

"Feminism" is one of the foreign words that, unlike postmodernism and kitsch, was not easily adopted in late Soviet and post-Soviet Russia even among women. Many factors influence this reluctance: negative connotations associated with the Soviet history of feminism, a visceral dislike on the part of the Russians for any "isms" and ideologized discourses, a fear of exclusion and new ghettoization on the part of female artists, and a stoic position taken by the majority of Russian working women who do not believe that Russian men could undergo any kind of mental perestroika.[39] While many Russian women writers and artists spoke against feminism and other "isms," they continued to comment explicitly on the feminine mythologies in Russian culture as well as on the mythologies of byt and banality. Contemporary Russian women artists have inherited and often internalized the conceptions of effeminate "bad taste" and are still haunted by the grotesque female figures of Madame Poshlost'. For Tatyana Tolstaya, "women's prose" is synonymous with superficiality, philistinism, materialistic psychology, and an excess of sentimentality—a "saccharine air."[40] Mass culture is defined along the same dismissive lines. In response to a questionnaire on mass culture Tolstaya wrote that mass culture is "not a culture by definition" but a contradiction in terms, and she derogates its Soviet variant as "kitsch."[41] Yet in her own work, as well as in the works of many other contemporary women artists, poshlost' mingles with poetry, and the boundaries between irony and banality are often blurred.

In Tolstaya's stories everyday trivia, minor rituals, and tacky domestic objects with an aura of time past occupy a central place and provide a major writerly "pleasure of the text."[42] In this respect Tolstaya follows the tradition of Gogol, Flaubert, and Nabokov: she both decries poshlost' and takes a special writerly delight in describing it. Yet the references to high culture do not fully illuminate Tolstaya's fictional world; her central subtext is Soviet urban folklore, especially the slightly outmoded urban romances and sentimental songs. The "Okkerville River" is a story about a man's dream romance with a singer in an imaginary place on the banks of the Okkerville River. The Okkerville River is at once the dream of blue mists and beautiful Petersburgian bridges and the actual margin of the city, the place of urban trash, pollution, excrement and residues, and "of something else desperate, provincial, trite."[43] It is the limit of Simeonov's everyday existence, with its bachelor's feasts of pasteurized cheeses and bits of bacon served on yesterday's newspaper. The river has two banks: the bank of the misty ideal and the bank of poshlost'.

At first glance a similar duality is to be found in the images of two women: the singer Vera Vasilievna, the heroine of Simeonov's heroic solitude, who sings about withering chrysanthemums, the ephemerality of being, and unrequited love, and the ordinary woman Tamara, with her flower-patterned curtains and home cooking. (Both women have their flowery attributes, but the flowers are distinctly different: Vera Vasilievna's are the pseudo-aristocratic chrysanthemums while Tamara's are the standard Soviet flowers of homey curtains.) This opposition of ideal beauty and poshlost', however, does not hold throughout the story. In fact, the ideal Vera Vasilievna is at first depicted as a queen of turn-of-the-century poshlost', a "languorous naiad" like the turn-of-the-century soft-porn postcards and Nabokov's busty German bathing beauties. At the end of the story, the queenly Vera Vasilievna, bathing in the aura of past ideals, is dethroned. What remains is only the tacky, vulgar Soviet prima donna Verunchik, taking a real bath in Simeonov's house.

The story reframes old-fashioned romances that were branded as the embodiment of bad taste throughout Soviet history. Here is a refrain from "Chrysanthemums," which resounds through Tolstaya's story: "The chrysanthemums have withered in the garden long ago, but love is still alive in my ailing heart."[44] The other romance begins like this: "No, it's not you I love so passionately, it's not for me the shining of your beauty, I love in you my past suffering and my perished youth."[45] The second song is in fact based on a poem of Lermontov's. This romance has had an interesting journey: from high culture to people's oral culture, to urban and middle-class folklore, and then down to a meshchanskii object that the new high culture wishes to suppress. Eventually, it is recovered, once it is completely outmoded, within the eclectic texture of a self-conscious artistic text. The last paragraph of "Okkerville River" incorporates some lines from old romance songs, and recycles and poetically rewrites clichés about rivers, lives, loves, and beautiful stories that wither like autumnal chrysanthemums.

Tolstaya's "Sonia" is yet another meditation on romance and bad taste. Let us examine the first paragraph of the story:

A person lived—a person died. Only the name remains—Sonia. Remember, Sonia used to say . . . "A dress like Sonia's . . ." "You keep blowing your nose all the time like Sonia . . ."—then even the people who used to say that, died, and there was only a trace of her voice in my head, incorporeal, seeming to come from the black jaws of the telephone receiver. Or all of a sudden, there is a view of a sunny room, like a bright photograph come to life—laughter around a set table, like those hyacinths in a glass vase on the tablecloth, wreathed too with curly pink smiles. Look quickly before it goes out. Who is that? Is the one you need among them? But the bright room trembles and fades and now the backs of the seated people are translucent like gauze, and with frightening speed, their laughter falls to pieces, recedes in the distance—catch it if you can.[46]

The first sentence of the story is a cliché, a trivial statement about life and death: "a person lived—a person died." It could be uttered by a skaz narrator or a wise woman story-teller from the communal apartment. In this first paragraph the narrator does not merely describe but acts out the difficulty of recovering the story and the characters from oblivion. The first cliché actually reveals to us what the story is about—about death and revival by fiction of what is poetically called "festively dressed immortality" *(nariadnoe bessmertie)*. The disembodied voices, the traces of overheard conversations have conjured up a visual memory: "All of a sudden there is a view of a sunny room, like a bright photograph come to life." It emerges like a scene from an amateur home movie, and the characters appear as projections of light, fragile and semi-transparent. The space of the story is not the perspectival three-dimensional space of realist conventions, but the space of a memory that is fragile and fleeting. But what this fragile representation brings us is a picture of an old-fashioned meshchanskii byt, a private banal scene with tacky objects. The little glass vase and the hyacinths with their curly pink smiles remind us of some evil flowers of poshlost'. It is difficult to say whether this poshlost' is with or without quotation marks. (The color pink, beloved at the time of NEP and then again in the 1950s, and then abandoned for the primary colors and the new red of the 1960s, figures prominently in Tolstaya's fiction.) The smiling curly hyacinths in their little vase function as the main triggers of memory.

Sonia, whom the female narrator of this story wishes to recover from the blurred background of an old photograph, is radically un-photogenic, as are her fictional sisters—old women from a different era who inhabit tiny rooms in god-forsaken communal apartments in Leningrad. Sonia is a kind of blessed fool who is viewed by everyone as unattractive, stupid, and always in bad taste. The two main female characters of the story are described in terms of taste: Ada Adolfovna (a hellish tautology: *ad* means hell in Russian) is said to possess "a serpentine elegance," while Sonia is dressed very "unbecomingly." One detail of Sonia's clothing becomes particularly important: the little brooch representing an enamel dove, which she never takes off. In the context of the history of Soviet taste this little enamel dove is regarded as an emblem of bad taste and poshlost'. In the story it is ridiculed as the ultimate embodiment of Sonia's lack of style. Sonia falls victim to a party joke orchestrated by the powerful Ada Adol-fovna, who invents a passionate epistolary lover for Sonia named Nikolai. The clichés of a tacky romance work for poor Sonia, who falls in love with Nikolai, a product of Ada's powerful "feminine prose." At the moment when Ada is ready to "kill" Sonia's imaginary romantic lover, Sonia sends him in one of her letters her enamel dove, her most intimate and sacred object. This act allows the epistolary romance to continue just a bit longer. At the end, the narrator, wishing to reconstruct Sonia's story from anecdotes and old blurred photographs, asks Ada for Sonia's letters. A lot of time has passed—there had been a war, a blockade; Sonia and her mythical love died their natural or unnatural deaths, and Sonia's letters might have been burnt, along with books, to heat the houses during the deadly winter of the Leningrad blockade. At the end the only thing that survives, or is believed to have survived, is the enamel dove. The last line of the story: "It's just that the fire does not take the little doves" is introduced by the colloquial and affective Russian *ved'* ("just," "you know"). This is also a paraphrase of the proverbial phrase from Bulgakov's *The Master and Margarita*—"manuscripts do not burn"—repeated throughout the novel to perpetuate the myth that art survives all purges and repression. In Tolstaya's story, however, it is not the artistic object but a tacky enamel dove that does not burn.

The adventures of the little dove in this story are parallel to the adventures of poshlost' and the complex shifts in the narrative per-spective on it. Not only does the little dove make the epistolary romance more physical, saving the imaginary lover from his premature death, but it also triggers the romance and the narration of the story itself. From being an emblem of ridiculed old-fashioned tackiness, it turns into a sympathetic sentimental object, a souvenir, imbued by a personal warmth. At the end it is reframed as the poetic thing *par excellence*, the last eccentric romantic survivor of the world of daily poshlost'. Sonia's little brooch suggests the infinite powers of poetic metamorphosis: of poshlost' into poetry and back again. The dove can be regarded as a symbol of spirituality, but it is a mass-reproduced symbol and a cliché element of decoration frequently used in book illustrations, architectural bas-reliefs, and women's cheap jewelry. It is associated with popular versions of the eclectic and *art nouveau* styles in applied arts and crafts, strongly disliked by the intellectual arbiters of taste but beloved by many people, denigrated for having the tastes of meshchanstvo. It is a bit of "trashy" jewelry, not valuable but priceless. Tolstaya told me about her particular affection for trash; she said that she found the inspiration for her first story, "Shura," in discarded souvenirs from a communal apartment in one of Leningrad asphalt-paved yards. Sonia's dove can be seen as this kind of trashy found object, with special fictional charisma, a metaphor for the protean powers of fiction. It shifts from spiritual symbol to romantic cliché, then reveals itself as a pregnant poetic metaphor, a powerful and suggestive trigger of memory and narrative. The little dove acquires a different narrative adornment and different meaning depending on the context; it defies a clear-cut opposition between everyday byt and spiritual bytie. The dove appears as an ideal narrative gift that ensures the imaginary exchange between the fictional lovers of the story and between the writer and her readers. But gifts should not be overinterpreted. The little enamel brooch will "burn" and disappear the moment we attempt to reduce its poetic suggestiveness and rich textuality to any kind of universal symbolism.

Tolstaya's stories present wonderful exhibits of kitsch as well as of the Soviet ordinary marvelous. Most of the kitschy items in Tolstaya's stories are not contemporary; they belong to another time and are colored by the aura of memory and nostalgia for that vanished world, as tacky and unoriginal as it might have been.[47] Tolstaya's framing of trivial souvenirs and jewels and her affection for artifice and for the outmoded might qualify her for Sontag's "camp." Yet a quick comparison between the campy "eroticization of daily life" as described by Sontag, and Tolstaya's poetics of banality, will reveal that in fact they belong to quite different camps. First, since "psychopathology of affluence" is hardly a feature of Soviet life in Tolstaya's stories, the objects are eroticized as a consequence of material scarcity, not material oversaturation. Second, camp's key metaphor—that of *theatrum mundi*—would hardly apply to her fiction. And sexual playfulness is not her forte either. In Tolstaya's fictional world, sympathy and morality are as important as literary artifice.

Her stories invite us to rethink the one-sided mockery of sentimental kitsch. Full of ornamental excesses and artistic density, Tolstaya's own writing vacillates between poetic clichés and poetic discoveries, and the clear distinction between the two tends to evaporate in the "blue mist" of narrative streams.

Larisa Zvezdochetova

The artist Larisa Rezun-Zvezdochetova is an affectionate collector and archeologist of Soviet trash. Zvezdochetova said that she wanted to recover in her work everything that has been forgotten by art history: women's embroideries made in the collective farms, 1950s postcards, "deer" carpets from the communal apartment, matchbox labels with the label of the cruiser *Aurora,* chocolate foils with Ivan Shishkin's painting of the "Three Bears"; badges reading "Be Ready for Labor and Defense," the gilded sportsman covered with rust; black-and-white reproductions of Queen Nefertiti, who became the most popular Soviet pin-up after Hemingway—all those found objects that were the minor aesthetic delights of a bleak Soviet everyday culture, objects that were doubly censored, by high art and high politics. Like Tolstaya, Zvezdochetova makes "art" out of "domestic trash." In her works "femininity" and "bad taste" are placed within quotation marks and creatively reinterpreted.

Zvezdochetova wishes to confront the high avant-garde culture predicated on originality with everyday culture of mass-produced feminine arts and crafts, communal-apartment decoration, and Soviet wallpaper designs that frame one's memories of childhood. The dialogue with the avant-garde and that conducted between the lines with some Soviet conceptualists of the older generation are played out in some of Zvezdochetova's key works. Her installation of fragile paper

Larisa Zvezdochetova and her art (photo by the author)

Larisa Zvezdochetova, "Conceptual Carpet" with Soviet badges (courtesy of the artist)

angels hanging from the trees, entitled programmatically "The End of the Avant-Garde," was presented at the exhibition "Aptart—Beyond the Fence" (1983).[48] Here the angels, cut out of white paper like the ready-made snowflakes familiar to any Soviet school student, evoke both children's art and the turn-of-the-century mass culture populated by angels and other whimsical winged creatures like the "fat flirtatious cupids" that the avant-garde fought so ferociously.[49] The flimsy angels in their natural setting signal the end of the humorless worship of the historical avant-garde. Among her creative influences, Zvezdochetova mentions an amateur "aesthetic therapist" from the province of Odessa, who crafted large embroideries reproducing classical Russian and Soviet paintings. When Zvezdochetova asked the "aesthetic therapist" why she embroidered portraits of Lenin and not her own designs, she was told that this was the true way of bringing art to the masses; while the women embroiderers follow the lines and brush strokes of the great artists, they are both propagating art and raising the prestige of embroidery. Zvezdochetova wishes to do exactly the opposite—to transform embroidery into art and challenge cultural hierarchies. Moreover, unlike the women constructivists of the 1920s such as Varvara Stepanova, she is not trying to impose her pure, nonobjective patterns on mass design but rather to learn from the unofficial women's mass culture itself.

In a recent installation Zvezdochetova touches and invites us to touch, in a literal sense, one of the main avant-garde icons. Imagine Malevich's *Black Square,* meant to be the ultimately pure, nonobjective painting, "zero degree of form," as an attractive object of soft velour in a gilded frame, an avant-garde antique. Zvezdochetova offers us a "zero degree" of painting; the suprematist surface is nothing but a velour curtain inviting us not to search for avant-garde absolutes but to look right underneath—only to find an enlarged reproduction of a common embroidery. Moreover, the black squares themselves are reproduced and repeated three times. The frame, seemingly of sumptuous gold, is made out of a glittering tablecloth Zvezdochetova found at a Turkish flea market in Germany.[50] The embroideries are the actual found objects: one was found on an old pillowcase, the others were rescued from trash or inexpensively purchased. They are the products of craftswomen, collective and anonymous. Moreover, they are incomplete, nothing but fragments, unfinished or simply badly preserved, ruined, unvalued and invaluable. The three black square velour curtains cover the enlarged photographs of the embroideries as if they were the most precious museum artifacts; but they are merely mechanical reproductions, even less original than their anonymous originals. Hence the work creatively "plagiarizes" not only Malevich, the suprematist master, but also the master of embroidery, the amateur aesthetic-therapist from the Odessa province.

In a museum a painting is untouchable; its aesthetic distance is carefully patrolled and protected by watchful museum guards. In contrast, Zvezdochetova's installation is supposed to be touched. The artist told me that the installation was an attempt to make "erotic art," by which she means a particular kind of tactile feminine eroticism. It does not consist of sexual explicitness on the level of visual representation—the necessary nude scene in every recent Soviet and post-Soviet film–nor is it eroticism in quotation marks, a kind of intertextual eroticism. Her erotic art is playful; it consists of a variety of tactile experiences, including tactile *trompe-l'oeil,* the games of revealing and concealing the "body of work." The installation plays with arts and crafts, high and low styles, and with the aesthetic distance itself. Zvezdochetova's is the art of tactile conceptualism. Of course, it is up to the viewer to decide whether to touch or not to touch.

The installation is one of her more explicitly conceptual works; most of her work presents fragmented souvenirs, metal badges on a velour carpet, repainted dolls, silhouettes cut out of paper and covered by a lacy curtain. Her exhibition reminds one of a child walking through the streets of her native city, glancing through the brightly lit windows, eavesdropping on the lives of strangers, and never resolving the plots of their dramas. Zvezdochetova brings together clashing tactile experiences (the metal of the badge against the rich velour of the carpet) or else plays with the memories of the tactile experiences (her metal badge is only a reproduction). Her playful, postmodern irony and eclecticism occasionally reveal a nostalgia for the premodern—for the time before the distinction between Art in the singular, with a capital "A," and arts in the plural, including manual crafts. It is a nostalgia for a lost tactility, that elusive tactility that plays hide-and-seek with us.

One of Zvezdochetova's mottoes is the coarse saying that might have originated in prisoner jargon: "to make sweet out of shit." *The*

Encyclopedia of Bad Taste, which deals exclusively with American mass culture, treats "treasures from trash" with a sly humor, as a common occupation among lower-class suburban American housewives, something that has moved from the art and counterculture of hippies into the suburban mass culture.[51] In the United States this is a kind of popular recycling program and a reaction against a culture of wasteful overabundance of disposable goods; by contrast, in Russia the idea of making something out of nothing is a result of material scarcity and an expression of need, not simply material but also the need for minimal aesthetic self-affirmation. In the Soviet context, where there were hardly any nonworking housewives (they begin to emerge only now and in the new entrepreneurial upper class), Zvezdochetova associates these needs with "prison art and prison mentality—it was a kind of all-Soviet aesthetic therapy—making something out of nothing, turning 'shit into a sweet.'"

Zvezdochetova is not particularly interested in the official Socialist Realism of high Soviet political icons and the media and Western mass culture. "Mickey Mouse is uninteresting," she told me once. "He is just too cold." Instead of working with major political events or major historical figures, like the artists of the Sots Art movement who play ironically with Socialist Realist icons, she recovers the everyday, the forgotten and yet familiar level of culture where there are no heroes and antiheroes, but countless tacky ornaments from communal apartments, standardized Soviet children's books, women's needlework, and official festivities. The everyday resists artistic defamiliarization; it is both too familiar and too uncanny. Yet in contrast to Kabakov, the strikingly antiaesthetic and stark Soviet conceptual artist and master of communal-apartment art, Zvezdochetova enjoys the banal ornaments of the old-fashioned Soviet communal carpet and the material details of standard Soviet furniture and mass-produced objects. It is not Kabakov's metaphysical "emptiness" but the material particularity of detail, with its aura of the outmoded ordinariness of the totalitarian past, that motivates her work. Her creative recuperation of the everyday is not totalizing, just an invitation to a forgotten child's game, a game of secrets framed by glittering foil.

The works of women artists from the former Soviet Union demonstrate that the relations between irony and sympathy, estrangement and engagement, the material and the conceptual, are far from simple: poshlost', like beauty, is in the eye of the beholder. Women's artistic works creatively reinvent that illegitimate and untranslatable Russian and Soviet everyday which is so often blurred in the background of a larger historical tableau.

Yet, the slightly outmoded and precommercial everyday culture of the communal apartments, framed by the cheap gilded foil paper of conceptual art, remains "everyday" in quotation marks; while challenging aesthetic distance, it remains an aesthetic gesture. It subverts the ideals of culture and kul'turnost' alike, yet preserves a certain nostalgia for the importance of art. Like the film makers Soloviev and Aranovich, Tolstaya and Zvezdochetova are *auteurs,* original individual players with unoriginality and communal life. But the challenge to cultural unity—or, as some perceive it, to the autocracy of kul'turnost'—is flung not only by artists but also by newcomers to Russian public life: the entrepreneurs, advertisers, and those who trace their pedigree to the trashed group of the petty bourgeoisie and the much-insulted Russian merchants. Art and literature are no longer the only paradigms of culture, and the artistic intelligentsia is no longer the voice of the nation (in the last seventy years the intelligentsia has been playing hide-and-seek with its cultural mission; at times it has been ostracized, but only to be redeemed later, in the unofficial or dissident culture). New cultural diversity can be found in the happenings of the "new merchants," in entrepreneurial art and commercials. This kind of post-Soviet cultural recycling, the everyday reappropriation of aesthetics (often for practical purposes), questions the prestige and the boundaries of culture as such.

Merchant Renaissance and Cultural Scandals

The nostalgic revival of the style and behavior of native Russian capitalism from prerevolutionary times is one of the major historic revisions of the post-Soviet era. The Russian bourgeoisie that came to the public arena in the second half of the nineteenth century has a bad name in Russian literature. Tolstoy's favorite hero, Konstantin Levin, refuses to shake hands with the merchant Rakitin, claiming that he would not shake hands with a lackey, and a merchant is worse than a lackey.[52] Not only aristocrats like Tolstoy but also members of the democratic intelligentsia, like Dobroliubov, felt morally superior to the merchants. In his programmatic essay on Ostrovsky's play

The Storm, an obligatory text in Soviet high schools, Dobroliubov describes the everyday life of the merchant class as a "kingdom of darkness," personified in the play's main character, Kabanikha (*kaban* means "wild pig, boar"). The merchants were denigrated from the right by the aristocracy, and from the left by the intelligentsia; they were insulted even in some popular gypsy romances, one with the refrain, "Moscow merchant, torn-up stitch, you aren't a son of the Fatherland, you're just a son of a bitch."[53]

Yet at the end of the nineteenth century Moscow merchants began to play an increasingly important role in society, building hospitals and schools, organizing charities, supporting arts and crafts. Russian merchants were not philosophical Slavophiles although some came from the families of Old Believers. They were patriots of another kind, patriots without metaphysics. They sponsored exhibits of modernized Russian craftwork produced by *kustars* and encouraged the revival of interest in national folk culture. If in the late nineteenth century certain distinguished members of the merchant class, like Pavel Tretiakov, helped Russian realist artists through the Society of Travelling Exhibits, in the early twentieth century many Maecenas-like merchants supported the modernists. According to John Bowlt, the merchants represented the "social avant-garde" that was more open to sponsoring the artistic avant-garde. (Of course the artists never lost their slightly condescending attitude toward their sponsors.)

The merchants' mansions changed the Moscow cityscape; unlike the neoclassical estates of Western-oriented nobility, they had a style of their own called Byzantine Revival or (in Soviet art-history books) pseudo-Russian. It featured eclectic fantasies on pre-Petrine architecture, and they were often much more sumptuous than the imagined originals. While merchants of the older generation were known for their frugality and traditional Russian ways, their children were famous for wild banquets with roasted pork and kasha, broken champagne glasses, and all-night revels of gypsy romances. One of the wildest characters of the time, Misha Khludov, lived an exemplary picturesque Russian merchant biography: he gave enormous feasts, trained Central Asian tigers, fought for Serbian independence in the 1880s, and ended up in a Moscow mental institution. The young merchants' behavior was often wilder than that of the self-proclaimed hooligans and self-consciously outrageous avant-garde artists.

After the Revolution, merchants disappeared as a social group: some left, others were killed. Their mansions, which Soviet tour-guides uniformly condemned as "without artistic value," have since been renovated and imitated. The "Russian style" is fashionable again, and the uncomfortable prefix "pseudo" is frequently dropped. Russian merchants, once dismissed by literature and purged by Soviet power, are in fashion again, and the new entrepreneurs are proud to reclaim their historic pedigree. Advertisements and shop signs fre-quently use the pseudo-Slavonic script common at the turn of the previous century, and the provocative debaucherie of some members of the new elite resembles not only the lifestyles of their predecessors but also their fantasies. Some of the post-Soviet *nouveaux riches* inherited the old inferiority/superiority complex which is one of the main characteristics of Russian and Soviet Russian culture, and which drives each new group of *nouveaux riches* to engage in taste wars in order to assert itself in the public sphere. If the Russian and Soviet intelligentsia pretended to be the new aristocracy, not of blood but of the spirit, the post-Soviet entrepreneurs pretend to be new merchants. Like the old merchants who struggled against the condescension of the impoverished and powerless gentry, some new merchants find themselves in a cultural war with the now-disempowered Soviet-Rus-sian intelligentsia mourning its loss of cultural prestige.

One interesting example of an odd symbiosis of avant-garde and merchant cultures is the famous Moscow gallery, proudly named Regina. Artist and curator Oleg Kulik and owner Ovcharenko flaunt imaginary pedigrees of wild Russian entrepreneurs. Yet they also flirt with the prestige of high conceptual art, which has had a prominent dissident role since the 1970s. Perhaps they present the most power-ful challenge to the exclusive aesthetic community of the Moscow conceptualists. Instead of shocking the bourgeois, the new masters of Regina wish to shock the intellectuals, to challenge the artistic intel-ligentsia and their taste (which is not exactly like the avant-garde's "dictatorship of taste," but is something like a liberal ministry of culture). Curator Oleg Kulik believes in the art of patronage and is committed to the new post-Soviet economic power. He is an obedient servant to the successful Russian businessman, self-made man of perestroika, Ovcharenko, whom Kulik fashions as a new great patron of postmodern art. Kulik wishes to reeducate the new rich along with the high-minded intellectuals by putting economic pressure on them and forcing them to abandon their arrogant ideals of artistic autonomy and elite aesthetic distance.

Regina's two shows, "Bestiary" and "Transparency," were among the most scandalous and most talked-about in Moscow in 1992. They offered an ample opportunity for a real fight between the "new merchants" and the artists. It is difficult to determine whose side these shows take: are they an artistic subversion of the new culture of entrepreneurs or an expression of merchant contempt for aesthetics; indeed, are we speaking of aesthetics at all? Kulik's installation in the "Bestiary" exhibition offered an exercise that had less to do with "tactile conceptualism" than with conceptual violence, even visceral violence directed against the artistic intelligentsia.

The Regina exhibit proposed a vision of society and art as a violent and all-inclusive banquet where the rich are free to cross as many boundaries as they wish. "Bestiary" violated conceptions of taste, both literal and figurative. The first part of the brutal happening was the slaughter of a pig, which the audience had to watch as it occurred on a video screen. This was considered a conceptual "installation" among other installations, which were more traditionally avant-garde. The televised slaughter was followed by a sumptuous banquet in the good tradition of the Russian merchants, during which guests (artists, intellectuals, sponsors, and businessmen) were treated to freshly barbecued pork, elegantly arranged on a platter complete with the pig's head—to facilitate recognition of the slaughtered animal, the video artifact. The audience thus had to devour its aesthetic object, to the point of nausea. The general shortages of food in Moscow and enormous price increases made the formerly well-fed intellectual élite and their children especially vulnerable to culinary seductions. The audience was disgusted and seduced by culinary luxuries, as well as by the violence of the gesture. (The animal-rights movement is very unpopular in Russia, where it is commonly perceived that people are frequently treated worse than animals and where the *human*-rights movement hardly accomplishes its goals.) Was the violence of slaughter, or the culinary pleasure, the more disturbing element of the event? Was this a dadaist gesture—a slaughter of the very institution of both traditional humanist culture and of postmodern conceptual art, or only a sophisticated Russian debaucherie?

The antithesis to Regina's "Bestiary" was Joseph Bakshtein's conceptual art show in the Butyrki prison. This one also made the headlines in 1992 but for a different reason. It presented now-established artists of the Moscow underground of the 1980s, known as the Moscow Conceptualists, and celebrated again the Soviet dissidents' perception of art as an underground activity, made for and by marginalized members of the society. In the post-Soviet era, however, formerly dissident conceptual art became a new canon for intellectual art critics, hence the artists' and the curators' search for new contexts of marginalization, trespassing the boundaries of the literary and metaphorical and entering the prison space. If, during the opening of "Bestiary," the artists and their friends were made uncomfortable mixing with the new merchants, during the opening of the exhibit in the Butyrki prison the visitors were made uncomfortable mixing with actual prisoners (only those who had light prison terms were invited to the reception). Some prisoners remained indifferent to conceptual pursuits, but many expressed appreciation for the artists' invasion, for aesthetic and practical reasons alike (hoping to draw media attention and shorten their sentences).

The second Regina show, "Transparency," took place in the open air and instead of tempting the artists with luxurious pork, it put them through a trial of hunger. Like the first exhibition, this event was in some respect thoroughly conceptual. It advertised itself as a mock anniversary of the 1983 underground exhibition outdoors called "Apt Art beyond the Fence." "Transparency" was set up in the ideal *sots art* space, the Pioneer Camp, rented especially for the occasion for a large sum of money. Again, the viewers came not only for the art but also for the banquet, and again their taste was upset and their expectations disrupted. Instead of mixing democratically as at the opening of "Bestiary," this time artists and sponsors were segregated during dinner. The artists were offered mashed potatoes with tomatoes (some said half-rotten), while the entrepreneurs and businessmen enjoyed a sumptuous meal. The next day a football match was scheduled between artists and businessmen, with a prize of one million roubles. Perhaps it was the result of heavy overeating the night before, but the businessmen lost the game while the artists and intellectuals celebrated victory (thus upsetting some of the prejudices about intellectuals playing sports). But at that point Oleg Kulik declared that there would be no prize; since the artists had won, it was only a joke. Outraged and starving, the artists went back to

Moscow planning their own institutional revenge. One of the intellectual players was a well-known anchorman of the unconventional
TV news program "Vesti" (Messages). He told the story on the air
and made a wry joke about "the deceitful little merchants" *(kup-
chiki)*, while the artists decided to boycott the gallery and to exclude
it from the Moscow Gallery Association for cheating them. In 1993
Regina merged with the new European Bank of Moscow and radically changed its self-image, from merchant renaissance to high-tech
commercial postmodernism, European style. (Even their furniture is
1980s corporate postmodernist chic.) Yet their collection is much
more sophisticated, eclectic, and provocative than any collection to
be seen in a Western bank, which usually consists of predictable
pastel abstracts or realistic portraits of the owners. Among Regina's
future plans are two ambitious undertakings: to rebury Lenin in a
glass coffin and leave it hanging forever in Regina's basement, and to
open a restaurant on the premises of the bank. The architecture of
the Regina restaurant will didactically illustrate the new social hierarchies: the rich will eat on the second level and below them the poor
will be fed for free. The floor between the two levels will be made of
glass, so that two categories of "clients" can observe each other. I did
not engage the curator into a discussion of the possible ethical implications of this kind of voyeurism. I only asked: "And what about the
middle class?"—"When and where did you see a middle class in
Russia?"—sardonically remarked the curator.[54]

So much for Moscow's artistic and culinary gossip. The two 1992
happenings at the Regina only prove that in Russian culture many
metaphors are taken literally: Kabanikha, the boar-merchant of the
"dark kingdom," materializes as an actual pig; the intellectual football game is played out in the field; and violence is not merely metaphorical either. Sometimes "transparency" is more transparent than
we would like it to be. Indeed, in Russian culture it is often hard to
distinguish between boorish behavior as a conceptual gesture and
boorishness as such, without quotation marks. As Freud remarked,
at times a pipe is just a pipe. Moreover in the case of Regina, the
avant-garde gesture of transferring the practice of art into real life
reveals more about life than about art. Violence and boorish behavior
are hardly strange in the contemporary Russian context—they are all
too familiar. It is marked politeness and civilized manners that produce the effect of de-familiarization. The show did not celebrate the

diversity of cultures but rather assaulted the borders of culture and cultural behavior. The problem is that in a society without a structure, destructive gestures are no longer subversive; post-Soviet everyday life is often more absurd than the theater of absurdity, and an ordinary street scene frequently resembles a dada happening.

The Obscure Object of Advertisement

In 1920 the revolutionary avant-garde artists drew up a design for a tram, the most progressive new means of Soviet transportation. It would carry the "visual propaganda" slogan "Long Live World Revolution!" surrounded by red and white geometrical shapes, embodiments of revolutionary nonrepresentation. In the 1990s the post-Soviet tram carries another slogan: "The New Generation Chooses Pepsi," illustrated by a larger-than-life "realistic" representation of the Western drink. I try to take a picture of it, to capture the present moment, but the tram makes its inevitable turn and moves beyond the frame.

The way commercial culture travels seems to know no borders. Yet the Western language of advertisement has not become the global commercial Esperanto. On the contrary, it reveals more acutely national mythologies, special ways of communication and cultural myths.[55] To understand commercial communication Russian style, one has to remember the old practices of reading between the lines, of using Aesopian language, of speaking with half-words, and maintaining exclusive imagined communities through language.

In effect the new advertisements in Russia often physically displace the old Soviet slogans, just as they had replaced commercial advertisements in the late 1920s, when commercial culture was prohibited. In the place of the slogan on Red Square, "Strengthen the Unbreakable Friendship of the Peoples of the Soviet Union," there now hangs an advertising banner: "Visit the Canary Islands." This is a celebration of a different kind of "international friendship," which, in view of the economic situation of Russian citizens, appears as authentic and unbreakable as the friendship of the Soviet people. The Canary Islands stand for an earthly paradise that is as inaccessible to the average Russian citizen as was the Soviet ideological one. As escapist as the advertisement might appear, nowhere in the world would the invitation to visit the Canary Islands have produced such an outburst of rage; the ad was one of the main targets of curses in the demonstration in May 1992 by Communists and nationalist-Stalinists, who carried portraits of Lenin and Stalin.

Sometimes the former Soviet slogan and the new advertisement coexist more or less peacefully. Right under the slogan "We Built Communism," done in mosaic tile on the side of a building in Moscow in the optimistic time of Khrushchev's thaw, there is a new announcement in the red and blue colors of the Russian flag: "We Build a New Russia!" signed in small letters by "Trust Russia." In their structure of communication the two statements have a lot in common. The "we," for instance, has no referent in actuality. Indeed, they are not communications at all but incantations that tap the magical subliminal power which any promise of future happiness offers. ("Russia" or the poetic old-fashioned "Rus" is the most frequent word in the new advertisements. One of the central food stores near the Barricade subway station is called "Rus," but the goods sold in the store are mostly foreign and so are the prices. But in ads the name need not correspond to reality.) The new Russia sounds almost as abstract as the old Communist Soviet Union.

In the summer of 1992 the best known slogan-punchline was not "We Build a New Russia" but "MMM—No Problem!" ("MMM— *net problem!*"). There were plenty of problems that summer, and nobody could tell me what exactly the triple M stood for, but everyone joyfully recited the optimistic punchline. MMM was another cheerful abbreviation like RSFSR or CPSU, only better sounding. The expression "no problem" is quite un-Russian, so by using it the slogan invokes what is assumed to be Western ease in dealing with the world. But the communication remains incomprehensible. Yet my desire to find out what MMM actually sells and my belief that that knowledge can contribute to my understanding of the slogan's popularity appeared Western and naïve to my Russian friends. (It turned out that the MMM firm sold computer hardware, stocks, and semifictional "broker's seats," thus engaging in a kind of traditional Russian trade in "dead souls.") In 1993 MMM invaded a sacred Soviet space by renting the third floor of the Lenin Museum on Red Square (where the largest map of the Soviet Union was kept). The money paid by MMM allowed the old state-run museum to survive—if only for a few more years—and MMM enjoyed the central location facing

Above, "We Build Communism," on a mural from the 1950s; below, "We Build a New Russia" (photo by the author)

the Kremlin. The fate of the largest map of the Soviet Union is unknown.

The new Russian commercials are strange hybrids and reflect a peculiar *ménage à trois*—on the one hand, the postcommunist romance with the West, and on the other, the perpetual love affair with old Russia, which often unfolds in that so-called pseudo-Russian style. The eclectic Russian commercial market includes the items one would never encounter in any other country in the world. In post-Soviet Moscow a plastic, second-hand Mickey Mouse faces a full-sized cartoon of Gorbachev and Yeltsin, with the Pushkin monument in the background. Near Mickey Mouse vendors sell Alexander Solzhenitsyn's *The Gulag Archipelago,* cheap Ukrainian beer, and hand-made Jesus Christ Easter eggs. The post-Soviet marketplace is a display of Russian cultural myths, a jumble of old and new conceptions of prestige and cultural hierarchies. In the new dialect of the old Aesopian language, Russian commercial communication has its own esoteric side that does not easily translate into the Western mode.

Moreover, advertisements always sell more than they promise to sell and reveal more about the culture than they mean to reveal. There is always a certain excess, a surplus value to them that constitutes the residue of cultural myth. A popular American ad for Encore Pizza can serve as a parable for commercial communication Western style. The central character of this long-running TV ad is a middle-aged Italian man, exuding cordiality, who offers us *more of* a pizza and *more than* a pizza. In a series of completely improbable scenes shot in a mildly comic realistic style, various individuals—a "confirmed bachelor," a single old woman, and other desperates—come to the shop to complain that they've got "too much pizza." In response to this serious complaint, the jovial pizza-man explains that his is a family-size pizza and if they haven't got a family, he will happily bring his own for dinner. This is presented as a chat between common people in some imaginary friendly neighborhood. American commercials frequently use humor and self-reflexivity, which, however, never make fun of or disrupt the main communication: the sale of the product. Here, along with the pizza, we get a helping of family values. They come as a little extra on the multiethnic family dinner. The anglicized French word "encore" serves as a marker of cordial "Italian spirit"; it ciphers commercial and cultural communication.[56] The televisual "encore" goes to the core of the American dream; the pizza is cooked in the mythical melting pot.

Alas, this simple-minded, seemingly populist, and innocuous ad is completely untranslatable into the Russian context. In Russia the promise that a dark stranger will come over for dinner is not happily received unless followed by an ad for safety door locks and iron doors (recently the most profitable business in Russia). Solitude is not a major Russian problem; overcrowdedness is. The word "neighborhood" would not have very friendly connotations in Russian, where it would be associated with obnoxious communal apartment neighbors or with the Soviet propaganda terms "fraternal neighboring countries" (referring to Eastern Europe or Afghanistan) or "neighboring nations" (referring to the Caucasus), which now sound more than merely ironic. In Russia pizzas of any size do not need any elaborate promotion. Moreover, the populist democratic approach of "real common people from the neighborhood" has little appeal to Russian audiences. A TV anchorman, Sergei Sholokhov, explained to me that nobody wants to see "common people" on television because their representation has been overused: Soviet propaganda had promised that the "kitchen cook will rule the country," yet nowadays too many common people and kitchen cooks stand in the food lines. This also explains the virtual absence of Donahue-style talk shows in Russia; the only collective events are extrasensory sessions, Russian Orthodox services, yoga, rock, aerobics. The Russian viewer turns on the TV to see something spectacular, not common.

To appeal to its audience, the new Russian TV ad dramatizes excess. A new ad for beer shows a rather overweight but very Russian-looking popular comedian taking a beer bath (literally, bubbling in the bathtub full of beer) and laughing hysterically. He tells us that this beer is so cheap that it is simply unprofitable for him to sell it. He would rather bathe in it. Giggling ferociously, he repeats the commercial refrain: "Oh these prices are just so funny!" *(Ochen' smeshnye ceny!)* In this appeal to black humor the viewers share in the masochistic laughter; they too think that prices in the context of contemporary Russian hyperinflation are very funny—so funny that many people can no longer afford soap for a bath, let alone foreign beer.[57]

If American commercials masquerade authenticity and use the de-

vice of "sincere communication" (that is, one group of common
people speaks directly to another group of common people, pretend-
ing there is no camera) to realize the sale of something which is
frequently (but not always, of course) affordable to the TV viewer,
Russian commercials are explicitly theatrical, exaggerated, and spectacular. Many ads try to be as vague and mysterious as possible, since
the culturally acceptable manner of communication is between the
lines. The viewers of the ad must be able to feel they belong to an
imagined, exclusive community. Instead of sincerity, straightforward-
ness, and authenticity, post-Soviet commercials appeal to exclusivity
and power, and promise protection. They use neither believable real
people nor real things. They are not interested in the direct sales pitch
but engage in a more esoteric form of communication. Many commercials represent pictorial symbols such as lions, dollar bills, or
butterflies, recovering well-established techniques of the Soviet political poster—not from the avant-garde period, but from the Brezhnev
era. And rather than advertise generally affordable consumer goods,
ads usually sell something immaterial like stockmarket seats, patent
protection, or something so carefully codified in layers of pseudo-foreign neologisms that nobody is quite sure what it is.

Let us examine a few ads from the journal *Ogonek*. Since the
1930s *Ogonek* has represented Soviet mass culture throughout its
official phase and into glasnost', of which it has been the most prominent exponent. Now, while barely surviving financially, it continues
to be one of the few remaining old journals for the general public;
since 1991 it has begun to print ads on the cover of every issue,
without which the journal could not afford to exist. A large ad placed
by a firm called Binitec/nol presents an image of a medieval knight in
armor with his entire face hidden behind the visor, and the caption
reads "We guard your intellectual property."[58] The picture looks like
a film still redolent of Eisenstein's *Alexander Nevsky* or some forgotten Estonian adventure film from the 1970s. The identity of the
heavily armed man is unknown, but he is definitely ready to guard
something as immaterial as "intellectual property"—doubly immaterial because there are hardly any laws in the country that would
protect author's rights and cultural property. To increase the impact
of the image, the company's logo appears as the knight's shield—a
visual metonymy turned into a metaphor further emphasizing the
idea of protection. Many ads, directly or indirectly, advertise a form

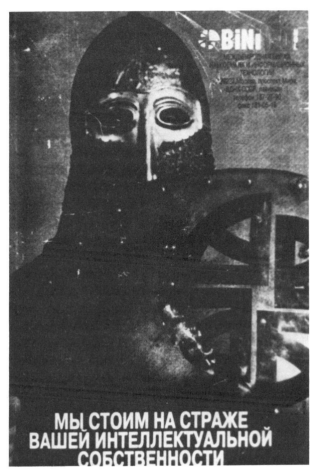

"We Protect Your Intellectual Property," *Ogonek*, 1991 (courtesy of *Ogonek*)

of protection or protectionism, perhaps because this is the single most crucial source of anxiety in the post-Soviet society. An earlier ad from *Ogonek*, placed by the mysteriously named SKF *Kiss*, is for building roads and concrete constructions—hardly something the average journal reader plans to do.[59] The name of this promising enterprise, "Complex International Symbiosis Service" (the Russian abbreviation spells KISS), is excessive and tautological; the idea, apparently, is that everything has to be international and offer service with a foreign accent. The ad shows a bright pastel sketch of a perfect

anytown and two portraits. One is of a smiling Western-style execu-
tive; the other is of a broad-shouldered, scowling, and fearsome man
in a black jacket whose very Russian demeanor signals "force" or
"enforced protection." This tells the reader that the euphonic "international symbiosis service" has the power to protect itself. And it
may need it: current business practices in Russia remind one more of
those of the American Wild West than of present-day business practices. The business manager of *Ogonek* told me that many ads are
aimed not at the magazine's readers but at other businessmen. It is
prestigious to place an advertisement in *Ogonek*. The ads are therefore not about selling to the consumers but about self-promotion to
the esoteric networks of the new post-Soviet entrepreneurs and their
peculiar systems of prestige and hierarchy. For this purpose, they
communicate in an esoteric language which the majority of the utterly
impoverished and perplexed consumers cannot understand—to say
nothing about buying. The structures of address and the ways of
communicating between the lines seem to be preserved from the
previous era. Before glasnost' the Soviet dialect of the Aesopian language was used in literature and journalism to cipher political sub-
texts, and it was shared by the intelligentsia and the artistic elite; now
the Aesopian language that ciphers mysterious business transactions
seduces many but is accessible to very few.

I asked if the readers of *Ogonek* ever respond to the commercials.
Yes, at one time there was an overwhelming response to an ad that
promised another kind of "international symbiosis"—international
matchmaking. The ad asked the readers to send $25; the price guar-
anteed eternal marital bliss Western style. But most people complained that although they had lovable qualities they did not have
$25 or did not know how to send it. There is no checking system in
Russia, all hard currency accounts are under constant threat, and the
mail system hardly works. That makes the act of *sending* $25 even
more completely impossible than simply having it, which is only
virtually impossible. The readers of *Ogonek* could not board the
foreign love boat.

If the Russian ways of communicating with and addressing the
consumer appear quite esoteric to a Western observer, the forms of
seduction, conversely, are obvious, naïve, and old-fashioned. One of
the more explicit MMM commercials placed in *Ogonek* reads "Give
us a chance to save your time and money!" It depicts a young woman

scantily dressed in green lingerie with black lace sitting in a sea of roubles (very patriotically, they *are* roubles!).[60] Although the currency around the green lingerie is not very hard, the image is familiar to Western consumers; it looks like a playboy bunny outfit of the 1970s. Glamorous (or would-be glamorous) ads featuring half-dressed girls and technological gadgets seduce Russians as much as Americans, though the Russian consumers' attitude toward the ads is that of purely aesthetic escapism, since most of the products (and personal

"MMM—No Problem!" *Ogonek,* 1991 (courtesy of *Ogonek*)

computers in particular) are inaccessible. At any rate, the Russian consumers look for exoticism and foreign glamour rather than for everyday familiarity and homeyness.

The MMM ad does not consider women as potential buyers of the appliances. (Who would wish to work at a computer in this uncomfortable tight outfit?) The ad is pitched at male entrepreneurs who can afford a secretary—and her green sexy costume as well. Like the ad for "international symbiosis," this one unfortunately also reveals something about Russian business practices. I have learned that many female secretaries in the new firms perform more than their professional duties. Moreover, many job announcements include comments on age, hair color, and the length of legs for the potential female employees, as well as the comment "without inhibitions" *(bez kompleksov)*. The concept of sexual harassment, like that of legal protection, is absent, and it is assumed that a woman knows what she is getting herself into when she takes a well-paid secretarial job in the private sector. The idea of women's privacy is not part of the "intellectual property" of the new entrepreneurs. So it is hardly the case that there are "no problems" with MMM.

Russian ads rarely make fun of themselves. Even the popular newspaper *Kommersant,* which represents the new generation and pokes fun at all the greats—Bush, Clinton, Madonna, Yeltsin—takes its commercial ads very seriously. The commercial culture in Russia is still young and cannot afford to be self-mocking.

What are the icons of this new culture? What are those little extras, "encores," the surplus of value systems that it sells? Many ads use the old signs of Russian cultural prestige; many bring together Russian high culture and Western technology, eliminating the Soviet period completely. The first page of an artsy computer ad features an old-fashioned typewriter, a pair of pince-nez glasses, an old watch, and a nineteenth-century file cabinet, adorned with spirals of whimsical handwriting.[61] The ensemble evokes the writing ambiance of the nineteenth century; indeed, some of those things are said to have come from the house of the poet Afanasii Fet. On the next page we see a computer and the old watch with a gold chain surrounded by colorful high-quality Western journals. "Quality and reliable partnership," reads the ad. There is a suggestion of continuity between the early high culture scene and the new high-tech scene, which the ad bridges through a peculiar historical leap of faith, thereby erasing the

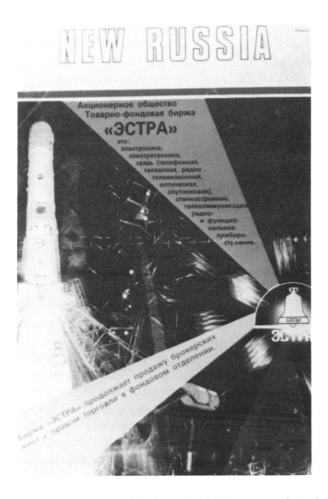

"Extra: New Russia," *Vosskresenie*, 1991 (courtesy of *Vosskresenie*)

whole of Soviet history. The new ads frequently use very high-quality art photographs that offer new commercial opportunities to many unemployed ex-Soviet artists. Yet there are no artistic traces here of the Russian avant-garde that have become (in a tame form, of course) a commonplace of Western design. The style of revolutionary futuristic art is completely passé; what is current is the very style the avant-gardists themselves considered "passé-ist" and conservative— the so-called pseudo-Russian style favored by the merchants and Maecenases of the turn of the previous century.

My final ad comes from the international edition of the journal *Voskresenie* (in Russian the title means both "Sunday" and "resurrection," so it could be a cross between the "Sunday Times" and "Resurrection Weekly").[62] The cover advertises the stockmarket auction "Extra," a Russian parallel to "encore" that can serve as the last, rather contradictory, parable of Russian advertisement. "Extra" sells brokers' seats, and the caption reads "'Extra' is electronic communications, telecommunication, etc." The image is a faerie tower that looks like something out of *Star Trek, the Next Generation*. The tower bathes in laser beams and is covered by attractive foreign labels. But this fairy tale is not entirely foreign-made. The word "stock market," as well as the name "Extra," are written in Slavonic letters reminiscent of the prerevolutionary popular journal *Niva* and the style of the merchant revival. The word "stock market" is framed by a blue church bell, reassuring the client that the market of Extra is not foreign but native, Russian. At the top of the ad, though, a caption reads in English: "New Russia." So we begin to wonder if the ad is in fact addressed to potential foreign clients who would invest in the new Russia but have to indulge in a bit of Russian exoticism. The language of the new post-Soviet advertisement is at once pseudo-Russian and pseudo-Western; it plays hide-and-seek with the viewer, concealing and revealing unexpected things. "Extra" offers us another extra glimpse at the fusion and confusion of Western special effects and pseudo-Russian revivals that are part of the excitingly chaotic present of post-Soviet Russia.

An ironic postscript to the discussion of Russian mythologies of everyday life comes in the form of an optimistic 1993 advertisement that redeems Mayakovsky's tragic line and promises a happy denouement to all problems of daily existence: "Your love boat will not crash against the daily grind if it is equipped with technology for everyday use made by Siene."[63]

Conclusion
Nostalgia for the Common Place

A reflection on nostalgia must begin with a joke. I confess occasionally feeling nostalgic for the imagined community of Soviet joke-tell-
ers, ghost writers of the unofficial text of Soviet culture. In this
collection of humorous Soviet commonplaces the Civil War hero
Vasily Ivanych Chapaev chats with the eternal Jew Rabinovich,
Pushkin walks with Khrushchev, Brezhnev encounters Brigitte Bardot
on a desert island, and the "Armenian radio" reports on Eskimo
toilets and other home improvements. Here is a joke that celebrates
Soviet joking:

> At a time when there are very few jokes left *(bezanekdot'e)*, Rabi-
> novich meets Chapaev and Anka, the machine-gunner.
> Rabinovich says, "Joke number 12."
> Chapaev laughs.
> Rabinovich: "Joke number 67."
> Chapaev laughs.
> Rabinovich: "Joke number 31."
> Chapaev can't stop laughing. "How can you, Abram Abramych, tell
> such obscene jokes in front of a lady . . ."

This story dates from the Brezhnev era, and its very premise that
there are few jokes left was then very funny. It was the one commodity of which there had never been any shortage; it could have been a
tongue-in-cheek reference to the political persecution possible for
telling jokes. Moreover, this joke is not about the lack of jokes:
rather, it shows that there is no need to tell them; it is enough to give

283

a hint, and the listener will know. Soviet jokes reflected a habitual way of cultural survival within an oppressive official communality— an all-Soviet communion through laughter and an unshaken belief in those exclusive imagined communities that understood each other "with half-words," those imagined communities that corrode and exist as parasites on, the totalitarian state. But Soviet culture had ended more quickly than my book on Soviet culture. In post-Gorbachev times the old joke becomes nostalgic; its premise that there are "few jokes left" has become true. Now these joke numbers are nostalgic ciphers for the vanishing cultural text, the souvenirs of minor everyday dissent and easily available comic relief.

In the 1990s a touch of nostalgia has affected many residents and scholars of the former Soviet Union: nostalgia of old Stalinists for the cheerful marches of their youth; of young film directors for the grand style; of the people who came of age during Khrushchev's thaw of the early 1960s and had dreamed of alpinist romances and journeys in search of fog, without thinking about money and border crossings; the nostalgia of some residents of the ex-USSR for the mythical *Russia That We Lost* (the title of a popular neomonarchist film which could be renamed "the Russia that never existed"); nostalgia of some immigrants and Soviet dissidents for the clear sense of what was the empire of evil; of aging left intellectuals in the West who began to realize there is no way "back in the USSR"; and, finally, the nostalgia of Western Sovietologists for the long-lasting value of scholarship.

Nostalgia (from *nostos* and *algia*) is a longing for home, but often for a home that no longer exists or perhaps has never existed. One has to distinguish between two kinds of nostalgia: utopian (reconstructive and totalizing) and ironic (inconclusive and fragmentary). The former stresses the first root of the word, *nostos* (home), and puts the emphasis on the return to that mythical place on the island of Utopia where the "greater patria" has to be rebuilt, according to "its original authentic design." Ironic nostalgia puts the emphasis on *algia*, longing, and acknowledges the displacement of the mythical place without trying to rebuild it. This type of nostalgia is—to quote Susan Stewart—"enamoured of distance, not of referent itself."[1] If the utopian nostalgic sees exile, in all the literal and metaphorical senses of the word, as a definitive falling from grace, the ironic one accepts (if not enjoys) the paradoxes of permanent exile. In some ways the *nostos* of nostalgia is always utopian; it exists nowhere (even if we return to our birthplace it is not the same place that we inhabited in the past, we are not the same people who inhabited it, and the borders of the motherland have changed as well), but utopian nostalgia does not reflect upon itself and tries to remedy the temporal gap by reconstructing the home and providing home improvements.

Nostalgia makes us acutely aware of the irreversibility of time; but if one cannot travel back in time, one can travel in space to the place that feels like home. The nostalgic reinvents her or his own imaginary affective geography that does not coincide with any scientific maps. Utopian nostalgia tends to be collective—it is at the core of national- ist and communist ideologies—while ironic nostalgia tends to be more singular and particular; one remembers the city of one's birth or the neighbors, but not the abstract ideas of citizenship or neigh- borhood. Utopian nostalgia, however, coöpts and builds on the per- sonal. Utopian nostalgia is a nostalgia for the Common Place, which is both a memory place and a rhetorical topos (the two intimately connected), but the utopianist forgets the rhetorical side of the com- mon place. Nostalgia for the Common Place becomes particularly pronounced during a time of crisis, a crisis of the previous forms of community and communication, whether the Greek polis, a feudal empire, a totalitarian state, a personal or national home, a commu- nity of spirit, or a community of blood. Ironic nostalgia dwells on the commonplace of daily life and the rhetoric of distance. Nostalgia might appear somewhat kitschy, but so long as it does not objectify the original *nostos,* the utopian home, so long as it remains a longing, nostalgia is "a fundamental part of the human condition" (to para- phrase Kundera's words about kitsch). So there is simply no choice; the antinostalgic campaign might be another modernist utopian ges- ture to effect a hygienic purge of affection, memory, and longing.

Both kinds of nostalgia might appear hostile to the traditional task of a historian: instead of reconstructing the chronology of events, the nostalgic wishes to forget or to rewrite them, to defy the linear progression of time. This helps to sustain personal and national myths that could be questioned by a historian. On the one hand, elusive nostalgic affects undermine the historians' dispassionate at- tempts to write their chronicles; on the other hand, these affects help them to understand people's relationship to the lived or imagined experience and the infatuation with things past, because most of us experience history as nostalgia. Moreover, the figure of the traditional

An Orthodox priest exorcizes the evil spirits from Moscow's KGB building
(photo by Mark Shteinbok)

historian itself is now somewhat antiquated and nostalgic, since history has turned into a self-reflective discipline with diverse methodological approaches. Narrative history feeds on personal nostalgias, so it is better to acknowledge them.

Utopian nostalgia could easily converge with totalitarian nostalgia: this reveals both nostalgia for totalitarianism and the totalitarian nature of nostalgia itself—the longing for a total reconstruction of a past that is gone. It is not accidental that in most postcommunist countries today nationalism takes the place of communist ideology. Nationalism is the only other available modern ideology (although it explicitly opposes certain forms of modernity) that modifies capitalist individualism and gives people an imaginary sense of community, a mythical map of rewritten history. In fact, nationalism builds on the unfaithful reconstruction of the past; it relies on faith, not on faithfulness. At the same time, historians of postcommunist nationalism frequently fall into the nationalist trap; they explain present-day wars and ethnic conflicts as if they were similar to tribal conflicts of the past. Despite the many uncanny similarities between the new and the old-style nationalism, this approach obscures the political and economic struggles that occur behind the national banners.[2] The seduction of nationalism is the seduction of homecoming and total acceptance: one doesn't even have to join the party; one simply belongs. Nationalist ideology mobilizes the nostalgia for the old Common Place lost and individual nostalgias and family histories, and it also proposes a plan of action for the purification and rebuilding of the collective home. It offers a comforting collective biography instead of a flawed individual story full of estrangements and disappointments; it promises to recover the blissful childhood of a nation, without the alienation and loss experienced in adult years. Utopian nostalgia—both Communist and nationalist—operates on the principle of "who is not with us is against us." It engages in various practices of exclusion and scapegoating. According to Danilo Kiš, nationalists do not see people as particular individuals but as nationalists of a different kind, members of a different group, and hence for a nationalist the motto "nothing human is alien to me" is meaningless; it is, rather, "whatever is not mine (Serbian, Croatian, French) is alien to me."[3] Kiš regards nationalist nostalgia as similar to kitsch and both as inimical to humor and irony. Indeed, while it is relatively common to tell anticommunist jokes and laugh at them (even if one unselfconsciously shared a lot of its ideology), it is still fairly uncommon to laugh at nationalist nostalgia. This new version of nostalgia takes itself very seriously and blurs the distinction between official and unofficial discourse.

One feature of cultural mentality common to both Soviet and pre-Soviet Russia is the cult of a strongly guarded national border; it is celebrated in a popular Soviet song: "On the border the clouds float somber, the severe country is steeped in silence; on the high banks of the Amur River, the guardians of the motherland are standing." The national border has been as idolized as the national map, as it strengthened the cultural oppositions between native and alien, order and chaos. But in the contemporary global context the extremes of a sealed national cultural autonomy versus a complete erasure of cultural differences and universal homogenization has to be rethought. According to cultural anthropologist Ulf Hannerz, for example, the fact that Nigerian natives drink Coca Cola does not mean that they have stopped drinking their native drink, burukuto. Hannerz observes that "the world system, rather than creating massive cultural homogeneity on a global scale, is replacing one diversity with another; and the new diversity is based relatively more on interrelationships and less on autonomy."[4] In other words, the binary opposition native/foreign has to be reconsidered, since the national borders have become permeable; moreover, the Russian cultural particularities have always developed in interrelationship with other cultures. So Russians might drink burukuto the Russian way, the same way that they drink English tea from a samovar, turn Japanese dolls into matreshkas, or export the cult of Russian classics to a blasé Western audience. Yet the idea of cultural interrelationship remains a very foreign concept for many present-day Russian intellectuals fascinated by the idea of Russian exclusivity and often driven by ethical extremism. The end of the totalitarian order does not have to mean the end of order as such, however; the present time of confusion is not the same as chaos, and, finally, everyday life in democracy, like everyday life in totalitarianism, does not come naturally but has to be learned. What in the post-Soviet press is called "legal nihilism," meaning total permissiveness, is not a trait of democracy but a legacy of the authoritarian past.

The Russian critic Mikhail Epstein made an interesting discovery about the conventional and ritualistic aspect of American democracy that is completely unknown to the ex-Soviet citizens.[5] He attended a rally protesting the Gulf War and, after the rally, walked away with one of the protesters. The protester continued beating the drum and shouting slogans and insults about President Bush, but when they came to an intersection, the protester automatically stopped at the red light although there were no cars at the intersection. The Russian critic, accustomed as he was to seeing red (accustomed to seeing and not believing), proceeded to cross the street. It is at this point, not at the time of the protest, that the American took on the fascination of an exotic ethnographic species in the eyes of the Russian critic. For an American, the protest and the stopping at the red light were both part of the democratic ritual; in fact both his protest and his everyday behavior were lawful. For a Russian accustomed to routine violations of everyday prohibitions and cynical about the laws because they were part and parcel of the official order, this combination of simultaneously protesting and observing the rules is nearly inconceivable.

In Russia driving through the red light when the police is not watching is an acceptable practice; there, public opinion would be more critical of eating ice cream on the subway, a practice classified as foreign or "uncultured" behavior. This disparity tells us much about the all-Soviet campaign for kul'turnost' launched in Stalin's times, a campaign that politicized the psychopathology of everyday life, elevated everyday misconduct into a political crime, and later provoked the cynical attitude toward all kinds of laws and prohibitions. It also exacerbated the traditional Russian aversion to "theatrical" or conventional behavior, an attitude fostered by some of the Russian writers of the nineteenth century. According to Dostoevsky's conception of "sincerity and truth," any democratic ritual, legal trial, or conventional rule observance is "a lie." So after the collapse of the Soviet empire not only do the official borders have to be redrawn, but many democratic partitions and conventions have to be rebuilt as well. To do this successfully it is necessary to understand the central structuring principle of Russian life, which consisted of finding elaborate ways of surviving by means of resisting structure. And in devising the new laws, it is not enough simply to prescribe the single normal way of behavior (from which everyone will automatically deviate); it is also important to distinguish the acceptable deviations from inappropriate ones.

According to Iurii Lotman, the Russian binary cultural system, perpetuated by the ethical extremism of the Russian intellectuals and ideologues, was characterized by the opposition of byt and bytie, by the vision of history as alternating stagnation and explosion, and by the desire for a total destruction of the "old world" and for a new utopia. But "the price for utopia" is experienced only by the next generation; the contemporaries of the Revolution were intoxicated by the radical poetry of "new Earth and New Heaven" and were not aware of the ruthlessness of their historical experiment.[6] In his view, the end of the Soviet Union and the new relations between East and West offer a possibility of slow evolution toward an unpredictable historical future that would neither copy the West nor perpetuate the Russian apocalyptic predicament. Russia might gradually move toward the European tertiary system, in which changes are more evolutionary than explosive, and catastrophes do not affect all spheres of existence or shatter the entire life of the country. "To lose this chance would be a historical catastrophe"—this is the last line of Lotman's last book.

One could imagine the emergence of different kinds of communities that would allow participation without belonging and community without "isms" (nationalism, communitarianism, or utopian communism), as well as a careful rearrangement of the cultural commonplaces, no longer overshadowed by a single Common Place. But maybe this is another utopia—that of a perfect imperfection . . .

Everyone is always a bit nostalgic for the time and space of childhood, wherever and whatever that might have been, and whether this childhood was, or could have been, happy. I feel that I am lucky that I belonged to the last Soviet generation, and thus cannot be uncritically nostalgic for my beautiful childhood in a Leningrad Pioneer Camp and communal apartment, in the epoch of totalitarian decadence, in the skeptical age of late Brezhnevism. So I can only develop a genre of nostalgia mediated by irony, which combines estrangement with the longing for the familiar—in my case this happens to be a familiar collective oppression. It offers a good balance between homesickness and the sickness of being home that is necessary for a cultural mythologist.

I have always thought that the sentiment of nostalgia is ancient and originates somewhere in the Homeric epic (perhaps in the *Odyssey*). I was surprised to find out that, in fact, the word "nostalgia" was invented in the seventeenth century, roughly around the time of the famous quarrel between the Ancients and the Moderns, and that it is therefore only pseudo-Greek, or nostalgically Greek.[7] The disease of nostalgia was first diagnosed by seventeenth-century Swiss doctors and was detected in Swiss mercenary soldiers. The inventive doctors came up with a cure for the contagious nostalgic disorder which included leeches, hypnotic emulsions, opium, and trips to the Swiss Alps, where the special mountain air would cure homesickness. Modern homesickness was thus treated in a modern scientific manner; nostalgia was not regarded as destiny, nor as part of the human condition, but only as a passing malaise. And the post-Soviet nostalgia? Perhaps a collective sanatorium could be organized for the nostalgic citizens and expatriates of the former USSR, as well as for the doubly nostalgic émigrés, former citizens of the former USSR. In that post-modern Alpine resort life will be free from "inauthentic" conventions of Western civility, the nannies would be excessively emotional and rude, and nobody would ever answer "fine" to the question "how are you?" As a dietary supplement and a relief from healthy food, the eternal mashed potatoes will be served, together with the "Mikoyan cutlets" invented in Stalin's time, complete with the generic rosy "fruit drink."

And so it goes: one wishes to cure nostalgia through history, but ends up by simply historicizing one's own nostalgia.

A nameless town near the Arctic Circle. The man's shirt was thriftily made out of a discarded flag (photo by Mark Shteinbok)

Notes

Introduction

1. Vladimir Nabokov, "Philistines and Philistinism," in *Lectures on Russian Literature* (New York: Harcourt, Brace, Jovanovich, 1981), p. 313.

2. Roman Jakobson, "On the Generation That Squandered Its Poets," in *The Language in Literature,* ed. Krystyna Pomorska and Stephen Rudy (Cambridge, Mass.: Harvard University Press, 1987).

3. Even the word "neighborhood" does not have a comfortable Russian translation (the word *sosed* is now too compromised by communal apartment life, where a good neighbor is defined, in Soviet folklore, as someone who pees in the communal neighbor's teapot only occasionally. After glasnost', however, americanisms and gallicisms have begun to enter the language.

4. Dmitrii Likhachev quotes Nikolai Rerikh's complaint that the *Oxford English Dictionary* includes only two Russian words, *ukaz* and *sovet,* both connected to Russian and Soviet systems of power and bureaucracy. Likhachev, *Zametki o russkom* (Moscow: Soviet Russia, 1984), p. 11; conversely, *volia,* "freedom," and *udal,* "courage," are connected to the Russian landscape, and particularly to the great central Russian plain.

5. My conception of "cultural myth" derives from Lévi-Strauss and Roland Barthes, particularly the latter's *Mythologies* (Paris: Seuil, 1957). See also the revised preface to the 1970 edition, translated into English as "Change the Object Itself" in Barthes, *Image, Music, Text,* trans. Stephen Heath (New York: Hill and Wang, 1978). In a later revision of "cultural myth" Barthes writes that the task of the cultural mythologist is not to "demystify" but rather to reveal the process of myth-making.

6. Michel Foucault opens his discussion of the "order of things" with

an "icon" of early modern civilization: Velázquez's *Las Meninas*. It tests the rules and limits of representation, exposes visual *trompe l'oeil*, and at the same time, pays homage to the patrons of art, in his case the royal couple. *The Order of Things: An Archeology of the Human Sciences* (New York: Vintage Books, 1970).

7. Domestic scenes are not characteristic of Socialist Realism and appear only in the early 1950s. Among the best known are Fedor Reshetnikov's *You've Got a Bad Grade Again! (Opiat' dvoika)* and Nikolai Ponomarev's *New Uniform. The New Apartment* was also criticized for other details of domestic *byt* such as bright wallpaper, mandoline and paper flowers, as well as for the representation of the postwar Soviet woman (see N. Dmitrieva, "Bytovaia zhivopis'" in *Iskusstvo* (1953–54, pp. 13–22), although the mistress of the new apartment reminds one of the women portrayed in Socialist Realist paintings during the War, such as Sergei Gerasimov's *The Partisan's Mother* (1943.) I am grateful to art historian Musya Glanz for helping with my research on these paintings.

The iconography of the rubber plant in the Soviet literary and artistic tradition is quite ambiguous. In Mikhail Bulgakov's *The Master and Margarita,* Margarita the witch destroys the rubber plants in the apartment of Lopushansky, the Master's enemy, a critic who represents the new Soviet artistic bourgeoisie. Similarly, in the letters of women revolutionaries such as Larisa Reisner, rubber plants stand for hated domesticity. On the other hand, the plant is represented in a positive way in very diverse works. In one of the most popular films of the late 1930s beloved by Stalin himself, *The Illuminated Path (Svetlyi Put',* directed by Grigory Alexandrov), the Soviet Cinderella in the guise of a Stakhanovite textile worker carries a rubber plant to her new apartment. (This reveals the precarious position of Socialist Realist criticism as such, its frequent ideological inconsistencies and eclecticism.) In a still different context, in Alexander Solzhenitsyn's "Matriona's Home" *(Matrenin dvor),* the rubber plant is again "naturalized" and seen as a part of unpretentious country living in Mother Russia outside the taste wars of the 1960s led by urban intelligentsia. The foreign relative of the Soviet rubber plant is George Orwell's aspidistra. One could also speculate about the etymology of *phycus* and its relation to the fig tree—but this exploration lies outside the scope of this chapter. I leave any further discussion of the semiotics of the rubber plant to my readers.

8. On the "new deal" Stalin style, and the "new acquisitiveness" in the 1930s, see Vera Dunham, *In Stalin's Time* (Cambridge: Cambridge University Press, 1976). See also Sheila Fitzpatrick, "Becoming Cultured: Socialist Realism and the Representation of Privilege and Taste" in her *The Cultural Front, Power and Culture in Revolutionary Russia* (Ithaca, N.Y.: Cornell University Press, 1993), pp. 216–217.

9. Walter Benjamin, "A Berlin Chronicle," in *Reflections*, trans. Edmund Jephcott (New York: Schocken Books, 1978), p. 26. For the notion of "archeology" in contemporary theory see Michel Foucault, *The Archeology of Knowledge*, trans. M. Sheridan Smith (New York: Pantheon Books, 1982) and for a critical discussion of the concepts of "history" and "archeology" see *Modern European Intellectual History*, ed. Dominick LaCapra and Steven L. Kaplan (Ithaca: Cornell University Press, 1982).

10. Clifford Geertz, *The Interpretation of Cultures* (New York: Basic Books, 1973).

11. Thomas More, *Utopia*, ed. Edward Surtz (New Haven: Yale University Press, 1964), p. 12.

12. See Frances Yates, *The Art of Memory* (Chicago: University of Chicago Press, 1966).

13. Aristotle, *Topica* and *Rhetorica* in *Basic Works*, ed. Richard McKeon (New York: Random House, 1941).

14. More, *Utopia*. For the explanation of the linguistic neologism see Frank E. Manuel and Fritzie P. Manuel, *Utopian Thought in the Western World* (Cambridge, Mass.: Harvard University Press, 1979), p. 1.

15. Immanuel Kant, *Critique of Judgment*, trans. Werner Pluhar (Indianapolis: Hackett, 1987), p. 231.

16. Hans-Georg Gadamer, *Truth and Method* (New York: Continuum, 1975), pp. 19–29.

17. Ibid., p. 38.

18. Anton Zijderveld, *On Clichés: The Supersedure of Meaning by Function in Modernity* (London: Routledge and Kegan Paul, 1979), p. 66. See also Ruth Amossy and Elisheva Rosen, *Discours du cliché* (Paris: CDU SEDES, 1982) and Ruth Amossy, *Les Idées reçues: Sémiologie du stereotype* (Paris: Editions Nathan, 1991); see Umberto Eco, "The Structure of Bad Taste," in *The Open Work*, trans. by Anna Cancogni (Cambridge, Mass.: Harvard University Press, 1989), pp. 180–217.

19. Clement Greenberg, "Avant-Garde and Kitsch" in *On Art and Culture* (Boston: Beacon Press, 1965). Theodor Adorno, *Aesthetic Theory*, trans. C. Lenharardt (London: Routledge and Kegan Paul, 1984).

20. For a survey of the possible etymologies of kitsch and a bibliography, see Matei Calinescu, *Five Faces of Modernity* (Durham: Duke University Press, 1987), pp. 225–265.

21. Hermann Broch, "Notes on the Problem of Kitsch" in *Kitsch: The Anthology of Bad Taste*, ed. Gillo Dorfles (London: Studio Vista, 1969), pp. 69–70.

22. Clement Greenberg himself acknowledges his mistake in the 1970 edition of his essays and attributes it to intellectual ignorance of Russian art and its contexts. In a discussion of modern aesthetics Theodor Adorno made

an infamous attack on American jazz, which he evaluated with comparable acumen.

23. Greenberg, "Avant-Garde and Kitsch," p. 15.

24. Yaron Ezrahi, in *Salmagundi,* 85–86 (Winter-Spring 1990), p. 309. This is a special issue dedicated to kitsch. For the distinction between democratic and fascist kitsch see Saul Friedlander's preface to this issue. See also Abraham A. Moles, *Le Kitsch: l'art du bonheur* (Paris: Mame, 1971).

25. Hannah Arendt, *Eichmann in Jerusalem: Report on the Banality of Evil* (New York: Viking, 1963), p. 48.

26. For the contemporary discussion see Saul Friedlander, *Reflections of Nazism: An Essay on Kitsch and Death* (New York: Harper and Row, 1984).

27. If kitsch comes from the Bavarian slang word for "sketch," it illustrates Baudelaire's point that modern beauty can be captured only in the dynamic, unfinished sketches that embody transience itself. Kitsch-sketch is a kind of reification of that unrevelatory but gratifying transience that both mimics and mocks universal beauty.

28. Charles Baudelaire, "Fusées," in *Oeuvres complètes* (Paris: 1965), p. 23.

29. Rimbaud cultivates the aesthetics of bad taste, which is not at all satanic but the soft, sentimental seduction of provincial art, of the old-fashioned decorations of village churches, popular calendars, and postcards of the opera. Flaubert morally decries the banality of bourgeois life and at the same time perpetuates it within his perfectly crafted, beautiful sentences.

30. Susan Sontag, "Notes on Camp," in her *Against Interpretation* (New York: Pantheon Books, 1989), p. 117.

31. Ibid., p. 118.

32. Milan Kundera, *The Unbearable Lightness of Being,* trans. Michael Heim (New York: Harper and Row, 1989), p. 256.

33. Stanley Cavell, *In Quest of the Ordinary: Lines of Skepticism and Romanticism* (Chicago: University of Chicago Press, 1988). Cavell acknowledges a special relationship between the everyday and American philosophy.

34. Here I am referring specifically to the Annales School in France, which emerged after World War II in reaction against teleological interpretations of history and the privileging of modernity. The Annales School began to promote interest in the "long duration" and the history of mentalities. It was a way of thinking about survival, and of subverting many metadiscourses in history and theory. (For the formulation of the concept of mentality and the Annales approach to the study of the everyday see Fernand Braudel, *On History,* trans. Sarah Matthews (Chicago: University of Chicago Press, 1980)). At the same time, Henri Léfèbvre proposed an alternative look at everyday life from a revised Marxist perspective, and many postwar artists following in the Surrealists' footsteps, the Situationists, for example, were

interested not merely in studying the everyday but in transforming it; it is how a passive study of the everyday can turn interventionist. See Henri Léfèbvre, *Everyday Life in the Modern World,* trans. Sasha Rabinovitch (New Brunswick, N.J.: Transaction Press, 1984). For the development of Léfèbvre's theories see the special issue of *Yale French Studies* on the everyday (*YFS*, 73, ed. Kristin Ross and Alice Kaplan, New Haven: Yale University Press, 1987). On the situationist conception of the everyday see Raoul Vaneigem, *The Revolution of Everyday Life,* trans. Donald Nicholson-Smith (London: Aldgate Press, 1983).

35. In the German context, where the cult of domesticity is a crucial part of national and nationalist iconography, recent histories of the everyday have a different accent. They often recover the tradition without rewriting it, perpetuating its blind spots which can lead to telling historical omissions, and to forgetting the disasters of World War II and the Holocaust. The "non-Aryans," primarily the Jews, did not share the same history of everyday life as did the Germans, and therefore cannot partake in the same forgetting. The debate about representation of the everyday and history reopened after the showing of "Heimat" (1984, dir. Edgar Reitz). See Martin Broszat et al., *Alltagsgeschichte der NS-Zeit, Neue Perspektive oder Trivilisierung?* (Munich: Oldenbourg, 1984), Martin Jay, "Songs of Experience: Reflection over the Debate over Alltagsgeschichte" in *Salmagundi,* 81 (Winter 1989), pp. 29–41, and Anton Kaes, *From Hitler to Heimat: The Return of History as Film* (Cambridge, Mass.: Harvard University Press, 1989), pp. 161–193.

36. Michel de Certeau, *L'Invention du quotidien/Arts de Faire* (Paris: Union Générale d'Éditions, 1980). Unfortunately, I am not sufficiently familiar with the study of modern everyday life outside Europe and the United States. The study of Asian conceptions of the everyday would have been particularly useful, since Russia was often presented as a mythical threshold of the Eurasian continent. For recent ethnographic discussion of everyday practices see the interdisciplinary journals *Public Culture,* and *Diaspora.*

37. Maurice Blanchot, "La Parole quotidienne," in *Entretien infini* (Paris: Gallimard, 1959), pp. 355–366. Reprinted in *Yale French Studies,* 73, pp. 12–20.

38. See Jorge Luis Borges, "The Two Kings and Their Two Labyrinths," "The Circular Ruins," "Ibn-Hakkan al-Bokhari, Dead in His Labyrinth," in *Aleph and Other Stories* (New York: Bantam, 1971), "La Biblioteca de Babel" in *Ficciones* (Buenos Aires: Alianza/Emecé, 1977) and *El Libro de Arena* (Buenos Aires: Alianza/Emecé, 1975).

39. Vladimir Mayakovsky, "Bania," in *Sochineniia v dvukh tomakh,* (Moscow: Pravda, 1988), vol. 2, p. 585. The line about Volga and the Caspian Sea is from Chekhov's "The Literature Teacher."

40. Benjamin, *Reflections,* p. 118.

41. Jacques Derrida, "Back from Moscow, in the USSR" in *Politics, Theory and Contemporary Culture*, ed. Mark Poster (New York: Columbia University Press, 1993), pp. 197–237.

42. For true cross-cultural communication to take place it is necessary to have something resembling Slavoj Žižek's "ethics of fantasy": to recognize cultural particularity in specific terms of cultural hate and cultural enjoyment. See Slavoj Žižek, *Looking Awry: An Introduction to Jacques Lacan through Popular Culture* (Cambridge, Mass.: MIT Press, 1991). Žižek writes: "What confers on the other the dignity of a 'person' is not any universal symbolic feature but precisely what is 'absolutely particular' about him that we can be sure we never share" (p. 156).

It would be useful to examine comparatively other "borderline" European cultures, Spain or Greece for instance, which are free from the messianic paradigm. The differences between cultures will help to expose the heterogeneity within one culture, a variety of cultural levels not visible in the dominant cultural histories which tend to perpetuate mythical paradigms of the culture they describe.

43. James Clifford, *The Predicament of Culture: Twentieth-Century Ethnography, Literature and Art* (Cambridge, Mass.: Harvard University Press, 1988), p. 17.

1. Mythologies of Everyday Life

1. According to Lotman and Uspensky, "Earthly life [in the West] is correspondingly conceived of as admitting three types of behaviour: the unconditionally sinful, the unconditionally holy, and the neutral, which permits eternal salvation after some sort of purgative trial. In the real life of the medieval West a wide area of neutral behaviour thus became possible . . . the Russian medieval system was constructed on the accentuated duality . . . Intermediate neutral spheres were not envisaged. Behaviour in earthly life could, correspondingly, be either sinful or holy." The question is: is a "neutral sphere" of behavior missing in early modern Russia, or was it simply not sufficiently described by Russian cultural historians, and hence not integrated into the Russian national identity as it was constructed in literary and political writings in the nineteenth century? See Iurii Lotman and Boris Uspensky, "Binary Models in the Dynamics of Russian Culture," in Alexander Nakhimovsky and Alice Stone-Nakhimovsky, eds., *Semiotics of Russian Cultural History* (Ithaca: Cornell University Press, 1985), p. 32. But in his *Culture and Explosion* Lotman suggests that the binary system is not Russia's inevitable fate and that it is possible to move away from the dangerous slogan, "who is not with us is against us." The binary system of Russian thought could only lead to a catastrophic explosion. A more gradual historical evo-

lution does not necessarily have to be seen as a mere copy of the West. The last words of the book are: "History does not know repetitions. She likes new, unpredictable routes." (Moscow: Gnosis, 1992), p. 265.

2. A belief in cultural uniqueness and a contempt for dailiness are not unique to Russian culture, but it seems that in Russia these attitudes came into being later than in other countries and persisted longer.

3. Dal's *Dictionary* has no entry for *byt;* it is included together with *byvat,* hence the word does not seem to carry any derogatory meaning. *Byt* is described through a number of synonyms, some of which share its root: *bytnost', byt'e, zhit'e rod zhizni, obychai, i obyknoveniia* (vol. 1, p. 148). Obviously the opposition between *byt* and *bytie* is not featured there.

4. Edward Keenan, "Moscovite Political Folkways," *Slavic Review,* 45 (1986), p. 128.

5. Keenan writes, "Not 'justice,' as the Slavophiles and many city-bred ethnographers have thought, not 'progress' or accumulation of wealth, not the 'preservation of a way of life,' but the preservation of life itself—human life, life of vital lifestock, the life of life-giving field culture" (ibid., p. 125).

6. Aleksandr Blok, "Bezvremen'e," in *O literature* (Moscow: Khudozhestvennaia literatura, 1980), p. 29. For more on apocalyptic imagery in Blok see David M. Bethea, *The Shape of Apocalypse in Modern Russian Fiction* (Princeton: Princeton University Press, 1989), pp. 123–125.

7. "Russians are either apocalypticists or nihilists . . . That means that the Russian people, according to their metaphysical nature, and calling in the world, are a people of the end"; see Nikolai Berdiaev, *Russkaia ideia* (Paris: YMKA Press, 1946), p. 195. In *The Shape of Apocalypse in Modern Russian Fiction,* Bethea draws a very interesting parallel between Berdiaev and Lotman in their thinking about cultural dualism.

8. In the epilogues of the great Russian nineteenth-century novels, including *War and Peace* and *Crime and Punishment,* as well as in the posthumous praises for Pushkin and Chekhov, the emphasis on "the end" and on the battle between *byt* and *bytie* looms exceedingly large. In the Russian critical tradition a didactic reading tends to prevail over an aesthetic one.

9. M. O. Gershenzon, "Creative Self-Consciousness," in *Vekhi, Sbornik Statei o russkoi intelligentsii* (Moscow: Novosti, reprint of 1909 in 1990), pp. 84–85.

10. In other words, while criticizing the everyday life of an *intelligent,* Gershenzon does not question the intelligentsia's historic war against philistinism, *meshchantstvo,* and bourgeoisie, a war that is partly responsible for the intelligentsia's militant attitude toward the everyday. In the 1990s the first postrevolutionary publication of *Vekhi* (Landmarks) provoked a serious debate on the role of the intelligentsia in the Russian culture.

11. Nikolai Zabolotsky, "Novyi Byt," in *Stolbtsy, stikhotvoreniia, poemy* (Leningrad: Lenizdat, 1990), p. 28.

12. Postanovlenie TsK VKP(b) "O Perestroike Byta," May 16, 1930.

13. Sergei Tretiakov, propagandist of the *Left Front,* redefines the dynamism of *bytie,* turning it from a spiritual into a revolutionary force. He opposes revolutionary bytie to materialistic *byt,* the realm of the petit-bourgeois kitschy objects, "enemies of the people," which do not simply compose a private world but also profane the Revolution.

14. Andrei Sinyavsky, *Soviet Civilization: A Cultural History,* trans. Joanne Turnbull (Boston: Little, Brown, 1990), p. 153.

15. Vladimir Mayakovsky, "O driani," in *Sochineniia v dvukh tomakh* (Moscow: Pravda, 1988), vol. 1, p. 145.

16. Ibid.

17. In the symptomatically entitled "Idyll" (1928), Mayakovsky invents monstrous new words, derivatives from the much cursed *byt*—*bytishche,* like *chudovishche* (monster)—and offers us another image of an ideologically incorrect petty peasant way of life: "The samovar / boils with a whistle / The gramphone / screeches a romance / Two / comrades-communists / sat down to / a game of preference / clubs and hearts and suits and cards / The ritual / is performed in full / From a little shelf / For happiness and luck / Three porcelain elephants / Are / watching."

These lines have the rhythm of popular teasing-songs called "chastushki." But the contagious peasant rhythm acquires the beat of revolutionary propaganda that parodies the new "elegant life" of the former peasants and of the new, barely emerging Soviet lower-middle class. Mayakovsky establishes himself as the chief poetic designer of the New *Byt* and a *maître* of revolutionary taste.

18. *Komsomolskaia Pravda,* Nov. 4, 1928.

19. Ibid.

20. *Komsomolskaia Pravda,* July 28, 1928.

21. On the same page of the newspaper denunciations of the "imperialist conspiracy" mingled with pleas of young fellow Communists in Greece and Lithuania and reports of rebellion in Afghanistan. Occasionally it seems that the arguments and the arms-race of metaphors were the same in all those campaigns.

22. *Komsomolskaia Pravda,* July 28, 1928.

23. Ibid.

24. Mayakovsky, *Polnoe sobranie sochinenii* (Moscow: 1958), vol. 8, p. 38.

25. *Komsomolskaia Pravda,* Nov. 4, 1928.

26. *Komsomolskaia Pravda,* Dec. 4, 1928. Alfred Kurella too tells about "cutting the curves of his furniture, of tearing off the wallpaper with roses

and little birdies." Alfred Kurella, *Krasivaia zhizn'*, pp. 40–41, quoted in V. I. Khazanova, *Sovetskaia arkhitektura pervoi piatiletkii* (Moscow: Nauka, 1980), p. 160.

27. Ibid.

28. In Mayakovsky's fantastic play *The Bedbug,* the exemplary post-revolutionary philistine complains about the utopian design of his new room with semi-transparent glass walls in the year 2030; "What kind of life is this when I can't even tape a photo of my girlfriend to the wall?"

29. Mayakovsky, "Vladimir Il'ich Lenin," in *Sochineniia v dvukh tomakh,* vol. 2, pp. 232–301.

30. El Lissitsky, "Kul'tura Zhil'ia," in *Stroitel'naia promyshlennost',* 12 (1926), p. 881. A general objective in the war against bourgeois objects, this type of curved furniture in the "fat-bellied traditional commode" style is characteristic of European design trends. The ideology inspiring the war was in fact pioneered by Le Corbusier and the founders of the Bauhaus. But in no other country of the world was it taken so literally as to organize public burnings and destruction of these objects by the thousands; nowhere else were the theories of total design put into practice on such a mass scale. However, Le Corbusier and Mayakovsky himself express much more ambiguity with respect to the utopia of the new byt than do the campaign editorials.

31. Vera Dunham, *In Stalin's Time* (Cambridge: Cambridge University Press, 1976).

32. Ibid., p. 42.

33. Ibid., p. 250.

34. Anton Chekhov, "Dama s sobachkoi" in *Dama s sobachkoi i drugie rasskazy* (Moscow: Russkii iazyk, 1981), p. 13.

35. The Dictionary of the Soviet Academy of Science marks the following usages of *poshlost'*: "Lacking in spiritual qualities, ordinary, insignificant, worthless, paltry. Not original, worn-out, banal. Indecent, obscene, tasteless, vulgar." *Akademicheskii Slovar' Russkogo Iazyka* (Moscow: 1957), p. 476. I argue that these multiple meanings of the word develop by the end of the nineteenth century.

36. The word is rarely used in the feminine, so it appears that in this cultural mythology women are objects rather than users of obscene language; women who behave like their male counterparts are called worse names.

37. Vladimir Nabokov, *Nikolai Gogol* (Norfolk, Conn.: New Directions, 1944), p. 70.

38. Ibid.

39. Nevertheless Nabokov insists that Western Europeans tend to be more guilty of poshlost' than Americans.

40. Vladimir Dal', *Tolkovyi slovar' zhivago velikorusskogo iazyka* (St.

Petersburg: Volf Editorial, 1882), p. 374. These are the Russian synonyms of *poshlyi* offered by Dal: *davniy, starodavnii, cto isstari vedetsia, drevnii.*

41. In the Russian cultural imagination, as shaped by nineteenth-century literature, the *kupets* is an embodiment of conservatism, "the reign of darkness." The merchants primarily traded with the Orient, and preserved a very traditional Russian way of life reminiscent of the old *boyars,* whose beards Peter the Great so ruthlessly cut. *Poshlyi kupets,* once of the earlier usages of the term given by Dal, refers to a merchant who belonged to the community of *sotnia,* and who was able to pay the *poshlina*—a tax taken by the tsarist administration, the meaning of which is similar to "ban" (summon, order) of banality. For etymology see Max Vasmer, *Russisches Etymologisches Wortebuch* (Heidelberg: Carl Winter, Universitats Verlag, 1979), p. 423.

There is an inherent connection between *poshlost'* and language: poshlost' cannot be studied merely thematically; it has as much to do with the style, with the way things are done, as with the things themselves. The metamorphosis of the word is closely linked to the development of Russian and Soviet languages, particularly the omnipotent language of the bureaucracy. Bureaucracy operates on the notions of precedent, custom, order, and their preservation and recycling. The old procedures, rituals, and orders from above remained almost unmodified even after the Revolution.

42. This is only one of the legends about Ivan the Terrible, and most probably it is apocryphal. But I am interested in both myths and facts surrounding *poshlost'.* The legend was told to me by Boris Uspensky.

43. "Onegin s Ol'goiu poshel. Vedet ee, skol'zia nebrezhno, / I naklonias'; ei shepchet nezhno kakoi-to poshlyi madrigal." Alexander Pushkin, "Evgenii Onegin," chap. 5, sect. 43, in *Sochineniia v trekh tomakh* (Moscow: Khudozhestvennaia literatura, 1955), vol. 3, p. 99. Pushkin's use of *poshlyi* is ironic; it marks the critical distance of the stylized author of the novel-in-verse from his characters. This linguistic genius gives us in two lines two words of the same root—*poshel* and *poshlyi*—hinting at the etymology of *poshlost'.* On the range of culture and creative conventionality in "Evgenii Onegin" see William Mill Todd III, "Eugene Onegin: Life's Novel," in *Literature and Society in Imperial Russia,* ed. William Mill Todd III (Stanford: Stanford University Press, 1978).

44. Although the *Dictionary of Pushkin's Language* reports only the old definition of the word: "ordinary, common, unremarkable," I claim that Pushkin's usage of the word affected its later use. V. V. Vinogradov, ed., *Slovar' iazyka Pushkina* (Moscow: Gos izdatel'stvo slovarei, 1956–1961), p. 626. Iurii Lotman follows this definition in his *Roman Pushkina "Evgenii Onegin"* (Leningrad: Prosveshchenie, 1983), p. 285.

45. Attaching poshlyi to "madrigal" is crucial: this verse form represents a ritual flirtation between an aristocratic man and an aristocratic woman. Obviously, Pushkin himself was not completely averse to writing occasional madrigals and poems for a lady's album—he was not a heroic martyr to "pure" writing.

46. Alexander Pushkin, "Pikovaia dama," *Sochineniia v trekh tomakh,* vol. 3, p. 402.

47. On the uses of "vulgar" and "comme il faut" in Pushkin see Lotman, *Roman Pushkina Evgenii Oneguin,* p. 352. Pushkin's use of Chateaubriand's pronouncement is discussed in Lotman, *Roman Pushkina Evgenii Oneguin,* pp. 350–351. Pushkin's attitude toward common places will be explored further in Chapter 3 below.

48. As much as Pushkin liked to joke about his fear of the Slavophile Shishkov, who censored all the foreign expressions in his Russian, the poet was never accused of "russophobia." He was never seen as "a rootless cosmopolitan" *(bezrodnyi kosmopolit)*—a peculiar Russian insult that originates in the nineteenth century and gains popularity during the Stalinist purges of 1948–1952.

49. Zinaida Gippius, "Vliublennost'," in *Russkii eros* (Moscow: Progress, 1991), p. 175. The quote comes from a discussion of Vasilii Rozanov. She goes on to reject both asceticism and the idea that "everything is permitted" and proposes a more holistic spiritual approach that integrates flesh and spirit. Russian "eros," in the philosophical writings of the Symbolist writers and philosophers, is different from French eighteenth-century eroticism and from Freud's sexuality. It does not exist by itself but merges with spirituality and compassion, with *agape* and *caritas.* In this neo-Platonic philosophy, love has to be Christian and transcendent; falling out of love is deadly; human affection, sympathy, and attraction have no place outside that global cosmology. Many Russian native speakers perceive poshlost' in relationship to *pokhot'* (lust), although there is no etymological connection between the two. Others, on the contrary, would deny the sexual connotations of the word (explicitly stated in the dictionary); they do not perceive sexuality as an independent cultural sphere.

50. *Le Grand Robert,* p. 510. This is only one of the possible etymologies of the word; *The Oxford English Dictionary* points at the medieval "trivium." This is an interesting intersection of the prostitutes' space and the academic curriculum.

51. Lev Tolstoy, "Iunost'," in *Sobranie sochinenii* (Moscow: Khhudozhestvennaia literatura, 1978), vol. I, p. 287.

52. Iurii Lotman and Boris Uspensky, "Binary Models in the Dynamics of Russian Culture," pp. 32–33.

53. It is possible that the abstract noun from the old word *poshlyi,* which is registered only in the nineteenth century, is to some extent a foreign influence in itself.

54. Hermann Broch, "Notes on the Problem of Kitsch" in *Kitsch: The Anthology of Bad Taste,* ed. Gillo Dorfles (London: Studio Vista, 1969), pp. 69–70.

55. Nabokov's invective against *poshlost'* is an ironic twentieth-century rewriting of Tolstoy's aristocratic principle of distinction; it laments the disappearance of "good taste" in an era of mechanical reproduction of arts and lifestyles.

56. A recent and insightful reflection on *poshlost'* that came to my attention when this chapter was already completed is Grigorii Pomeranz's "Akafist poshlost." Pomeranz connects poshlost' to theatricality as well as to posing and fashions, including the fashions of democracy, of liberalism, of nationalism, or of religious practice. *Iskusstvo Kino,* 3 (1991), pp. 6–7.

57. "Vystavliat' tak iarko poshlost' zhizni, umet' ochertit' v takoi sile poshlost' poshlogo cheloveka . . ." Nikolai Gogol, *Sobranie sochinenii* (Moscow: 1937–), vol. 8, p. 292.

58. Donald Fanger, echoing Pushkin, sees Gogol's main talent "in the vivid exhibition of the ordinary in characters and their lifestyles, the ordinariness which, being low in quality, common and of little significance in life, constitutes a special challenge to the artist who would endow its representation with high poetic value." Fanger discusses this reference to Pushkin in *The Creation of Nikolai Gogol* (Cambridge, Mass.: Harvard University Press, 1979), p. 19.

59. Vissarion Belinsky, "O Russkoi povesti i povestiakh N. Gogolia" in *Polnoe sobranie sochinenii,* vol. I (Moscow: 1953).

60. Nikolai Gogol, "Starosvetskie pomeshchiki," in *Vechera na Khutore bliz Dikan'ki i Mirgorod* (Moscow: Khudozhestvennaia literatura, 1984), p. 214.

61. With a current awareness of the national distinctions, it is important to note that the old-fashioned land-owners are Malorussian (now the Ukraine), while Gogol's elegy is composed in Russian. This language shift might add another level to the edifice of Slavic poshlost'.

62. Nabokov, *Nikolai Gogol',* p. 104.

63. Nikolai Gogol, *Mertvye dushi* (Tbilisi: Ganatleba, 1987), pp. 46–47. Although Gogol immediately admits his difficult in describing women, his women always embody one or another type of poshlost' and enjoy none of the redeeming sympathetic moments occasionally offered to his male heroes.

64. Nabokov, *Nikolai Gogol',* p. 73.

65. The links between them (as well as the configuration of the devil

himself) are somewhat exaggerated by later critics and writers who often conflate Gogol's pronouncements in his letters and essays with his fiction.

66. Boris Eikhenbaum, "O Chekhove," in *O proze, o poezii* (Leningrad: Khudozhestvennaia literatura, 1986), p. 225: "His contemporaries did not understand that Chekhov wrote about trifles not because he did not see or did not wish to see anything big. . . . Chekhov's method displaced the distinctions between social and private, historic and intimate, large and small—all those contradictions with which Russian literature wrestled so torturously and fruitlessly in search of the renewal of life" (p. 227).

67. S. Shchukin, *Iz Vospominanii o Chekhove* (Moscow: Russkaia mysl', 1911), p. 44. Quoted in Boris Eikhenbaum, "O Chekhove," p. 233.

68. Anton Chekhov, "Uchitel' slovesnosti," in *Sobranie sochinenii v dvenadsati tomakh* (Moscow: Khudozhestvennaia literatura, 1962), vol. 7, p. 402.

69. Ibid., p. 403.

70. The few "happy families" (usually of the older generation) depicted in Chekhov's stories are not presented as idyllic; rather, their charming little rituals—such as, in "Ionych," the wife's reading melodramatic novels about things that "never happen in life" and her husband's funny salutation, "Hello, please"—are repeated mechanically throughout the story and gradually lose their charm. This repetitiveness and temporality of boredom kills the charm of domesticity. See Cathy Popkin, *The Pragmatics of Insignificance: Chekhov, Zoshchenko, Gogol* (Stanford, 1993).

71. Anton Chekhov, "Nevesta," in *Sobranie sochinenii v dvenadsati tomakh*, vol. 8.

72. In other stories, however, the very narrative of a "new woman" or a "new man" is itself often presented as another set of clichés. Nadia is a little like Chernyshevsky's Vera Pavlovna from *What Is to Be Done*, but she is an independent thinker, not an imitator of role models from revolutionary literature. I am grateful to Catherine O'Connor for bringing the story of the escape from poshlost' to my attention.

73. Anton Chekhov, "Dama s sobachkoi," in *Sobranie sochinenii v dvenadsati tomakh*, vol. 8.

74. Lev Tolstoy, "Iunost'," p. 285.

75. Ibid.

76. Although Tolstoy is explicitly critical of the *comme-il-faut* principle, in his later moral philosophy he will not entirely undo its fundamental structure of exclusion. He just changes his allegiance from *comme-il-faut* people to the "common" people. The *nouveaux riches* like Berg from *War and Peace* do not fail to be morally wrong. And women, like Liubochka and Katen'ka in *The Youth*, still rarely take part in boys' exclusive conversations,

and when they do, they end badly—on the murderous rails of Tolstoy's fiction.

77. Quoted in Irina Paperno, *Chernyshevsky and the Age of Realism: Study in the Semiotics of Behavior* (Stanford: Stanford University Press, 1989), p. 16. She writes that "rudeness and curt manners, negligent styles of dress and even untidiness of the intelligentsia were important ideological signs, and markers of their distinction from the members of the opposing camps (the traditionalists, the reactionaries)."

78. Ibid., p. 17.

79. Sasha Cherny, *"Poshlost'"* in *Stikhotvoreniia* (Moscow: Khudozhestvennaia literatura, 1991), pp. 27–29. ("Lilovyi lif i zheltyi bant u biusta, / Bezglazye glaza—kak dva pupka. / Chuzhie lokony k viskam prilipli gusto / I maslianisto svesilis' boka," trans. John Henriksen.)

80. She is also like Hélène, a poshlyi character from Tolstoy's *War and Peace*. The last stanza turns into a scandalous theatrical interaction between the poet-author and his readers—also, he suspects, a group of vulgar-genteel poshlyi characters.

81. Alexandr Blok, "Tam damy shchegoliaiut modami . . ." (1906–1911), in *Stikhotvoreniia i poemy* (Moscow: Khudozhestvennaia literatura, 1984), pp. 130–131. Blok's Symbolist poems continue the rhythms and themes of popular urban songs about unrequited love, white tablecloths splashed with wine or blood, hot dark eyes, and withered chrysanthemums. These romances were severely scolded by the Futurists and seen as an epitome of meshchanski and middle-brow taste. Even Blok's contemporaries, including the poet Sasha Cherny, wrote parodies of his verse. Indeed, by turning poshlost' into mystery, by enveloping it with his whispering poetic alliteration, Blok risks exposing a bond between the two. This, however, is precisely what constitutes the aesthetic delight of his poetry.

82. In the essay "Literary Moscow," Osip Mandelshtam poetically synthesizes the attributes of the cultural mask of the poetess, calling the "feminine poetry" of Tsvetaeva and Parnok "a parody of poetic invention." See Svetlana Boym, *Death in Quotation Marks: Cultural Myths of the Modern Poet* (Cambridge, Mass.: Harvard University Press, 1991).

83. Jeffrey Brooks, *When Russia Learned to Read* (Princeton: Princeton University Press, 1985), p. 323.

84. According to Brooks, this led to a postrevolutionary abolition of competitive commercial culture in Russia that limited cultural production, whereas pluralism could have helped to carry ordinary people "into the world of more modern thought and imagination."

85. Alexandr Blok, "Bezvremen'e" in *O literature* (Moscow: Khudozhestvennaia literatura, 1980), p. 25.

86. Nikolai Bukharin, "Lenin i problema kul'turnoi revoliutsii" in *Put'*

k socializmu v Rossii (New York, 1967), p. 375. Quoted in Mikhail Geller and Aleksander Nekrich, *Utopia in Power* (New York: Summit Books, 1986), p. 221.

87. "Poshchechina obshchestvennomu vkusu," in *Literaturnye manifesty* (Munich: Wilhelm Fink Verlag, 1969), vol. 1, p. 78.

88. Sergei Tretiakov, "Perespectivy futurizma," in *Literaturnye manifesty,* pp. 239–240. In his battle for taste Tretiakov sets up a series of oppositions: between "inventors" *(izobretateli)* and "acquisitors" *(priobretateli),* two words that in Russian differ only in prefix; between Futurists and Passéists (from the past and passé), between revolutionary dialectics and "æstheticizing and reifying" metaphysics. "Æstheticization" refers not to art in general, but only to the "ideologically incorrect" practice of art, understood as the creation and fetishization of beautiful objects. Art is supposed to change life; it is not the purpose of art to cherish beautiful objects.

89. Edward Brown suggests "Pont" could have come from "Pierpont Morgan"; see his *Vladimir Mayakovsky: A Poet in the Revolution* (New York: Paragon House, 1988), p. 333. Also, in the slang of the 1960s "pont" means pretentiousness and snobbish arrogance, so the name "Pont Kitsch" has retroactively become doubly parodic. Mayakovsky worked with a celebrated translator, Rita Right, to create Mr. Pont's language, the language of homonyms. He was looking for English words that could be transposed into Russian. This was very important for Mayakovsky, for despite his extensive travels abroad as emissary of the Revolution, he spoke hardly any foreign language (or rather spoke it as Mr. Kitsch spoke Russian).

90. In the range of attitudes toward the West, the LEF member occupies an ambiguous position: on the one hand he praises the "Americanization of personality," Taylorism, and American utilitarianism and efficiency; on the other hand, America also represents the mentality of cherishing material things. The "Mr. West" type (a character from Kuleshov's celebrated film of the 1920s, *Mr. West in the Land of Bolsheviks)* appears in many works of the Russian avant-garde, incarnating many clichés of foreignness.

91. In the film *Our Contemporary* (dir. Raizman) one of the central conversations between the father, a scientist and factor manager, and his student son hinges on the issue of poshlost'. According to the father, the youth is ruining his life by deciding to get married to a factory girl, older and socially inferior to him, who might entrap him in the webs of domesticity and jeopardize his career. The "irresponsible" son thinks only about "little love angels in the sky." Unsurprisingly, the son defends love. As the son attempts to dissociate love and poshlost', the father wishes to dissociate poshlost' from Communist politics.

92. Evgenii Evtushenko, "Dve Liubimykh," in *Vzmakh ruki* (Moscow: Molodaia Gvardiia, 1962), p. 126.

93. It is not accidental that the first postrevolutionary publication of the writings of Nikolai Berdiaev became very fashionable in the 1980s among the intelligentsia of the previous generation.

94. *The American Heritage Dictionary*, p. 1158.

95. Mayakovsky, "O driani," in *Sobranie sochinenii v dvukh tomakh*.

96. See Vera Dunham, *In Stalin's Time*. For a discussion of the lower echelons of the Russian intelligentsia see Jeffrey Brooks, "Popular Philistinism and the Course of Russian Modernism" in *Literature and History*, ed. Gary Saul Morson (Stanford: Stanford University Press, 1986), pp. 90–110. For the most recent rethinking of the Russian middle-class see Edith W. Clowes, Samuel D. Kassow, and James L. West, eds., *Between Tsar and People: Educated Society and the Quest for Public Identity in Late Imperial Russia* (Princeton: Princeton University Press, 1991).

97. On the intelligentsia see Isaiah Berlin, *The Russian Thinkers* (London: Penguin Books, 1956), Richard Pipes, ed. *Russian Intelligentsia* (New York: Columbia University Press, 1961), and more recently S. Frederick Starr, "The Waning of the Russian Intelligentsia," plenary address at the AAASS meetings, Miami, 1991. (Abridged version published in the AAASS Newsletter, March 1992). In 1991–92 an interesting debate took place in the post-Soviet journals on the redefinition of Russian intelligentsia. One of the best informed and provocative articles is by Lev Gudkov, "Intelligenty i intellectualy," in *Znamia* 3/4 (1992), pp. 203–220. I am grateful to Nataliya Ivanova for bringing it to my attention.

98. Alexander Herzen, "Koncy i nachala, pis'mo pervoe," in *Sochineniia v dvukh tomakh* (Moscow: Mysl', 1986), p. 354. Poshlost' for Herzen is directly connected to meshchanstvo. Thus the urban crowds on the Champs Elysées and in Kensington Garden are described as "poshly faces" (p. 355).

99. Maxim Gorky, "Meshchane" in *Sobranie Sochinenii v tridcati tomakh*, vol. 7 (Moscow: 1953–1956).

100. Dmitrii Filosofov, "Zavtrashnee meshchanstvo," in *Novyi put'* (1904). Dmitrii Merezhkovski, "Griadushchyi kham," in *Polnoe Sobranie Sochinenii* (Moscow, 1912), first published on the eve of the first Russian Revolution, December 30, 1905. These texts are discussed in detail by Edith Clowes in "Gorky, Meshchanstvo and the Changing View of Society in Literary Debate, 1902–1913," an unpublished paper presented at the AAASS meetings in Boston, 1987. I am grateful to Edith Clowes for sharing with me her ideas on this subject. Consider also the early debates in *Novyi Zhurnal* and *Vestnik Znaniia* and the confrontation between modernist intelligentsia and "people's intelligentsia" discussed in Jeffrey Brooks, "Popular Philistinism and the Course of Russian Modernism" in *Literature and History*, ed. Gary Saul Morson.

101. Maxim Gorky, "Zametki o meshchanstve," in *Sobranie Sochinenii v tridsati tomakh*, vol. 28, pp. 405–404; vol. 23, p. 341. As Edith Clowes

observes, Gorky and Merezhkovsky were focusing on the opposition of intelligentsia and *meshchanstvo* from two different sides. While Merezhkovsky suggests that the "people" have been superseded by a semi-cultivated, semi-urbanized meshchanstvo, Gorky wishes to show that the modernist intellectual elite has betrayed the people and hence turned into *meshchanstvo*. While Merezhkovsky rewrites the issue as "modernist intelligentsia versus meshchanstvo," Gorky rewrites it as "meshchanstvo (disguised as modernism) versus the common people (and their few true leaders, revolutionary intellectuals like himself)."

102. Vladimir Mayakovsky, "Marusia Poisoned Herself" in *Sochineniia v dvukh tomakh,* vol. 1, p. 485.

103. Anton Chekhov, "Three Sisters," in *Sobranie sochinenii v dvenadsati tomakh,* vol. 9, pp. 543, 549. Masha says: "Oh, look how she dresses. It's not just that it's not pretty or fashionable; it is pathetic! This weird bright yellowish skirt with poshly decoration and this red blouse . . . and her cheeks are so scrubbed, so scrubbed" (p. 543).

104. Andrei Platonov, "Fro," in *Povesti i rasskazy* (Moscow: Kudozhestvennaia literatura, 1983), p. 58.

105. Ibid.

106. Mikhail Ancharov, "Odnazhdy ia pel na vysokoi estrade," *Pesni,* vol. 2, p. 71. Quoted in Petr Vail' and Alexander Genis, *60s: Mir sovetskogo cheloveka* (Ann Arbor: Ardis, 1988), p. 313.

107. Mikhail Shatrov, "Imenem revoliutsii," in *P'esy* (Moscow: 1974), p. 257.

108. Petr Tkachev wrote a very influential essay entitled "The People of the Future and the Heroes of Meshchanstvo." He sees "the people of the future" as the revolutionary intelligentsia that dedicates itself entirely to the cause of the future revolution. *Liudi budushchego i geroi meshchanstva* (Moskva: Sovremenik, 1986).

109. See Daniel Orlovsky, "The Lower Middle Strata in Revolutionary Russia," in *Between Tsar and People,* pp. 248–268.

110. S. Frederick Starr, "The Waning of the Russian Intelligentsia," p. 1.

111. Walter Benjamin, "Moscow," in *Reflections* (New York: Schocken Books, 1978). Benjamin rushes to explain that he is not for any "bourgeois coziness" or "completeness of bourgeois interiors"; nevertheless, the abolition of private life appears to him to be a radical measure. For Benjamin, the "collectivization" of private life and the disappearance of cafés are connected, and both conspire to turn a critically thinking intellectual into an endangered species. The free-floating *flaneur,* someone who can move from engagement to estrangement and back, becomes virtually impossible within the boundaries of Soviet communality. Even foreign visitors become progressively compromised, estranged, or coopted.

112. This might have an analog in French, where *la vie privée* and *la vie*

particulière are synonymous. The Russian *"chastnaia"* comes from *chast'*—part, only a part of a collective whole.

113. Vladimir Dal', *Tolkovyi slovar' zhivago velikorusskogo iazyka*, p. 259. "Samotnik lichnoe blago predpochitaet obshchemu." Other examples include "personal insult" and "personal responsibility." If a clerk is insulted in the workplace or because of his position, this is not a personal insult. While personal responsibility is not defined in opposition to the community, the responsiveness to the community is internalized. Some words that belong to the Western European or American conception of the public sphere are also missing, such as "institution" and "neighborhood." In the eighteenth and early nineteenth centuries, the gallicism *privatnaia zhizn'* was used in educated speech. Thus Andrei Bolotov writes about Tsar Pavel I's *privatnaia zhizn'* in his *Pamiatnik pretekshikh vremian*, in *Zapiski ochevidca* (Moscow: Sovremennik, 1989), p. 198. *Chastnyi* is also defined in opposition to *obshchii* (common) and is often used to express exception. *Chast'* is also related to *u-chast'*—fate, lot. "Private life" in Russian carries less emphasis on individual life in the Western sense of the word and more stress on the conception of the "human lot," which does not fully depend on individual will.

114. Denis Fonvizin, *Izbrannye sochineniia i pis'ma* (Moscow: Ogiz, 1947), pp. 236–237. Three quarters of a century later, this phrase of Fonvizin inspired Dostoevsky's "Winter Notes on Summer Impressions." Moreover, the journey abroad makes Fonvizin, like Custine fifty years later and like Dostoevsky after him, more tolerant toward his own motherland.

115. Ibid., p. 239.

116. "L intérieur des habitations est également triste, parce que malgré la magnificence de l'ameublement, entassé à l'anglaise dans certaines pièces destinés à recevoir du monde, on entrevoit dans l'ombre une saleté domestique, un désordre naturel et profond qui rappelle l'Asie." Marquis de Custine, *Lettres de Russie* (Paris: Gallimard, 1975), p. 67.

117. Ibid., pp. 167–168.

118. Petr Chaadaev, *Philosophical Letters and Apology of a Madman*, trans. and introduced by Mary-Barbara Zeldin (Knoxville: University of Tennessee Press, 1969), p. 37. In Russian, *Stat'i i pis'ma* (Moscow: Sovremennik, 1989).

119. See Andrzej Walicki, *History of Russian Thought: From Enlightenment to Marxism* (Stanford: Stanford University Press, 1978), pp. 87–91. Walicki traces Chaadaev's thought to the French traditionalists like de Bonald and de Maistre, as well as to German conservative Romantics.

120. "He was a 'private' *(chastnyi)* man, what is called 'privatier.'" Osip Mandelshtam, "Chaadaev," in *Sobranie sochinenii* (New York: Inter-Language Associates, 1974), vol. 2, p. 284.

121. Ibid. "As if realizing that his personality did not belong to him, but to posterity, his attitude towards it was humility. Whatever he did, it was as though he did not simply do it but served or performed a service."

122. P. Ia Chaadaev, *Stat'i i pis'ma* (Moscow: Sovremennik, 1989), p. 350.

123. Ibid., p. 188.

124. Alexander Herzen, "Koncy i nachala, pis'mo pervoe," in *Sochineniia v dvukh tomakh* pp. 353–356.

125. Ibid., p. 356.

126. Paul Veyne, "Introduction" in *History of Private Life* (Cambridge, Mass.: Harvard University Press, 1987), vol. 1, p. 1.

127. Ibid., p. 163.

128. See Philippe Ariès, "Introduction," in *History of Private Life* (1988), vol. 2, pp. 6–8.

129. Yet to think of Russian (Muscovite) culture as merely deprived of the familiar stages of Western social development (such as the Renaissance, the Reformation, or Roman law) is to miss its central mechanism, its ability to turn what might appear as a deficiency into a merit, and to create an effective political culture suited to its needs. See Edward Keenan, "Moscow Political Folkways."

130. Louis Dumont, *Essai sur l'individualisme, Une perspective anthropologique sur l'idéologie moderne* (Paris: Editions du Seuil, 1983), pp. 303–304. Translation mine.

131. Vladimirsky-Budanov, quoted in *Encyklopedicheskii Slovar'* (St. Petersburg: Brokgauz and Efron, 1898), p. 532.

132. Vassily Kliuchevsky, "Nedorosl' Fonvizina" in *Istoricheskie portrety* (Moscow: Pravda, 1990), p. 353. I am grateful to Thomas Barran for his help and advice on this matter.

133. Lidiia Ginzburg, "The Human Document and the Formation of Character," in *The Semiotics of Russian Cultural History,* p. 208.

134. Louis Dumont, *Essai sur l'individualisme,* p. 30.

135. Feodor Dostoevsky, "Zimnie zametki po letnim vpechatleniiam" in *Iskaniia i razmyshleniia,* p. 186.

136. Ibid.

137. Virginia Woolf, *The Common Reader* (New York: HBJ, 1953), p. 182.

138. Mikhail Bakhtin, *Problemy poetiki Dostoevskogo* (Moscow: Sovetskaia Rossiia, 1979), p. 71. I am grateful to Alexander Etkind for this insight. See *Eros Nevozmozhnogo: Istoriia Psikhoanaliza v Rossii* (St. Petersburg: Meduza, 1993).

139. This might not be the argument of Herder himself, as Dumont argues, but of his later interpreters. See *Essai sur l'individualisme,* pp. 134–152.

140. Berdiaev writes: "Germans, English and French are chauvinists and nationalists on the whole; they are full of national self-assuredness and self-complacency. What is national about Russia is precisely her supernationalism, her freedom from nationalism . . . Aggressive nationalism, forceful russification, is alien to the Russian people. This is what makes Russia original *(samobytna)* and different from any other country in the world. Russia has to become a liberator of the world" ("Dusha Rossii," p. 65). This is a rather gross mythical distortion of Russian and Soviet imperial history, from Ivan the Terrible's "liberation" of Siberia on.

141. Quoted in Nikolai Riazanovsky, *A Parting of Ways; Government and the Educated Public in Russia 1801–1855* (Oxford: Clarendon Press, 1976), p. 192.

142. Robert Belknap, *The Genesis of Brothers Karamazov: Aesthetics, Ideology and Psychology of Text Making* (Evanston: Northwestern University Press, 1990), p. 31. I am grateful to Greta Slobin for bringing this description of the "Russian soul" to my attention.

143. Nikolai Berdiaev, "Dusha Rossii," in *Iskusstvo kino*, 3 (1990), p. 68. See also George Kline, *Religious and Anti-Religious Thought in Russia* (Chicago: University of Chicago Press, 1968).

144. Berdiaev, "Russkaia ideia," in *O Rossii i russkoi filosofskoi kul'ture*, p. 87. The conception of *sobornost'* was first developed by the Slavophile writer, Khomiakov. Berdiaev opposes the Russian "communitarian spirit" to Western European knighthood.

145. Ibid., p. 189.

146. Nikolai Berdiaev, "Volia k zhizni i volia k kul'ture" in *Smysl istorii* (Moscow: Mysl', 1990), p. 170. The will to life and the will to culture are opposite in Berdiaev: culture is defined as the "great disaster of life." The enjoyment of life is thus the major enemy of "culture," and the most unspiritual, philistine, anti-communal, and anti-democratic (in Berdiaev's "spiritual sense") thing one could imagine. Society is based on association—a limited and voluntary connection between individuals that allows for their relative autonomy. It is not a fraternity of soul-mates.

147. "Russian intelligentsia always tried to develop a holistic or totalitarian *(totalitarnoe)* world view where the truth *(pravda-istina)* will be united with fairness *(pravda-spravedlivost')*." Berdiaev, "Russkaia ideia," p. 69.

148. The peasant commune as a uniquely and exclusively Russian community and communion of souls was discovered in the 1840s by Slavophile nationalists and popularized by the German historians. It was believed that the peasant commune embodied a human communality devoid of the possessive egoistic instincts that characterize other European traditions; hence the organization could help to resolve all the social problems of humanity. Conversely, the Westernizers as well as various scholars and historians since

the nineteenth century, saw the commune not as an ancient Slavic institution but as a fairly recent form of autocratic control, organized not by the mystical Russian soul but by the Russian tsars. The peasant *obshchina* was neither centered on an extended family nor was it a "society or association" of individual cultivators of land. Rather, it was a kind of neighborhood community of several peasant families. Property, owing to a peculiar inter- action of law and custom, was a communal right, while its cultivation and tools were individual. Peasants were united by communal responsibility *(kru- govaia poruka).* While the peasant commune has inspired many mythologies of Slavophiles, Social-Democrats and Bolsheviks, to date there is very little proof as to its existence before the eighteenth century, when it may have been established by the Russian monarchy for the purpose of taxing and control- ling. The Russian peasant commune has been idealized as an image of uniquely Russian communality, with its communitarian spirit, charity, and anti-individualism, and likewise denigrated as an embodiment of Russian conservatism, backwardness, and exploitation. See Richard Pipes, *Rossiia pri starom rezhime,* trans. Vladimir Koslovsky (Cambridge, Mass.: Harvard University Press, 1980) for a sobering and incisive account of the history of *obshchina,* and Frances M. Watters, "The Peasant and the Village Com- mune" in *The Peasant in Nineteenth-Century Russia* (Stanford: Stanford University Press, 1988), pp. 133–157. The word "mir" (with "i" in the prerevolutionary orthography) signifies both "the world" and the "peasant commune" and is defined as "the element in space and the force in time." So in Russia the world was always perceived in a peasant image as a Rus- sian-style "global village" and the peasant commune was seen as a universal "element" and force. (Dal', *Tolkovyi slovar',* vol. 2, p. 330. Here Dal' refers to Khomiakov.) Many proverbs reflect the unique power of *mir* in the Rus- sian cultural imagination: "For *mir* there is no judgement" *(Na mir i suda net),* or "You cannot argue with *mir (S mirom ne posporish')"*—Dal', vol. 2, p. 331. After the Revolution, the new orthography made the word for "world" and "peace" the same.

149. "God-building," which Lenin considered to be a socialist heresy, was the main subtext of Soviet culture of the 1930s. According to Katerina Clark, the early-twentieth-century philosophy of "god-building" was built on Sla- vophile rather than Western ideals of communal hagiography. See *The Soviet Novel: History as Ritual* (Chicago: University of Chicago Press, 1981), pp. 152–155. See also Nina Tumarkin, *Lenin Lives! The Lenin Cult in Soviet Russia* (Cambridge, Mass.: Harvard University Press, 1983) and Richard Stites, *Revolutionary Dreams: Utopian Vision and Experimental Life in the Russian Revolution* (Oxford: Oxford University Press, 1989). While in the works of Western scholars the continuity between Slavophile ideals of uto- pian community and Russian Marxism has long been accepted, contempo-

rary Russian historians and intellectuals tend to emphasize the break between the Russian and the Soviet ideas. The latter is frequently perceived by the nationalist intelligentsia as the work of ethnically non-Russian (mostly Jewish) revolutionaries imposed on the Russian people. This is a distortion of both Russian intellectual history and the historical record.

150. Alexander Bogdanov, "The Paths of Proletarian Creation," in *Russia of the Avant-Garde*, ed. John Bowlt (New York: Thames and Hudson, 1988), p. 181.

151. See Alexander Etkind, *Eros nevozmozhnogo: Istoriia psikhoanaliza v Rossii* (St. Petersburg: Medusa, 1993).

152. Vladimir Voloshinov, *Marxism and the Philosophy of Language* (Cambridge, Mass.: Harvard University Press, 1973), p. 12. According to Voloshinov, Freud overestimates the sexual side of human behavior at the expense of the social side. Vladimir Voloshinov, *Freidizm* (New York: Chalidze Publications, 1983), pp. 178–185.

I would suggest reading Voloshinov's critique of Freud not only as a Marxist critique of psychoanalysis, but also as a Russian cultural critique of Western individualism, a kind of cross-cultural reading or even a mis-reading that hinges on the notions of "sexuality," "self," and "society." This way Voloshinov's argument may be turned against itself, and his somewhat obsessive critique of Freud's sexuality read as a reflection and an enactment of the Russian and Soviet "everyday ideology," which consistently deemphasize the sexual dimension of the individual.

153. See Irina Paperno, *Chernyshevsky and the Age of Realism: Study in the Semiotics of Behavior* (Stanford: Stanford University Press, 1989).

154. On the making of a new Soviet man see Rufus W. Mathewson, Jr., *The Positive Hero in Russian Literature*, 2nd ed. (Stanford: Stanford University Press, 1975) and Robert Maguire, *Red Virgin Soil* (Princeton: Princeton University Press, 1968).

155. Dziga Vertov, *Stat'i, dnevniki, zamysly,* (Moscow: 1966), pp. 54–55.

156. Unlike the "new Adam," the image of a "new Eve" can hardly be found in the Russian literature of the 1920s but only in the beginnings of cinema as it was imagined in Villiers-d'Isle Adam's fantastic tale "The New Eve."

157. G. Belykh and L. Panteleev, *Respublika Sh.K.I.D* (Moscow: Molodaia Gvardiia, 1932). On education, see Sheila Fitzpatrick, *Education and Social Mobility in the Soviet Union 1921–1934* (Cambridge: Cambridge University Press, 1979).

158. A. Zalkind, "The Pioneer Youth Movement as a Form of Cultural Work among the Proletariat," in *Bolshevik Visions*, 2, p. 90.

159. Nadezhda Mandelshtam, *Kniga Vtoraia* (Moscow: Moscow Worker, 1990), p. 12. Translation mine.

160. Ibid., p. 13.

161. Ginzburg writes that the tragedy of the Russian modernist intelligentsia consisted in their occasional blindness toward the changes that took place by the late 1920s caused by their "contradictory impulses and great incompatibility between the modernist complex of individualism and elitist spiritual life and the complex of the populist tradition and the will for a just social system." Lidiia Ginzburg, *Chelovek za pis'mennym stolom* (Leningrad: Sovetskii Pisatel', 1989), p. 310. Translation mine. (The words "individualism" and "elitism" are used here without common derogatory connotations—S.B.)

162. Ibid., p. 335.

163. "Your pedestrians are not big people / With their pounding heels they hurry on their way / Oh Arbat, my Arbat, you are my religion / Your roadway lies beneath me. // I will never get over loving you / Even loving forty thousand other streets / Oh Arbat, my Arbat, you are my fatherland / No one could ever come to the end of you." (The English rendering does not transmit the poem's colloquialisms, intonation, or the peculiar melancholy ironic voice.)

164. For those outside the inner circle of Soviet jokers, *Truth* and *Labor* are just the names of Soviet dailies.

165. Dal', *Slovar'*, vol. 3, p. 379.

166. *Slovar' russkikh poslovic i pogovorok*, ed. V. P. Zhukov (Moscow: Russkii Iazyk, 1991), p. 265.

167. Dal', *Slovar'*, vol. 3, p. 379.

168. Vladimir Nabokov, "Leo Tolstoy," in *Lectures on Russian Literature*, p. 141. This insightful observation reflects upon the author as well as upon the Russian tradition he describes: "Essential truth, *istina*, is one of the few words in the Russian language that cannot be rhymed . . . Most Russian writers have been tremendously interested in Truth's exact whereabouts and essential properties. To Pushkin it was of marble under the noble sun; Dostoevsky, a much inferior artist, saw it as a thing of blood and tears and hysterical and topical politics and sweat; and Chekhov kept a quizzical eye upon it, while seeming engrossed in the hazy scenery all around. Tolstoy marched straight at it, head bent and fists clenched, and found the place where the cross had once stood, or found—the image of his own self."

169. "Koli grek na pravdu poshel, derzhi ukho vostro." Dal', *Slovar'*, vol. 3, p. 379.

170. Max Vasmer also suggests the relation between *iskrennost'* and the old Russian *iskren* meaning close or nearby, from *iz* and the root of the word *koren'* (root). See *Etimologicheskii slovar' russkogo iazyka*, vol. 2 (Moscow: Progress, 1986), pp. 140–141.

171. Denis Fonvizin, *Izbrannye sochineniia i pis'ma*, p. 255. Translations are mine.

172. Ibid., p. 237, April 1778.

173. Ibid. The problem with Lotman's description is that it posits a neutral "middle class European behavior" in the eighteenth and nineteenth centuries. But this is understood only in sharp contrast to the Russian situation. In fact, the history of Western private life shows that attitudes toward private behavior changed depending on class and the specific cultural context. For example, for the Anglo-Saxon or Scandinavian traveler the everyday behavior of middle-class Italians and Spanish appeared clearly marked and theatrical. So the Russian reaction was less extreme than is often portrayed.

174. Iurii Lotman, "The Poetics of Everyday Behavior in Eighteenth-Century Russian Culture," in *The Semiotics of Russian Cultural History,* ed. Alexander D. Nakhimovsky and Alice Stone Nakhimovsky, p. 70.

175. Quoted in Andrzej Walicki, *A History of Russian Thought from the Enlightenment to Marxism,* p. 93.

176. Richard Sennett, *The Fall of Public Man* (London: Faber and Faber, 1974), p. 37. On the concept of public sphere, see also Jürgen Habermas, *The Structural Transformation of the Public Sphere,* trans. Thomas Burger (Cambridge, Mass.: M.I.T. Press, 1989).

177. Whereas in Europe, particularly in Italy and France, there was a tradition of playful appreciation of theatricality and virtuosity of style, in Russia there was a strong prejudice against them. In pre-Petrine Russia theatricality was regarded as a kind of pagan revelry, and this attitude persisted throughout the eighteenth and nineteenth centuries. Unlike Poland and the Ukraine, Russia developed a secular tradition of theater very late, and changing costumes was often perceived as diabolical or magic and permitted only during strictly designated times of year. This religious and ethical attitude colored the popular response to Russian nobility.

178. Feodor Dostoevsky, "Dnevnik pisatelia," in *Sobranie sochinenii v tridsatikh tomakh* (Leningrad: Nauka, 1984), vol. 26, pp. 53–54. See Gary Saul Morson, "Introduction," Feodor Dostoevsky, *Diary of a Writer,* trans. Kenneth Lantz (Evanston: Northwestern University Press, 1992), and *The Boundaries of Genre: Dostoevsky's Diary of a Writer and the Traditions of Literary Utopia* (Austin: University of Texas Press, 1981).

179. Lionel Trilling, *Sincerity and Authenticity* (Cambridge, Mass.: Harvard University Press, 1971), pp. 1–26.

180. Feodor Dostoevsky, "Winter Notes on Summer Impressions," pp. 205–207. I am grateful to Donald Fanger for an enlightening conversation about Dostoevsky's attitudes toward eloquence and tongue-tiedness.

181. Friedrich Nietzsche, *Beyond Good and Evil,* trans. Walter Kaufman (New York: Vintage, 1966), Aphorism 244.

182. A. Bossart, "A ia ostaiusia s toboiu," *Ogonek,* 44 (1989), p. 31. Quoted in Irina Corten, *Vocabulary of Soviet Society and Culture* (Durham:

Duke University Press, 1992). Corten offers many wonderful examples of the Soviet usage of the word "culture." Apparently the word entered the post-perestroika slang and now *kul'turno* is synonymous with "cool."

183. This explains why the word "culture" does not get much attention in Dal's *Dictionary* where the first meaning of the word is given as "cultivation" *(obrabotka i ukhod, vozdelyvanie, vozdelka),* and the second as moral and intellectual "education" *(obrazovanie umstvennoe i nravstvennoe).* Vol. II, p. 217.

184. Vissarion Belinsky, "Thoughts and Notes on Russian Literature" (1846).

185. Norbert Elias, *The History of Manners,* trans. Edmund Jephcott (New York: Pantheon Books, 1982), p. 5.

186. See Jean Starobinski, "The Word Civilization" in *Blessings in Disguise; or The Morality of Evil,* trans. Arthur Goldhammer (Cambridge, Mass.: Harvard University Press, 1993), pp. 1–36.

187. Ibid., p. 31. He writes that in mapping civilizations and cultures, "what matters is the shifting patterns of boundaries and distinctive systems of value, not the qualitative judgement we might make."

188. On the concept of *kul'turnost'* see Vera Dunham, *In Stalin's Time* (Cambridge: Cambridge University Press, 1976) and Sheila Fitzpatrick, "Becoming Cultured: Socialist Realism and the Representation of Privilege and Taste," in *The Cultural Front, Power and Culture in Revolutionary Russia* (Ithaca: Cornell University Press, 1992), pp. 216–217. I am grateful to Golfo Alexoupoulous for bringing Sheila Fitzpatrick's new project to my attention.

189. I do not exclude a possibility that the box was an artful fake made for the foreign market.

190. Quoted in G. Zhidkov, "Laki" in *Iskusstvo,* No 2 (1947), March-April, p. 33.

191. Walter Benjamin, "Moscow" in *Reflections,* p. 114.

192. N. Sobolevsky, "Iskusstvo Palekha," in *Iskusstvo,* No 6 (1955) Nov.-Dec., p. 28.

193. Ibid., p. 26.

194. Evgenii Dobrenko sees "varnishing of reality" as "a mechanism of literary politics": "Everything that was later called 'the theory of the lack of conflicts' *(bezkonflictnost')* was a part of an apology of the system, characteristic for totalitarian culture. On the other hand, the system itself was based on the mentality of conflict and confrontation, the cult of struggle and the search for the enemy." "Evgenii Dobrenko, 'Pravda Zhizni' kak formula real'nosti" in *Voprosy literatury* (1992), p. 23.

195. Vladimir Mayakovsky, "Khorosho!" in *Sobranie sochinenii v dvukh tomakh,* vol. 2, p. 419.

196. I am grateful to Felix Rosiner for sharing with me the information

about this song. See Vladimir Frumkin, "Ran'she my byli marksisty: pesen-
nye sviazi dvukh socializmov" in *Obozrenie*, 17, to *Russkaia Mysl'* (Paris,
November 1985).

197. Grigory Alexandrov, *Epokha i Kino* (Moscow: Polit. literatura,
1976), p. 286.

198. Boris Groys, *The Total Art of Stalinism*, trans. by Charles Rougle
(Princeton: Princeton University Press, 1992). The relation between the
avant-garde and Socialist Realism is one of the central issues in the contemporary debate about Soviet postmodernism. Indeed, what did occupy the
space between the prefix "post" and the root of the word "modernism"?
What is the place of Socialist Realism, which comes directly after modernism
in Soviet culture? The interpretation of the relation between the avant-garde
and Socialist Realism itself changes through history. In the 1960s and 1970s
many writers and critics emphasize the break between the two, the war of
languages and tastes between the nomadic avant-garde and the Socialist
Realist establishment. In the 1980s it is more fashionable to emphasize the
continuity between the two, while insisting on the radical discontinuity between "Russian" and "Soviet." Perhaps this contemporary remapping of
Russian and Soviet history has to do with the same problem of old and new,
and the difficulty of understanding change, that plays such an important role
in the discourse of the ordinary.

At first glance, avant-garde art seems to be about reflection on language
and defamiliarization, while Socialist Realism seems to be about precisely the
opposite: a cover-up of rhetoric, and an attempt at a new familiarization.
This attempt is even more uncanny than the avant-garde's defamiliarization,
because it seeks to make the the impossible and the fantastic into the familiar.
The "realism" part of Socialist Realism has virtually nothing to do with the
everyday existence of Soviet citizens; it does not even attempt to mime or
imitate it. The point is to visualize the mythical and utopian world and thus
bring it into existence. This leads some Russian postmodern theorists to
claim that Russians have invented postmodernism and the practice of simulation as described by Jean Baudrillard. Socialist Realism is postmodern in
one sense only: historically, it comes after modernism; ideologically, it dis-
cards its heritage.

On the other hand, what Socialist Realism shares with the avant-garde is
its total—and potentially totalizing—vision and the rejection of art as an
autonomous domain of the beautiful in favor of the idea of art as a "road
to life," to use the title of another popular film of the 1930s. Of course, the
avant-garde has never achieved, and perhaps never could have achieved, its
project of bringing art into the praxis of life; it was too caught up in the
creative search for a new language and a new, antisubjective subjectivity. See

Peter Burger, *The Theory of the Avant-Garde* (Minneapolis: University of Minnesota Press, 1984). Yet Boris Groys's position on the avant-garde, based not on the French or German but on the Russian model, is different.

199. Ibid., p. 67.

200. Saul Friedlander proposes a distinction between the kitsch of death characteristic of Nazi Germany and the more innocuous and "life-affirming" kitsch of Stalinist Russia. See his "Kitsch and Apocalyptic Imagination," in *Salmagundi* (Winter-Spring 1990), pp. 201–206. Indeed, in the Socialist Realist universe the emphasis on death is not crucial, while after the war it is (as there is no love). Early Socialist Realist novels written before World War II are motivated neither by love nor by death—*pace* Freud—but rather by the drama of labor, of overcoming the petit-bourgeois self and partaking of the heroic collective spirit. (See Katerina Clark, *The Soviet Novel.*) After the war, however, many war heroes enter the Soviet pantheon, and the scene of the death of a hero becomes crucial for postwar iconography—be it Alexander Matrosov, the pilot Gastello, or the partisan Zoia Kosmedem'ianskaia. Not death as such, but a heroic feat, an ultimate victory, and the official resurrection of the tortured hero are brought into the foreground. In spite of this difference in emphasis, victory over death in the Communist Socialist Realist universe and the glorification of death in Nazi art manipulate the same emotional and behavioral structures. Milan Kundera describes a beautiful Socialist Realist revolutionary march in which the French Communist and Surrealist poet Paul Éluard joins the Czech people in a dance around a scene of public execution (*The Book of Laughter and Forgetting* [London: Penguin, 1983]; the executed is the Czech Surrealist Kalandra.) So the dancing ring of a new generation of youthful enthusiasts hides the scene from view. After all, it is hard to say whether there is much difference between being killed with Wagner's "Death of Isolde" in the background or with the sounds of a life-affirming collective march. (This is speaking metaphorically, of course, because most of the victims of Hitler and Stalin were killed in much less theatrical settings.)

201. The words are by Lebedev-Kumach, music by Isaak Dunaevsky. Translation is mine.

202. The words of the songs are written down from the albums or personal tapes. Minor variations in their texts do not alter the argument.

203. The parody was reported to me by Felix Rosiner who has a truly encyclopedic knowledge of the 1960s urban folklore.

204. Bella Akhmadulina, "Aprel'," in *Izbrannoe* (Moscow: Sovetskii pisatel', 1988), p. 31.

205. The rock band uses the name of the legendary ship from Jules Verne's novels that provided escapes into both science fiction and the foreign

seas for several generations of Soviet citizens. Nineteenth-century French and English popular novels became an unofficial mass culture for the Soviet intelligentsia children, an escape from endless stories of Young Pioneers.

2. Living in Common Places

1. The anecdote is from *Istoriia SSSR v anekdotakh* (Smolensk: 1991), p. 77.

2. Alexander Kabakov, "Na chuzhom pole," in *Moskovskie novosti*, 49, December 6, 1992, p. 5.

3. Quoted in Vladimir Paperny, *Kul'tura Dva* (Ann Arbor: Ardis, 1984), p. 83.

4. Joseph Brodsky, "Room and a Half" in *Less Than One: Selected Essays* (New York: Farrar, Straus & Giroux, 1986).

5. El Lissitsky, "Basic Premises, Interrelationships between Arts, the New City and Ideological Superstructure" in *Bolshevik Visions,* ed. William Rosenberg (Ann Arbor: The University of Michigan Press, 1990), vol. 2, pp. 194–195.

6. The evolution of the concept of place was similar to that of photomontage itself, which recreates the revolutionary topos with its deliberate cuts and seams. At first, as in the early photographic experiments of Klutsis, Lissitsky, and Rodchenko, the construction of space calls for a radical reversibility of perspectives and multiplicity of viewpoints: "to be looked at from all sides," reads the caption on Gustav Klutsis's first revolutionary photomontage, "Dynamic City." Later, the play of perspective becomes more fixed, the montage more explicitly ideological, and the organization of space more hierarchical. By the 1930s the photomontages are dominated by the figures of the party leaders, Lenin and Stalin, who indicate one route through the space, the route of "communist victory." See Margarita Typitsyn, "From the Politics of Montage to the Montage of Politics," in *Montage and Modern Life,* ed. Matthew Teitelbaum (Cambridge, Mass.: MIT Press, 1992), pp. 82–128.

7. Walter Benjamin, "Moscow," in *Reflections,* p. 109.

8. Grigorii Kozintsev, Leonid Trauberg, Georgii Kryzhitsky, Sergei Iutkevich, *Ekstcentrism 1922* (Ekscentropolis (formerly Petrograd): 1922), p. 10. Cafés, like salons, could be seen as institutions of artistic communication, and revolutionary artists wished to avoid this mode of artistic self-reference.

9. The "boulevard," like the "street" is often personified; it appears as a metonymic substitution for the "crowd." The emphasis on the crowd as the main actor of modernity brings us back to Baudelaire's "The Painter of the Modern Life," Apollinaire's Parisian "Calligrams," and Mayakovsky's

early poems "Street," "Street Signs," and others. In other words, boulevard brings us back to the prerevolutionary international avant-garde, while the crowd is too anarchistic a concept to serve the new order. A short time later, however, the ideas of the eccentric manifesto become marginal in Soviet culture, and the foreign word "boulevard" ceases to be relevant to the Soviet public place. For an inspiring article on Surrealist topography and the movement from the street to the salon, see Susan Suleiman, "Between the Street and the Salon: The Dilemma of Surrealist Politics in the 1930s" in *Visual Anthropology Review,* 7, 1 (Spring, 1991).

10. For a historical description of revolutionary utopias, see Richard Stites, *Revolutionary Dreams: Utopian Vision and Experimental Life in the Russian Revolution;* V. E. Khazanova, *Iz istorrii sovetskoi arkhitektury, 1917–1925* (Moscow: A.N.S.S.S.R., 1963); *Sovetskaiia arkhitektura pervykh let oktiabria* (Moscow: Nauka, 1970); *Sovetskaiia arkhitektura pervoi piatiletki* (Moscow: Nauka, 1980); Christina Lodder, *Russian Constructivism* (New Haven: Yale University Press, 1983); Moisei Ginzburg, *Style and Epoch* (Cambridge: MIT Press, 1982). For theory and comparative views on utopia see Frank and Fritzie Manuel, *Utopian Thought in the Western World* (Cambridge, Mass.: Harvard University Press, 1979) and Lars Kleberg and Richard Stites, eds., *Utopia in Russian History, Culture and Thought* (Special issue of *Russian History,* 11/2–3, Summer–Fall 1984).

11. The authors of the project were the architects Vengerov, Tverskoi, and Buryshkin. See Richard Stites, *Revolutionary Dreams,* pp. 200–204.

12. See Walter Benjamin, "Paris, the Capital of the Nineteenth Century," in *Charles Baudelaire: A Lyric Poet in the Era of High Capitalism* (London: Verso, 1983), pp. 155–177.

13. Many revolutionary architects who called themselves "dis-urbanists" planned socialist suburbs. Among the most interesting projects are Leonid Vesnin's garden court apartment complex, and Konstantin Melnikov's Green City (1929)—a peculiar suburban Arcadia in which people lived in private rooms in hotels, and communal interaction took place in the huge railroad station. Melnikov, who comes from a peasant background, was one of the more "individualist" among the designers of the house communes: he paid special attention to the areas of transition between public and private and created long corridors that connected small private sleeping rooms with the communal spaces. One of the most imaginative of Melnikov's spaces were aroma-therapeutic sleeping chambers called euphonically "sonnaia sonata" (sleep sonata) where the air would be crystal clean and the poets and musicians would sing ideologically correct lullabies to the fatigued laborers. The idea was partially plagiarized by the American architect Wallace Harrison and his benefactor and New York showman "Roxy" Roth. It led them to create a special atmosphere of ozoned, ultra-solarized air in

Radio City Music Hall—another kind of workers' paradise. Melnikov's sleeping chambers were both poetic and imaginative yet imbued with revolutionary teleology: in the very center of Green City there was an Institute for Changing the Form of Man, a behaviorist laboratory that was supposed to model an ideal socialist laborer of the future. Russian utopias in general tend to be less pleasure- and leisure-oriented than their Western counterparts. (Nobody could compete with the grand gourmet Fourier's imagined pleasures of eating and of leisure.) And in contrast to the French Surrealists' program, especially the first manifesto published four years before Melnikov's project for the Green City, which centers on the unconscious, Russian utopian dreams were both more outlandish and more controlled, subservient to the overruling teleology of the revolution. See S. Frederick Starr, *Melnikov: Solo Architect in the Mass Society* (Princeton: Princeton University Press, 1978), pp. 49–50.

14. Alexandra Kollontai in her novellas presents working women caught between their intimate and their public life, matters of the heart and matters of duty. Vasilisa Malygina, the heroine of one of Kollontai's stories, leaves her unfaithful husband, a new Soviet apparatchik who has a petit-bourgeois mistress, and finds her self-realization in the building of collectives for women and men. The story ends at the start of the construction of a house-commune; we learn about the difficulties of dreaming but not about the consequences of those dreams. The novella is also a didactic lesson, a moral tale in the Tolstoyian tradition of fairy tales for the common people. Yet it reveals some of the crucial ambiguities in the foundations of the new byt.

Housing dreams were not limited to writers or avant-garde architects. The newspapers of the 1920s were full of the amateurish utopian projects suggested by the readers. One of the articles, "Give Us the House-Commune," quotes the workers from the "Red Chemist" factory: "We don't need little English houses, we don't need private apartments, give us a whole house where a worker's family could be in touch with the other workers' families, where they could meet in one common room." See *Komsomolskaia Pravda,* Oct. 13, 1928. The writer stresses that this is "not a matter of utopia" but a project for the future. Many authors of utopian projects preferred to emphasize collective authorship and the rational and practical base of their ideas.

15. I am grateful to Maya Turovskaya, a specialist on everyday life of Stalin's times, for bringing this to my attention.

16. Lidiia Ginzburg, *Chelovek za pis'mennym stolom* (Leningrad: Sovetskii pisatel', 1989), pp. 492–493.

17. There is a game theory of utopia: it is presented as a playground for the escapist ideas of a specific historical period and an enactment of political programs. But utopian thinking has to pass through a non-playful leap of

faith that cuts the connection between everyday life and imaginary existence. Utopias often present a "paradise on earth" in a corrupt land, which might help to redeem it. Hence utopias tend to be didactic rather than playful. See James Michael Holquist, "How to Play Utopia: Some Brief Notes on the Distinctiveness of the Utopian System" in *Science Fiction,* ed. Mark Rose (Englewood Cliffs: Prentice Hall, 1976).

18. Evgenii Zamiatin, *We* (New York: Inter-Language Literary Associates, 1967), pp. 26–27. I offer only a few sketches for the future analysis of the Soviet communal home in art.

This "ancient house" has a literary ancestor in the room of Sofia Petrovna from Andrei Bely's *Petersburg,* equally overcrowded with useless orientalia. But that room expresses a stifling Asiatic mentality, decadent and excessively feminine; it is a room from which one goes directly to join the revolution, in its most radical anarchist form. In *We* the values are reversed: the apartment turns into a refuge. Here the interior is feminized; guarded by an old woman and worshiped by a young one, it becomes a site of seduction.

19. Mikhail Zoshchenko, "O chem pel solovei," in *Izbrannoe v dvukh tomakh* (Minsk: Narodnaia Asveta, 1983), vol. 1, pp. 403–422.

20. Ibid., p. 411.

21. Bylinkin is a perfect postrevolutionary hypocrite. He happily abuses the hospitality of his landlady, Liza's mother, who is afraid that the apartment will turn communal; and at the same time, he never misses a chance to criticize *meshchanski byt,* the Soviet petit-bourgeois existence. Hence the critique of meshchanstvo appears, as it were, in quotation marks, since it is placed in the mouth of one that the reader will identify as a self-righteous meshchanin himself. Because of the narrative's hide-and-seek it remains unclear whether Zoshchenko is looking for some kind of unhypocritical critique of meshchanstvo, whether he is laughing at that critique as such, or simply offering us the Soviet common place and a slice of Soviet sentimental life. In a similar manner, the hypocrisy of the wars against meshchanstvo is revealed in Mayakovsky's poem "Marusia Got Poisoned." See the discussion of meshchanstvo in Chapter 1.

22. Mario Praz, *An Illustrated History of Interior Decoration from Pompeii to Art Nouveau* (London: Thames and Hudson, 1981).

23. On the cultural "fuss around the bed" see Olga Matich, "Sueta vokrug krovati: Utopicheskaia organizatsiia byta i russkii avant-gard" in *Novoe literaturnoe obozrenie,* 11 (1991), pp. 80–84. Olga Matich discusses the cultural "making of the bed" and its role in the mythology of new byt. I am grateful to Irina Paperno for bringing this article to my attention.

In the context of a complex cultural paradigm sofas are placed against minimalist revolutionary beds such as the "archetypal" bed of the exemplary revolutionary Rakhmetov, the hero of *What Is To Be Done,* who used to sleep on nails.

24. Iurii Olesha, *Envy* (Ann Arbor: Ardis, 1977).

25. Ilia Ilf and Evgenii Petrov, *Zolotoi telenok (Golden Calf)* (Moscow: Khudozhestvennaia literatura, 1990).

26. The authors' attitudes toward the character and his narrative framings are slippery. Unlike Zoshchenko's stories, Ilf and Petrov's novel does not have a narrator present; its objects of satire, although no less comical, appear less ambiguous.

27. While composing poems to his unfaithful wife, Vasisuali "rolls like an old Jew during prayers" (p. 419). But it is not clear how this allusion should be interpreted in the context of the time, since the word "Jew" did not yet have the same connotations it would carry in the late 1930s, when it turned into one of the "obscene" or never uttered words in the Soviet press.

Nadezhda Mandelshtam sees in Lokhankin a parody of the liberal Russian intelligentsia playing up to the official propaganda of the time until it fell victim to the purges. At that time every intellectual was in danger of becoming not merely a pseudo-intellectual but a nonperson. Nadezhda Mandelshtam, *Vospominaniia* (New York: Chekhov Publishing Corporation, 1970), pp. 345–346.

28. In 1993 a new Russian film was made based on a free adaptation of *The Golden Calf* entitled *The Idiot's Dream* (dir. Pichul). The film made a point of being unfunny, which was its primary artistic conceit.

29. Iurii Lotman, *Universe of the Mind: A Semiotic Theory of Culture*, trans. Ann Shukman (New York: I. B. Tauris, 1990), p. 191.

30. One of Bulgakov's early stories has a satirical description of the transformation of fashionable Elpit House, under the devilish number 13, into a workers' commune. This is what the "dwelling comradeship" looked like: "Seventy five apartments were occupied by incredible populace; the pianos were silent, instead the gramophones were alive and sang in malevolent voices. Across the living rooms they hang laundry lines with their sheets and underwear. The stoves were hissing like serpents, and day and night piercing smoke enveloped the staircases. All the lamps disappeared and darkness settled in. Human shadows stumbled upon each other and sadly call: 'Mania, Mania, are you there? What the hell.' In the apartment 50 the parquet was burned to heat the room . . . As for the elevators . . . Oh well . . . what can I tell you . . ."

The "dwelling comradeship" is protected and guarded by "the greatest genius of all housemasters," a survivor from prerevolutionary times, the "swarthy" Boris Samoilovich Christi who hides in the basement apartment. But even he is unable to perform the necessary miracle to save workers' commune no. 13. The expropriation adventure culminates with a destructive

Soviet carnival, a "hellish" fire that burns away the "dwelling comradeship." In Bulgakov's fiction the Soviet communal home turns into a site of counter-revolutionary orgies and ritual destructions. Mr. Christi metamorphoses into Devil Voland, the protector of poets and intellectuals in *The Master and Margarita.* It seems that in Bulgakov's fictional universe the unconventional Mephistopheles and the unconventional Christ forget their traditional antagonisms and join forces as fellow heroes of the old mythology and romantic civilization to fight the complacent Soviet brutes, masters of the new world order. Mikhail Bulgakov, "Dom No 13. Elpit Rabkommunna" in *Diavoliada* (Moscow: Nedra, 1925; repr. New York: Russica, 1980), p. 127. Translation mine.

31. Alexander Zholkovsky makes an original suggestion that perhaps one should not oppose the "compromised" writers, who in a broad sense wished to be the fellow travelers of the Soviet regime (including Olesha and Ilf and Petrov), to the "uncompromised" and "morally pure" writers like Bulgakov and Mandelshtam, who became martyrs of the dissident intelligentsia in the late Soviet period. In fact, they partake of many of the same myths of Russian intelligentsia. See Zholkovsky, "Popytka zavisti u Mandel'shtama i Bulgakova" in *Bluzhdaiuschie sny: Slovo i Kul'tura* (Moscow, 1992), pp. 177–211. In fact, some of the Bulgakov heroes participate in the romantic rebellion against everyday life that is structurally similar to the rebellion against byt promoted by left revolutionary artists like Tretiakov.

32. I am indebted to Moscow writer and journalist Alla Gerber, who told me about kitchen culture.

33. See Erving Goffman, *The Presentation of Self in Everyday Life* (New York: Doubleday, 1959).

34. Edward Keenan, "Moscow Political Folkways," p. 128.

35. Alexander Etkind, "Psychological Culture of the Soviets," paper presented at the Conference on Soviet Culture, Las Vegas, November 1992.

36. Igor Kon, "The Soviet Moral Culture," paper presented at the Conference on Soviet Culture, Las Vega, November 1992.

37. Walter Benjamin, "Paris, the Capital of the Nineteenth Century," in *Reflections,* p. 155.

38. The Russian word for furniture, *mebel',* comes from the French *meuble* meaning movable property, in contrast to land or buildings. Gradually a mere storage chest turned into an object of craft and art, a prototype of the modern chest of drawers and glass cabinets.

39. Mario Praz, *An Illustrated History of Interior Decoration,* p. 56. The glassed cabinet, a stronghold of bourgeois coziness, was locked with a key to protect the private treasures and opened only to the private delights of the family and of selected guests. By the end of the century, the glass cabinets turned into a home *kunstcamera,* a private collections of curios and

bric-à-brac, a privileged site of bibliomania and occasionally of rarefied and morbid fin-de-siècle erotomania. The private collection was the primary display of bourgeois self-fashioning. See Emily Apter, "Cabinet Secrets: Peep Shows, Prostitution and Bric-a-Bracomania," in *Feminizing the Fetish: Psychoanalysis and Narrative Obsession in Turn-of-the-Century France* (Ithaca: Cornell University Press, 1991), pp. 15–39.

40. Walter Benjamin, "Paris, the Capital of the Nineteenth Century," p. 154.

41. Norman Bryson, *Looking on the Overlooked: Four Essays on Still Life Painting* (Cambridge, Mass.: Harvard University Press, 1990), p. 8.

42. Pierre Bourdieu, *Distinction: A Social Critique of the Judgement of Taste,* trans. Richard Nice (Cambridge, Mass.: Harvard University Press, 1984), p. 9.

43. Ibid., p. 5.

44. For an extensive theoretical discussion of fetishism see William Pietz, "The Problem of Fetish I," *Res* 9 (Spring 1985); "The Problem of Fetish II," *Res* 13 (Spring 1987), pp. 23–45; and "The Problem of Fetish IIIa," *Res* 16 (Autumn, 1988), pp. 105–123. Emily Apter, *Feminizing the Fetish,* p. 5. Sigmund Freud, "On Fetishism," in *The Standard Edition of Complete Psychological Works and Letters,* 24 vols., trans. James Strachey (London: Hogarth Press, 1953–1974), vol. 21, pp. 152–157. Karl Marx, *Capital,* trans. Samuel Moore and Edward Aveling, ed. Frederick Engels (New York: Modern Library, 1906). For a discussion of the fetishization of the concept of fetish, see W. J. T. Mitchell, "The Rhetoric of Iconoclasm: Marxism, Ideology and Fetishism," in *Iconology: Image, Text, Ideology* (Chicago: University of Chicago Press, 1986), pp. 160–208. See also Naomi Shor, "Female Fetishism: The Case of George Sand" in *The Female Body in Western Culture,* ed. Susan Suleiman (Cambridge, Mass.: Harvard University Press, 1986). British psychoanalyst D. W. Winnicot has a useful and complex theory of the "transitional object." See also Jean Baudrillard, *For a Critique of the Political Economy of the Sign,* trans. Charles Lewin (St. Louis, Mo.: Telos Press, 1981), and *De la séduction* (Paris: Galilée-Denoel, 1979). For the discussion of culture collecting see James Clifford, *The Predicament of Culture* (Cambridge, Mass.: Harvard University Press, 1988).

45. Osip Mandelshtam, "Egipteskaia marka," in *Sobranie sochinenii v trekh tomakh,* vol. 2, p. 5.

46. Mandelshtam reacts against both Futurist utopianism and Symbolist metaphysics, commenting that the latter were "the bad house sitters" of language, who wished to transcend the materiality of language and of the world too quickly.

47. A kind of empathetic everyday aesthetics is needed to account for the cultural significance of ordinary precarious possessions. This aesthetics is

not ahistorical and universally human: the appeal to the precariousness and preciousness of the objects can in itself be rhetorically abused. Yet this aesthetics ought to be developed alongside theories of commodity fetishism.

48. Elaine Scarry, "The Interior Structure of the Artifact," in *The Body in Pain: The Making and Unmaking of the World* (Oxford: Oxford University Press, 1985), pp. 278–326. Following from the context of alienated labor and economic production, thinking about things is displaced into the context of reception, projection of reciprocity, responsibility, and responsiveness. The object is seen as a projection of human sentience, as a projection of the awareness of aliveness. The denial of the object is not only a social deprivation but also a sensory deprivation, a thwarting of sentience, human contact, powers of projection, and reciprocity. Although Scarry does not wish to draw a clear distinction between art objects and artifacts, it seems that a creative impulse is crucial for her reading, and this creative impulse and affirmation of aliveness constitute the aesthetics of daily existence.

49. Susan Stewart, *On Longing: Narratives of the Miniature, the Gigantic, the Souvenir, the Collection* (Baltimore: Johns Hopkins University Press, 1984).

50. Ilya Kabakov, *Ten Characters* (London: ICA, 1989), p. 32. See also a catalogue from the Ronald Feldman installation of April 1991. For more on Kabakov, see Boris Groys, "Ilia Kabakov," in *A-Ya,* 2 (1980), pp. 17–22; Claudia Jolles and Viktor Misiano, "In Conversation with Eric Bulatov and Ilya Kabakov," *Flash Art,* 137 (November–December 1987), pp. 81–83; Margarita Tupitsyn, "Ilia Kabakov," in *Flash Art,* 142 (October 1988), p. 115.

51. In 1988 Soviet ministers approved an amendment allowing citizens to buy their apartments, but the process went exceptionally slowly: only 0.03 percent in 1989, and 0.07 percent of apartment residents, turned their apartments into their "private property." Only in July of 1991 did the Supreme Soviet adopt the law allowing for full privatization of apartments. *Ogonek,* 38 (September 1991), p. 18.

52. See Celestine Bohlen, "Moscow Privatization Yields Privacy and Problems," *Sunday New York Times,* Feb. 28, 1993.

53. This statistic was given in a Russian news program (*Novosti,* August 10, 1993).

3. Writing Common Places

1. For a discussion of the "literary institution" and its functioning in the prerevolutionary Russian context, see William Mills Todd III, "Institutions of Literature in Early Nineteenth-Century Russia: Boundaries and Transgressions," in *Literature and History: Theoretical Problems and Rus-*

sian Case Studies, ed. Gary Saul Morson (Stanford: Stanford University Press, 1986), pp. 57–89, and William Mills Todd III, "Literature as an Institution: Fragments of Formalist Theory" in *Russian Formalism: A Retrospective Glance,* ed. Robert Louis Jackson and Stephen Rudy (New Haven: Yale University Press, 1985), pp. 25–26. See also *Literature and Society in Imperial Russia,* ed. William Mills Todd III (Stanford, 1978) and his *Fiction and Society in the Age of Pushkin* (Cambridge, Mass.: Harvard University Press, 1986).

2. Boris Eikhenbaum, "Literaturnaia domashnost'" in *Moi vremennik: slovesnost', nauka, kritika, smes'* (Leningrad, 1929), pp. 82–86. Eikhenbaum's example is Iazykov, a poet of Pushkin's time, who resisted the publication of his poems, and did not wish to become a professional *litterateur,* a new type of writer promoted by Pushkin.

3. *Le Grand Robert* dictionary dates "graphomanie" from 1782, while the adjective "graphomane" appears only in the early twentieth century. *The Oxford English Dictionary* cites "graphomaniac" in a book title in 1827, and "graphomania" in a journal article from 1840.

4. Max Nordau, *Degeneration* (New York: H. Fertiq, 1968). I am grateful to Charles Bernheimer for bringing this to my attention.

5. Plato, *Phaedrus* (New York: Macmillan Publishing Company, 1956), 244–245, p. 26.

6. Milan Kundera, *The Book of Laughter and Forgetting,* trans. Michael Heim (London: Penguin Books, 1986), p. 92.

7. Ibid. Elsewhere, Kundera also offers many fictional images of totalitarian graphomaniacs, particularly romantic poet-conformists, although he does not use the term "graphomaniac" explicitly in relation to them.

8. Abram Tertz (Andrei Sinyavsky), "Grafomany" in *Fantasticheskie povesti* (Paris, New York: Inter-Language Literary Associates, 1967), p. 80.

9. *The Third Wave,* ed. Olga Matich with Michael Heim (Ann Arbor: Ardis, 1984). I am grateful to Donald Fanger for bringing this to my attention.

10. The word "graphomania" is not registered in *The Russian Dictionary of the Academy* of 1822, yet the Russian poets of the time might have been familiar with it, either from French or from their own playing with the classical roots to create comic neologisms for prolific writers. Even if the linguistic ambiguity of Khvostov's nickname was not perceived at the time, this turned out to be a *mot juste* that pioneered the trend of theoretical jargon on bad writing. William Mills Todd III actually uses the word "graphomaniac" in his description of Khvostov in his *The Familiar Letter as a Literary Genre in the Age of Pushkin* (Princeton: Princeton University Press, 1976), p. 56.

11. Iurii Tynianov, *Poetika, Istoriia literatury, kino* (Moscow: Nauka, 1977), p. 306. For a discussion of Pushkin's "Ode to Count Khvostov" see *Pushkin i ego sovremenniki* (Moscow: Nauka, 1968), pp. 105–108. For the uses of the name "Khvostov" as a synonym for an outmoded, excessively prolific and ridiculous writer see the letters of Karamzin, Pushkin, and Kiuk-helbekker discussed in William Mills Todd III, *The Familiar Letter as a Literary Genre in the Age of Pushkin*, pp. 55–56, 96–97, 175–176.

12. Alexander Pushkin, *Evgenii Onegin*, in *Sochineniia v trekh tomakh*, trans. John Henriksen (Moscow: 1955), vol. 3, ch. 6, p. 107.

13. For a detailed examination of the intertextual references of Lensky's elegy see Iurii Lotman, *Roman Pushkina Evgenii Oneguin* (Leningrad: Pros-veshchenie, 1983), p. 299. Lensky's poetry is first described as an enumera-tion of the fixed idiomatic expressions of Romanticism. All the similes and comparisons here are conventional: "as clear as the thoughts of a simple-hearted maiden"; "like a moon"; "the moon is the goddess of mystery." Here the similes and metaphors are presented as completely automatized, almost reduced to absurdity. Pushkin's italics further distance the commonplace, mark it as alien speech which the narrator is parodying. "Je ne sais quoi" (néchto) and "misty distance" are quotations of the elevated romantic style which Pushkin intertwines into the playful, colloquial, and almost prosaic style of his novel in verse. On the other hand, in the early version of the novel, Lensky was portrayed as a political free-thinker, sharing many views with Pushkin's exiled friends, the Decembrists. This further complicates Pushkin's relationship to Romanticism and its self-fashioning, which includes an assumption of anti-autocratic political views and the struggle for freedom.

14. Ibid., pp. 350–351.

15. Alexander Pushkin, "Istoriia sela Goriukhina," in *Sochineniia*, vol. 3, pp. 288–304.

16. Ibid., p. 294.

17. For a discussion of the double texts of history and fiction in the Russian tradition see Andrew Wachtel, *An Obsession with History: Russian Writers Confront the Past* (Stanford: Stanford University Press, 1993).

18. Pushkin, "Istoriia sela Goriukhina," p. 299.

19. On the extensive literature of Pushkin's canonization as a national genius see Marcus Levitt, *Russian Literary Politics and the Pushkin Celebra-tion of 1880* (Ithaca: Cornell University Press, 1989) and his article "Pushkin in 1899" in *Cultural Mythologies of Russian Modernism: From the Golden Age to the Silver Age*, ed. Boris Gasparov, Robert Hughes, and Irina Paperno (Berkeley: University of California Press, 1992).

20. Abram Tertz, *Progulki s Pushkinym* (London: Overseas Publication Interchange Ltd., 1975). For an excellent discussion of Sinyavsky's reception

in the late Soviet press and the controversy over his image of Pushkin see
Catherine Theimer Nepomnyaschy, "Andrei Sinyavsky's 'Return' to the Soviet Union" in *Formations*, 6, 1 (Spring 1991).

21. See Iurii Tynianov, "O literaturnoi evoliutsii," in *Poetika, Istoriia
literatury, kino.*

22. Feodor Dostoevsky, *Bednye liudi* (Moscow: Khudozhestvennaia literatura, 1986), p. 117. For a discussion of the relationship between Gogol
and Dostoevsky, see Donald Fanger, *Dostoevsky and Romantic Realism*
(Chicago: University of Chicago Press, 1967), pp. 152–159.

23. Ibid., p. 69.

24. Feodor Dostoevsky, *Besy* (Leningrad: Lenizdat, 1990), part I, chapter V, pp. 155–156. "Zhil na svete tarakan, / Tarakan ot detstva / I potom
popal v stakan / Polnyi mukhoedstva . . ."

25. Vladimir Nabokov, "Crime and Punishment," in *Lectures on Russian Literature* (New York: Harcourt Brace Jovanovich, 1981).

26. Peter Brooks, *The Melodramatic Imagination* (New York: Columbia
University Press, 1985).

27. *Sochineniia Koz'my Prutkova* (Moscow: Khudozhestvennaia literatura, 1976), p. 121.

28. Ibid., p. 120.

29. "Biograficheskie svedeniia o Koz'me Prutkove," in *Sochineniia*,
p. 290. The notion of "kazennye poshlosti" is quite revealing.

30. Iurii Tynianov, "O parodii" in *Poetika, Istoriia literatury, kino*,
pp. 284–310.

31. Koz'ma Prutkov, "Iunker Shmidt," in *Sochineniia*, p. 32. "Vianet
list. Prokhodit leto. / Inei serebritsia . . . / Iunker Shmidt iz pistoleta / Kho-
chet zastrelit'sia."

32. Gustave Flaubert, *Bouvard et Pécuchet* (Paris: Gallimard, 1979),
p. 535.

33. Ibid., pp. 537, 489. "Littérature: occupation des oisifs."

34. Ibid., p. 489. "La femme-artiste n'est peut-être qu'une catin."

35. Anton Chekhov, "Ionych," in *Sobranie Sochinenii v dvenadsati
tomakh*, vol. VIII (Moscow: Khudozhestvennaia literatura, 1962).

36. Jeffrey Brooks, *When Russia Learned to Read* (Princeton: Princeton
University Press, 1985), p. 159.

37. Vladimir Nabokov, *Pnin*, p. 181. I am grateful to Elizabeth Klosty
Beaujour for reminding me of the prominent female graphomaniac Liza Pnin.

38. Ibid., p. 182.

39. Ibid., p. 45.

40. French Surrealists in the early stage of their movement dreamed of a
pure writing or a pure graphomania, a writing unadulterated by plot, character, and other superfluous elements: "automatic writing." In the first Sur-

realist Manifesto, André Breton gives us an exact prescription of how to achieve genuinely automatic writing. (This kind of "ukaze" on automatic writing is in itself a paradox.)

41. Mikhail Zoshchenko, "Sentimental'nye povesti" in *Izbrannoe v dvukh tomakh* (Minsk: Narodnaia Asveta, 1983). I am grateful to Donald Fanger for reminding me of these prominent graphomaniacs.

42. Ibid., p. 365.

43. Ibid., p. 366.

44. Ibid., p. 421.

45. Ibid., p. 435.

46. Nikolai Oleinikov, *Ironicheskie stikhi*, p. 91.

47. Lev Losev, "Ukhmylka Oleinikova," in *Ironicheskie stikhi*, p. 10.

48. For further discussion of Oleinikov and Zabolotsky, see Lidiia Ginzburg, "O Zabolotskom kontsa dvadtsatykh godov" in *Vospominaniia o Zabolotskom,* ed. E. B. Zabolotskaia and A. B. Makedonov (Moscow: Sovetskii pisatel', 1977), pp. 120–131.

49. Daniil Kharms, *Izbrannoe,* ed. George Gibian (Wurzburg: Jal verlag, 1974), p. 253. "Konduktor chisel, druzhby zloi nasmeshnik, / O chem zadumalsia? Il' vnov' porochish' mir? / Gomer tebe poshliak, i Gete glupyi greshnik, / Toboi osmeian Dant. Lish' Bunin tvoi kumir," trans. John Henriksen.

50. Quoted in Lev Losev, "Ukhmylka Oleinikova," p. 7.

51. On the Stalinist policy of folklorism see Richard Stites, "Stalin by Starlight" in *Russian Popular Culture: Entertainment and Society since 1900* (Cambridge: Cambridge University Press, 1992), pp. 64–97.

52. Grigorii Alexandrov, *Epokha i Kino* (Moscow: Politizdat, 1976), p. 216.

53. I have benefited greatly from conversations with Maya Turovskaia and from her paper "Volga, Volga," presented in New Orleans in 1991. Her research points out the film's subtleties, as well as the not-so-subtle disappearance of Erdman's and Nilsen's names.

54. See Nikolai Erdman, "Stikhi i intermedii," in *P'esy, intermedii, pis'ma, dokumenty* (Moscow: Iskusstvo, 1990), pp. 165–171.

55. On the relationship between Sinyavsky and Tertz and on the making of the pseudonym see Donald Fanger, "Conflicting Imperatives in the Model of the Russian Writer: Sinyavsky/Tertz" in *Literature and History,* ed. Gary Saul Morson, pp. 111–124.

56. Pavlik's writing is actually quite remarkable, and appears to be more interesting than that of his father. It reminds us of the absurdist children's literature written by former avant-garde writers and poets of the 1930s— Kharms, Oleinikov, Chukovsky.

57. Abram Tertz (Andrei Sinyavsky), "Grafomany," p. 95.

58. Ibid., p. 77. "Bylo zharko i dushno."

59. The novella was published in *Iskusstvo kino*, 6 (1990).

60. Ibid., p. 120.

61. Ibid., p. 115.

62. Dmitrii Prigov and Svetlana Beliaeva-Konegen, "Krepkogo vam zdorov'ia, gospoda literatory," *Strelec*, 3, 70 (1992), p. 209.

63. *Lichnoe Delo No*, ed. Lev Rubinstein (Moscow: Soiuz-Teatr, 1991), p. 266.

64. One of Prigov's paintings actually represents his signature in big letters in the middle of a black inkspot on the front page of the newspaper *Pravda*. His name is the "magic text" in the words of the author, and the only signifying one in the midst of the meaningless sentences of the journalistic account of life in the 1980s.

65. *Lichnoe Delo No*, ed. Lev Rubinstein, p. 207.

66. Dmitrii Prigov, *Slezy geral'dicheskoi dushi* (Moscow: Moscow Worker, 1990), p. 25.

67. Mikhail Aisenberg, "Vmesto predisloviia," in *Lichnoe Delo No*, p. 17.

68. Dmitrii Prigov, *Slezy geral'dicheskoi dushi*, p. 21.

69. Dmitrii Prigov, "Milicioner guliaet v parke," in *Lichnoe Delo No*, p. 206. "Milicioner guliaet v parke / osennei pozdneiu poroi / I nad pokrytoi golovoi / Vkhodnoi beleet nebo arkoi. / I budushchee tak nelozhno / Iavliaetsia sredi allei / Kogda ego ischeznet dolzhnost' / sredi osmyslennykh liudei. / Kogda mundir ne nuzhen budet / Ni kobura, ni revol'ver / I stanut brat'iami vse liudi / I kazhdyi—Milicioner."

70. From this point on Krasivaya's draft begins to ramble: "In the West one rarely 'writes': one either publishes or perishes (in any order), or engages in 'graphomoneya': not writing whatever comes to mind, but writing whatever makes money . . ." I allowed myself to cut this part, because I think Krasivaya draws here a rather simple opposition of Russia and the West, graphomania and "graphomoneya." In the end it sounds like some outmoded graphomaniac of the old world is simply envying the fame and success of the new-world graphomoneyac.

4. Postcommunism, Postmodernism

1. *Boston Globe*, Aug. 20, 1991.

2. In Susan Sontag's view, a love for *Swan Lake* is among the things that define those belonging to the exclusive "camp" of aesthete connoisseurs of "bad taste" and all things outmoded. Susan Sontag, "Notes on Camp," in *Against Interpretation* (New York: Doubleday, 1990), pp. 275–292. Though some elements of refined aestheticism can be found in late Soviet and

post-Soviet Russian art, nobody would yet consider Tchaikovsky's ballet, a piece of official virtuosity, to be particularly campy. And American aesthetes would be surprised that their young Russian peers might prefer *Terminator 2* to *Swan Lake*.

3. *Smena,* Leningrad, August 22.

4. The use of commercials during the coup reveals some old and new clichés of American-Soviet relations. Independent Soviet entrepreneurs, under the pretext of putting out a new advertisement for Stolichnaya Vodka, smuggled to the West on the day of the coup a photograph of the crowds massed in protest on Palace Square, with the caption "Stolichnaya Vodka: Proud to Be Russian." This in many ways paradoxical incident uncovers old underground political tactics in the new commercial framing.

5. Jean Baudrillard, "La guerre n'aurait pas lieu," in *Liberation,* 4 Janvier, 1991. I am grateful to Martin Roberts for bringing this article to my attention.

6. As Mary Ann Doan remarks, "catastrophe is on the cusp of the dramatic and the referential, and this is indeed part of its fascination." Mary Ann Doane, "Information, Crisis, Catastrophe," in *Logics of Television,* ed. Patricia Mellencamp (Bloomington: University of Indiana Press, 1990). Several other essays in the same collection are relevant to my topic: Stephen Heath, "Representing Television"; Margaret Morse, "An Anthology of Everyday Distraction: The Freeway, the Mall, and Television"; Meagan Morris, "Banality in Cultural Studies"; and Patricia Mellencamp, "TV Time and Catastrophe or Beyond the Pleasure Principle."

7. The concepts of disaster and catastrophe, as well as the separation between natural and political, are different in the two cultures. While at the time of the coup some of my Soviet friends—journalists—were laughing at the American preoccupation with health and their fear of natural disasters, the American press was somewhat ironic about the Soviet manias for "political" catastrophes. In fact, on August 17, 1991, the *New York Times* characterized Alexander Yakovlev's warning about the impending military coup as a "melodramatic flourish." (Yakovlev was one of Gorbachev's old friends and among the founders of glasnost'.) Unfortunately, what appeared to the *New York Times* journalist as melodrama and as a typically Russian apocalyptic prediction, was enacted as history. Melodrama and black comedy, or sometimes black tragicomedy, appear to be the dominant genres of Soviet history. For a third-party perspective on political forecasting on August 19, 1991, consider Radio Beijing, which did not offer much information about the events of the August 19 coup in the Soviet Union, but instead gave a detailed report of "major storms in the United States" depicted as contributing to the country's economic crisis.

8. Alexey Tarkhanov, "How the Post-Modernist Revolution Has Built

Art-Historical Barricades," *Seance,* 5 (St. Petersburg, 1991), pp. 9–10. I am grateful to my Leningrad and Moscow friends for sharing their coup experiences with me: Viktor Misiano, Sergey Sholokhov, Liubov' Arcus, Joseph Bakstein, Tatiana Arzamasova, Leonid Gozman, Nadezhda Azhgikhina, Daniil Dondurei, Zara Abdullaeva, Nina and Oleg Il'insky.

9. Ibid, p. 10. The translation of the quotations is mine.

10. Ibid., p. 10.

11. A good example of this approach is Mikhail Epstein's "After the Future: On the New Consciousness in Literature," in *Late Soviet Culture: From Perestroika to Novostroika,* ed. Thomas Lahusen with Gene Kuperman (Durham: Duke University Press, 1993), pp. 257–289. Epstein's other writings, however, reveal a variety of creative and playful philosophical approaches. For a stimulating debate on Russian postmodernism on E-mail see *Post-Modern Culture* (November 1992). The essays by Marjoree Perloff and Arkadii Dragomoschenko offer interesting critiques of the master narrative of Russian postmodernism.

12. While some postmodern theorists like Baudrillard and Frederic Jameson lament the loss and failure of the modern(ist) project, the loss of what they perceive as a possibility of historical change and a utopian dream, others, like Jean-François Lyotard, Craig Owens, James Clifford, and Hal Foster celebrate the new diversity and heterogeneity of recovered voices, along with liberation from the claims of originality and the seductions of utopia.

13. Republished in *Moscow Diary,* trans. Richard Sieburth, ed. Gary Smith (Cambridge, Mass.: Harvard University Press, 1988), p. 132. Benjamin's fragile search for Moscow facts has some affinities with Tretiakov and Pilnyak's notions of the "literature of facts," with Dziga Vertov's attempts to capture life unawares, and with Osip Mandelshtam's desire to transmit "the noise of time." "Facts" have a very tentative existence in Benjamin's universe and are always on the verge of turning into artifacts and suggestive allegories. Yet unlike allegories, facts demand the suspension of proliferating interpretative chains, relays of literary and theoretical speculations.

14. Among some neo-Slavophiles, especially from among the Moscow intelligentsia, Peter the Great's reign is seen as a first step toward the devilish internationalization and westernization of which the Bolshevik Marxist revolution was a climax. But then if we were to push this theory to its logical albeit absurd conclusion, Leningrad/St. Petersburg (the "window to Europe") should be forever closed as a shameful page of Russian history, and the swamps of the Neva delta returned to Sweden. (As a former Leningrader and a St Petersburgian-in-absentia I would never wish that to happen.)

15. A former dissident, Alexander Galich, wrote a very popular song about the post-Khrushchev order to destroy monuments of Stalin, which was

to be carried out by the prisoners of Stalin's labor camps—the same people who had to put those monuments up only a few years earlier.

16. *Moscow News* (Oct. 13, 1991).

17. Flying monuments are not all that surprising. In Russian culture statues do not stay still. Indeed, in the Russian Orthodox tradition statues are associated with sin and incarnation of the devil. (The art of sculpture developed at the time of Peter the Great and was one of the arts imported to Russia from the West.) The statue to Peter the Great comes alive in Pushkin's fantastic Petersburg tale "The Bronze Horseman" and chases the little man along the flooded streets of the imperial capital. Pushkin's own statue in Moscow, unveiled in 1875, went on a brief fantastic journey in the 1930s: from his original site in the Square of Christ's Passion (Strastnaia) facing the Passion Monastery, it was moved across the street and turned around because it was considered inappropriate for the greatest Russian (Soviet) genius to face the "citadel of religion." The monastery was pulled down and the monument was positioned in such a way that it would face the main thoroughfare of Moscow, formerly Tverskoi Boulevard, renamed Gorky after another "great Soviet literary genius," the founder of Socialist Realism. The square was subsequently called Pushkin Square.

18. Walter Benjamin, "Moscow," in *Reflections,* trans. by Edmund Jephcott (New York: Schocken Books, 1978), p. 102.

19. Quoted in Dmitri Volkogonov, *Triumf i tragediia: Politicheskii portret I.V. Stalina* (Moscow: Novosti Press, 1988), p. 87. I am grateful to Russian historian Viktor Listov for bringing this quote to my attention.

20. On historicism in cinema see Leonid Kozlov and Viktor Listov in *Iz Proshlogo v budushchee: Proverki na dorogakh* (Moscow: VNIIK, 1990). I benefited greatly from my conversations with Jeremy Kuehl and from reading his essay "The Camera Never Lies." See also Svetlana Boym, "Stalin's Cinematic Charisma: Between History and Nostalgia" in *Slavic Review* (Fall 1992); Anna Lawton, "The Ghost That Does Not Exorcise," and Svetlana Boym, "Stalin Is with Us: Soviet Documentary Mythologies of the 1980s," in *Stalinism in Soviet Cinema,* ed. Richard Taylor and Ian Christie (London: Routledge, 1993); and Andrew Horton and Michael Brazhinsky, *Zero Hour: Soviet Cinema of Glasnost'* (Princeton: Princeton University Press, 1992).

21. On the dual texts of history and fiction in Russian culture see Andrew Wachtel, *An Obsession with History: Russian Writers Confront the Past* (Stanford: Stanford University Press, 1994). See also *Literature and History: Theoretical Problems and Russian Case Studies,* ed. Gary Saul Morson (Stanford: Stanford University Press, 1986).

22. Roland Barthes, *Mythologies,* trans. Richard Howard (New York: Farrar, Straus, and Giroux, 1979). Yet it seems to me that the distinction between old and new cultural myths, myths on the right and myths on the

left, or "depoliticized" and "political" myths is as problematic as is the definition of right and left, which continuously alternates as we move from West to East and from the 1950s, when Barthes published his book, to the 1990s. Soviet cultural myths, especially the cult of the great party genius, defy clear distinctions of right and left; they are heterogeneous and impure; they are old myths in new trappings or new ideology building up on old beliefs and prejudices.

23. Nina Tumarkin, *Lenin Lives! The Lenin Cult in Soviet Russia* (Cambridge, Mass.: Harvard University Press, 1983). In the early 1990 investigations into Stalinism were superseded by investigations into Leninism. One of the first films reflecting this change is Vyacheslav Govorukhin's film *One Should Not Live Like That* (1990). At the center of the film is a forceful analogy between petty, seemingly disparate individual crimes and the global Crime committed by the Soviet government. Like many other Soviet documentaries, this film uses many explicit allegories. The Russian Revolution, which destroyed the churches, is the source of all evil, and the image of Lenin recurring at various crucial moments in the film is the visual embodiment of it. (For polemical reasons, perhaps, Stalin is not even mentioned in the film.) However, unlike *I Served in Stalin's Bodyguard,* the film uses an authoritative narrative that offers the viewer an overwhelmingly authoritarian vision that is itself representative of the same cultural tradition it denounces.

24. Aranovich remarked that he had an idea for a documentary a long time ago, and had a character in mind, but could not find a good candidate for the role. Thus the initial impulse for Aranovich's film is both mythological and documentary: Rybin himself is a mythical image of a devoted Stalin bodyguard, and at the same time, he is a unique character, whose minute gestures and facial expressions are commemorated in cinematic close-up.

25. Milan Kundera, *The Book of Laughter and Forgetting,* trans. Michael Heim (London: Penguin Books, 1986), pp. 65–68.

26. Tofik Shakhverdiev, "Stalin Is with Us?" in *Soviet Film,* 9 (1989), p. 7. The suggestion was made by then Vice-President of Goskino, Oleg Uralov.

27. The film does not rely only on cinema verité techniques but uses reenactment and staging.

28. "Stalin Is with Us?" p. 7.

29. Andrei Konchalovsky, *The Inner Circle,* trans. and ed. Jamey Gambrell (New York: Newmarket Press), p. 142.

30. Like *I Served in Stalin's Bodyguard, The Inner Circle* presents the events from the point of view of a believer, without making any immediate moral or ethical denunciations; yet whereas *I Served in Stalin's Bodyguard* exposes the oxymoronic configuration of documentary and myth, *The Inner Circle* veils it. Konchalovsky's film is freely based on the story of Stalin's projectionist, Alexander Ganshin, but the director is less interested in a

specific story than in the parable of an "innocent believer, a regular Russian guy, a real *homo sovieticus*." The director attempts to understand the nature of emotional manipulation, totalitarian seduction, and the mutual complicity of victim and victimizer. In fact, the most successful moments of the film depict this "totalitarian seduction" and self-imposed fear that result in the internalization of official myths, as in the remarkable scene in which Beria seduces Anastasia, Ivan's wife, with delicatessen, vodka, and children's games. The mythical melodramatic plot of the film develops around the love triangle of Ivan, Anastasia, and Stalin. In a crucial scene Anastasia asks Ivan whom he loves more, her or comrade Stalin, and receives the answer: "Comrade Stalin, of course." At the end, after many tragic events, it is her voice that Ivan remembers at Stalin's funeral, finally realizing that she was his "true love." The viewers of the film are not left guessing as to what the story is about, and rather like schoolchildren are taught "the truth." And as it happens in Russian artistic tradition, from Dostoevsky to Tarkovsky, the truth is spoken by a deranged woman right before her death (and by an old professor, who announces that "Satan is in the Kremlin"). Konchalovsky is not satisfied with subtle glimpses into totalitarian myths; he wishes to assert myths of his own. His Ivan Sanshin is "Ivan the Everyman," or "a symbol of the petrified spirituality of the Russian people, the hypnotized people who are willing to justify every horror" (*The Inner Circle*, p. 138). The film fits into the genre of "docudrama" or Hollywood "human-interest story," a subtle tearjerker in a historical setting. *The Inner Circle* could have been an exemplary genre film had it not aspired to be "a parable of Russian history."

The issues of conformism, of totalitarian myths and mystique, were crucial to the European cinema of the 1970s—especially for German, Italian, and Eastern European filmmakers who had lived under fascism or Stalinism. One remembers the brilliant film by Andrzej Wajda, *The Man of Marble,* and Bernardo Bertolucci's tantalizing *The Conformist,* which inquire in various—and far from straightforward—ways into the nature of totalitarian charisma by questioning the cinematic language and the language of emotions while still remaining engaging emotional spectacles. These films present ethical and aesthetic challenges, flirt with and estrange seductive totalitarian images, and expose the process of myth-making.

Konchalovsky himself relies on the language of emotions and the fast pace of professional editing. But isn't it true that precisely such calculated emotional seduction by figures of power made conformism possible in the first place? Deliberate emotional appeal and its universal reification are at the core of "totalitarian kitsch," once defined as the "dictatorship of the heart" and the "universal brotherhood of men." Despite some remarkable scenes, the film is full of Russian exoticism.

31. *The Abyss* offers the most recent twist in post-Soviet reflection on

representing history. A "retro" genre flourished in the Soviet cinema of the late 1970s; Nikita Mikhalkov's *The Slave of Love* or *Unfinished Piece for Player Piano* are excellent examples of this. The genre was frequently regarded as an aesthetic escape into the time before the Revolution, into the world of Chekhov, which had enormous resonance with the present but was much more beautiful.

32. Russian cultural critic and sociologist of art, Daniil Dondurei, wrote a wonderful essay on the topic entitled "Marianna—Protectress" in *Nezavisimaia Gazeta*, Fall 1992.

33. The only other national cinema that could compete is the Indian.

34. For the miraculous economic survival of the late Soviet cinema see Daniil Dondurei, "Soviet Cinema: Life after Death," forthcoming in *Slavic Review*.

35. The film was made during the period of late glasnost', when the decentralization of major studios had already occurred and the Union of Cinematographers began to lose its powers, but the post-glasnost' system of film distribution (frequently called the "producers' mafia"), which favored third-rate American movies and controls, was not yet in place.

36. From Sergei Soloviev's introduction to his film at its Boston premiere in the Coolidge Corner Theater, 1989. See also the interview with Sergei Soloviev in *Sovetskii Ekran*, 17 (1989).

37. The song is part pop gypsy and part sentimental love song of "feminine culture," treated with a mixture of parody and endearment: "black rose is the emblem of sadness; red rose is the emblem of love; the demons strummed to us about the black rose, the nightingales sang to us about the red one." In its own kitschy way the song's refrain is about the opposition of good and evil, demons and nightingales, sadness and love. The song is in the same genre as the film itself: the genre of so-called romantic cretinism. But the elements of kitsch and poshlost' are not all on the side of the demons. The song is performed with exaggerated playfulness by the young heroine right after a funny sex scene. Her lover echoes it with his own ironic imitation of the Soviet singer-superstar and queen of popular culture, Alla Pugacheva: "a million, million, million red roses." Thus the red roses seem to bridge two fin-de-siècle "feminine cultures." The performance is in the end a carnival of poshlost'—of sentimentality, bad taste, and rediscovered sexuality.

38. The scene of baptism is not without some elements of humor: the baby winks, the provincial girlfriend of Mitia's uncle from Liubertsy gets undressed to show her black-market black lingerie. However, this is neither black humor nor satire but merely good-natured friendliness that lightens the romantic intensity of the scene.

Religious kitsch is one of the oldest kinds of kitsch. The issue of popular representation is at the very core of many Christian theological debates. See *Kitsch: The Anthology of Bad Taste*, ed. Gillo Dorfles (London: Studio Vista, 1969). The issue of the kitschification of religion is very delicate in the late Soviet context. For a few instances of the debate see *Iskusstvo Kino*, 6 (1990), in which Tatiana Tolstaia talks about religion as kitsch and the director Andron Konchalovsky remarks that the most popular hero of mass culture is Jesus Christ. Among the few late Soviet films that address this issue at that time is *Sidewhiskers* (dir. Iurii Mamin).

39. There is, however, a slowly growing number of new artistic and feminist endeavors. Examples include the journal *Zhenskoe chtenie* published in St. Petersburg by Olga Lipovskaya, the Russian-American journal *Idioma* published in Moscow, and the women's club "Transfiguration." On misunderstandings between Russian and American feminists see the illuminating paper by Beth Holmgren, "Gender Troubles: Russia and the West," presented at the symposium on postcommunism at the University of California, Santa Cruz, March 1993, and Helena Goscilo, "Domostroika or Perestroika, The Construction of Womanhood in Soviet Culture under Glasnost'," in *Late Soviet Culture: From Perestroika to Novostroika*, ed. Lahusen with Kuperman, pp. 233–257.

40. Sigfrid McLaughlin, "Soviet Women Writers," in *Canadian Women Studies* (Winter 1989).

41. *Iskusstvo Kino*, 6 (1990), pp. 69–70.

42. See Helena Goscilo, "Tat'iana Tolstaia's 'Dome of Many-Coloured Glass': The World Refracted through Multiple Perspectives," in *Slavic Review*, 47, 2 (Winter 1988), p. 283.

43. Tatiana Tolstaia, *Na zolotom kryl'tse sideli* (Moscow: Molodaia gvardiia, 1987), p. 20.

44. These songs are still known by heart and sung in Russia. I quote the texts from the collection *Russkie Pesni i Romansy* (Moscow: Poeticheskaia biblioteka, 1989).

45. Ibid., p. 390.

46. Tatiana Tolstaia, "Sonia," in *Na zolotom kryl'tse sideli*, p. 136. This story was translated into English by Jamey Gambrell.

47. In Walter Benjamin's conception aura is the experience of distance, of involuntary memory and historical temporality, and of the uniqueness of art objects. See "Some Motifs in Baudelaire" and "The Work of Art in the Age of Mechanical Reproduction," in *Illuminations* (New York: Schocken Books, 1981), pp. 188–189 and pp. 222–223.

48. For a discussion of the new developments in late Soviet conceptual art see Margarita Tupitsyn, "The U-Turn of the U-Topian," in *Between Spring and Summer: Soviet Conceptual Art in the Era of Late Communism*, ed. David Ross (Cambridge, Mass.: MIT Press, 1991), pp. 35–53.

49. Kazimir Malevich, "From Cubism and Futurism to Suprematism," in *Russian Art of the Avant-Garde*, ed. John Bowlt (New York: Thames and Hudson, 1991), p. 123.

50. The installation is called "Classical Genres of Art: Portrait, Landscape, Still Life." The work itself is a kind of *trompe-l'oeil* or *trompe-genre*. It appears at first as a perfect classical ensemble: a gray monumental pedestal in the center and three black squares. On the three sides of the pedestal are three little embroideries—a portrait of a girl, a landscape, and a still life.

51. Jane and Michael Stern, *The Encyclopedia of Bad Taste* (New York: Harper Perennial, 1991), pp. 293–294.

52. My examples are taken from Pavel Burykin, *Moskva kupecheskaia* (Moscow, 1991), p. 5. See also V. A. Giliarovsky, *Moskva i moskvichi* (Moscow: Pravda, 1979) and *Between Tsar and People: Educated Society and the Quest for Public Identity*, ed. Edith W. Clowes, Samuel D. Kassow, and James L. West (Princeton: Princeton University Press, 1991).

53. Pavel Burykin, *Moskva kupecheskaia*, p. 70. I took some liberty with the translation here. The original reads: "Moscovskoe kupechestvo, izlomannyi arshin, kakoi ty syn otechestva, ty prosto sukin syn." "Arshin" here may refer to both the measure of a meter and to a fabric sample.

54. I am grateful to Katerina Degot' for introducing me to Regina.

55. It would be unfair to claim that Russian advertising is exclusively of Western pedigree. Russia has its own history of commercials, from prerevolutionary to postrevolutionary times. Soon after the Revolution free trade was prohibited, but the new Soviet propaganda used the charisma of advertising. Mayakovsky wrote many wonderful postrevolutionary ads: "I will swear in front of everyone, / the capitalist tea is nasty indeed, / what a wonderful thing / is Central Tea Management. / You can see / the tea is awesome; / the house smells / like a garden in blossom"; or "There are and there will be no better suckers *(soski);* I am ready to suck them till the end of my days!" These ads, from the *Windows of ROSTA*, preserve Mayakovsky's distinct poetic rhythm and his language, especially the neologisms he coined in a desperate search for originality at a time of organized conformity. Mayakovsky's advertisements lack the characteristic feature of commercial culture all over the world, the anonymity of authorship. Soviet advertisements obviously did not keep up with the standard set by the language of the "poet of the Revolution." Nevertheless, Soviet products were advertised until the Brezhnev era, when consumer items became too scarce, attitudes too cynical, reading between the lines even more skillful, and the black market in Western goods began flourishing conspicuously.

56. The advertisement has a particularly American history of televisual evolution; four years after the pizza ad was aired originally, the same jovial

TV cook appears again in 1992, but this time he promotes "On-Core Steaks." Instead of the desperado-singles from the previous ad, well-known TV characters come in search of an ideal TV dinner. The ad becomes more self-referential, and "encore" turns into an even more anglicized "on-core" that goes to the very *core* of American dream. Of course, these ads reflect only one genre of advertisement. There are also glamorous and spectacular ads, usually for perfumes and expensive cars.

57. It is a curious coincidence that the pioneer of the new television commercials that use many "postmodern" video techniques is the son of Bondarchuk, the established Soviet movie director of many Soviet epics. This is an indication of continuity between the Soviet and post-Soviet elite and style (the post-Soviet elite might be more humorous but its activities are certainly no less lucrative).

58. *Ogonek,* 9, February 1992. I am grateful to Nadezhda Azhgikhina and Igor Pergamenschikov.

59. *Ogonek,* 41, October 1991.

60. *Ogonek,* 18–19, May 1991.

61. Ibid.

62. *Voskresenie,* International Edition, 3, 1992.

63. "Vasha liubovnaia lodka ne razob'etsia o byt, esli na ee bortu bytovaia tekhnika Siene," *Kommersant,* 18 (1993).

Conclusion

1. Susan Stewart, *On Longing* (Baltimore: Johns Hopkins University Press, 1985), p. 145. On nostalgia see also Vladimir Jankelévitch, *L'Irréversible et la nostalgie* (Paris: Flammarion, 1974).

2. Brilliant elaboration of this issue can be found in Slavoj Žižek's article, "Caught in Another's Dream in Bosnia" in *Alphabet City,* 2 (Toronto, 1992), pp. 42–46.

3. "Nationalism is a negative spiritual category, because it thrives on denial and by denial. We are not what they are. We are the positive pole, they are the negative . . . we are nationalists but they are even more so, we slit throats . . . but they do too and even more; we are drunkards, they are alcoholics; our history is proper only in relation to theirs." Danilo Kiš, "On Nationalism," in *Why Bosnia?* ed. Rabia Ali and Lawrence Lifschultz (Stony Creek, Conn.: The Pamphleteer's Press, 1993), p. 127.

4. Ulf Hannerz, "The World System of Culture and Its Local Management," unpublished, quoted in James Clifford, *The Predicament of Culture* (Cambridge, Mass.: Harvard University Press, 1988), pp. 16–17.

5. Mikhail Epstein, "O ritualakh," in *Strelec,* 3 (1991), p. 247.

6. Iurii Lotman, *Kul'tura i vzryv* (Moscow: Gnosis, 1992), pp. 265–270.

7. David Lowenthal, *The Past Is a Foreign Country* (Cambridge: Cambridge University Press), 1985. I am grateful to Paul Holdengräber for sharing with me the origins of "nostalgia."

Index